TWENTY-FIVE YEARS OF ARCHAEOLOGY IN GLOUCESTERSHIRE
A REVIEW OF NEW DISCOVERIES AND NEW THINKING IN GLOUCESTERSHIRE
SOUTH GLOUCESTERSHIRE AND BRISTOL
1979–2004

Edited by Neil Holbrook and John Juřica

ISSN 1479–2389
ISBN 0 9523196 8 3

C.A.G.

Bristol and Gloucestershire Archaeological Society	Committee for Archaeology in Gloucestershire	Cotswold Archaeology	English Heritage

COTSWOLD ARCHAEOLOGY

Bristol and Gloucestershire Archaeological Report No. 3

This report is distributed free to members of the Bristol and Gloucestershire Archaeological Society

This publication has been generously supported by grants from the Bristol and Gloucestershire Archaeological Society, the Committee for Archaeology in Gloucestershire and English Heritage.

1513

Front cover: Aerial photograph of Saintbury, Gloucestershire (photograph by Damian Grady, November 2003, © English Heritage, National Monuments Record 23275/24)

Series Editor: Martin Watts
Typeset and printed in Europe by the Alden Group, Oxfordshire

CONTENTS

CONTRIBUTORS

Mark Bowden BA FSA MIFA
Senior Investigator
Archaeological Survey and Investigation
English Heritage
NMRC
Great Western Village
Kemble Drive
Swindon
Wilts. SN2 2GZ

Timothy Darvill BA PhD DSc FSA FSA Scot RPA MIFA
Professor of Archaeology
Archaeology and Historic Environment Group
School of Conservation Sciences
Bournemouth University
Fern Barrow, Poole
Dorset BH12 5BB
Email: tdarvill@bournemouth.ac.uk

David R. Evans BA
Historic Environment Record Officer
South Gloucestershire Council
Civic Centre
High Street
Kingswood
Bristol BS15 9TR
Email: david.evans@southglos.gov.uk

Carolyn Heighway BA FSA MIFA
Past Historic
6 Church Street
King's Stanley
Stroud
Glos. GL10 3HW

Neil Holbrook BA FSA MIFA
Chief Executive
Cotswold Archaeology
Building 11
Kemble Enterprise Park
Cirencester
Glos. GL7 6BQ

Robert H. Jones BA MIFA
City Archaeologist
Bristol City Council
Dept. of Planning, Transport and Sustainable Development
Planning Services
Brunel House
St George's Road
Bristol BS1 5UY
Email: bob_jones@bristol-city.gov.uk

John Jurica BA PhD
Honorary Editor BGAS Transactions
27 Moorend Road
Leckhampton
Cheltenham
Glos. GL53 0ER

Tom Moore BA PhD
Lecturer
Department of Archaeology
University of Durham
South Road
Durham DH1 3LE
Email: t.h.moore@dur.ac.uk

Richard Reece BSc PhD FSA
The Appleloft
The Waterloo
Cirencester
Glos. GL7 2PU

Andrew Reynolds BA PhD FSA FSA Scot
Reader in Medieval Archaeology
Institute of Archaeology
University College London
31–34 Gordon Square
London WC1H 0PY

Alan Saville BA FSA FSA Scot MIFA
Senior Curator, Earliest Prehistory
Archaeology Department
National Museums of Scotland
Chambers Street
Edinburgh EH1 1JF
Email: a.saville@nms.ac.uk

Jan Wills BA MIFA
County Archaeologist
Environment Department
Gloucestershire County Council
Shire Hall
Westgate Street
Gloucester GL1 2TH

ABBREVIATIONS

For abbreviations in bibliographies standard conventions have been observed. The forms listed below concern only a few of the organisations and publications mentioned in this volume.

AOC   Areas of Competence

BaRAS   Bristol and Region Archaeological Services

BAR   British Archaeological Reports

BGAS   Bristol and Gloucestershire Archaeological Society

CAB   Council for British Archaeology

CRAAGS   Committee for Rescue Archaeology in Avon, Gloucestershire and Somerset

HBMCE   Historic Buildings and Monuments Commision for England

RCHME   Royal Commision on Historical Monuments (England)

WAT   Western Archaeological Trust

Introduction and Acknowledgements

Neil Holbrook

In 1991 I applied for a job in Cirencester with the newly formed Cotswold Archaeological Trust. At the time I was working in Newcastle-upon-Tyne and knew next to nothing of Gloucestershire or its archaeology. In preparation for the interview I went into Newcastle University library in search of a book that I could read on the train to give the appearance of being prepared. That was the first time I came across *Archaeology in Gloucestershire* edited by Alan Saville, but in the last 14 years it has been a regular companion as I have endeavoured, sometimes in vain, to place new discoveries into some kind of context. The 25th anniversary of the original day conference held on 8 September 1979 fell in 2004, which was also conveniently the 20th anniversary of the publication of Alan's 'green book' (as I always think of it). Inevitably much has changed in Gloucestershire archaeology in the last quarter of a century and it seemed a good time to hold another day conference to review new discoveries and ideas. I was conscious that in 1984 the region served by the Bristol and Gloucestershire Archaeological Society (BGAS) was split between the counties of Avon and Gloucestershire, a division reflected in the archaeological literature. *Archaeology in Gloucestershire* was concerned solely with the post-1974 county, Bristol and the southern part of historic Gloucestershire being covered in *The Archaeology of Avon* edited by Mick Aston and Rob Iles and published in 1987. This time round I thought it would be useful to include the unitary authorities of Bristol and South Gloucestershire created in 1996 upon the demise of Avon County Council in our discussions. The conference was held on 6 November 2004 at the University of Gloucestershire in front of an enthusiastic audience. Two of the original participants (Tim Darvill and Carolyn Heighway) returned and along with a number of younger scholars demonstrated the vitality of the subject at the start of the 21st century. It was a particular pleasure to invite Alan Saville and Richard Reece to chair the conference sessions, and Alan concluded the day with a frank assessment of the successes, and failures, of archaeology in the county over the last couple of decades. I am pleased that both have contributed papers to this volume.

The constraints of a day conference dictated that we could not cover all chronological periods, and the decision was taken to halt the review at the end of the Middle Ages (although Mark Bowden's discussion of the medieval countryside strayed into the post-medieval period and Bob Jones's paper on Bristol took us almost up to the present day). The cut-off was made purely on practicality, for there has been an upsurge in interest in the archaeology of the post-medieval and modern periods over recent decades, and there is a fine tradition of work by the Bristol Industrial Archaeology Society and the Gloucestershire Society for Industrial Archaeology. Interest in the historic environment has never been so catholic, and a future conference and publication covering these more recent periods in our area would be welcome. The last 25 years have also witnessed a revolution in local authority archaeology with the development of Sites and Monuments Records (or Historic Environment Records as many are now called) and effective control of the impact of development upon archaeological remains. There was no time to include a review of these developments in the conference, but two new papers (Wills and Evans) place these achievements on record. It is pleasing that three of the four local authorities in our area that maintain an archaeological staff (Bristol City Council, Gloucestershire County Council and South Gloucestershire Council) are represented in this volume.

Without doubt the major change that has occurred in archaeology since 1979 has been the introduction of Planning Policy Guidance Note 16: Archaeology and Planning (PPG 16) in 1990.

Combined with other guidance and legislation (such as the 1979 Ancient Monuments and Archaeological Areas Act and ratification of European Union directives on Environmental Impact Assessment) the effect has been largely to halt the widespread destruction by development of archaeological sites without record. Of course the picture is not perfect. Managing the detrimental effects of agriculture on archaeological remains, for instance, is still a challenge, although Jan Wills paints a hopeful picture for the future in her paper. But we should not forget just how much progress has been made. Archaeology is now a material consideration in the planning process, a state of affairs that has caused the nature of archaeological fieldwork to change dramatically. Many contributors review and discuss the evidence that has accrued under this new regime, which is both larger in volume and somewhat different in character from that familiar to us in the 1970s and 80s. In terms of our knowledge of the archaeology of the historic county, 25 years ago Cotswold evidence dominated the scene. In this volume it is the Severn Vale where many new discoveries have been made. This should be no surprise. Fieldwork now largely follows development, and the Cotswolds is both an Area of Outstanding Natural Beauty and contains 144 Conservation Areas, more than any other local authority in England. Understandably it has not been a focus for such activity, with the notable exception of investigations in advance of the improvement of the A417/A419 trunk road in 1996-7. Rather it has been the two main river valleys of the county where most work has taken place. In the Upper Thames Valley investigation over many hectares in advance of mineral extraction continues to make a major contribution to our understanding of the interplay of past human activity and environmental processes. The corridor of the M5 motorway running through the Severn Vale has served as a focus for much new residential development, with extensive housing schemes around Tewkesbury, Bishop's Cleeve and Gloucester. In the 'Greater Bristol' conurbation extensive urban developments have occurred at Bradley Stoke and Emersons Green, preceded by varying levels of investigation, while the construction of the M48 motorway and the Second Severn Crossing provided an opportunity to examine the Avonmouth Levels. As Alan Saville highlights in his paper, new discoveries in these areas throw into sharper relief the gaps in our knowledge of the archaeology of the county west of Severn, where the level of work has been less. An ongoing archaeological survey of the Forest of Dean promises much.

Just as the nature of archaeological fieldwork has changed over the last 15 years, so have the bodies that execute it. In the 1980s archaeological investigation was undertaken by local authority units in Bristol and Gloucester, the long-established Cirencester Excavation Committee (CEC) in Cirencester, and regional units such as the Committee for Rescue Archaeology in Avon Gloucestershire and Somerset (CRAAGS) (1973–82) and its successor the Western Archaeological Trust (1982–5) dealing largely with rural projects. The introduction of PPG 16 was eagerly awaited by archaeologists, but few perhaps fully anticipated its consequences. For archaeologists to be able to react to the pace of development, and for the requirements of newly found clients who rightly expected value for money and efficiency from their consultants in return for funding, existing structures and working practices had to change. In Cirencester, the CEC recognised the wind of change earlier than some other urban units, and in 1989 Cotswold Archaeological Trust was created to take responsibility for new fieldwork. Today Cotswold Archaeology, as it is now called, is one of the ten largest archaeological companies operating in Britain, with work in Gloucestershire and Avon at the core of a geographically widespread portfolio of projects. The breakdown of territorial monopolies over the last 15 years or so has caused some angst within the archaeological profession, but it is a situation that is likely to continue for the foreseeable future. Intelligent and rigorous regulation is essential, however, for the free market to function successfully.

So far this introduction has focused on changes in government policy and professional structures. All the while, however, we must note the achievements of the local archaeological societies which have done so much to further our understanding of the past in our region. In addition to the BGAS, three local groups produce annual journals that are packed with the results of fieldwork and research. The Bristol and Avon Archaeological Society has been led inspirationally for several decades by James Russell. Dean Archaeological Group continues in the tradition of Bryan Walters and still undertakes research excavation (their current project at Rodmore Farm, St Briavels, is now drawing to a close). The third member of this triumvirate, the Gloucester and District Archaeological Research Group (GADARG), has prospered under the twin leadership of Eddie Price and the late Bernard Rawes. Bernard and his colleagues tirelessly recorded many sites in and around Gloucester before destruction, while Eddie has been directing research excavation at Frocester Court for over 40 years, an achievement now recognised and celebrated beyond the bounds of Gloucestershire (see, for instance, *Current Archaeology* **169** (2000), 11–19). The triumphant publication of the first two Frocester monographs in 2000 is as good a testament as one could ask for the quality and professionalism of Eddie and GADARG. A scan through the bibliographies contained in this volume shows just how much important information is to be found in the pages of *Bristol and Avon Archaeology*, *Dean Archaeology* and *Glevensis*. And this is in addition to the BGAS *Transactions*. Few other counties can demonstrate a comparable level of active archaeological research undertaken by individuals in their free time simply because they are interested. It is a humbling thought for all of us who earn our living by practising archaeology.

The 1984 volume was dedicated to Helen O'Neil and Elsie Clifford, two redoubtable figures of mid 20th-century Gloucestershire archaeology. Twenty years on this volume is dedicated to three individuals who have achieved much in the final quarter of that century from a local base: Eddie Price, the late Bernard Rawes, and James Russell. Their research stands comparison with that of the very best of their peers, 'professional' or 'amateur'.

Many people contributed to the success of the conference and helped in bringing its proceedings to publication. First I must thank the main partners in the venture: the Committee for Archaeology in Gloucestershire (CAG), Cotswold Archaeology, English Heritage and the University of Gloucestershire. Martin Ecclestone, the Secretary of CAG, did much behind the scene to ensure the success of the conference, assisted on the day by staff of Cotswold Archaeology. Professor Neil Wynn, head of the Department of History, and Lorna Scott, archivist, at the University of Gloucestershire generously arranged for the facilities at The Park campus to be put at our disposal. English Heritage supplied a grant to allow the Cotswold Archaeology drawing office to produce many of the illustrations contained in this volume. They are the work of Peter Moore, Lorna Gray and Liz Hargreaves. The index was compiled by Susan Vaughan. This publication was produced by Cotswold Archaeology with grant aid from English Heritage, CAG and the BGAS. I am particularly grateful to my fellow editor John Jurica, editor of the BGAS *Transactions*, for offering to share the burden of editorial duties. My main thanks, however, go to the contributors, both those who spoke at the conference and those who produced papers subsequently. I believe their papers show that archaeology in Bristol and Gloucestershire is alive and well at the start of the 21st century. It will be fascinating to see what people in 2029 will make of our progress in the next 25 years.

Cirencester – *Corinium Dobunnorum*
June 2005

Early Prehistory

Timothy Darvill

INTRODUCTION

Twenty-five years is a long time in the study of prehistory. Since the first *Archaeology in Glouce-stershire* conference in September 1979 there have been numerous excavations, surveys, chance finds, reviews of earlier work, and the publication of investigations carried out in previous decades. Results from some of this work were incorporated in the conference's published papers which appeared in 1984 (Saville 1984), and there was another opportunity to update these accounts in a volume on prehistory for the County Library Service published three years later (Darvill 1987). In drawing together this overview covering the quarter century of archaeological endeavour between 1979 and 2004 attention is focused on three questions. What has been done over the last 25 years? What has been found? And what do the results of these investigations and discoveries mean for our understanding of early prehistory in Gloucestershire?

Chronologically, the period covered spans the earliest colonization of the area by human communities during the late Pleistocene through to about 1000 BC, the beginning of the late Bronze Age in the conventional terminology of the expanded Three-Age System. Although, geographically, the 1979 conference confined its view to the then 'new' county of Gloucestershire established in 1974 (see Aston and Iles 1987 for a comparable overview of Avon) subsequent changes to local government administrative areas now make it appropriate to return to something appro-aching the historic counties of Bristol and Gloucestershire. These embrace the local government districts of Cotswold, Stroud, Tewkesbury, Forest of Dean, Cheltenham, and Gloucester, and the unitary authorities of Bristol (north of the river Avon) and South Gloucestershire.

Space precludes no more than passing recognition of the changing theoretical basis of archaeological studies that have drifted from the predominantly processualist (positivist) perspectives of the New Archaeology that prevailed through the 1970s and early 1980s to the interpretative post-processual (relativist) thinking of the late 1980s and beyond (Hodder 1984; Champion 1991). Nor is great consideration given to the changing environment of the region, evidence for which is gradually emerging through studies of deeply stratified sequences in essentially natural accumulations as well as of short-duration deposits preserved within or below archaeological sites (see Bell 1984 for a summary of work to 1983; Lewis and Maddy 1997 on Quaternary geomorphology and palaeoecology; and numerous papers in successive issues of the annual reports of the Severn Estuary Levels Research Committee published from 1990 onwards as *Archaeology in the Severn Estuary*).

DISCOVERY AND EXCAVATION 1979–2004

Research investigations, whether in the field, laboratory, museum store, record office, or library, provide the life-blood of archaeology and over the last 25 years all these sources and others have proved fruitful. More than a score of monographs explicitly relaying aspects of prehistoric archaeology in the county have appeared in those years and evidence of activity in prehistoric times creeps into many other reports concerned principally with later sites. The immensely rich and diverse range of journals springing from all quarters of Bristol and Gloucestershire include more than a 100 papers on aspects of early prehistory in the area, and national journals have carried a fair quota of papers and reports too.

The Annual Review of archaeology in Gloucestershire that started in 1977 and has appeared ever since in the *Transactions of the Bristol and Gloucestershire Archaeological Society* provides a useful, and fairly complete, overview of fieldwork and discovery over the past quarter century. Figure 1A shows an analysis of the work reported. In total, about 2,300 separate fieldwork events are recorded, of which about 12 per cent relate wholly or partly to prehistoric archaeology. As can be seen on the graph, there is a marked overall upward trend in the number of events recorded over the period even though the year-on-year totals fluctuate considerably. The number of reported events that include prehistoric material has increased only slightly over the period, which means that the proportion of events relevant to understanding prehistory is declining. This is probably caused by expanding interests in the increasingly broadly defined 'historic environment' which naturally tend to favour the archaeology of later periods.

The number of chance discoveries of prehistoric material reported in the Annual Review is generally low. It is certainly not a true reflection of the range of material coming to light, but a rather pale picture of the material coming to the attention of museums or archaeological organisations. There are many reasons for this, and much valuable information has been lost as a result. It is to be hoped, however, that improvements to the ancient laws of Treasure Trove from the late 1990s (DCMS 2002) and the expansion of the Portable Antiquities Scheme to Gloucestershire in 2004 (Miles 2002; Parsons 2003) will together provide a reliable and systematic long-term source of information about stray finds and chance discoveries. Certainly the discovery and reporting of what seems to be one of the largest hoards of early prehistoric goldwork yet found in England, discovered in a field near Cirencester, shows what can be achieved through vigilance and co-operation (Anon. 2005). In the first year of operations, 2004–05, some 1772 finds were recorded from Gloucestershire (MLA 2005, 94), of which about 10 per cent are of earlier prehistoric date.

So far as investigations of known and potential archaeological remains are concerned there have been fundamental and far-reaching changes over the last 25 years in the way work is carried out, its funding, and its purpose (Darvill 1999; 2004a). Critical here was the introduction in November 1990 of Planning Policy Guidance Note 16 (PPG 16 as it is usually called) which covered archaeology and planning (DoE 1990), followed in September 1994 by PPG 15 covering planning and the historic environment (DoE 1994). These, supported by the primary legislation that stands behind them and related guidance and legislation standing alongside, fully integrate archaeological interests with England's powerful town and country planning system (Darvill and Russell 2002). As such, it complements the protection offered to nationally important ancient monuments under the Ancient Monuments and Archaeological Areas Act 1979 (as amended for England) and to historic buildings by the Planning (Listed Buildings and Conservation Areas) Act 1990, and many other aspects of the historic environment covered by a plethora of other statutes. Proposals brought forward by the Government in June 2004 (DCMS 2004) may eventually consolidate these protective designations, but this will still leave a remarkably strong dual structure involving, on the one hand, protection for identified elements of the historic environment, while, on the other hand, providing planning tools that allow reasonable controls over the impact of proposed changes to our towns and countryside.

Fig. 1: *Charts showing (A) archaeological investigations in Gloucestershire 1979–2004 as reflected in the annual Archaeological Review published in the* Transactions of the Bristol and Gloucestershire Archaeological Society; *and (B) investigations 1990–2003 recorded by the Archaeological Investigations Project (various sources).*

(*A*)

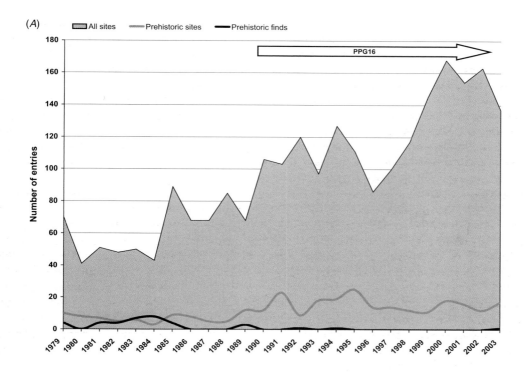

(*B*)

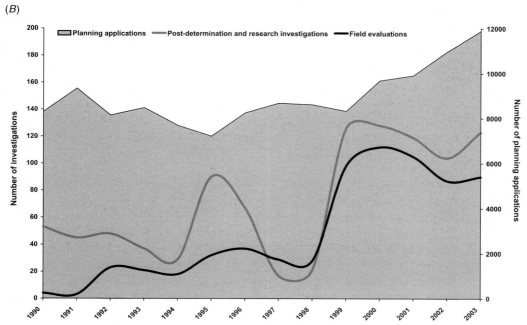

A fundamental concern of the planning system in England that is clearly expressed in PPG 16 is the provision of appropriate information as the basis for informed and transparent decision-making at all stages in the planning process. This involves the translation of principles ultimately derived from environmental impact assessment procedures developed in the United States and now widely applied across the European Union (Darvill 2004a, 418–19). With reference to *strategic planning* this means mapping and defining known archaeological constraints and potential alongside policies that set out how these factors will be balanced against other conflicting demands. More visible is the approach to *development control* where detailed information about archaeological impacts from specific proposals is collected in advance of determining planning permission or consents related to particular designations (e.g. Scheduled Monument Consent). Such works are usually referred to as 'pre-determination studies' and may typically include archaeological appraisals, desk-based assessments, field evaluations, and environmental impact assessments. The work is generally paid for by the individual or organisation seeking the relevant permissions (the 'developer') and the results are usually presented separately as technical reports to accompany the application or wrapped together within an Environmental Statement. In all cases they become public documents when deposited with a planning application, and can be consulted by any interested party while the application is open for comment. When determining a planning application a planning authority can, if it so chooses, insist that the applicant mitigates the impact of the proposals on the historic environment either by making arrangements for the preservation of remains *in situ* (the preferred option) or by carrying out an agreed programme of investigation, recording and reporting. Such works, usually called 'post-determination operations' or 'mitigation works', are again paid for by the developer and may be enforced either through a planning condition or a legally binding agreement of some kind. Through each successive stage of this process a series of reports will be prepared, but most are not typical of the kind of reports familiar from the pre-PPG era. Rather, each step in the process has a clearly defined purpose in supporting decision making and the reports produced reflect these objectives and needs.

Making wider use of such papers requires an adjustment to our expectations and new skills in extracting and digesting the data and information they contain. Moreover, each must be judged on how well it meets its purpose. Only at the end of the whole process, when all post-determination studies have been carried out, can a full archaeological report be produced. This takes time, but because the work is carried out within a contractually controlled environment and is adequately funded many reports appear within a few years of the fieldwork coming to an end. Archaeological contractors working in Gloucestershire have generally set a good record by making their activities known and reporting their findings promptly. Even though PPG 16 has only been in place for a little over a decade, several major projects have come through to completion and the value of the staged approach can clearly be seen. Exemplary cases in Gloucestershire include the improvement of the A419/417 road across the Cotswolds (Mudd *et al.* 1999, 1: 2–5), the construction of a link-road between the Brockworth Bypass and the former Gloucester Trading Estate at Hucclecote (Thomas *et al.* 2003), gravel extraction at Thornhill Farm (Jennings *et al.* 2004) and Shorncote (Hearne and Heaton 1994; Barclay *et al.* 1995; Hearne and Adam 1999; Brossler *et al.* 2002), and housing development at Bishop's Cleeve (Enright and Watts 2002). All these projects, and many more beside, have made major contributions to our understanding of ancient communities living in the region, and serve to illustrate the value of carefully planned and fully implemented work of this kind.

Nationally, the nature and extent of archaeological investigations in England since 1990 have been recorded for English Heritage by the Archaeological Investigations Project which carries out an annual census of projects. Gazetteers and web-based lists of all the projects recorded to date are available, and the first synthesis of general trends covering the period 1990 to 1999 has been published (Darvill and Russell 2002). Figure 1B shows an analysis of recorded archaeological events in Gloucestershire between 1990 and 2003. Approximately 1,500 archaeological investigations took place over that period, including 495 field-evaluations and 760 post-determination or research-oriented excavations and surveys. Since more than 95 per cent of these studies were prompted through the planning system it is instructive to compare underlying trends in the pattern of planning applications (shown as the background to the graph). Because much archaeological work takes place before planning applications are made it is notable that changes in the level of archaeological activity precede by a year or two changes in the level of development activity visible as formal planning applications.

Figure 2A shows the distribution of these projects within the county, Figure 2B picking out only those which identified prehistoric monuments, deposits, features, or finds. In both cases it is clear that while there are some obvious hot-spots there is a good spread of archaeological work of all kinds right across the county. Since the collective pressure of development from all sources (e.g. housing, roads and mineral extraction) is not itself influenced by archaeological factors they effectively randomise the range of places where archaeological remains are sought and investigated. This in turn leads to new insights simply as a result of looking in sectors of the landscape that may seem archaeologically unattractive. Just as the motorway boom of the 1960s and 70s changed perceptions of the nature and density of archaeological remains in areas such as the Severn Valley (Fowler 1979) so in turn have new opportunities since 1990 opened our eyes to the significance of areas such as the Forest of Dean and the gravel islands around Lechlade, Tewkesbury, Barnwood, and Bishop's Cleeve. Compared with other counties in western England, Gloucestershire saw a relatively high level of archaeological investigation between 1990 and 2003 with an overall score of 0.56 investigations per square kilometre. Berkshire saw slightly higher levels of activity, but Somerset, Oxfordshire, Wiltshire, and Herefordshire were all lower (Table 1).

More than 20 substantial excavations that include the investigation of early prehistoric remains took place between 1979 and 2004 (Table 2). Of these about 30 per cent could be described as research excavations in the sense that they were not promoted by the planning system or closely connected with specific threats from development, agriculture, or forestry. The remainder were rescue excavations or post-determination mitigation studies. Four of these major projects were prompted by linear threats – pipelines and major road schemes – and these provide valuable cross-sections through adjoining landscape zones. Work along a 25-km stretch of the A419/417 road from Latton on the Wiltshire border through to Birdlip east of the Cotswold escarpment is especially illuminating since it revealed evidence for every part of early prehistory from the Palaeolithic through to the middle Bronze Age (Mudd *et al.* 1999, 2: 513–17).

Extensive surveys of various kinds, including fieldwalking and large-scale geophysical surveys, have also played a key role in understanding the distribution and extent of early prehistoric activity even though their aims are more general (Table 3). Special note may be made here of work in the eastern part of the county by the Cotswold Archaeological Research Group (Marshall 1985 and notes in the Archaeological Review) and west of the Severn by the Dean Archaeological Group (Walters 1988; 1989; 1992). A survey of the Malvern Hills undertaken by English Heritage includes a small part of north-west Gloucestershire (Bowden 2005).

Publication of reports relating to important excavations of early prehistoric sites carried out before 1979 has also made a significant contribution to changing interpretations. Table 4 summarises the main achievements in this area. Thankfully, very little pre-1979 excavation

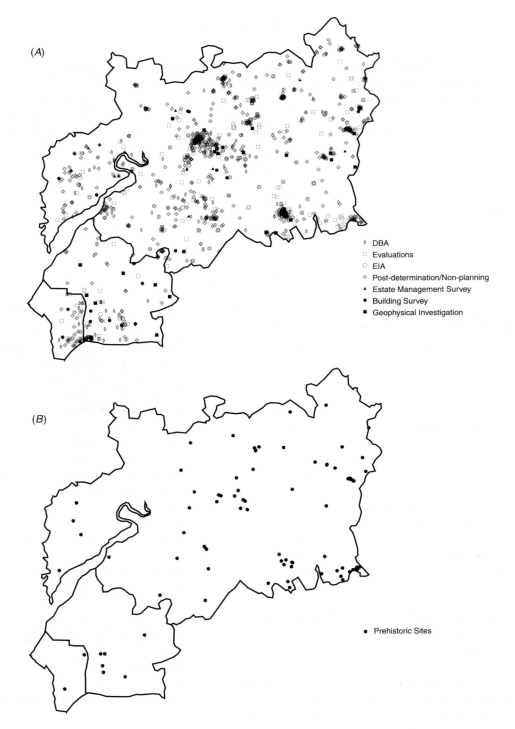

(A)

◇ DBA
□ Evaluations
○ EIA
✧ Post-determination/Non-planning
▲ Estate Management Survey
● Building Survey
■ Geophysical Investigation

(B)

● Prehistoric Sites

Fig. 2:   Maps showing the distribution of (A) archaeological investigations in Gloucestershire 1990–2003 (DBA = Desk-based Assessment; EIA = Environmental Impact Assessment) and (B) investigations yielding evidence of prehistoric features, deposits, or finds (Archaeological Investigations Project).

Table 1: Archaeological investigations in Gloucestershire and surrounding counties 1990–2002 (data supplied by the Archaeological Investigations Project)

County	Number of investigations 1990–2002	Investigations per square kilometre
Berkshire	1,003	0.79
Gloucestershire	1,513	0.56
Oxfordshire	1,053	0.40
Somerset	1,014	0.29
Wiltshire	879	0.25
Herefordshire	124	0.05

Table 2: Major excavations in Gloucestershire 1979–2003
 †Summary account only

Site / Project	Dates	References
Frocester Court, Frocester	1958 to date	Price 2000a; 2000b
Crickley Hill, Coberley	1969–93	Dixon 1979; 1980†; 1981†; 1982†; 1983†; 1984†; Savage 1986†; Dixon 1987†; 1998a; 1988b†; 1990†; 1992†; 1994†
West Hill, Uley	1977–79	Woodwood and Leach 1993
Hazleton North, Hazleton	1979–82	Saville 1990
Hazleton South, Hazleton	1980	Saville 1990, 137–40
Peak Camp, Cowley	1980–81	Darvill 1981; 1982a
Saintbridge	1983	Garrod and Heighway 1984, 23–8; Darvill and Timby 1986
Druid Stoke long barrow, Bristol	1983	Smith 1989
Guiting Power ring-ditches	1984	Marshall 1989
The Buckles, Frocester	1984–87	Darvill in Price 2000a, 193–209
Lechlade (Butler's Field)	1985	Boyle *et al.* 1998
Lechlade cursus	1985	Barclay *et al.* 2003, 189–214
Esso Midline	1985	Smith and Cox 1986†
West Tump, Rodmarton	1988	Saville 1989a
Shorncote Quarry and Cotswold Community	1989–2001	Hearne and Heaton 1994; Barclay *et al.* 1995; Hearne and Adam 1999; Brossler *et al.* 2002; Laws 2002†; Weaver 2004†
A417/419 road improvements	1990–91 & 1996–97	Mudd *et al.* 1999
Guiting Power round barrow G3	1991–92	Marshall 1992a; 1992b†; 1993†; 1994†
Stow-on-the Wold	1991–92 & 1994	Parry 1999
Lechlade (Gassons Road)	1993	King in Boyle *et al.* 1998, 269–81

(*Continued*)

Table 2: *Continued*

Site / Project	Dates	References
Hucclecote	1993–4	Parry and Cook 1995†
Lechlade (Memorial Hall)	1995	Thomas and Holbrook in Boyle *et al.* 1998, 282–88
Guiting Power round barrow G1	1996	Marshall 1993†; 1997†
Tirley to Wormington pipeline	2000	Coleman and Hancocks forthcoming
Fairford	2002	Lamdin-Whymark 2003†
Blenheim Farm, Moreton-in-Marsh	2002	Hart 2004†

Table 3: *Large-scale survey projects in Gloucestershire 1979–2003*

Site / Project	Dates	References
Frocester area	*c.*1970 to date	Price 2000a, 210–20
Cotswold Survey	*c.*1981 to date	Marshall 1985
Birdlip Bypass	1983–84	Darvill 1984b
Severn Levels	*c.*1987–2002	Summarised in Bell *et al.* 2000 with earlier references mainly in annual volumes of *Archaeology in the Severn Estuary* starting in 1990
Salmonsbury Camp	2002–03	
Malvern Hills	2003–04	Bowden 2005

relevant to early prehistory remains unpublished, the two key sites being the early phases of Crickley Hill investigated over 25 seasons between 1969 and 1993 (Dixon 1979; 1988a; summary reports in idem 1980; 1981; 1982; 1983; 1984; 1987; 1988b; 1990; 1992; 1994) and the five ring-ditches investigated by Professor Richard Atkinson at Netherhills, Frampton on Severn in 1948 (O'Neil and Grinsell 1960, 114, and Chouls 1993, 17, for summary details). As noted above, work carried out after 1979, and especially after 1990, has generally been well publicised and published with reasonable dispatch either fully or in interim form.

Table 4: *Excavations carried out before 1979 and published in the period 1979–2004*

Site / Project	Fieldwork dates	Publication
Roughground Farm, Lechlade	1957–65	Allen *et al.* 1993
The Loder's, Lechlade	1964–66	Darvill *et al.* 1986
Lechlade Cursus, Lechlade	1965	Barclay *et al.* 2003, 189–214
Sandy Lane, Cheltenham	1971	Leah and Young 2001
Cinema Site, Tewkesbury	1972–74	Hannan 1993
Condicote Henge, Condicote	1977	Saville 1983

Since the disappearance in March 1985 of Western Archaeological Trust (formerly CRAAGS, the Committee for Rescue Archaeology in Avon, Gloucestershire and Somerset) as the government-supported regional rescue archaeology unit (WAT 1985, 4–5) the greatest proportion of contract archaeology in Gloucestershire has been carried out by three of England's largest archaeological organisations: Cotswold Archaeology, Oxford Archaeology, and Wessex Archaeology. Amateur archaeology remains strong in the county and many of the dozen or so archaeological and local history societies undertake or support fieldwork of various kinds. Disappointingly, few university departments have chosen to focus their research in the area. This may, in part at least, be a reflection of the changing priorities and funding patterns in the delivery of Higher Education over the past two decades. Overall, the perpetuation of well-considered research-oriented archaeology and the repositioning of contract archaeology over the last 25 years has meant that much new high-quality data has become available which allows our understandings of early prehistory in the area to be considerably revised.

EARLY PREHISTORY REVISITED

A wider context for the discoveries and advances in understanding Gloucestershire's early prehistory can be found in the resource assessments accompanying the published research frameworks in Wales (Martin and Phipps 2004), the West Midlands (WMRRF 2004), and South-West England (SWARF 2005). In the following sections attention is closely focused on Gloucestershire and its immediate borderlands through an essentially chronological review of the accumulating evidence for human activities in the area during the later Pleistocene and early Holocene.[1]

Pleistocene People and Environments

Prior to the main last glacial phase, the Devensian (c.110,000–10,000 BC), the landscape of western and central England looked rather different to that of today. Sea level was generally lower, and research into river patterns, for example, has shown that within what is now the Severn Estuary there was a network of streams cut into the underlying bedrock. These were plugged and diverted by deposits of fluvial gravels during the Ipswichian interglacial (c.135,000–111,000 BC) when sea levels rose to c.6 m AOD and much of the low-lying ground was flooded (Allen 2000b, 14–15). Further north, investigations through the Shotton Project (2005) are building on work by Professor Fred Shotton and colleagues which showed the presence of an ancient river system sealed below glacial deposits in what is now the Avon Valley. In Pleistocene times this river system, known as the Bytham River, flowed north-eastwards through the midlands to join other rivers in the area now covered by the North Sea.

Human settlement at this period was peripatetic, sporadic, and distributed across barely imaginable periods of time. During warmer periods (the Hoxnian and Ipswichian geostratigraphic stages of the Pleistocene) communities seem to have favoured riverside and lakeside sites. During cold periods (the Wolstonian and Devensian stages) they exploited the periglacial tundra and extensive icesheets as hunting grounds from semi-permanent camps and temporary shelters much as modern-day circum-polar arctic communities such as the Inuit and Sami still do (Brody 2000). Preserved material culture from these early periods represents just a tiny fraction of what must once have existed and this naturally dulls our appreciation of the richness and diversity of these small-scale communities. Devensian and earlier occupation sites are extremely rare in the British Isles and generally depend for their survival on exceptional circumstances such as protection by rock overhangs, cave systems, or the superimposition of stable cover-deposits. Although it has sometimes been suggested that King Arthur's Cave, Whitchurch, in the Wye Valley was occupied during Ipswichian or early Devensian times (conventionally the middle Palaeolithic), ApSimon (2003) has demolished the case and shown that the earliest occupation here belongs to the mid Devensian (*c*.40,000–20,000 BC).

Stray finds of flint tools originating from the Hoxnian, Ipswichian, and Devensian stages of occupation and exploitation of the landscape do survive, mainly as residual components in gravels and drift deposits resulting from subsequent glacial or fluvio-glacial action. Fourteen handaxes/bifaces were reported by Saville (1984a, fig. 1), mainly from gravels along the Severn at Barnwood east of Gloucester and the Upper Thames between Lechlade and Latton. To these can now be added a further five examples which both thicken existing clusters and expand the overall distribution.[2] Curiously, no significant new finds appear to have been made either in the Barnwood area or along the Bristol Avon (cf. Wymer 1996).

In the south-east of the county an Acheulian handaxe found in gravel hardcore used in the construction of the A419 road at Latton is believed to be from the adjacent quarry at Latton Lands (Mudd *et al.* 1999, 1: 15, fig. 7.3.24). Although the exact context is lost it may be similar to that of a comparable handaxe found in April 1977 at South Cerney which probably became incorporated into the gravel beds in which it was found before 42,000 BC as a result of erosion on the higher ground to the north or south (Whitehead 1979). Both tools were probably made and used more than 200,000 years ago.

Early tools remain rare on the Cotswolds. The Acheulian handaxe from near Charlton Abbots (Saville 1984a, 75 item 6) was returned to the local area from a collection in Buckinghamshire Museum and is now in Cheltenham Museum (Saville 1984b). New finds are occasionally made and in 2003 a well-preserved Acheulean/Mousterian type sub-cordate form handaxe was recovered from high-level drift gravels at Blenheim Farm, Moreton-in-Marsh (Hart and McSloy 2004; Fig. 3). The position of this site on the south shore of the putative proglacial Lake Harrison (Roe 1981, 49) accords neatly with the idea that waterside locations were preferred by early hunter-gatherer groups.

Two important finds in the Severn Valley serve to illustrate the potential for further discoveries in this area and emphasise the need for close monitoring of gravel extraction along the Severn and its tributaries. In the north, an Acheulian handaxe found at Harwick Bank, Bredon, was acquired by Tewkesbury Museum (Rawes 1981, 179) and early handaxes have been recorded in the Colwall area just outside the county in Herefordshire (Bowden 2005, 11). In the Severn Estuary implements have been found associated with gravel spreads near Sudbrook, Gwent. These include a crude elongated ovate handaxe from Sedbury Cliffs (Green 1989, 196). Equally significant is the Acheulian handaxe from Welsh Newton (Walters 1989) which extends the known distribution of finds deep into the river valleys west of the Severn.

Faunal remains contemporary with the flint tools appear from time to time, but again there is much potential for further discoveries through monitoring and closer liaison with quarry operators. Amongst recent finds are the remains of a woolly mammoth, dated to *c*.100,000 BC, uncovered during gravel extraction in the Cotswold Water Park (Anon. 2004a).

The later part of the Devensian stage of the late Pleistocene broadly equates with the Upper Palaeolithic, which itself is conventionally divided into earlier (EUP: *c*.38,000–20,000 BC) and later (LUP: *c*.15,000–10,000 BC) phases (Campbell 1977, 199–201). The start of the EUP broadly coincides with the appearance in Europe of anatomically modern humans (*Homo sapiens sapiens*) and it is notable that some of earliest dated remains of this period lie in the west country (Jacobi and Petit 2000) even though relatively little comes from Gloucestershire itself (Saville

Fig. 3: Palaeolithic handaxe from Blenheim Farm, Moreton-in-Marsh. The handaxe is 87 mm high. (photograph Cotswold Archaeology: copyright reserved).

1984a, 66–7). King Arthur's Cave near the river Wye on Great Doward, Whitchurch (Hereford), includes EUP artefacts and hearths in three levels (Campbell 1977, 43–5) and is a critical site for the late glacial prehistory of the region. The discovery by Alf Webb of what appears to be a tanged Solutrean point while walking near Offa's Dyke in Autumn 2004 may, if genuine, emphasise the importance of the Wye Valley at this period (Hughes 2004; Webb pers. comm.). The findspot lies close to a possible rock-shelter at Pen Moel (Hart 1967, 3–4) and may suggest the presence here of a late Pleistocene occupation broadly contemporary with the small open-air camp at Forty Acre Field, Barnwood, to the east of the Severn (Campbell 1977, 146).

The sparse array of LUP material culture from the Gloucestershire area in 1984 (Saville 1984a, 67) can now be expanded slightly with the discovery of a Cheddarian-type point at Llanishen and a core at Woolaston (Walters 1989), west of the Severn, and a possible worked flint from Grumwell Close, Shirehampton (Bryant 1994a), east of the Severn. Supposed LUP cave art at Symonds Yat in the Wye Valley, first published in the *Illustrated London News* in 1981, has since proved entirely natural. Genuine cave art has, however, now been recognised at Creswell Crags, Derbyshire (Bahn *et al.* 2003). This reinforces the possibility that other caves in southern Britain might contain comparable images and underlines the need for further searches in the Wye Valley cave systems.

Early Holocene Hunter-Gatherers

Following the end of the last major cold phase of the Devensian glacial cycle about 10,000 BC, the familiar landscape zones of the Upper Thames Valley, Cotswold uplands, Severn Valley, and Forest of Dean began to take on their current topography and form. Of the four, the most dynamic area in the early Holocene and beyond was the Severn Valley, especially what is now the Severn Estuary. Here, as John Allen has shown, sea level has risen unevenly during the Holocene, significant temporally limited fluctuations being superimposed on the underlying upward trend which was at first rather rapid (Allen 2000b, 13). As a result of these changing conditions, a deep sequence of transgressive estuarine silts alternating with layers of intertidal and terrestrial peats in places up to 15 m thick accumulated within and around the estuary between about 10,000 BC and recent times. These peats are highly variable in their development, both regionally and locally, but in general get thicker with increasing distance from the sea and the main rivers that crossed the levels. Understanding these deposits has been one of the main objectives of the Severn Estuary Levels Research Committee and many important results have been reported in their annual reports, *Archaeology in the Severn Estuary* (e.g. Allen 2000b; Haslett *et al.* 2000).

Occupation dating to the 9th, 8th and 7th millennia BC is usually characterised by the presence of broad obliquely blunted microlithic points (Saville 1984a, 69). To date these are rather few in number and, in common with the late Pleistocene occupation of the area, are represented mainly as stray finds. The discovery of an early microlith at the Cherry Tree Lane site east of Cirencester during the improvement of the A417 road (Mudd *et al.* 1999, 1: 15, 311–13) adds a little to the picture and emphasises the need for further research into the early post-glacial colonization of the region.

On present evidence it was during the 6th and 5th millennia BC that a significant number of communities established themselves in the area. Saville (1984a, 75–6) listed about 40 sites that have yielded microliths in the form of small and narrow scalene triangles and other geometric shapes. Most of these sites were on the Cotswold uplands, and four included substantial assemblages: Syreford Mill, Whittington; Troublehouse Covert, Cherington; Bowldridge Farm, Long Newnton; and Barrow Ground, Hazleton. Of these, only the last-mentioned includes *in-situ* material recovered through systematic excavation. Here, excavations at Hazleton North revealed that the area later used as the site for a substantial long barrow had been occupied in the 6th or 5th millennium BC as a short-lived camp by a hunter-gatherer group, perhaps for retooling equipment during a hunting trip (Saville 1990a, 13–14, 240). A scatter of about 80 microliths and a small amount of working debris was found spread over an area of 70 square metres. No certain features could be associated with this occupation, although it is tempting to link it with several small areas of burning recorded within the area of the flint scatter.

In the Upper Thames Valley sites datable to the 6th and 5th millennia BC remain scarce. A microlith from Leaze Farm, Lechlade (Moore 2002), starts to fill the void in known distributions (cf. Saville 1984a, fig. 4), but part of the problem may be geomorphological. Changes to river patterns and later sedimentation have sealed large tracts of low-lying landscape that were occupied in this period. Opportunities to investigate these deposits are rare, but can be very fruitful. At Rissington, for example, a watching brief during the construction of a pipeline in 1992 recorded late Devensian/early Flandrian palaeochannels adjacent to the river Windrush with red deer and horse remains in the underlying gravels (Morton 1993). Subsequent studies of bulk samples and a single soil monolith taken during the watching brief have provided a rare glimpse of late Devensian and early–middle Flandrian environments in this part of the Cotswolds (Wilkinson 1994). A radiocarbon determination of 11,200–10,350 BC (OxA-4150: 10710±110 BP) dates the lower part of the sequence while a second determination 5880–5550 BC (OxA-4149: 6820±80 BP) dates the main phase of peat development. Over the five millennia or so represented by the sequence the environment changed from fen carr and reed swamp, through a period when the riverside was dominated by birch woodland, a phase of more open grassland, and, towards the end of the sequence, alder woodland.

Several additional findspots of worked flints dating to the 6th and 5th millennia BC have been recorded on the Cotswolds over the last 25 years. Fields 10 and 15 on the line of the Northleach Bypass (Rawes 1984, 40–1) both yielded small assemblages, and a single microlith was found during a fieldwalking survey over a causewayed enclosure recognised from aerial photography at Southmore Grove, Rendcomb (Trow 1985, 19). Two small clusters of worked flints from this period were identified by fieldwalking along the line of the Birdlip Bypass at one of the highest points on the Cotswolds (Darvill 1984b, 25). During the construction of the A419/417 road, three sites on the Cotswold uplands yielded possible 6th- and 5th-millennium BC flintwork, but no features of the period were recorded (Mudd *et al.* 1999, 1: 15, 307–15).

In the Severn Valley a handful of sites discovered or published in the last 25 years serve to expand considerably our understanding of settlement in this area. Microlithic, micro-core blades, scrapers and blades of 6th–5th-millennium BC date were recovered during the investigation of a medieval, Romano-British and later prehistoric site at King's Stanley (Heighway *et al.* 1988, 37). Fieldwalking at Frocester revealed an extensive scatter of worked flint beside a small stream in Big Nutfield which included 6th- and 5th-millennium BC microliths and core tools (Darvill in Price 2000a, 210–14). Implements of similar date were also recorded in colluvium sealing a 2nd-millennium BC land surface in The Buckles to the south (Ibid. 202), and in ploughsoil and as residual finds in later deposits at Big Stanborough to the west (Darvill in Price 2000b, 178). Worked flints of the period have also been reported from development work at Archway School, Stroud (Anon. 1982), and Westward Road, Ebley (Barber and Walker 2000, 3–4). Changing water levels in the Severn had consequences for sedimentation patterns in both east and west bank tributaries and here, as in the Upper Thames Valley, some early prehistoric sites are sealed by later prehistoric alluvium and colluvium. Post-glacial alluviation up to 2 m thick was reported, for example, beside the Horsbere Brook at Hucclecote where a microlith was found residual in a later feature (Thomas *et al.* 2003, 8).

In the south of county worked flints of the 6th or 5th millennium BC have been reported from Bradley Stoke Way, Bradley Stoke (Samuel 2002a). Changes in topography in this region are even more marked than elsewhere in the county. Land surfaces dating to the 7th, 6th and 5th millennia BC have been noted during the archaeological monitoring of groundworks for development along the Bristol Avon, as for example at Canon's Marsh, Bristol, where an old river channel sealed below alluvium at a depth of 11.2 m below present ground level was recorded (Longman 1999). A piece of mature alder wood from within the channel was radiocarbon dated to 4800–4450 BC (No reference given: 5770±80 BP). At Katherine Farm, Avonmouth, a soil ripening horizon formed amid accumulating alluvial deposits represented a hiatus in alluviation dated to 5840–5640 BC (NZA-12495: 6866±50 BP) and 4910–4540 BC (NZA-12478: 5879±70 BP); no direct evidence of occupation was found (Allen *et al.* 2002). The soil lay about 4.8 m AOD and comparable stabilisation horizons have been identified at a handful of other sites in the Avonmouth Levels (see Allen *et al.* 2002, table 3).

Archaeologically, the most significant change in our understanding of settlement patterns of this period results from fieldwork west of the river Severn. No sites between the Severn and the Wye were listed by Saville (1984a, fig. 4), but systematic walking of 165 fields between January 1985 and August 1988 revealed that 89 per cent of them yielded prehistoric worked flints, 28 fields yielded microliths, and 12 contained cores and waste of 6th- and 5th-millennium BC date (Walters 1988). Four main concentrations were recognised: Nedge Cop, St Briavels; Barnfield, English

Bicknor; Great Howle Farm; and Bream. Most of these sites seem to lie on higher ground that is generally well-drained. The assemblage from Nedge Cop was the focus of a note by Alan Saville (1986b; see Walters 1985) who emphasised that, although the worked flints range widely in date, 6th- and 5th-millennium BC material, including 13 microliths, represents a significant element. Later, two further dense scatters of worked flint were discovered at Huntsham Hill (James and Walters 1988) and on the lower slopes of May Hill. Core tools of 6th- and 5th-millennium BC date have been found west of the Severn at Elton Road near Littledean, Newnham (Walters 1985; Saville 1986b, 229–30), and on a rocky beach near Symonds Yat, English Bicknor (Price 2001). By the early 1990s at least nine substantial settlement areas and a wide scatter of other material of the 6th and 5th millennia BC could be claimed in the Forest of Dean and Lower Wye Valley (Walters 1989; 1991; 1992, fig. 8), neatly balancing what is known from the Cotswolds and the valley lands east of the Severn.

Taken as a whole, the nature and extent of activity dating to the 6th and 5th millennia BC across all four landscape zones in Gloucestershire is impressive, especially when taking account of the 'hidden landscapes' of the Upper Thames and Severn valleys. Research into the content and structure of some of the known sites on the Cotswolds and in the Forest of Dean is urgently needed, and in due course a well-preserved site with structural remains will no doubt be discovered and examined. In the Lower Severn Estuary, however, such work is already underway with a major research programme directed by Martin Bell that began in 2000 and focuses on the transition from hunter-gatherer to early farming communities (Bell *et al.* 2001; 2002; 2003). To date, work has mainly focused on the Goldcliff and Redwick areas on the western shore of the estuary in Monmouthshire, but the results have much wider implications. The basic geostratigraphic sequence in the area has been documented and seems to have seven basic elements (Table 5). Activity areas of the 5th millennium BC at Goldcliff East include evidence for the use of heat-fractured stones, a probable hearth with evidence of aurochs butchery, and an area with a concentration of fish bones. There was also evidence for burning oak trees perhaps in connection with forest clearance or woodland management. Animal and human footprints were revealed in the banded silts around about (Bell *et al.* 2003, 1), while deer trails have been recognised in broadly contemporary deposits at Oldbury Flats, Gloucestershire (Allen *et al.* 2003, 58).

4000–3000 BC: Early Farming Communities

Although there is much debate about the reasons why, it is now widely accepted that in the century or two either side of 4000 BC communities in Britain switched from an essentially hunter-gatherer way of life to one dominated by simple farming systems involving husbandry of cattle, pig and sheep and the cultivation of wheat and barley. Sites which span this transitional period are hard to find (Darvill 2003), but a number of strands of evidence from a range of different sources help understand this critical period in the development of the landscape and the re-organisation of settlement patterns and social relations.

Environmental sampling in the Upper Windrush Valley shows that minor clearances were taking place in the later 5th and early 4th millennia BC (Marshall and Allen 1998) and much the same was happening in the Lower Severn Valley. An 8-km transect provided by pipeline construction between Pucklechurch east of Bristol and the gas-powered power station at Seabank north of Avonmouth provides a complete record of Holocene alluvial sediments (Carter *et al.* 2003). An ancient course of the Severn was recognised between Spaniorum Hill and Seabank with a lowest recorded level of –8.5 m AOD. By the early Holocene its course would have been a marshy

Table 5: Summary stratigraphic sequence of the main Pleistocene and Holocene sedimentary and organic units in the Severn Estuary (based on Bell et al. 2002, table 1)

Stratigraphic unit	Details
vii	Upper peat and upper submerged forest overlaid by raised bog. Radiocarbon dates on wood peat from Goldcliff East range from 4910–4490 BC (Car-658: 5850±80 BP) to 4350–3990 BC (Car-656: 5360±80 BP).
vi	Estuarine silts up to 1.5 m thick. Laminated silts with partings of sand, associated with many animal and human footprints.
v	Lower peat and submerged forest. Radiocarbon dates in Trench D at Goldcliff include 5800–5530 BC (Beta-60761: 6770±70 BP), 5740–5620 BC (OxA-12359: 6790±38 BP), and 5729–5560 BC (OxA-12358: 6726±33 BP) at about –4 m AOD; the peat in Trench T40 at Redwick is dated 5630–5480 BC (OxA-12360: 6625±40 BP)
iv	Palaeosol with charcoal, artefacts, and localized occupation (Holocene): a radiocarbon date of 5610–5310 BC (Car-1502: 6480±70 BP) relates to charcoal from the old land surface at a depth of about –3.9 m AOD.
iii	Stoney head containing Trias Red Marl (Devensian)
ii	Stoney head containing Lias Limestone (Devensian)
i	Raised beach: sandy and pebbly matric locally cemented as sandrock (Ipswichian)
	Bedrock

depression with an island of raised ground at Seabank/Pilning between the old Severn to the east and the new channels of the Severn to the west. Eastwards of the old channel, peat deposits up to 4.5 m thick show the formation of fenland in the Avonmouth Levels, progressively affected by rising sea level. An undated palaeochannel at the Kendleshire Golf Club, Westerleigh, loosely associated with worked flint datable to the 4th to 2nd millennia BC may also be of this period (Samuel 2002b). An area of occupation dating to the early 4th millennium BC was noted at Farm Lane, Easter Compton, and may correlate with comparable surfaces found nearby at Pilning and in other recently exposed sequences (Carter *et al.* 2003, 81–4).

Two settlement areas dating to the first few centuries of the 4th millennium BC are known, and others suspected. The more fully investigated is at Barrow Ground, Hazleton, where the later long barrow preserved an extensive area of occupation that included a midden over 10 m across, a hearth, the postholes of a small structure (?house), and a possible fenceline (Saville 1990a, 14–22). Dating to around 3900 BC, the material culture of the site included at least 25 ceramic vessels of plain bowl and carinated style, quernstones and rubbers for grain processing, broken flint tools, and flint-working waste. Carbonised grain attests to the use of wheat and barley. Hazlenuts show the collection of wild foodstuffs, and bones representing cattle, sheep, and pigs indicate the presence of domesticated livestock. In the 50 years or so between the abandonment of this settlement and the construction of the long barrow the area seems to have been cultivated for a few seasons and then left to develop a light cover of hazel scrub (Ibid. 240–1).

A second very early site may be glimpsed through excavations in Big Stanborough, Frocester, where a piece of animal bone dated to 4500–3500 BC (GU-2685: 5180±210 BP) was the only find in a rectangular pit-like feature (F4) that seems to have been truncated by a later prehistoric sunken trackway (Price 2000a, 39–43). Parts of seven stone axes and over 100 recognisable flint implements of the 4th and 3rd millennia BC came to light as residual finds in later contexts on the site suggesting that occupation in the area at this time may be more extensive than currently thought (Darvill in Price 2000b, 177–83). These two recently investigated sites complement the evidence from a handful of other early occupations east of the Severn known through previous work, including Sale's Lot, Withington (Darvill 1982b, 60–1); Cow Common, Swell (Darvill 1984a, 86–7); and Crickley Hill, Coberley (Dixon 1988a, 78). In most cases, however, these sites have been dated on the grounds that they stratigraphically pre-date substantial stone-built monuments; more research is needed to locate and investigate contemporary sites not sealed in this way.

Monument building is a characteristic of early farming groups of the 4th millennium BC throughout Britain and may be linked to changing relationships between people and the land they occupy. Some of the earliest known structures are portal dolmens, oval barrows, and simple round barrows or rotunda graves (Darvill 2004b, 46–66) which serve to link communities in the Cotswold area with groups living on the near continent, in Wales, and in Ireland. These small simple structures also stand at the head of a development sequence that leads to a series of larger and more complicated monuments, of which long barrows are the most well known in Gloucestershire.

About 60 long barrows were known in Gloucestershire in 1979. Examples continue to be discovered from time to time, ten being recognised between the listing published by Helen O'Neil and Leslie Grinsell in 1960 and a resurvey in 1988 (Darvill and Grinsell 1989). A new study of Cotswold-Severn long barrows suggests that, contrary to earlier views, this distinctive class of monument had a relatively short life in terms of the period over which they were built and used (Darvill 2004b). Their longevity in the landscape should not be confused with the duration of their popularity, construction, and use which probably spanned less than five centuries. In a sense then they seem to be part of a fashion or social imperative, some being elaborations of earlier simple ceremonial structures while others were built from scratch to a single design.

Excavations took place at four long barrows in Gloucestershire over the last 25 years, adding considerably to our understanding of these monuments and providing a series of reliable radiocarbon dates for their construction and use. At Druid Stoke (GLO 28),[3] evaluations in 1983 (Smith 1989; see Grinsell 1979) included a geophysical survey which revealed evidence of the shape of the mound and the presence of a possible quarry on the south-east side. Four small excavation trenches and a later watching brief confirmed the general form of the mound and revealed the high impact of cultivation during the Roman period. A single human toe-bone apparently sealed below traces of the mound provided a radiocarbon date of 2880–2450 BC (HAR-8083: 4070±80 BP) which sits rather late in the overall sequence for similar sites and perhaps suggests that it in fact derives from a secondary burial. At Windmill Tump, Rodmarton (GLO 16), small-scale clearance following tree-fall in 1988 revealed the existence of a previously unknown third chamber on the north-west side of the barrow (Saville 1989a).

The most important investigation of a Cotswold long barrow took place at Hazleton North (GLO 54) over four seasons between October 1979 and August 1982 (Saville 1990a) and served not only to provide a very detailed study of a well-preserved example but also called into question many long-held assumptions about such monuments. The excavation revealed a trapezoidal mound 53 m long and 19 m wide at the broader 'business end' which, uncharacteristically, faced west. Two simple 'L'-shaped lateral chambers lay in the central part of the mound. The south chamber contained a scatter of human bones throughout its length: 14 adults and 6–11 pre-adults.

The north chamber contained the disarticulated remains of 4 adults and 6 pre-adults. The final burial lay in the north entrance: an adult male accompanied by grave goods suggesting a flint worker. Quarry pits lay both north and south of the mound and it was from these that most of the stone and soil used in the construction of the barrow came. Numerous radiocarbon dates showed that the long barrow was built as a unity about 3800 BC, and that use of the monument spanned little more than a century. Environmental evidence suggested that the barrow had been built in a small-scale clearance that had been cultivated and subject to some hazel-scrub colonization in the years before construction began. As already noted, the area had previously been used by a mobile hunter-gatherer community of the 6th or 5th millennium BC and some kind of occupation in the early centuries of the fourth millennium BC. It is these activities that might have given the place special meaning to local people when they selected the spot for the construction of their long barrow.

Hazleton South (GLO 33), which lies about 80 m south-east of Hazleton North, was surveyed and sampled in 1980. This revealed that both barrows had a similar plan. Hazleton South had at least one lateral chamber and flanking quarry pits (Saville 1990a, 137–40), but the surviving deposits were not investigated.

Alongside these excavations research has also been carried out on finds from earlier investigations and on the broader social issues raised by the construction and use of these magnificent monuments (Darvill 2004b). Renewed interest in the human remains has included the application of techniques from forensic science to explore the health of the populations represented, possible causes of death, and the post-mortem treatment of the corpse and skeletal remains. An analysis of bone excavated at West Tump (GLO 8), for example, revealed cutmarks on a right clavicle that had been inflicted during the perimortem period and were consistent with decapitation (Smith and Brickley 2004). Under re-analysis the same assemblage was shown to contain more animal remains than previously thought, and what may be the earliest case of a person buried with their dog (Brickley and Thomas 2004). Cranial trauma has been examined by Schulting and Wysocki (2002) while Mary Baxter (1999) looked at how long-barrow using communities handled and circulated the remains of their dead.

In the field, both intensive and extensive surveys of long barrows have been carried out. A survey of archaeological sites in the Avon and Gloucestershire Cotswolds by Alan Saville in 1976–77 provided a base-line account of the survival and condition of all kinds of monuments on the Cotswolds with long barrows singled out for special attention in light of their generally ruinous and eroding state (Saville 1980, 26–7). At a more detailed level the Cotswold Archaeological Research Group led by Alistair Marshall has carried out geophysical surveys and remote sensing at several long barrows (Marshall 1998) including Pinkwell, Chedworth (GLO 65: Marshall 1996b; 1997a); Hazleton South (GLO 33: Marshall 1996d; 1997c); Lodge Park, Farmington (GLO 5: Marshall 1996c); Northleach (GLO 30: Marshall 1996e); and Oak Piece, Temple Guiting (GLO 43: Marshall 1996g). These surveys variously revealed details of quarry pits, confirming that many Cotswold long barrows are in fact flanked by quarries of rather irregular shape and form. Some surveys showed evidence for the position of chamber areas and confirmed the structured nature of the barrow mound. Work at Shawswell Farm barrow, Rendcomb (GLO 97), suggests that this might in fact be two round barrows or a multi-component structure (Marshall 1996f).

It has long been recognized that long barrows did not contain the remains of the whole population that built them, but finding the missing people is far from easy (Darvill 2004b, 203–5). During excavations along the Wormington to Tirley pipeline a grave containing a single burial of the mid 3rd millennium BC was discovered in Wormington just over the county boundary in

Worcestershire (Coleman and Hancocks forthcoming). The pit grave was 2 m long by 0.49 m wide and 0.49 m deep. It contained the fairly well-preserved skeleton of a female aged between 25 and 40 years, placed in a flexed position on her left side (Fig. 4). Examination of the skeleton revealed that she had suffered from degenerative joint disease and had an oblique fracture to the right ulna. No grave goods were found, but there was a flint flake in the fill of the grave. There was no evidence of a covering mound and the burial must be considered an isolated flat grave. Samples of bone have been radiocarbon dated to 3640–3370 BC (WK-15335: 4747±48 BP). Such burials are rare, but in part this is because relatively few unaccompanied inhumations are adequately dated. One important parallel is the grave of adult male found in 1988 below the bank at Windmill Hill, Wiltshire (Whittle *et al.* 1999, 79–81). Lying on his right side, the skeleton was largely complete and articulated, although some bones had been displaced perhaps during a period when the grave was left open. One of the ribs from this man was radiocarbon dated to 3650–3360 BC (OxA-2403: 4745±70 BP), contemporary with the Wormington woman. Further afield, 4th-millennium BC flat graves have been identified at Pangbourne, Berkshire, where the remains of an old woman were associated with a round-bottomed ceramic vessel (Piggott 1928, 30–3), and Fengate (Cat's Water Site), Cambridgeshire, where an adult male, an adult female, a child, and an infant lay in an oval pit 4 by 2 m, the adult male having been killed by an arrow tipped with a leaf-shaped flint point (Pryor 1976; 1984, 19–25).

The other main class of monument known from the 4th millennium BC in Gloucestershire is the causewayed enclosure. Five certain and probable examples were known in 1984, all on the

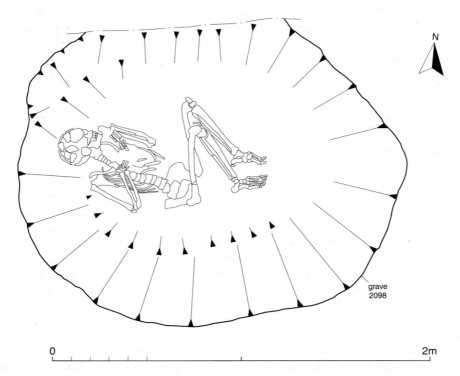

grave 2098

0   2m

Fig. 4:   Early Neolithic burial at Bank Farm (Site B), Wormington (Cotswold Archaeology).

Cotswolds (Darvill 1984a, fig. 3). Since that time a further two examples have come to light: Southmore Grove, Rendcomb (Trow 1985), and Salmonsbury (Marshall 1995a; 1996a).

The Southmore Grove enclosure was recognised as a result of aerial photography. It lies on a hill spur at 220 m AOD and has two concentric rings of ditches with a maximum diameter of 125 m thus enclosing about 1 ha. Fieldwalking confirmed a high incidence of worked flint in the field. Finds ranged in date from a microlith of the 6th or 5th millennium BC through to a barbed and tanged arrowhead of the 2nd millennium BC, but included an abundance of 4th- and 3rd-millennia BC flintwork, among which was a flake from a polished flint axe (Trow 1985, 19). Aerial photography has enhanced our understanding of other sites in the region (e.g. Darvill and Locke 1988; Oswald et al. 2001) and it must be hoped that the National Mapping Programme will eventually bring other examples to light (Bewley 2001).

Salmonsbury lies on relatively low-lying land on the interfluve between the rivers Eye/Dickler and Windrush. Marshall's initial work used resistivity survey, but gradiometry has recently been applied in connection with the development of an integrated management plan for the site (Fig. 5). The interrupted ditch runs around the contour and comprises at least two roughly concentric lines of ditch with segments between 5 and 15 m in length.

Neither Southmore Grove nor Salmonsbury has been tested through excavation, although features containing pottery and worked flint of the 4th and 3rd millennia BC were revealed by Dunning's excavation of the later prehistory hillfort/oppida at Salmonsbury in the early 1930s. His Site IV contained two segments of ditch and lies very close to the south-western terminal of what can now be seen as the inner causewayed ditch (Dunning 1976, 77–8, fig. 7).

Excavations at Crickley Hill, Coberley, started in 1969 and continued each summer until 1993. In the seasons that took place within the period covered by this review important progress was made with the definition of the two main phases of Neolithic occupation on the hilltop. At least three small sub-circular buildings were recognized as related to the early phase of the site, while rectangular buildings seemed to relate to the later phases. Internal subdivisions of the hilltop in the form of fences, and a rubble platform perhaps forming a ceremonial structure were also explored. Numerous hearths associated with scatters of pottery and worked flint were found beneath the long mound at the west end of the site (Savage 1986; Dixon 1990; 1994). During the nineteenth season in 1987 a series of platforms was recognised on the slope of the hill beside which were rows of small pits, some with deposits of cremated human bone (Dixon 1988b).

Nearby, at Peak Camp (also known as Birdlip Camp), Cowley, small-scale excavations were carried out in 1980 and 1981 (Darvill 1981; 1982a). Heavily truncated by medieval and later quarrying, this hilltop supports the remains of a promontory enclosure perhaps with two widely spaced lines of segmented ditch (Oswald et al. 2001, fig. 4.14). A single trench through the eastern side of the outer circuit revealed three main phases of ditch cutting, all associated with plain bowl style pottery (Fig. 6). Radiocarbon dates for the first phase centre on 3650–3100 BC (OxA-445: 4670±90 BP) while a single date for the second phase of 3350–2550 BC (OxA-638: 4290±80 BP) suggests that use of the enclosure continued for several centuries. A small cutting at the extreme western end of the promontory revealed what appears to be an internal ditch later sealed below a layer (? surface) of stone rubble. Dates from the primary fill of this feature overlap with the first phase of the enclosure boundaries. A rich material culture including flint arrowheads, scrapers, knives, part of a polished stone axe (Group VI), a shale arc-pendant, and abundant plain pottery was recovered from the fill of the internal ditch. Animal bones include cattle, sheep, pig, and red deer, but very little carbonised grain was present in the samples examined. Like its close neighbour Crickley Hill, Peak Camp appears to have been occupied either on a permanent or temporary

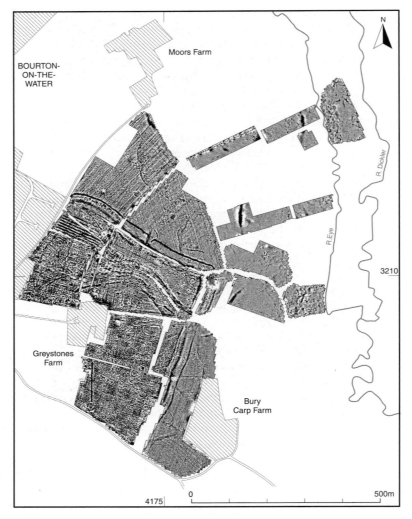

Fig. 5: Salmonsbury Camp, Bourton-on-the-Water: geophysical survey showing the Iron-Age enclosure and underlying Neolithic causewayed enclosure (Cotswold Archaeology and GSB Geophysics Ltd).

basis, although this does not preclude it also being the setting for ceremonial and ritual activities. The close proximity of the two enclosures invites comparison with the arrangement at Hambledon Hill, Dorset, where a pair of enclosures stands just under 1 km apart on adjacent parts of the same hill (Mercer 1988; Healy 2004).

Since 1979 there has been a marked increase in the number of recorded flint scatters and small groups of features and associated artefacts seemingly detached from known enclosures. Under excavation many of these comprise a single pit, or small cluster of pits, which could be interpreted as places for ceremonial depositions or, more likely, as remnants of settlement sites. Traditionally it was thought that the Upper Thames Valley was rather poor in such remains, a view

Fig. 6: Peak Camp, Cowley: excavations through the boundary earthwork in Area I in 1981 (photograph Timothy Darvill: copyright reserved).

supported by work in 1979–89 at the 40-ha site at Thornhill Farm, Fairford, which failed to reveal any early prehistoric activity on the first lowest-lying gravel terrace (Jennings *et al.* 2004). But on higher terraces the picture is rather different. Fourth-millennium BC occupation was found on the second terrace at Horcott Pit, Fairford, where more than 20 pits in pairs or threes, some containing plain bowl pottery, were recorded (Lamdin-Whymark 2003). Single sherds of 4th-millennium BC style pottery were found at two sites south-east of Cirencester during improvement works to the A419/417 road: St Augustine's Lane, Ampney Crucis, and Court Farm, Latton (Mudd *et al.* 1999, 1: 17–19; 2: 316). A posthole with putatively 4th-millennium BC pottery was discovered during a test-pit survey at RAF Fairford, Kempsford (Barber 1999; Hoad 2002).

On the Cotswolds excavations at Guiting Power 1 round barrow[4] revealed evidence of activity on the underlying ground surface which was dated to 3950–3530 BC (no reference: 4929±78 BP), but no features were recorded (Marshall 1997b). By contrast, the investigation of a Romano-British site at Vineyards Farm, Charlton Kings, revealed what seems to be a pit filled with pieces of burnt stone and ash-rich soil together with part of a round-bottomed cup typical of the mid 4th millennium BC (Rawes 1991, 32). Something of the likely density of such finds across the Cotswolds can be gauged from the results of surveys and excavations during improvements to the

A419/417 road: two sites yielded evidence of 4th-millennium BC occupation in the 12 km roadline between the river Churn and Birdlip (Mudd *et al.* 1999, 1: 17–25). At Duntisbourne Grove work for the same road-scheme revealed a handful of pits and associated postholes containing a rich assemblage of pottery, worked flint, fired clay, and animal remains (Mudd *et al.*1999, 1: 18–24; 2: 315–17). The pottery includes sherds from plain bowls and, in pit 94, pieces of what appears to be a Peterborough series vessel (possibly Fengate Ware sub-style). Hazelnut shells from the fill of this pit produced a radiocarbon date of 3650–3370 BC (NZA-8671: 4761±57 BP), which neatly accords with what is known of the plain pottery and flintwork but seems rather early for the Peterborough pottery (cf. Gibson and Kinnes 1997). North-westwards, a cluster of eight pits and a couple of outliers at Birdlip Quarry were associated with a few fragments of pottery and worked flint characteristic of the 4th millennium BC (Mudd *et al.* 1999; 1: 17–19; 2: 316).

An extensive campaign of fieldwalking in the northern Cotswolds has identified and mapped a large number of flint scatters representing the remains of early settlements. Because a robust sampling methodology was applied it is possible to predict that about 300 such sites must be expected across the area (Marshall 1985). Some have been examined through more detailed fieldwalking and geophysical surveys, including one south of Belas Knap, Sudeley, which confirms the potential of hillspurs as prime sites for extensive early settlements (Marshall 2003). Increased density of worked flint was also recorded in the area of the Burn Ground long barrow (GLO 60) during investigations in advance of the construction of the Northleach Bypass (Rawes and Rawes 1984). Investigations along the A419/417 revealed the presence of flint scatters at Hare Bushes North, Middle Duntisbourne, Norcote Farm, and St Augustine's Farm South, but excavation revealed very little by way of features associated with the use or deposition of the lithic material (Mudd *et al.* 1999, 1: 18–25). This is entirely typical of such sites across southern England and strongly suggests the existence of activity areas which yield few substantial sub-surface features and which may only ever have comprised debris deposited on the contemporary ground surface that through later cultivation and bioturbation has become today's topsoil.

In the Severn Valley, excavations by David Evans on the site of a medieval moated manor near St George's Church, King's Stanley, has revealed an earlier Romano-British villa, later prehistoric pits and occupation debris, and more than 600 worked flints of the 5th to 2nd millennium BC (Heighway *et al.* 1988). Excavations in 2003–4 revealed pits of later 4th- or early 3rd-millennium BC date (Evans 2005) and it may be speculated that the density of material here suggests the possibility of an enclosure of some kind. Flint scatters on other gravel terraces and gravel islands within the Severn Valley have been reported east of Tewkesbury (Walker *et al.* 2004, 35), at Arlingham (Curtis 1998), and in the Frome Valley west of Stroud (Anon. 1982). Further south occupation has been recorded in what is now the intertidal zone at Hills Flats, Oldbury-on-Severn (Allen 1997). At Oldbury occupation on a buried ground surface has been dated to 4330–3980 BC (Beta-84850: 5310±70 BP) with wood from nearby submerged peat beds that seal the surface dated to 3650–3100 BC (Beta-44057: 4630±70 BP) and still later peats above (Allen 2000a). Quartz pebbles from these 3rd- and 2nd-millennia BC silts have been interpreted as sling-shot (Allen 2000a), but could equally have been collected for their magical qualities (Darvill 2002). Elsewhere along what were then the margins of the Severn Estuary there is abundant evidence for occupation around palaeochannels and on ground surfaces now flooded as a result of subsequent sea level rises (Allen 1998).

No recent excavations appear to have yielded 4th-millennium BC pottery or features at sites west of the Severn, but intensive fieldwalking between 1985 and 1988 showed that flint scatters broadly datable to the 4th and 3rd millennia BC were present. High-density scatters were noted at

Longstone Field, St Briavels, and Huntsham Hill, English Bicknor (James and Walters 1988; Stait 1990; Walters 1992, 22–5; see Bowden 2005 for Malvern Hills area).

Another useful indicator of the extent of settlement in the 4th and 3rd millennia BC is finds of flint and stone axes. More than 20 stone axes and some 18 flint axes have been reported over the last 25 years from right across the county. A hoard of three axes was found about 1 m down in the garden of Oakfield Road, Bishop's Cleeve (Kilminster 1990; 1995), two being of Group I greenstone from Cornwall and the other of Group VII rock from North Wales. This is the first such hoard from Gloucestershire but on the basis of examples elsewhere in Britain may be interpreted as a ceremonial deposit (Thomas 1999, 85–6).

Two stone axes originally found *c.*1939–40 near Nailsworth were recorded, although it is not clear whether they were found together (Walrond 1986). A fragment of a Group I axe with contemporary flintwork was found during fieldwalking at Manor Farm, Daglingworth (Ecclestone 2001, 77; 2002), and part of a Group VI axe was found during field survey for the Birdlip Bypass (Darvill 1984b, 33; 1984c). A Cornish axe with a pointed butt was found near Chipping Campden (Clews 1984a), and another greenstone axe with a pointed butt, also probably Cornish, was found at Driffield (Ibid. 225). Other axes have been found east of the Severn at King's Stanley (probably Cornish: Heighway *et al.* 1988, 37); Uley (Price 2004a and b); Wickwell, Chedworth (Marshall 1992b); The Gables, Broadwell (Saville 1989b, 46–7; 1990b); and London Street, Fairford (Phillips 1979). Three axes were found on the intertidal foreshore of the Severn Estuary at Hills Flats near Oldbury; one each of Groups I, VIII, and XXI (Allen 1990). From west of the Severn two polished stone axes were found in flood debris at Lower Lydbrook (Anon. 1997, 10); a fragment of Group VI axe was found at Huntsham Hill, English Bicknor (Walters 1988, 37; James and Walters 1988); a Cornish axe came from Littledean in 1993 (Johns 1993, 39); and unidentified examples were found at Town Farm, Newent (Hutton and Hutton 1994; 1995); Bull's Hill, Walford (Walters 1992, 29 and fig. 17); and Oxenhall (Bick 1980; Saville 1987).

Complete flint axes, or substantial parts thereof, have been found at Somerford Lakes Reserve, Poole Keynes (Clews 1985); Dumbleton (Smith 1986a; Smith and Cox 1986, 4–5); Lechlade (Darvill 1985); Wickwell, Chedworth (Marshall 1992b); Middle Down, Hampnett (Marshall 1992c); Woodlands, Rendcomb (Marshall 1992d); Gulf Scrubs, Withington (Marshall 1992e); Newland (Walters 1990); Haymes, Southam (Saville 1986d); Barmer's Land Farm, Tytherington (Roe 1985); Long Cross, Lawrence Weston (Parker 1984, 28); Tresham, Hawkesbury (Iles and White 1986, 51); Bearse, St Briavels (Walters 1992, 25 and fig. 12); and Little Blacks Field, Taynton (Anon. 1997, 11). Two pieces of polished flint axe were found during field survey for the Birdlip Bypass (Darvill 1984b, 33; 1984c) and one piece was found during fieldwalking over the causewayed enclosure at Southmore Grove, Rendcomb (Trow 1985, 19). A large part of a rather unusual flint chisel or pick came to light at Haymes, Southam (Saville 1986d).

Taken together, these monuments, small groups of features, stray finds, and flint scatters provided valuable source material for two studies of settlement patterns on the Cotswolds (Holgate 1988; Snashall 2002). Holgate's work (1988, 150–3) focused on the Thames Basin and emphasised the essential continuity of settlement on the calcareous upland soils from the 6th and 5th millennia BC through into the 4th and 3rd millennia, with small cleared areas within the woodland providing a series of small-scale settlement zones. Snashall (2002, 129–34), by contrast, adopts a post-processualist approach that focuses on the experience of understanding, memorialising, and reshaping the world. She suggests that different kinds of short-term and long-term residence areas can be identified by the presence of particular kinds of flintwork assemblages. Both studies emphasise continuity in the use of the landscape from the 6th through to the 3rd millennia

BC and the way in which successive communities engraved their identity on the spaces they used and the places they created. One way this seems to have been achieved in northern and western parts of the British Isles was by signing the land with rock art (Bradley 1997).

Rock art was unknown in Gloucestershire 25 years ago, but several certain and a few possible panels have come to light since. A local block of limestone found on the northern side of Nottingham Hill is the most southerly example of a type of decorated mobiliary stone normally found in northern England (Morris and Marshall 1983). The decoration comprises a large central cup-mark 155 mm across surrounded close to its lip by a penannular channel or ring. A shallow radial groove links the central cup with the edge of the stone. A smaller cup-mark is fitted into one corner of the block and through this motif there is another channel or ring more or less concentric with the larger central ring (Fig. 7). All the motifs on the stone were produced by hammering or pecking, a technique common to much prehistoric rock art in the British Isles. A single possible cup-mark has been recognised on a columnar block of limestone from Cleeve Hill just a few kilometres away from the Nottingham Hill find (Marshall 1978), and further stones have been reported from Rook Pool, Swell, and Oxpens, Yanworth (Marshall 1986). All four decorated slabs from the Cotswolds were found on the mid-slopes of stream valleys in positions marginal to adjacent spurs (Marshall 1986, 225). Other such stones might await discovery within the Cotswolds. Cup-marked rocks have also been identified in the Forest of Dean (Walker 1991; Johns 1990; Johns 1992) at the Drummer Boy Stone (2 cups), Blakeney Hill Woods (at least four panels: (a) with 5 cups; (b) with 14 hollows/?cup-marks; (c) with one cup; (d) with one cup), Broom Hill (4 cups), near the Drummer Boy Stone (2 cups), and Brockweir (1 bowl). However, at least some of these last-mentioned finds should be treated with caution as a stone from Edge Hills, near Cinderford, with what appears to be a large cup-mark was in fact a hollow filled with iron-working slag and somehow connected with heating metal during forging (Price 1991). These caveats aside, the emergent group of rock art in the county suggests that there is more to find which will perhaps allow its cultural context to be more precisely tied to comparable traditions in Wales (Darvill and Wainwright 2003) and midland/northern England (Beckensall 1999, 79–82).

Fig. 7: Decorated stone from Nottingham Hill, Gotherington (photograph Corinium Museum, Cirencester: copyright reserved).

3000–2000 BC: New Horizons and the First Metal Working

Long barrows and causewayed enclosures had mainly fallen out of use by about 3000 BC, although people still visited them and they remained distinctive features in the changing landscape. Environmental evidence from the fill of the quarry pits at Hazleton North (GLO 54) suggests some regeneration of woodland cover after the main use of the monument ceased, showing perhaps that woodland clearance during the 4th millennium BC was not that extensive (Bell in Saville 1990a, 222). Much of the evidence for occupation in Gloucestershire during the early third millennium BC comes from pits and pit clusters.

New finds of Peterborough Ware, which spans the end of the 4th and the beginning of the 3rd millennium BC, have been relatively few, but include the Mortlake bowl from Tewkesbury recovered during excavations in 1972–4 (Hannan 1993, 29–30, 47); Horcott Pit, Fairford (Lamdin-Whymark 2003); Bourton-on-the Water Primary School (Nichols 2001); and the Duntisbourne Grove site already mentioned (Mudd *et al.* 1999, 1: 19; 2: 316–17). Grooved Ware, current mainly during the middle and later 3rd millennium BC has recently been reported from five sites. At The Loders, Lechlade (Darvill *et al.* 1986), the remains of two vessels were associated with a small flint assemblage comprising mainly broken tools and a small amount of working debris, an oblong sarsen boulder, and 17 pieces of animal bone including a cattle sacrum with evidence of butchery and a red deer metatarsus with evidence of groove and splinter working. Nearby, at Roughground Farm, Lechlade, a cluster of four pits yielded Grooved Ware pottery together with flint-working waste, animal bone, fired clay, the remains of bone working, and a hammerstone that had probably been used for flint knapping (Darvill 1993). More than half the animal bones were from pig and about a quarter from cattle. Sheep/goat were poorly represented; one fragment of dog/wolf was present. Red deer remains suggested that they had been hunted by the occupants of the site. A few fragments of freshwater mussel add another interesting dimension to life at the site. Three radiocarbon dates of 2950–2350 BC (HAR-5498: 4100±100 BP), 2700–2100 BC (HAR-5500: 3940±80 BP) and 2600–1950 BC (HAR-5501: 3820±90 BP) show good clustering around the middle centuries of the 3rd millennium BC.

Possible Grooved Ware has been reported from Saintbridge (Darvill in Garrod and Heighway 1984, 72–3) but it may be similar-looking later Bronze-Age decorated post Deverel-Rimbury ware (Darvill and Timby 1986, 54). Grooved Ware associated with worked flint, bone, and hazlenut shells has been reported from investigations in advance of gravel extraction at the Cotswold Community site, Somerford Keynes (Laws 2002; Weaver 2004), and Horcott Pit, Fairford (Lamdin-Whymark 2003). Less well-defined features of the same period have also been located at Babdown Farm, Beverstone (Parry 2000), and Harry Stoke Lane, Stoke Gifford (Samuel 1997).

One of the biggest changes in our understanding of the 3rd millennium BC in Gloucestershire over the last 25 years results from the increased incidence of evidence associated with Beaker pottery. Although no occupation sites with structural remains have yet been found, pits and spreads of domestic debris have come to light at 17 sites east of the Severn, especially on the lower ground of the Cotswold dip-slope and in the Upper Thames Valley.

Small amounts of Beaker pottery have been found as residual items at a handful of sites: in a mid 2nd-millennium BC boundary ditch at Rudgeway Lane, Tewkesbury, possibly contemporary with a small hearth found 75 m south-west of the south end of the ditch (Walker *et al.* 2004, 59); in an early 1st-millennium BC context at Shorncote (Hearne and Heaton 1994, 34); in the fill of a Romano-British grave at Hucclecote (Thomas *et al.* 2003, 8); in various later prehistoric contexts at Shorncote, Somerford Keynes (Mepham in Hearne and Adam 1999, 59); and in colluvium overlying a late 2nd-millennium BC old ground surface at The Buckles, Frocester (Darvill in Price 2000b, 204). All these usefully fatten-up the distribution of known activity of the period and serve to alert us to the possibility of finding more substantial occupation in these areas in future.

Pits and pit clusters associated with Beaker pottery have been recorded at two sites on the route of the Esso Midline: Toddington and Yanworth (Smith 1986b; Smith and Cox 1986, 5–6). At Station Road, Kemble, Beaker pottery was found in one of two early pits (Nichols 2002), while at the rugby ground on the Whiteway, Cirencester, Beaker pottery was found in the fill of a large stone-filled pit (Hicks 2000). At Horcott Pit, Fairford, pits variously containing Beaker pottery and Grooved Ware have been excavated but only some of the early work here is fully reported (Pine and Preston 2004, 5; see Lamdin-Whymark 2003). The same applies to investigations in advance of gravel extraction at the Cotswold Community, Somerford Keynes, where pits associated with Beaker pottery also contained worked flint and hazlenut shells (Laws 2002).

During the improvement of the A419/417 road in 1996–7 no less than four sites yielded pieces of Beaker pottery, mainly in the southern section of the road corridor away from the limestone uplands (Mudd *et al.* 1999, 2: 317). Of these four sites just one, Trinity Farm, produced a substantial assemblage estimated at 14 separate vessels (Ibid. 1999, 25–7; 317–19). The pottery derived from a cluster of three pits and an adjacent tree-throw hole; it comprises only fineware pottery with fingernail and comb impressed lines in bell-Beaker forms (Style 2: Case 1993, 244). In addition, worked flint, burnt limestone, charcoal, and hazlenut shells were represented. A few grains of wheat and barley were present, and environmental indicators suggested that the pits lay within an open landscape. Two radiocarbon dates of 2490–2140 BC (NZA-8673: 3876±57 BP) and 2470–2130 BC (NZA-8674: 3836±58 BP) accord well with other Style 2 Beaker-associated dates from the area and suggest this is a relatively early site of its kind.

At Roughground Farm, Lechlade, five widely scattered pits contained fineware and domestic Beaker pottery, an assemblage of flint tools dominated by scrapers and knives, a collection of stone rubbers, hammerstones, a cushion stone perhaps from metal working, and a few fragments of animal bone (Darvill 1993, 15–21). A single radiocarbon date of 2500–1750 BC (HAR-5499: 3710±100 BP) places the use of these features a few centuries later than the Grooved Ware activity on the site (see above). Nearby, at Gassons Road, Lechlade, a cluster of 15 pits spread over an area 6.5 by 4.5 m provides an insight into the kind of site that was more typical of the period (King in Boyle *et al.* 1998, 269–75). The pits varied in size between 0.75 and 1.25 m across and averaged 0.35 m deep. Red deer antler picks lay on the floor of two of the pits, while most contained small quantities of charcoal, worked flint, and burnt bone and stone. Fragments of six ceramic vessels of 'domestic' Beaker type came from one of the pits (Barclay *et al.* 2003, 190; and cf. Darvill in Boyle *et al.* 1998, 275–6 where misreported as Grooved Ware), suggesting a small-scale occupation site nearby.

The number of Beaker burials has also increased considerably with the discovery and excavation under modern conditions of four examples since 1979. At the Memorial Hall, Lechlade, two Beaker burials were discovered in 1995 (Thomas and Holbrook in Boyle *et al.* 1998, 282–88). Burial 1 comprised a mature adult male aged between 30 and 45 years that had been placed on his left-hand side in a tightly flexed position within a north–south oriented oval pit 1.90 by 0.95 m (Fig. 8A). A decorated Beaker of short-necked type (Style 2: Case 1993, 244) had been placed at his feet and a lot of charcoal was present within and around the remains of this broken vessel. A radiocarbon date of 2020–1690 BC (BM-2980: 3530±50 BP) was obtained from collagen in the bones of this burial. About 7.5 m to the north was a second slightly larger grave oriented east–west (Fig. 8B). This contained the fragmentary remains of an older infant aged 2–4 years radiocarbon

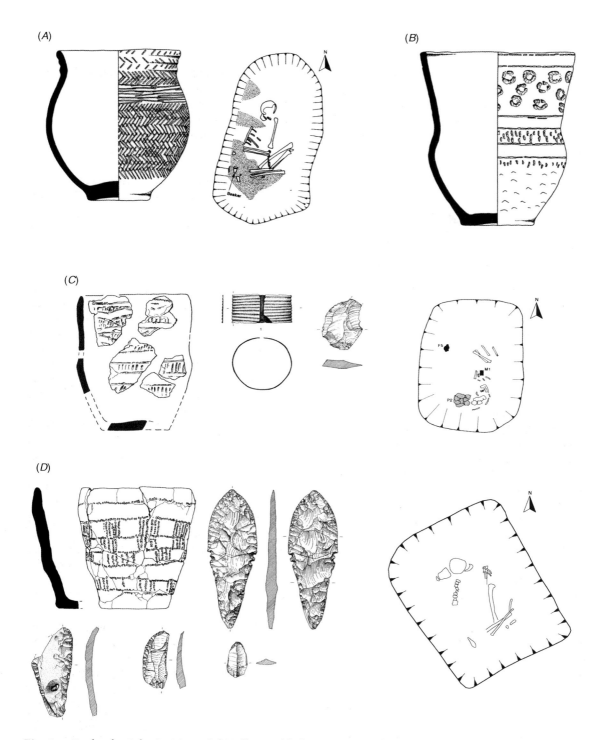

Fig. 8: Beaker burials. A: Memorial Hall I, Lechlade; B: Memorial Hall II, Lechlade; C: Shorncote Grave 1007, Somerford Keynes; D: Shorncote Grave 12, Somerford Keynes (A and B Cotswold Archaeology; C and D after Barclay et al. 1995, figs. 2–4). Scales = graves 1: 40; finds 1: 4.

dated to 1920–1630 BC (BM-2981: 3460±50 BP). Within the grave was a Beaker pot of long-necked type (Style 3: Case 1993, 244) with an unusual decorative scheme involving twisted-cord impressed rings, an unworked flint flake, and copper awl. Four fragments of an adult long bone were also recovered from the fill of the grave, perhaps suggesting that an earlier burial had been disturbed when the grave was dug or that excarnated remains had been used in the funerary rituals. Originally, both these burials may have lay beneath simple bowl barrows, but no traces of mounds survived.

At Shorncote Quarry, Somerford Keynes, also in the Upper Thames Valley, two Beaker burials were found, perhaps representing the start of a cemetery that continued through into later centuries (Barclay *et al.* 1995). In Area 1 a ring-ditch 9.5 m in diameter with a ditch about 1 m wide surrounded a central rectangular grave. Within the grave was the poorly preserved burial of an adult male aged upwards of 30 years placed on his left side with the head to the north-west and facing north-east. A rather crude long-necked Beaker (Style 3: Case 1993, 244) had been placed on its side next to the skull and nearby was a flint knife. A fine flint dagger was found near the position of the feet and a retouched flake and flint knife were found near the legs (Barclay *et al.* 1995, 25–9; Fig. 8D). A second grave was found 80 m away to the north in Area 2, in this case probably a flat grave with no surrounding ditch. The body, that of a adolescent aged between 14 and 16 years, had been laid in its grave with the head to the south, facing east. A long-necked Beaker (Style 3: Case 1993, 244) had been placed on its side next to the skull, a decorated bronze bracelet adorned the right wrist, and a flint flake lay near the feet (Barclay *et al.* 1995, 29–31; Fig. 8C). A sample of bone from the skeleton was radiocarbon dated to 1950–1620 BC (BM-2862: 3480±60 BP). The ribbed bronze bracelet is the first of its kind to have been found in the Cotswolds, although a handful of comparable pieces are known from Beaker graves elsewhere in the British Isles, mainly in Scotland.

About 400 m north of the two Beaker burials at Shorncote was a possible hengi-form monument: a penannular ring-ditch about 9 m across internally with an entrance gap opening slightly west of north (Barclay *et al.* 1995, 31–8). Few finds were recovered, but these included a fine barbed and tanged arrowhead. About 40 m east of the Beaker burials was another penannular ditched structure, about 12 m in diameter with a wide opening to the east. A large rectangular pit and several small round pits may be associated, but the exact date and purpose of this structure is far from clear (Barclay *et al.* 1995, 38–9). It may tentatively be considered as a ritual-funerary monument perhaps related to various 'U'-shaped sanctuary-enclosures found in the Upper Thames Valley and midlands which date to the later 4th and 3rd millennia BC (Darvill 2004b, 206–6). At West Hill, Uley, excavations in 1977–9 revealed such a 'U'-shaped ditched enclosure 25 by 18 m, open to the north. Three large pits and two smaller hollows lay outside the enclosure to the north. Although undated, all these features stratigraphically pre-date the later prehistoric and Romano-British cult centre and temple complex (Woodward and Leach 1993, 303–5). Whether the monument at Uley ever contained a mound of some kind is unknown, but it lies just 700 m south of Hetty Pegler's Tump (GLO 14). At Shorncote, the hengi-form and 'U'-shaped enclosure could be contemporary and suggest the emergence of a small local ceremonial focus during the later third millennium BC.

Some 20 km east of Shorncote the area around the confluence of the rivers Thames and Leach at Lechlade also seems to have developed a special significance during the 3rd millennium BC. Mention has already been made of the pits with Grooved Ware and Beaker pottery and of the Beaker burials at the Memorial Hall site. Two small henges are known through aerial photography, one either side of the Thames at Buscot to the south and Lechlade to the north (Benson and Miles

1974, map 3). Each is spatially associated with a cursus monument, although only the Lechlade cursus has been investigated through excavation.

The cursus on the north side of the Thames at Lechlade was discovered in the 1940s and excavated in 1965 and again in 1985 (Barclay *et al.* 2003, 190–213). As currently known, the Lechlade cursus is a square-ended example, although only the northernmost 300 m is represented. At 45 m wide this cursus fits well within the range represented at other Thames Valley sites, and shares with others the fact that the eastern side ditch is wider and deeper than its western counterpart. Neither excavation provided datable material from the primary ditch fills, but abundant Peterborough Ware and Grooved Ware were found in 1985 in the upper fill of the eastern ditch. This suggests a construction date of around 3000 BC or a little before. Environmental evidence indicates that it had been built in open grassland (Robinson in Barclay *et al.* 2003, 208–9), entirely consistent with a ceremonial function that involved processions along the axis of the monument perhaps beginning or ending at the confluence of the rivers some 850 m away to the south-east.

The Lechlade cursus and its companion, the Buscot Wick cursus south of the Thames in Oxfordshire, represent the westernmost such monuments along the river, standing well upstream of the larger cluster of six examples between Drayton and North Stoke (Barclay and Hey 1999, fig. 6.1). No cursus monuments are yet known on the Cotswold uplands, but the theme of linear ceremonial monuments is represented at Crickley Hill where investigations of the long mound during the final few seasons' work showed that its western focus lay over an earlier circular ceremonial platform (Savage 1986, 231).

Although more dispersed than the ceremonial centres already discussed, attention may also be drawn to the group of monuments clustered around the headwaters of the river Evenlode on the Gloucestershire/Oxfordshire/Warwickshire border. On the north-east side is the stone circle known as the Rollright Stones and its associated structures investigated in the early 1980s by George Lambrick for the Oxford Archaeological Unit (Lambrick 1988). To the south-west is Condicote Henge and a large number of putatively associated round barrow cemeteries (Darvill and Grinsell 1989, fig. 6). At Condicote excavations by Alan Saville for Western Archaeological Trust in the late 1970s significantly enhanced our understanding of the date and cultural affinities of this classic henge monument (Saville 1983). Rather unusually, the henge comprises two near-concentric ditches with a single bank between them (Class Ia); the internal diameter of the bank is about 112 m, enclosing an area of about 0.9 ha. Excavations in the north-west sector in 1977 established that much of the interior was open space, although one possible stone-socket was identified. The inner henge ditch was about 4.2 m wide and 2.4 m deep below the present surface. Analysis of a soil column through the ditch fill revealed that the monument had been built in a small clearing within an essentially wooded landscape. It was not until the later 1st millennium BC that major clearance of the landscape was represented. Radiocarbon dates of 2400–1850 BC (HAR-3064: 3720±80 BP) and 2400–1700 BC (HAR-3067: 3670±100 BP) suggest a construction date in the late 3rd millennium BC, according well with the small amount of pottery recorded from the ditch fills which seems to be mainly domestic Beaker. Animal bones from the lower fills of the ditch showed a dominance of cattle followed by sheep and pig. Dog was also represented.

More widely across the county stray finds and scatters of worked flint emphasise the extensive nature of occupation through the 3rd millennium BC. Many of the flint scatters recorded as essentially 4th-millennium BC in origin include substantial later components, and some of the flint and stone axes noted in the previous section may also be of later date. To these can be added occasional very specific 3rd-millennium BC finds, for example the rather rare Conygar Hill type of barbed and tanged arrowhead from Kilkenny, Dowdeswell (Saville 1986c), suggestive perhaps of a burial in the area. Perforated stone implements also mainly belong to the later 3rd and early 2nd millennia BC and while not especially numerous do show evidence of long-range trade networks. From west of the Severn two perforated maceheads have been reported from Walford (Herefordshire): a broken Group I (Cornish) example from Walford itself, and a complete specimen of unknown origin from Coleraine Farm, Coughton (Anon. 2004b). Part of a quartzite pestle macehead of Thames type was found in the 1950s at Stidcote Farm, Tytherington, but only came to wider attention in the 1980s (Howell 1980; Roe 1985). Reporting a battle-axe found in 1969 at number 5 Oatground, Sinwell, Wotton-under-Edge, Saville and Roe (1984) review the other finds of perforated implements from Gloucestershire known up until that time and note the varied and far-flung sources represented: the Whin Sill of Northumberland (Group XVIII); Corndon Hill on the Shropshire/Powys border (Group XII); and, rather unusually, flint perhaps from eastern England. The Wotton-under-Edge example, however, stands apart from the others in that its form suggests it was imported from Scandinavia (Saville and Roe 1984, 19–20).

Such long-distance connections may also be glimpsed in the important early metal-working finds that have come to light in the county in recent decades. At the Cinema Site in Tewkesbury an oval pit containing most of a broken Mortlake style pot and a copper awl was cut by a second rather smaller pit containing no finds and also by an oval grave containing the tightly flexed skeleton of an adult but slightly-built woman. The whole was covered by a spread of gravel which might just have been the remains of a low barrow but more likely simply the upcast from digging the pits and grave (Hannan 1993, 29–32). An interesting parallel for the earliest pit is known from Caversham, Oxfordshire, where part of a bronze awl was seemingly found with pottery datable to the 3rd millennium BC, although precise details of the find itself and the cultural affiliation of the pottery remain uncertain (Piggott 1928, 33–9). Mention has already been made of the possible cushion-stone from Roughground Farm, Lechlade (Allen et al. 1993, 21, fig. 18.1). Two early bronze axes were found during the construction of a new house at Oddington in 1979 (Needham and Saville 1981). Both have unbevelled and undecorated faces, narrow butts, and a wide blade and they fall within the earliest tradition of tin-bronze tools known from Britain, being probably the earliest reliably provenanced hoard of such pieces from southern Britain. Regionally, this group joins the early copper axe from Hawling (Ellison 1984, fig. 2), a fine decorated bronze axe from Whittington (Needham 1979, 267, fig. 2.5), and a small thin-butted copper axe of Stage I copper working found at Viney Hill, Blakeney (Needham et al. 1996).

With firm evidence now established for the early extraction of copper in central Wales around the headwaters of the river Severn (Timberlake and Switsur 1988) it is perhaps appropriate to see the lands flanking the Lower Severn as a gateway into the interior of Britain and an area closely connected with the early development of metallurgy. However, anyone visiting the lower Severn and its estuary would have found a river very different to that of recent times. Relative sea level changes continued during the third millennium BC with further flooding of existing land surfaces in the Lower Severn Valley. At Seabank, north of Avonmouth on the North Avon Levels, a trench revealed organic layers representing the two uppermost bands of peat in the Wentlooge Formation. The lower of these, sometimes known locally as the BARAS Layer because it was first recognised by the Bristol and Region Archaeological Services, lay at 4.32 m AOD (nearly 3 m below the present ground surface) and was dated to about 2200 BC (Insole 1997). Later investigations of the same sequence at Cabot Park, Avonmouth, provided additional radiocarbon dates of 2900–2570 BC (Beta-125794: 4170±70 BP) and 2700–2200 BC (Beta-125795: 3970±60 BP) and environmental evidence suggesting saltmarsh with woodland nearby (Locock 1999a, 3–4; Locock 2001). Related peats have been noted at Stup Pill, Avonmouth (Tavener 1996).

2000–1000 BC: Organising the Landscape

Traditionally, the archaeology of the 2nd millennium BC in Gloucestershire has been dominated by the study of round barrows (Drinkwater and Saville 1984). The last 25 years has seen a considerable improvement in our understanding of these monuments. In parallel, however, there has been a commensurate increase in evidence relating to other facets of life during that millennium, notably the excavation of settlements that can be considered contemporary with the construction and use of round barrows.

It is now well established that the first round barrows were built in southern England during the 4th millennium BC and that these sites stand at the head of a long tradition of barrow building that reached it peak in the first half of the 2nd millennium BC. A revised listing of Gloucestershire barrows, including ring-ditches (Darvill and Grinsell 1989), added more than 50 examples to the previous total (O'Neil and Grinsell 1960). More than 15 round barrows and ring-ditches datable to the 2nd millennium BC have been excavated over the last 25 years (see above for excavations relating to earlier round barrows) and these provide more secure dating evidence than was previously available and give good insights into the complexity of the funeral rituals and construction sequences of these monuments. Excavation has also shown that a number of putative upstanding barrows and ring-ditches are in fact natural features. Thus at Swell 13 (Catchpole 1994) and at two sites on the line of the Birdlip Bypass (Parry 1998, 25) round stone mounds were found to be modern dumps or natural outcrops, while at Guiting Power cropmark and soilmark indications suggesting the presence of sub-surface ring-ditches proved to be clay-filled periglacial features in the bedrock surface (Marshall 1989).

On the Cotswold uplands five round barrows/ring-ditches have been examined through excavation. Guiting Power 1 was shown by geophysical survey to be about 15 m in diameter with a stone envelope covering an earthen core. Two adjacent pits may be quarries (Marshall 1993). Excavations in 1996 revealed five main phases to the development of the site: (1) a large and intense pyre was built on a surface that showed evidence of activity extending back into the early Neolithic; (2) a pit was dug through the remains of the pyre, the beginnings of a stone cairn constructed in the pit, and the burnt and unburnt remains of an adult male and animals were added to this construction; (3) a clay core was built over the primary structure, incorporating various deposits of cremated bone and the remains of other pyres; (4) limestone slabs taken from an adjacent quarry pit were used to form a kerb around the central mound and perhaps a capping too; (5) the kerb was extended and the mound enlarged, accompanied by the deposition of a further burial comprising at least one adult and perhaps an immature individual along with a flint tool and a bronze point. Finally, a collared urn was placed against the modified kerb (Marshall 1997b).

Guiting Power 3 was completely excavated in 1991–2 (Marshall 1992a; 1992b; 1993; 1994). Six main phases were identified: (1) spreads of burnt material, posts and stakeholes within an area about 18 m across showed signs of trampling and subsequently became of the focus of the barrow; (2) a layer of clay about 0.25 m thick was spread over the earlier area of activity; (3) a free standing circle of 65 posts was driven through the clay floor to form an enclosure 13.4 m across. A biconical urn and another vessel were smashed and scattered across part of the interior of the enclosure. In (4) the post-ring was demolished and fires were lit in the centre and around about. A cremation pyre was probably burnt within the area to be occupied by the barrow and the cremated bones collected and deposited in a shallow hollow in the centre of the site. The remains of a mature adult female aged 30–45 years together with an almost full-term foetus were identified in the burial pit. A miniature ceramic vessel was found near the pit and charcoal from the cremation provided a radiocarbon date of 2120–1730 BC (RCD-726: 3560±60 BP). In (5) a low mound of soil and clay was built over the burial, working outwards from the centre. The core of the mound was augmented by domestic refuse including flint-working waste. The cremated remains of child about 3 years old were placed in a shallow pit on the flank of the primary mound during its construction. Finally (6), the mound was enlarged by the addition of stone rubble quarried from a surrounding ring-ditch. When completed the mound was about 20 m across and 2 m high, enclosed by a ring-ditch 39 m in diameter, 3 m across and 1 m deep, separated from the mound by a berm some 6 m wide. Several pits were dug into the berm as well as two smaller scoops that each held a cremation, one a child and one an infant. Overall, the sequence is rather similar to the complicated set of rituals represented at Bevan's Quarry (O'Neil 1967; and see Darvill and Grinsell 1989, fig. 8) and emphasises the point that many round barrows on the Cotswolds acted as cemeteries for several generations.

At Birdlip, a heavily eroded penannular ring-ditch about 20 m in diameter with its narrow entrance to the south-east was excavated on the route of the Birdlip Bypass in 1987–8 (Parry 1998, 30–1). The northern part of the circumference has been lost to later cultivation, but a nearby pit contained fragments of collared urn, burnt flint flakes, and burnt clay. Charcoal from this feature provided a radiocarbon date of 1250–500 BC (OxA-2544: 2700±100 BP). Palaeobotanical remains in the pit included fragments of hazlenut shell and hazel charcoal; much the same was found in the fill of the ring-ditch along with a few cereal grains and cherry or sloe stone (Parry 1998, 77).

Finally, two conjoined ring-ditches were investigated at St Augustine's Lane, Preston, as part of the A419/417 improvements (Mudd et al. 1999, 1: 28–33). The southern ring-ditch was the earlier and had an internal diameter of 18 m with a surrounding ditch 1.2–1.6 m wide. In the centre was a pit containing the remains of a cremation, perhaps originally associated with the collared urn that was represented by a single sherd discovered during the field evaluation of the site. The second ring-ditch, with an internal diameter of 15 m, had been added to the north side of the first, partly utilising the earlier structure to a create a monument with a figure-of-eight plan. Pieces of urn found in the ditch suggest that originally there had been a cremation here too. A radiocarbon date of 1960–1630 BC (NZA-8614: 3482±60 BP) relates to a piece of bone from the primary ditch fill. Both ring-ditches appear to form part of a small dispersed cemetery of perhaps four barrows (Mudd et al. 1999, 1: fig. 2.11).

Detailed surveys of at least 20 round barrows/ring-ditches have been undertaken. Condicote 2 was surveyed and subject to a resistivity survey which revealed the barrow to be oval, 20 by 13 m, with a central area of dense stonework at the core (Marshall 1995b). At Hawling 2 similar surveys revealed the barrow to be about 18–20 m in diameter but no substantial internal structures were found (Marshall 1995c). Surveys at Temple Guiting 2 and 3 revealed that the extant mounds were surrounded by ring-ditches, each about 15 m across, and that two further ring-ditches continued the line of barrows over a distance of 75 m. Temple Guiting 8 also proved to be surrounded by a ring-ditch some 2 m wide and 27 m in diameter. Temple Guiting 16 on the other hand proved to be oval in plan, 17 by 9 m. Here there was no surrounding ditch but possible quarry pits were located nearby (Marshall 1995d). Upper Slaughter 1 was shown to be 20 m in diameter, perhaps with an earthen core enveloped in stone and surrounded by an irregular and perhaps incomplete ditch (Marshall 1995e). Hazleton 3 was found to be 20 m in diameter (Marshall 1997b). Elsewhere on the limestone uplands, two possible ring-ditches were noted east of Condicote henge in an area known to be rich in flint scatters (Bateman and Walker 1993), and three ring-ditches were identified during field evaluations at Dryleaze Farm, Siddington, one with a central feature (Kelly and Laws 2002). Further south a ring-ditch was found at Trappels Farm, Cromhall (Erskine 1998), and at least four were noted at Acton Turville during the analysis of 1946 aerial photographs (Iles 1980).

In the Upper Thames Valley nine single ring-ditches/round barrows have been examined. At Lechlade one ring-ditch was excavated within a small compact cemetery of four monuments at Butler's Field (Jennings in Boyle *et al.* 1998, 9–13). Internally 9 m in diameter, the ditch was *c*.2.5 m wide and up to 1.8 m deep. The monument most likely included a central mound, but the pattern of silting in the perimeter ring-ditch suggested that an outer bank may also have been present as at some 'fancy-barrows' in Wessex. Near the centre was a shallow scoop containing the disturbed cremated remains of an adult probably over 30 years of age. Pottery fragments suggested that there may have been other burials in the barrow defined by the ring-ditch. Three cremations, some representing more than one individual, were found to the north-east of the ring-ditch and another to the north. Redeposited cremated remains were also found in seven later features. Together these remains emphasise the point that round barrow cemeteries are more than just the barrows; burials around about are important too. A ring-ditch with no evidence of a burial or central feature and a small barrow were examined in advance of gravel extraction at the Cotswold Community, Somerford Keynes (Laws 2002; Weaver 2004).

The largest group of round barrows/ring-ditches to be investigated in the county are those at Shorncote, Somerford Keynes. Here a cemetery of six barrows developed around the early ceremonial focus represented by pair of Beaker graves, a hengi-form monument, and 'U'-shaped enclosure. These barrows were excavated over several seasons and by different archaeological contractors as the quarry has expanded. Figure 9 shows the distribution of barrows known so far, most of which are represented as ring-ditches.

Two of the ring-ditches (A and B) were very small; one had an internal diameter of just 4 m with a central disturbed pit while the other was too badly damaged to be sure of its size (Barclay *et al.* 1995, 31). Ring-ditch C (2806) was a near-complete circle 5.7 m across with a single south-east facing gap. Heavily truncated by later agriculture, no central features survived. Ring-ditch D (2623) was 5.4 m in diameter with a small gap in the ditch opening to the north-west; the ditch was about 0.6 m wide. A slightly off-central pit may have held the primary burial, but the site was heavily truncated and no remains survived. Ring-ditch E (2607) was considerably more elaborate than the others. It had an external diameter of 8 by 9 m, a ditch 2.6–3.0 m wide and a small central hub of gravel measuring only 3.4 by 2.6 m. There was no central burial and the ditch fills contained little beyond what are probably residual sherds of Beaker pottery and a cache of 38 flint blanks. Environmental evidence suggested that it had been constructed in an open environment and while the excavators tentatively suggested some association with the hengi-form tradition (Hearne and Adam 1999, 38–42) the lack of a defined entrance and unusual proportions makes this unlikely. Ring-ditch F (2567) was penannular, 7 by 6 m with a ditch up to 1.2 m wide and a 3m-wide opening to the north-east. There were no internal features or finds. Ring-ditch G (2841) was also of penannular form, 9 by 5 m with a west-facing gap in the ditch *c*.6 m wide. It contained no primary finds or internal features.

The latest use of the Shorncote cemetery appears to post-date the use of round barrows and comprises a small cremation cemetery that focused on the hengi-form monument in the

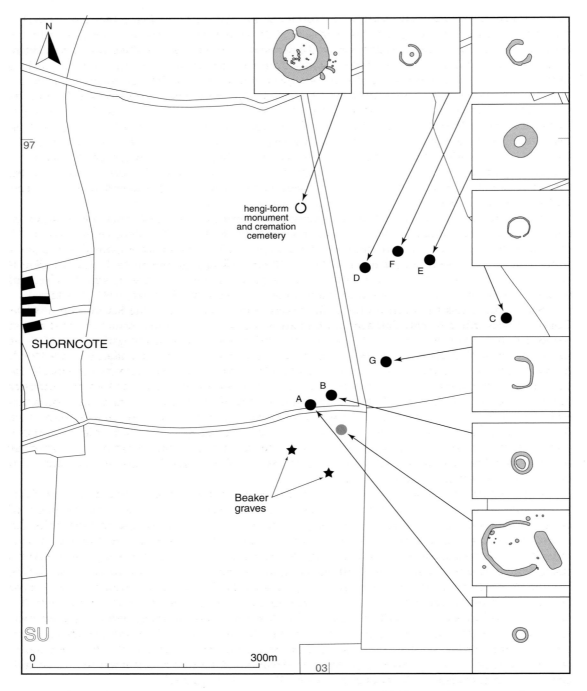

Fig. 9: Excavated barrow cemetery at Shorncote, Somerford Keynes (after Barclay et al. 1995, figs. 2, 8, 9 and 12; Hearne and Adam 1999, figs. 1, 4 and 9). The inset plans are at a scale of 1:1,000.

north-western part of the area examined (Barclay *et al.* 1995, 31–4). The original ditch of the monument was re-cut along the inside edge and 19 cremation burials were inserted into the southern part of the area enclosed by the ring-ditch, spilling out across the silted-up phase 1 ditch. Seven of the cremations had been deposited within inverted Deverel-Rimbury style urns. Two inhumations and a pit containing human bone were found outside the hengi-form monument. One grave was that of an adolescent aged 14–15 years, the body placed on its right side with the head to the north facing west. A radiocarbon determination on a sample of bone dates this burial to 1440–1110 BC (BM-2921: 3050±60 BP). The second grave contained an adult male placed on his left side, head to the west, facing towards the ring-ditch. A radiocarbon date of 1520–1300 BC (BM-2920: 3140±45 BP) was obtained from a sample of bone. A pit 4 m east of the first grave contained parts of an adult female. These burials, which overall span the period from 1500 BC through to about 1200 BC, can tentatively be associated with areas of settlement activity to the east and south-east (see below).

Single burials of the later 2nd millennium BC, seemingly without covering mounds or encircling ring-ditches, have been recorded. Among them are an infant dating to 1405–1010 BC (no details given) at Lechlade Manor, Lechlade (Longman 2001); an unaccompanied inhumation burial dated to 1270–820 BC (HAR-1157: 2840±90 BP) at Roughground Farm, Lechlade (Allen *et al.* 1993, 28); and, already referred to, a simple oval grave containing the tightly flexed skeleton of an adult but slightly-built woman at the Cinema Site, Tewkesbury (Hannan 1993, 29–32).

Sadly, rather less has been found in the Severn Valley and west of the Severn, but at Hunt Court, Badgeworth, a heavily damaged round barrow was investigated in advance of construction works for the A417 Brockworth Bypass (Parry and Cook 1995). Investigations in 1995 at the Kingsweston Roman villa revealed a small pit containing part of a collared urn (Burchill 1996). A small cremation cemetery dating to the 14th to 12th century BC was discovered at Hucclecote during the construction of a link-road between the Brockworth Bypass and the former Gloucester Trading Estate (Thomas *et al.* 2003, 8–9). Of the four burials recorded, two had been contained within biconical urns while the other two had simply been deposited in small shallow pits. A scatter of contemporary pottery residual in later contexts suggests the proximity of a settlement, but the earliest structures revealed on the site, five roundhouses adjacent to a droveway or double-ditched boundary, date to the turn of the 1st millennium BC and are associated with decorated post Deverel-Rimbury ceramics.

Investigations across southern England have shown that through the 2nd millennium BC it was common for burial grounds and settlements to be located within a few hundred metres of each other in such a way that a repetitive pattern of fairly compact farmstead-style units can sometimes be traced across the landscape (Bradley 1981). Such a pattern can be glimpsed in parts at least of Gloucestershire. At Guiting Power, for example, fieldwalking and geophysical surveys suggest the presence of a substantial settlement at Kennel Leasow about 400 m north-east of the Guiting Power 3 round barrow (Marshall 1994). Making the links secure, however, requires some evidence of contemporaneity and here changing ceramic styles become important. In the early 2nd millennium BC various styles of late Beaker and collared urns predominated, gradually giving way to bucket, globular, and biconical urns related to the Deverel-Rimbury tradition that characterises the period from about 1600 BC down to 1100 BC. In the last century or so of the 2nd millennium BC plain pottery of the so-called post Deverel-Rimbury (PDR) tradition predominated, in turn giving way to decorated PDR wares after about 800 BC (Barrett 1980).

In the Upper Thames Valley, the most intensively studied settlements are at Shorncote, Somerford Keynes, on the Gloucestershire/Wiltshire boundary. Here, about 450 m south-east of the 2nd-millennium BC cremation cemetery was an extensive area of settlement, spanning several centuries through the later 2nd and early 1st millennia BC. These have been recorded in considerable detail through a succession of field evaluations and excavations during the later 1980s and early 1990s in advance of quarrying. Three main areas of occupation were identified. The south-eastern settlement dates to the first century or two of the 1st millennium BC and comprised at least five roundhouses, four of post construction and one with a foundation trench for a timber wall (Hearne and Heaton 1994). Nearby were seven large pits, up to 2 m deep and 2–3 m across, which may have been wells or perhaps ritual pits. Pottery of plain PDR style was found together with a circular clay loomweight, pieces of a clay mould for the manufacture of bronze Ewart Park phase ribbed-socketed axes, and a small amount of metal-working slag. Carbonised plant remains were sparse in the samples examined, but included both wheat and barley, while the small animal bone assemblage indicated the presence of cattle and sheep/goats.

To the north (in Areas 1–4) are two further areas of settlement. That in Area 4 was excavated in 1995–6 (Hearne and Adam 1999) and comprises a scatter of about a dozen round structures (mainly post-built), four-posters, nine-posters, pits, and various fences and posthole alignments. Some are in small groups suggestive of farmsteads in which some buildings were replaced several times over (Fig. 10B). All can be dated to the early 1st millennium BC on the basis of plain PDR wares but the features are spread over an area more than 100 m across and are not necessarily contemporary. An additional building and a series of pits, wells and waterholes excavated in 1997 and 1998 are also probably part of this extensive settlement (Brosser et al. 2002). One of the wells had been lined with oak and ash stakes and was 1.10 m deep, and the primary fill retained organic material. A radiocarbon date of 1130–800 BC (NZA-10031: 2783±64 BP) sits neatly with what is known of the ceramics from this settlement. Plant remains from the well show that it was fully shaded by trees and shrubs; there were few indicators of cultivated plants. One of the nearby waterholes contained within its primary fill part of the skull of an adult male (Boyle in Brossler et al. 2002, 69). Fragments of a clay loomweight from one of the waterholes provide evidence for textile production within this area of occupation.

Equally dispersed is the third area of settlement at Shorncote, comprising more than a score of round buildings and associated structures in Areas 1–3 excavated in 1995–6. The only focus within this group is a cluster of five round buildings all with entrances opening to the south-east in Area 3 (Hearne and Adam 1999, fig. 11). Environmental evidence from all these structures was sparse but cattle was the prominent animal species represented. Wheat, barley, and a few weed seeds were noted, but artefacts were poorly represented and little can be said about this site even though it is the most extensive settlement of its period yet examined in the county.

To the south, in the area known as the Cotswold Community, Somerford Keynes, was an 'L'-shaped enclosure ditch within which were a number of roundhouses, a fence, and a series of rubbish pits. Ceramic moulds used in metal working were found here too (Weaver 2004), but full details of the discoveries must await completion of the excavation and post-excavation analysis.

Further afield, other sites are known in less detail. At Horcott Pit, Fairford, for example, three roundhouses, two four-posters, and a number of pits were found on the second terrace of the Thames; a tear-drop shaped post-built enclosure 30 by 50 m perhaps being contemporary (Lamdin-Whymark 2003). At Roughground Farm, Lechlade, a series of nine widely scattered pits contained Deverel-Rimbury related ceramics including bucket urns and biconical vessels (Allen et al. 1993, 27–35). A radiocarbon date of 1550–1000 BC (HAR-5504: 3040±100 BP) provides a glimpse of the chronology of these wares in the region. The small animal bone assemblage from these pits was dominated by sheep/goat, with a few cattle bones but no pig. A bone pin or needle, a small

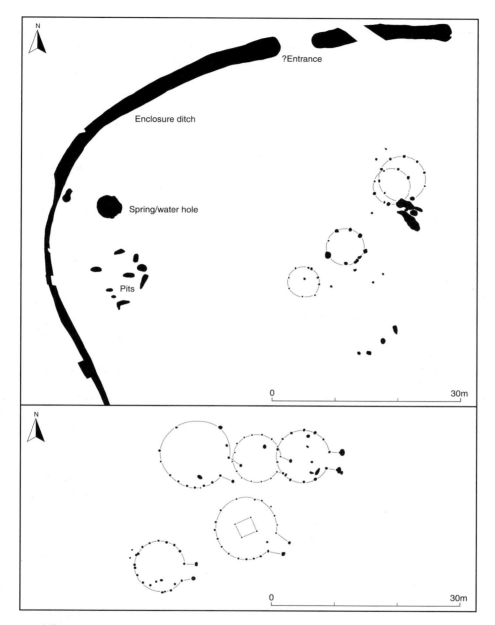

Fig. 10: Middle Bronze-Age settlements. A (top): Blenheim Farm, Moreton-in-Marsh; B (bottom): Shorncote, Somerford Keynes (A Cotswold Archaeology; B after Hearne and Adam 1999, fig. 11).

assemblage of worked flint, and various fragments of burnt clay and a stone rubber complete the finds. No houses or structures can be assigned to this phase of activity, but the burial referred to above shows another side to the picture. As with the skull fragments from the Shorncote settlement, the remains of the ancestors were never far from the day-to-day lives of the living community.

Several settlements of the early 1st millennium BC, characterised by plain PDR ware, have been found in recent decades. They include The Loders, Lechlade (Darvill *et al.* 1986), and, more recently, behind Sherborne House, Lechlade (Bateman *et al.* 2003). At the latter three roundhouses, pits, and lengths of boundary ditch belonged to this phase. One of the roundhouses was post-built; the others were represented by ring-grooves that are best interpreted as drip-gullies. A roundhouse of post-ring type was found at Butler's Field during the investigation of the Anglo-Saxon cemetery (Jennings in Boyle *et al.* 1998, 13) and is tentatively dated by a few rather undistinctive sherds of PDR ware. A small-scale coaxial field system was also noted at Butler's Field (Ibid. 13–14), a system of landscape organisation later succeeded by a multi-phase linear earthwork recorded by excavation at Butler's Field and by geophysical survey and excavation at Hambridge Lane (Barclay *et al.* 2003, 210). Its origins can be dated to the early 1st millennium BC but at Hambridge Lane its final phase was marked by a pit alignment loosely associated with decorated PDR pottery (Jennings in Boyle *et al.* 1998, 18). Slightly later is the single roundhouse and two four-post structures (possibly granaries) found during investigation of the Lechlade cursus in Hambridge Lane in 1985; these features may be tentatively assigned to the second or third quarter of the 1st millennium BC (Barclay *et al.* 2003, 196–8) and are probably contemporary with occupation at Roughground Farm, Lechlade, characterised by a decorated PDR ceramic assemblage (Allen *et al.* 1993, 36–47).

Overall, the late 2nd- and early 1st-millennia BC occupations in the Upper Thames Valley seem to be scattered across wide areas. Little or none of it is enclosed in the sense of being defended, and in total it suggests a gradual migration of attention from one area to the next as the successive generations rolled by.

On the Cotswolds evidence of 2nd-millennium BC settlement is more sparse and suggests generally smaller sites. Traces were revealed by the Esso Midline at Winson (Smith and Cox 1986, 6). More substantial remains have been recorded at Vineyards Farm, Charlton Kings (Rawes 1991, 32); Home Farm, Ebrington (Lankstead 2004); Bourton-on-the-Water Primary School (Nichols 2001); and The Cotswold School, Bourton-on-the-Water (Coleman and Leah 1999). The most substantial settlement of this period on the Cotswolds was discovered in 2002 at Blenheim Farm, Moreton-in-Marsh. Here excavations in advance of the construction of a major housing development brought to light a small semi-enclosed settlement of late 2nd- and early 1st-millennium BC date beside an old river channel (Fig. 10A). Within the enclosure were four circular post-built structures ranging from 5 to 7 m in diameter. A waterhole and several pit clusters were identified within and around the enclosure (Hart 2004).

At Stow-on-the-Wold, also in the north Cotswolds, a large roughly oval-shaped enclosure underlying the modern town centre has been known for many years and is designated a Scheduled Monument (Crawford 1933; Leech 1981; Fig. 11). However, its age was uncertain until a series of excavations in advance of small-scale development works in 1972, 1991, 1992, and 1994 on the northern side of the perimeter earthwork revealed the course a substantial ditch 4.3 m wide, but of unknown depth, with fills dating to the late 2nd millennium BC (Parry 1999). A single piece of plain PDR pottery was recovered from the fill of the ditch, along with pieces of animal bone that provided two radiocarbon dates which both calibrate to 1390–970 BC (OxA-3652: 2955±65 BP and OxA-3801: 2960±65 BP). Although the full extent of the enclosure is not yet known there are obvious points of comparison with a small group of late 2nd-millennium BC sites known as Rams Hill style enclosures after a type-site on the Berkshire Downs. These enclosures are generally regarded as high-status settlements and regional trading centres (Bradley and Ellison 1975; Ellison 1981). The presence of an example on the Gloucestershire Cotswolds

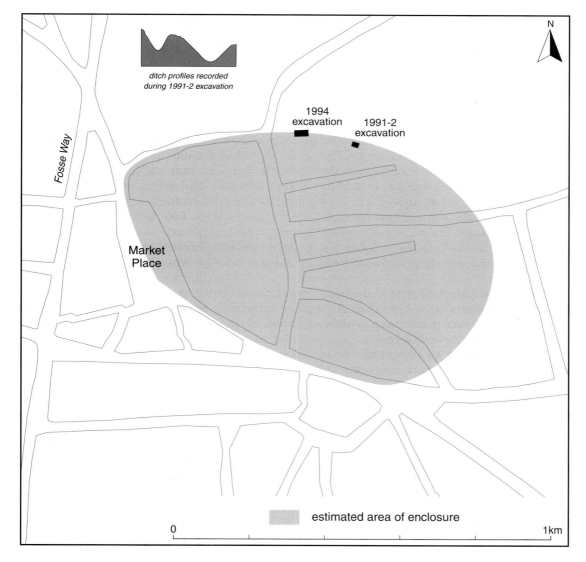

Fig. 11:   Bronze-Age enclosure at Stow-on-the-Wold (after Parry 1999, figs. 1 and 2).

serves to extend the known distribution northwards, but is not unexpected given the extent of occupation in the area, the presence of richly furnished warrior graves (Darvill 1987, 99–103), and trading connections to the east and west that are evident from the late 3rd millennium BC onwards. As with other enclosures of this type, it is likely that the Stow site was re-fortified during the later 1st millennium BC when it may have covered an area of *c.*12 ha (Parry 1999, 82).

In the Severn Valley 2nd-millennium BC settlements have been recognised at the Cinema Site, Tewkesbury (Hannan 1993, 32–3); The Wheatpieces, Walton Cardiff (Nichols 1999); Savages

Wood, Bradley Stoke (Erskine 2001); Lower Farm, Bishop's Cleeve (Holbrook 2000, 85–7); and Howsmoor Lane, Mangotsfield (Townsend 2002). In 1991 excavations in advance of the construction of a Tesco superstore at Bradley Stoke Way, Stoke Gifford, revealed a roundhouse, a pit alignment, ditches and postholes of 2nd-millennium BC date and further related discoveries have since been made in the vicinity (Russett 1993; see also Parry 2001). Two areas, Tewkesbury and Frocester, have been investigated more extensively and suggest a pattern of residence similar to that in the Upper Thames Valley.

Investigations in advance of road building and extensive developments south-east of Tewkesbury have revealed something of the widespread nature of 2nd-millennium BC occupation in this generally low-lying area east of the Severn. Site D on the Tewkesbury Eastern Relief Road scheme covered an area of locally raised ground on the interfluve between the Tirle Brook and the river Swilgate. Here was a small 'D'-shaped enclosure, 16.6 by 11.4 m, the interior of which was divided into two unequal parts by a shallow gully. Pits and postholes within the enclosure suggest a small occupation site on dry ground; globular-urn style pottery and a loomweight were associated with this activity. Outside the enclosure were a series of linear ditches and at least six fairly compact clusters of pits (Walker *et al.* 2004, 35–41). About 250 m to the north-east, on low-lying ground subject to periodic flooding along the valley of the Tirle Brook, excavations in Area F found more clusters of pits also dating to the 2nd millennium BC. Some of the 32 features in Pit Group A contained distinctive burnt fills and a handful of copper-alloy fragments was scattered across the area. Pit 4, initially located in the field evaluation, contained 18 fragments of mould and two bronze droplets within a fill of burnt stone and charcoal. The ceramic mould had been used for casting channel-bladed spearheads generally dating to 1500–1050 BC (Walker *et al.* 2004, 62–6). One of the unusual elements of the ceramic assemblage was the presence of Malvernian rock-tempered pottery from west of the site and Jurassic limestone tempered ware from areas to the east. This Deverel-Rimbury ware is the earliest Malvernian pottery yet recorded.

Further south, also on the interfluve of the Tirle Brook and river Swilgate, fieldwalking and evaluation trenching at Rudgeway Lane revealed a linear boundary ditch 3.5 m wide and more than 0.9 m deep which was traced for a distance of 100 m on a NW–SE orientation (Walker *et al.* 2004, 41). Animal bones, charcoal, burnt clay, and a small assemblage of pottery again suggest a middle to late 2nd-millennium BC date and serve to reinforce the picture of an organised and subdivided landscape. More mid to late 2nd-millennium BC boundary ditches were found at The Gastons west of the river Swilgate and about 1 km from Rudgeway Lane (Walker *et al.* 2004, 41). Again, pottery (bucket urn), animal bone, fired clay, and a few worked flints were found in association indicating the presence of nearby occupation. It is a system that might also connect with the linear ditch found at Holm Hill and provisionally dated to the later Bronze Age or early Iron Age (Hannan 1997, 113).

The location of this rich settlement area beside the Severn may be highly significant. As well as metal working, these communities clearly had wide connections as demonstrated by the presence of early cases of Malvernian rock-tempered pottery from 20 km away to the north-west and limestone tempered wares from the Cotswolds at least 5 km away to the east (Timby in Walker *et al.* 2004, 59–62). A little of the economy of the area is revealed by the small but significant assemblage of animal bones from four of the 2nd-millennium pits and a ditch which suggest that cattle were the dominant species (56%) followed by sheep/goat (35%) and pig (4%). Horse was also represented (Hambleton in Walker *et al.* 2004, 80).

Further south, at Frocester, occupation of the gravel spread that later became the focus of a major Iron-Age and Romano-British settlement began in the late 2nd millennium BC (Price

2000a, 37–9). A shaft or well, pits, and a linear boundary ditch are loosely associated with Deverel-Rimbury style pottery, wood from the shaft providing a radiocarbon date of 1520–1040 BC (GU-2230: 3070±90 BP). These features are about 1,100 m north-west of the slightly earlier stream-side activity at The Buckles, discussed below, and lay within an area of fairly intensive later 2nd millennium BC activity which also includes two or more possible round barrows.

West of the Severn settlements of the 2nd millennium BC remain illusive and their discovery and excavation must be a matter for urgent research.

Across the county as a whole some visible differences in the pattern of settlement are beginning to emerge. In the major river valleys of the Upper Thames and Severn occupation is extensive with little or no evidence of enclosures or major boundaries around the residential areas. Roundhouses predominate and there are numerous wells and waterholes providing fresh water. On the Cotswold uplands, by contrast, the sites seem smaller and at least some were enclosed. It is a set of differences that appears to continue down into the 1st millennium BC and which raises interesting questions about variations in social organisation, economy, and identity (Darvill 1987, 152–4; Moore this volume).

Although traces of metal working have been found at 2nd-millennium BC settlements at Tewkesbury, Shorncote, and the Cotswold Community site, and bronze items are occasionally found at settlements of the period, the majority of metal objects dating to the 2nd millennium BC occur as stray finds with little or no archaeological context. Leslie Grinsell (1985) provided a useful review of Bronze-Age metalwork and related sites in Avon while Bryan Walters (1989) listed 14 findspots of Bronze-Age metalwork in Dean (and see Walters 1992, 36–40). These studies and subsequent reports show that stray finds of metalwork of the 2nd millennium BC have been turning up at a steady rate over the last 25 years; more are likely in future as revisions to the *Treasure Act 1996* and the effects of the Portable Antiquities Scheme begin to be felt.

Recent finds from west of the Severn include a copper-alloy middle Bronze-Age spear tip from Boughspring (Walters 1991). An unlooped palstave of 'south-western type' connected with the Taunton industrial phase was found at Hawkwell brickworks near Steam Mills, Cinderford, in 1974 but was identified and published rather later (Walters 1985, 27–8, fig. 4; Saville 1986a). At the Common, Sling, Coleford, a series of discoveries has led to the recognition of a major hoard of palstaves. Since 1956 a total of five have come to light; of the two found in 1989 one contained scrap bronze in the socket suggesting perhaps that the whole group should be regarded as a founder's hoard (Walters 1991, 40; 1993) and perhaps the site of a workshop (Walters 1992, 40). Mention may also be made of a hoard of five looped palstaves found at Gamage Farm, Much Marcle, just a few metres outside Gloucestershire in Herefordshire. The first two were discovered during a metal-detector survey but with the findspot marked the remainder were uncovered through controlled excavation. Charcoal from the pit in which all five had been placed provided radiocarbon dates of 1690–1310 BC (OxA-1762: 3210±70 BP) and 1410–1010 BC (OxA-1761: 3000±70 BP). The later of these accords well with the typology of the palstaves in the Taunton industrial phase of the late 2nd millennium BC. The earlier date possibly results from the charcoal of old wood being incorporated into the feature.

Moving eastwards across the Severn, the tip of a middle Bronze-Age rapier was found at Hunt Court Farm, Badgeworth, in 1980 (Watkins 1982a), a bifid razor at Standish in 1981 (Watkins 1982b), and the tip of a socketed Penard phase spearhead on the northern extremity of the Lansdown plateau, Bath (Bird 1988). A hoard of 28 objects was recovered by metal detectorists in 1982 at Kingsweston. The group includes one complete and 19 broken socketed axes, casting jets, and parts of a possible socketed sickle. All belong to the Ewart Park phase, datable to the period *c*.920–700 BC (Locock 2001, 126).

Rather surprisingly, the Upper Thames Valley has yielded relatively few finds in recent decades, although wood preserved in the socket of large basal-looped spearhead from Dudgrove Farm, Fairford (Clews 1984b; Darvill 1987, 116), was radiocarbon dated to 1550–950 BC (OxA-1526: 3030±100 BP). This spear provides an interesting addition to the range of weapons of the Penard industrial phase known from the region. Equally important is the bronze Picardy pin discovered in 1997 during metal-detecting near Siddington (Enright 1999). About 20 cm long with a swollen perforated shank and a conical head (Fig. 12), this pin is either an export from a northern French workshop or was made in Britain in imitation of continental styles belonging to the so-called Ornament Horizon of the 13th–12th century BC (the Montelius II/III in the north European periodization, the Taunton industrial phase of the British Bronze Age). Only a handful of such pins are known in Britain (Lawson 1979, 49–50, 76–7) and the Siddington find serves to emphasise the long-distance contacts that communities living in the Cotswolds enjoyed during the late 2nd millennium BC. The strength of such links, and the wealth of the Cotswold area, is further illustrated by what must surely be the most remarkable chance discovery of prehistoric remains found in Gloucestershire. In September 2004 Steve Taylor of Hatherley unearthed a collection of 34 pieces of gold in a field near Cirencester (Anon. 2005). The find includes bar-twisted rings and bracelets, bullae, and pieces of scrap metal suggesting the stock-in-trade of an itinerant goldsmith.

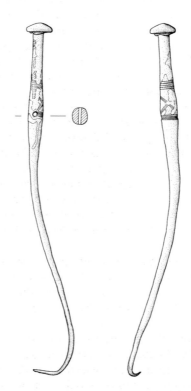

Fig. 12:   Picardy pin from Siddington (drawing Cotswold Archaeology) (scale 1: 2).

The increasing scale of settlement across Gloucestershire, evident in the size and intensity of occupation sites and the number of burial monuments, leaves no doubt that there were increases in the size of the population in the middle and late 2nd millennium BC. This in turn would have increased pressure on resources such as pasture, woodland, rivers and arable fields. The landscape was undoubtedly becoming more open and the economic evidence from settlement sites suggests more cultivation and an increase in arable land. The effect of these developments can also be seen in the landscape as the region's first big environmental disaster: soil loss and increased sedimentation in the main river valleys. In the Severn Estuary these changes were coincident with further local rises in relative sea level. An evaluation at the Western Approach Business Park, Severnside, in 2002, for example, provided a sea level change index point of 3.69 m AOD at 1520–1310 BC (NZA-15879: 3151±45 BP) which is a good marker (Moore *et al.* 2002). What are now intertidal landscapes in the Severn Estuary have produced tools and weapons of the later 2nd millennium BC (Green 1989, 196–7) which may be associated with extensive remains of occupation and economic exploitation around Goldcliff on the western shore more or less opposite the mouth of the Avon to the east (Bell *et al.* 2000).

Less investigation has been directed towards the eastern shore of the estuary, but within the last decade or so important sites have come to light. Investigations at Rockingham Farm, Avonmouth, for example, revealed a series of saltmarsh surfaces buried under alluvium and dated to 1220–820 BC (Beta-118378: 2830±70 BP) and 1190–820 BC (Beta-118379: 2810±70 BP) although details of the land use at that time are obscure (Locock 1999a, 3; Locock and Lawler 2000, 96). Investigations south of Oldbury Power Station revealed an old ground surface beneath about 2 m of estuarine clay. Pits and hollows were found; some contained worked flint, stone, charcoal and wood ash (Allen 1998, 105–7). One feature was dated to 1880–1520 BC (SRR-4777: 3400±45 BP). At Katherine Farm, Avonmouth, a soil ripening layer at about 5.1 m AOD was dated to 1050–800 BC (NZA-12725: 2778±55 BP) and 1380–1000 BC (NZA-12726: 2957±55 BP). On it was a spread of plain PDR pottery, imported micaceous sandstone and chert, fired clay, a few fragments of cattle bone, and very small amounts of wheat and barley grains (Allen *et al.* 2002, 97–9). At Kites Corner, Avonmouth, field evaluations and post-determination excavations in connection with the Cabot Park development (also known as The Severn Gate scheme) revealed evidence of a structure associated with plain PDR ware, burnt stone, and animal bone (Locock *et al.* 1998; Locock 1999b; Locock 2001). Radiocarbon dates span the later 2nd millennium BC and suggest a long period of intermittent use. Among the animal bones, cattle predominated, although deer was present along with some sheep/goat remains. Fish bones were found in sieved soil samples. The abundance of burnt stone from the site suggests it may be some kind of burnt mound, but an association with salt making cannot be ruled out. Traces of occupation dating to the later 2nd millennium BC have also been found at Barrow Hill Crescent, Shirehampton (Bryant 1994b).

Sedimentation of the river valleys and the resultant topographic changes were not confined to the coastal margins. Indeed, one reason why archaeological remains of the 2nd millennium BC and earlier are so illusive in some areas is the fact that they are buried below alluvium and colluvium that formed in later prehistoric times. This is especially the case with riverside sites as two examples clearly show.

At The Buckles, Frocester, an old ground surface sealed by up to 2 m of alluvium and colluvium was examined in 1984–7 (Darvill in Price 2000a, 193–210). Immediately below the Cotswold escarpment this surface included the eastern bank of a small stream that issued from the escarpment. The alluvium/colluvium contained a rich mix of early prehistoric worked flint and ceramics suggesting the heavy erosion of 6th- to 2nd-second millennium BC sites on nearby higher ground. A firepit, an extensive spread of charcoal and burnt stone, and a small circular pit suggested the presence of a burnt mound. A radiocarbon date from charcoal in the firepit of 1750–1430 BC (GU-2230: 3310±70 BP) indicates a mid 2nd-millennium BC date for this activity, broadly contemporary with the main use of round barrows in the area.

At Sandy Lane, Charlton Kings, a layer of silty clay sealed an old land surface on which was a small burnt mound up to 0.3 m thick and covering about 54 square metres (Leah and Young 2001). The matrix of the mound was burnt limestone, charcoal and ash-rich soil. It lay beside an old stream channel that would have been a tributary of the river Chelt. A handful of postholes to the east of the mound may have been the remains of some kind of structure. The small amount of pottery from the site suggests a late Deverel-Rimbury or plain PDR ware cultural association. This would accord with the discovery of part of a clay mould for casting fillet-defined spearheads characteristic of the Wilburton industrial phase. Animal bones were dominated by the remains of cattle (51%), but also included sheep/goat (22%), pig (15%), horse, dog, and red deer. The presence of deer is slightly unusual for a site of this date and may suggest that an animal was butchered here for meat and perhaps bone for tool-making. Indeed, two pieces of worked antler were amongst the small assemblage of worked bone from the site.

Various interpretations have been put forward for burnt mounds such as those at The Buckles and Sandy Lane, including cooking sites, sweat houses, saunas, or retreats in which hallucinogens were used (Barfield and Hodder 1987). As such they perhaps serve to emphasise the point that settlement, economy, ceremony, and ritual were intimately woven together in the way people lived in early prehistory. By the early centuries of the 1st millennium BC the landscape of Gloucestershire was already fairly full of farms and hamlets and the stage set for the emergence of several previously under-represented kinds of archaeological site and an upheaval in social relations.

CHANGING PICTURES

Looking over the results of archaeological work undertaken during the past 25 years it is clear that much has changed. There has been a massive expansion in the available data both in terms of volume and quantity. Opportunities to explore archaeological remains have dramatically increased as a result of contract archaeology so that the overall number of early prehistoric sites sampled has doubled. The distribution of sampled sites across the area has also improved, enabling us to begin to see real regional and local differences that are not simply the product of poor data. Indeed, we can now distinguish more clearly between the gaps in our datasets and the differences in the way prehistoric peoples occupied their landscapes. The scale of operations has also changed so that now we have a chance to review large areas, real spaces that were meaningful to the lives of prehistoric people. Instead of thinking only of sites in terms of the narrow confines of excavation trenches we can view sites as places in the landscape where people did particular things. We can begin to see the edges of activity areas, and realise the long-cherished dream that one day we can explore whole landscapes in terms of places and spaces that were meaningful to the populations we are looking at.

Chronological control is also better. The number of radiocarbon dates available for Gloucestershire's early prehistory has multiplied four or five times to the point that we can move away from the conventional culture-historical periodization of the past and explore people's activities in relation to an imposed real-time calendar such as the Gregorian system implicit to calibrated radiocarbon ages. This comprises solar years arranged in cycles of decades, centuries, and millennia extending backwards and forwards from a notional 'zero' point (the BC/AD divide) which is familiar to us and allows at least some appreciation of the passing of time and the relationships in time between different events even though we can be certain that prehistoric people had a rather different view of time and its passing. What exactly that view was is a matter for future research.

Less obvious is the way that different kinds of archaeology are being examined with the result that the range of material for any given period is commensurately richer. There is now less emphasis on familiar upstanding monuments and more attention to ephemeral but no less important sub-surface features and structures. Flat single graves are a case in point. Once considered of little interest because they rarely contain associated grave goods, it is now clear that this mode of burial was practised from at least the 4th millennium BC through into relatively modern times. Much the same applies to burnt mounds, alluvium/colluvium covered ground surfaces, submerged landscapes, and flint scatters. Dating and understanding these kinds of archaeology, and more that we can scarcely glimpse yet, are important because they reveal aspects of past ways of life that give context and meaning to the more visible monumental structures.

None of these developments in the quality of data available could have happened without the fundamental changes that occurred in the organization of archaeological work during the 1980s and 90s and the integration of archaeology with environmental concerns and spatial planning during the 1990s. Using this newly accessible data to take a long view across early prehistory in Gloucestershire there are three things that come into sharp focus.

First is the fundamental importance of the post-glacial colonization of the region. Certainly there were people here through the late Pleistocene and early stages of the Holocene, but it is not until the 6th or even 5th millennium BC that permanent, extensive, and seemingly fairly dense settlement seems to have been established. Territories were no doubt large and there was most likely a high degree of mobility, but it was perhaps the success of these communities in an economic and social sense that laid the foundations for the rapid expansion of early farming groups in the area during the 4th millennium BC. To judge from the number of causewayed enclosures and long barrows known, the Cotswolds were one of the most densely occupied areas of the British Isles during the 4th millennium BC and that is a matter that deserves explanation and understanding in terms of its 5th-millennium prelude.

A second period of considerable interest is the later 3rd millennium, especially the extensification of settlement associated with communities using Beaker pottery. With the exception of the area west of the Severn, where there is a gap in our data, all parts of the county seem to share a common material culture at this time and may be loosely associated with Humphrey Case's Group D Beaker province covering southern Britain, especially the Midlands, Wessex and Wales (Case 1993, 260–3). The clusters of ceremonial monuments around Lechlade in the Upper Thames Valley and Condicote/Rollright on the Cotswolds may represent important regional centres and it is notable that both are associated with river systems: the Thames-Evenlode confluence and the Windrush headwaters respectively. Around and between these foci a network of small dispersed farmsteads may be envisaged, each with nearby barrows or burial grounds that established a pattern of land use that continued through much of the 2nd millennium BC.

Finally, there is clear evidence for the intensification of settlement in the late 2nd millennium BC which in turn set the scene for the development of hillfort-based societies in the early centuries of the 1st millennium BC. By 1000 BC it is already possible to glimpse regional variations with open settlements dominant in the Upper Thames Valley and enclosures already starting to appear on the Cotswold uplands. The lands west of the Severn again show as a gap in our data in terms of settlement sites, although the wealth of contemporary metalwork from the area suggests that the investigation of possible occupation areas would be highly rewarding.

Each of these three insights are in a sense provisional observations which can be treated as models or propositions to inform the next phases of study, investigation, and analysis. As much as anything they serve to emphasise gaps that need to be plugged, and which could perhaps be addressed during the formulation of regional research frameworks. The environmental backdrop to these social trends needs filling in, and detailed sampling of raw materials such as clay, flint and stone that provide the essentials of early prehistoric material culture needs undertaking so that questions about sources and supply can be addressed. Artefact studies at the local and regional level are also needed to underpin discussions of identity and community in early prehistory. And from a different perspective it is clear that geographical balances in the availability of robust data need to be redressed. The good news is that such things can be achieved. There is now a solid and well-tested research process that harnesses the power and resources of the planning system to the curiosity and hard questioning of the archaeological community which seeks to record and understand the lives of earlier communities in the region. This paper shows how much has been achieved over the last 25 years as these new approaches to our past have worked up to speed; with the systems now in place the next quarter century promises to be a very exciting time for archaeology in Gloucestershire.

ACKNOWLEDGEMENTS

In preparing this paper I would especially like to thanks all those who over the years have kindly shared information about their discoveries and investigations in and around the county: Mary Alexander, Timothy Allen, Mick Aston, Malcolm Atkins, Alastair Barber, Alastair Barclay, Cliff Bateman, Don Benson, Humphrey Case, Mark Chapman, Mark Collard, Laurent Coleman, Mark Corney, Terry Courtney, Simon Cox, Wilf Cox, Philip Dixon, Partrick Garrod, Chris Gerrard, Leslie Grinsell, Chris Guy, Annette Hancocks, Alan Hannan, Carolyn Heighway, Gill Hey, Neil Holbrook, Robin Holgate, David Jennings, David Kenyon, Roger Leach, Alastair Marshall, Ed McSloy, Alan McWhirr, David Miles, Rick Morton, Stuart Needham, John Paddock, Julien Parsons, Arthur Price, Eddie Price, Barbara Rawes, Bernard Rawes, Richard Reece, John Rhodes, Richard Savage, Alan Saville, Rick Schulting, Isobel Smith, Nicola Snashall, Yvette Staelens, Ian Standing, Gail Stoten, Jane Timby, David Viner, Graeme Walker, Malcolm Watkins, Martin Watts, Alf Webb, Alasdair Whittle, Ann Woodward, and Richard Young. Most of the illustrations were prepared by Peter Moore and Lorna Gray. Figures 1 and 2 were prepared by Ehren Milner and Bronwen Russell using data collected by the Archaeological Investigations Project.

NOTES

1. Throughout this paper all dates are presented as conventional solar/calendar years BC or AD by notionally back-projecting the Gregorian Calendar conventionally used in western Christian societies today. Where radiocarbon determinations are cited they are expressed as a date-range at two standard deviations (c.95% probability) in calendar years BC, calibrated using OxCal version v.3.5 (2000). Radiocarbon dates are accompanied by their laboratory reference number and the original age-determination and accompanying standard deviation expressed in radiocarbon years Before Present (BP), conventionally taken as AD 1950.
2. It is uncertain whether a handaxe from the Forest of Dean that was recently reported by the Portable Antiquities Scheme (MLA 2005, 22–3) is amongst those noted below or a new find.
3. Long barrows are referred to by their county reference number (see Darvill 2004b, 244–9 for a full recent listing).

4. Round barrows are referred to by their parish reference codes (see O'Neil and Grinsell 1960, 99–138, and Darvill and Grinsell 1989, 70–83 for listings).

BIBLIOGRAPHY

Allen, J.R.L., 1990. 'Three Neolithic axes from the Severn Estuary', *Trans. BGAS* **108**, 171–4.

Allen, J.R.L., 1997. 'A scatter of Neolithic-Bronze Age flintwork from the intertidal zone at Hills Flats, South Gloucestershire', *Trans. BGAS* **115**, 265–70.

Allen, J.R.L., 1998. 'A prehistoric (Neolithic–Bronze Age) complex on the Severn Estuary Levels, Oldbury-on-Severn, South Gloucestershire', *Trans. BGAS* **116**, 93–116.

Allen, J.R.L., 2000a. 'Rounded pebbles in late Holocene estuarine silts, Oldbury-on-Severn: use as slingshot?', *Trans. BGAS* **118**, 183–212.

Allen, J.R.L., 2000b. 'Sea level, salt marsh and fen: shaping the Severn Estuary Levels in the later Quaternary (Ipswichian-Holocene)', *Archaeol. in the Severn Estuary* **11**, 13–34.

Allen, J.R.L., Bell, M.G., and Scales, R.R.L., 2003. 'Animal and human footprint-tracks in archaeology: description and significance', *Archaeol. in the Severn Estuary* **14**, 55–68.

Allen, M.J., Godden, D., Matthews, C., and Powell, A., 2002. 'Mesolithic, Late Bronze Age and medieval activity at Katherine Farm, Avonmouth', *Archaeol. in the Severn Estuary* **13**, 89–105.

Allen, T.G., Darvill, T.C., Green, L.S., and Jones, M.U., 1993. *Excavations at Roughground Farm, Lechlade, Gloucestershire: a prehistoric and Roman landscape* (Oxford Archaeol. Unit Thames Valley Landscapes: the Cotswold Water Park **1**).

Anonymous 1982. 'Observations in the Paganhill area', *Glevensis* **16**, 35.

Anonymous 1997. 'Lithic finds', *Dean Archaeol.* **10**, 10–13.

Anonymous 2004a. 'Mammoth skull was a chance discovery', *Gloucestershire Echo* 21 January 2004.

Anonymous 2004b. 'Lithic finds', *Dean Archaeol.* **17**, 32–3.

Anonymous 2005. 'Digger Steve strikes gold!', *Gloucestershire Echo* 28 February 2005.

ApSimon, A.M., 2003. 'Getting it right: no middle Palaeolithic at King Arthur's Cave!', *Proc. University Bristol Spelaeological Soc.* **23.1**, 17–26.

Aston, M., and Iles, R. (eds.), 1987. *The archaeology of Avon: a review from the Neolithic to the Middle Ages* (Bristol, Avon County Council).

Bahn, P., Pettit, P., and Ripoll, S., 2003. 'Discovery of Palaeolithic cave art in Britain', *Antiquity* **77**, 227–31.

Barber, A., 1999. 'RAF Fairford, Gloucestershire/Wiltshire: Field Evaluation' (Cirencester, Cotswold Archaeol. report 991016).

Barber, A., and Walker, G., 2000. 'Westward Road, Ebley, Gloucestershire', in N. Oakey (ed.) 2000, 1–14.

Barclay, A., Glass, H., and Parry, C., 1995. 'Excavation of Neolithic and Bronze Age ring-ditches, Shorncote Quarry, Somerford Keynes, Gloucestershire', *Trans. BGAS* **113**, 21–60.

Barclay, A., and Harding, J. (eds.), 1999. *Pathways and ceremonies. The cursus monuments of Britain and Ireland* (Neolithic Studies Group Seminar Papers 4, Oxford, Oxbow Books).

Barclay, A., and Hey, G., 1999. 'Cattle, cursus monuments and the river: the development of ritual and domestic landscapes in the upper Thames Valley', in A. Barclay and J. Harding (eds.) 1999, 67–76.

Barclay, A., Lambrick, G., Moore, J., and Robinson, M., 2003. *Lines in the landscape. Cursus monuments in the Upper Thames Valley* (Oxford Archaeol. Thames Valley Landscapes **15**).

Barfield, L., and Hodder, M., 1987. 'Burnt mounds as saunas, and the prehistory of bathing', *Antiquity* **61**, 370–9.

Barrett, J.C., 1980. 'The pottery of the later Bronze Age in lowland England', *Proc. Prehist. Soc.* **46**, 297–319.

Bateman, C., Enright, D., and Oakey, N., 2003. 'Prehistoric and Anglo-Saxon settlements to the rear of Sherborne House, Lechlade: excavations in 1997', *Trans. BGAS* **121**, 23–96.

Bateman, C., and Walker, G., 1992. 'Condicote, Condicote to Lasborough Sewer', in B. Rawes (ed.), 'Archaeol. Review 17', *Trans. BGAS* **111**, 220–1.

Baxter, M., 1999. 'Dancing with the dead in a mass grave', *Brit. Archaeol.* **50**, 6–7.

Beckensall, S., 1999. *British prehistoric rock art* (Stroud, Tempus).

Bell, M., 1984. 'Environmental archaeology in south west England', in H. Keeley (ed.) 1984, 43–133.

Bell, M., Allen, J.R.L., Nayling, N., and Buckley, S., 2001. 'Mesolithic to Neolithic coastal environmental change c.6500–3500 cal BC', *Archaeol. in the Severn Estuary* **12**, 27–53.

Bell, M., Allen, J.R.L., Buckley, S., Dark, P., and Haslett, S.K., 2002. 'Mesolithic to Neolithic coastal environmental change: excavations at Goldcliff East, 2002', *Archaeol. in the Severn Estuary* **13**, 1–29.

Bell, M., Allen, J.R.L., Buckley, S., Dark, P., and Nayling, N., 2003. 'Mesolithic to Neolithic coastal environmental change: excavations at Goldcliff East, 2003 and research at Redwick', *Archaeol. in the Severn Estuary* **14**, 1–26.

Bell, M., Caseldine, A., and Neumann, H., 2000. *Prehistoric intertidal archaeology in the Welsh Severn Estuary* (CBA Research Rep. **120**, York).

Benson, D., and Miles, D., 1974. *The Upper Thames Valley. An archaeological survey of the river gravels* (Oxford Archaeol. Unit Surv. **2**).

Bevan, L., and Moore, J. (eds.), 2003. *Peopling the Mesolithic in a northern environment* (BAR International Series **1157**, Oxford).

Bewley, B., 2001. 'Understanding England's historic landscapes: an aerial perspective', *Landscapes* **2.1**, 74–84.

Bick, D., 1980. 'Oxenhall', in B. Rawes (ed.), 'Archaeol. Review 4', *Trans. BGAS* **98**, 184.

Bintliffe, J. (ed.), 2004. *A companion to archaeology* (Oxford, Blackwell).

Bird, S., 1988. 'A Bronze Age spearhead fragment from Lansdown, Bath', *Bristol Avon Archaeol.* **7**, 37.

Bowden, M., 2005. *The Malvern Hills. An ancient landscape* (London, English Heritage).

Boyle, A., Jennings, D., Miles, D. and Palmer, S. (eds.), 1998. *The Anglo-Saxon cemetery at Butlers Field, Lechlade, Gloucestershire. Vol. 1: Prehistoric and Roman activity and Anglo-Saxon grave catalogue* (Oxford Archaeol. Unit Thames Valley Landscapes Monograph **10**.).

Bradley, R., 1981. 'Various styles of urn – cemeteries and settlement in southern England c.1400–1000 bc', in R. Chapman *et al.* (eds.) 1981, 93–104.

Bradley, R., 1997. *Rock art and the prehistory of Atlantic Europe. Signing the land* (London, Routledge).

Bradley, R., and Ellison, A., 1975 *Rams Hill: a Bronze Age defended enclosure and its landscape* (BAR Brit. Series **33**, Oxford).

Brickley, M., and Thomas, R., 2004. 'The young woman and her baby or the juvenile and their dog: reinterpreting osteological material from a Neolithic long barrow', *Archaeol. J.* **161**, 1–10.

Brody, H., 2000. *The other side of Eden. Hunter-gatherers, farmers and the shaping of the world* (London, Faber and Faber).

Brossler, A., Gocher, M., Laws, G., and Roberts, M., 2002. 'Shorncote Quarry: excavations of a late prehistoric landscape in the upper Thames Valley, 1997 and 1998', *Trans. BGAS* **120**, 37–88.

Brück, J. (ed.), 2001. *Bronze Age landscapes. Tradition and transformation* (Oxbow Books, Oxford).

Bryant, J., 1994a. 'Bristol, Shirehampton, Grumwell Close', in B. Rawes (ed.), 'Archaeol. Review 18', *Trans. BGAS* **112**, 198.

Bryant, J., 1994b. 'Bristol, Shirehampton, Barrow Hill Crescent', in ibid.

Burchill, R., 1996. 'Bristol, Lawrence Weston, Kings Weston Roman Villa', in J. Rawes and J. Wills (eds.), 'Archaeol. Review 20', *Trans. BGAS* **114**, 167.

Burgess, C., and Coombs, D. (eds.), 1979. *Bronze Age hoards: some finds old and new* (BAR Brit. Series **67**, Oxford).

Campbell, J.B., 1977. *The upper Palaeolithic of Britain* (Oxford University Press: 2 volumes).

Carter, S., Jones, J., and McGill, B., 2003. 'Pucklechurch to Seabank pipeline: sediment stratigraphy and palaeoenvironmental data from the Avonmouth levels', *Archaeol. in the Severn Estuary* **14**, 69–86.

Case, H., 1993. 'Beaker: deconstruction and after', *Proc. Prehist. Soc.* **59**, 241–68.

Catchpole, T., 1994. 'Swell, Swell Wold Quarry', in B. Rawes (ed.), 'Archaeol. Review 18', *Trans. BGAS* **112**, 211.

Champion, T., 1991. 'Theoretical archaeology in Britain', in I. Hodder (ed.) 1991, 129–60.

Chapman, R., Kinnes, I., and Randsborg, K. (eds.), 1981. *The archaeology of death* (Cambridge University Press).

Chouls, W., 1993. 'The Whitminster, Eastington and Frampton-on-Severn areas', *Glevensis* **27**, 8–20.

Cleal, R., and Pollard, J. (eds.), 2004. *Monuments and material culture. Papers in honour of an Avebury Archaeologist: Isobel Smith* (Salisbury, Hobnob Press).

Clews, S., 1984a. 'Chipping Campden', in B. Rawes (ed.), 'Archaeol. Review 8', *Trans. BGAS* **102**, 224.

Clews, S., 1984b. 'Fairford', in ibid. 225.

Clews, S., 1985. 'Poole Keynes, Somerford Lakes Reserve', in B. Rawes (ed.), 'Archaeol. Review 9', *Trans. BGAS* **103**, 236.

Coleman, L., and Leah, M., 1999. 'Bourton-on-the-Water, The Cotswold School', in J. Wills and J. Rawes (eds.), 'Archaeol. Review 23', *Trans. BGAS* **117**, 168–9.

Coleman, L., and Hancocks, A., forthcoming. *Four sites by the Carrant Brook and River Isbourne, Gloucestershire and Worcestershire: excavations on the Wormington to Tirley pipeline 2000* (Cotswold Archaeol. Occasional Paper **2**).

Crawford, O.G.S., 1933. 'An English hill-top town', *Antiquity* **7**, 347–50.

Curtis, M.L.K., 1998. 'Neolithic – Bronze Age flints from Arlingham', *Glevensis* **31**, 45–6.

Darvill, T., 1981. 'Excavation at the Peak Camp, Cowley: an interim note', *Glevensis* **15**, 52–6.

Darvill, T., 1982a. 'Excavation at the Peak Camp, Cowley: second interim note', *Glevensis* **16**, 20–5.

Darvill, T., 1982b. *The megalithic chambered tombs of the Cotswold-Severn region* (Highworth, Vorda Books).

Darvill, T., 1984a. 'Neolithic Gloucestershire', in A. Saville (ed.) 1984, 80–112.

Darvill, T., 1984b. 'Birdlip Bypass Project – first report: archaeological assessment and field survey' (Bristol, Western Archaeol. Trust report).

Darvill, T., 1984c. 'Cowley, Birdlip Bypass Project', in B. Rawes (ed.), 'Archaeol. Review 8', *Trans. BGAS* **102**, 225.

Darvill, T., 1985. 'A Neolithic flint axe from Lechlade', *Trans. BGAS* **103**, 207–9.

Darvill, T., 1987. *Prehistoric Gloucestershire* (Gloucester, Alan Sutton and Gloucestershire County Library).

Darvill, T., 1993. 'The early prehistoric period', in T. Allen *et al.* 1993, 9–25.

Darvill, T., 1999. 'Reeling in the years: the past in the present', in J. Hunter and I. Ralston (eds.) 1999, 297–315.

Darvill, T., 2002. 'White on blonde: quartz pebbles and the use of quartz at Neolithic monuments in the Isle of Man and beyond', in A. Jones and G. MacGregor (eds.) 2002, 73–93.

Darvill, T., 2003. 'Analytical scale, populations and the Mesolithic-Neolithic transition in the far northwest of Europe', in L. Bevan and J. Moore (eds.) 2003, 95–102.

Darvill, T., 2004a. 'Public archaeology: a European perspective', in J. Bintliffe (ed.) 2004, 409–34.

Darvill, T., 2004b. *Long barrows of the Cotswolds and surrounding areas* (Stroud, Tempus).

Darvill, T., and Grinsell, L.V., 1989. 'Gloucestershire barrows: supplement 1961–1988', *Trans. BGAS* **107**, 39–105.

Darvill, T., Hingley, R., Jones, M., and Timby, J., 1986. 'A Neolithic and Iron Age site at The Loders, Lechlade, Gloucestershire', *Trans. BGAS* **104**, 27–48.

Darvill, T., and Locke, R., 1988. 'Aerial photography in the Upper Thames Valley and eastern Cotswolds in 1986', *Trans. BGAS* **106**, 192–7.

Darvill, T., and Russell, B., 2002. *Archaeology after PPG16: archaeological investigations in England 1990–1999* (Bournemouth University School of Conservation Sciences Research Rep. **10**).

Darvill, T., and Timby, J., 1986. 'Excavations at Saintbridge, Gloucester, 1981', *Trans. BGAS* **104**, 49–60.

Darvill, T., and Wainwright, G., 2003. 'A cup-marked stone from Dan-y-garn, Mynachlog-Ddu, Pembrokeshire, and the prehistoric rock-art from Wales', *Proc. Prehist. Soc.* **69**, 253–64.

DCMS (Department of Culture, Media and Sport) 2002. *The Treasure Act 1996: Code of Practice (Revised), England and Wales* (London).

DCMS (Department of Culture, Media and Sport) 2004. *Review of heritage protection: the way forward* (London).

Dixon, P., 1979. 'A Neolithic and Iron Age site on a hilltop in southern England', *Scientific American* **241.5**, 142–50.

Dixon, P., 1980. 'Badgeworth/Coberley, Crickley Hill', in B. Rawes (ed.), 'Archaeol. Review 4', *Trans. BGAS* **98**, 179.

Dixon, P., 1981. 'Badgeworth/Coberley, Crickley Hill', in B. Rawes (ed.), 'Archaeol. Review 5', *Trans. BGAS* **99**, 173.

Dixon, P., 1982. 'Badgeworth/Coberley, Crickley Hill', in B. Rawes (ed.), 'Archaeol. Review 6', *Trans. BGAS* **100**, 258.

Dixon, P., 1983. 'Badgeworth/Coberley, Crickley Hill', in B. Rawes (ed.), 'Archaeol. Review 7', *Trans. BGAS* **101**, 223.

Dixon, P., 1984. 'Badgeworth/Coberley, Crickley Hill', in B. Rawes (ed.), 'Archaeol. Review 8', *Trans. BGAS* **102**, 223.

Dixon, P., 1987. 'Coberley, Crickley Hill', in B. Rawes (ed.), 'Archaeol. Review 11', *Trans. BGAS* **105**, 245.

Dixon, P., 1988a. 'The Neolithic settlements on Crickley Hill', in P. Topping *et al.* (eds.) 1988, 75–87.

Dixon, P., 1988b. 'Coberley/Badgeworth, Crickley Hill', in B. Rawes (ed.), 'Archaeol. Review 12', *Trans. BGAS* **106**, 220.

Dixon, P., 1990. 'Coberley/Badgeworth, Crickley Hill', in B. Rawes (ed.), 'Archaeol. Review 14', *Trans. BGAS* **108**, 195.

Dixon, P., 1992. 'Coberley, Crickley Hill', in B. Rawes (ed.), 'Archaeol. Review 16', *Trans. BGAS* **110**, 217.

Dixon, P., 1994. 'Badgeworth/Coberley, Crickley Hill', in B. Rawes (ed.), 'Archaeol. Review 18', *Trans. BGAS* **112**, 195.

DoE (Department of the Environment) 1990. *Planning Policy Guidance: Archaeology and Planning* (PPG **16**, London, HMSO).

DoE (Department of the Environment) 1994. *Planning Policy Guidance: Planning and the Historic Environment* (PPG **15**, London, HMSO).

Drinkwater, J., and Saville, A., 1984. 'The Bronze Age round barrows of Gloucestershire: a brief review', in A. Saville (ed.) 1984, 128–39.

Dunning, G.C., 1976. 'Salmonsbury, Bourton-on-the-Water, Gloucestershire', in D.W. Harding (ed.) 1976, 76–118.

Ecclestone, M., 2001. 'Fieldwalking a Roman site at Daglingworth', *Glevensis* **34**, 74–8.

Ecclestone, M., 2002. 'Daglingworth, Manor Farm', in J. Wills (ed.), 'Archaeol. Review 26', *Trans. BGAS* **120**, 245.

Ellison, A., 1981. 'Towards a socioeconomic model for the middle Bronze Age in southern England', in I. Hodder *et al.* (eds.) 1981, 413–38.

Ellison, A., 1984. 'Bronze Age Gloucestershire: artefacts and distributions', in A. Saville (ed.) 1984, 113–27.

Enright, D., 1999. 'A Bronze-Age pin from Siddington, Gloucestershire', *Trans. BGAS* **117**, 151–2.

Enright, D., and Watts, M., 2002. *A Romano-British and medieval settlement site at Stoke Road, Bishop's Cleeve, Gloucestershire* (Bristol and Gloucestershire Archaeol. Rep. **1**, Cirencester, Cotswold Archaeol.).

Erskine, J., 1998. 'Cromhall, Trappels Farm', in J. Rawes and J. Wills (eds.), 'Archaeol. Review 22', *Trans. BGAS* **116**, 200–1.

Erskine, J., 2001. 'Bradley Stoke, Savages Wood Primary School', in J. Wills (ed.), 'Archaeol. Review 25', *Trans. BGAS* **119**, 188.

Evans, D.C., 2005. 'Neolithic pits at King's Stanley, Gloucestershire', *Glevensis* **38**, 2–4.

Fowler, P.J., 1979. 'Archaeology and the M4 and M5 motorways, 1965–78', *Archaeol. J.* **136**, 12–26.

Gamble, C.S., and Lawson, A.J. (eds.), 1996. *The English Palaeolithic reviewed* (Salisbury, Trust for Wessex Archaeol.).

Garrod, P., and Heighway, C., 1984. *Garrod's Gloucester: archaeological observations 1974–81* (Gloucester, Western Archaeol. Trust).

Gibson, A., and Kinnes, I., 1997. 'On the urns of a dilemma: radiocarbon and the Peterborough problem', *Oxford J. Archaeol.* **16.1**, 65–72.

Green, S., 1989. 'Some recent archaeological and faunal discoveries from the Severn Estuary Levels', *Bull. Board Celtic Studies* **36**, 187–99.

Grinsell, L.V., 1979. 'The Druid Stoke megalithic monument', *Trans. BGAS* **97**, 119–21.

Grinsell, L.V., 1985. 'Bronze Age artifacts in Avon', *Bristol Avon Archaeol.* **4**, 2–5.

Hannan, A., 1993. 'Excavations at Tewkesbury, 1972–74', *Trans. BGAS* **111**, 21–76.

Hannan, A., 1997. 'Tewkesbury and the earls of Gloucester: Excavations at Holm Hill, 1974–5', *Trans. BGAS* **115**, 79–232.

Harding, D.W. (ed.), 1976. *Hillforts. Later prehistoric earthworks in Britain and Ireland* (London and New York, Academic Press).

Hart, C., 1967. *Archaeology in Dean* (Gloucester, John Bellows).

Hart, J., 2004. 'Moreton-in-Marsh, Blenheim Farm', in J. Wills (ed.), 'Archaeol. Review 28', *Trans. BGAS* **122**, 186.

Hart, J., and McSloy, E., 2004. 'Axe from Blenheim Farm', *Cotswold Archaeol. News* **6**, 3.

Haslett, S.K., Davies, P., Davies, C.F.C., Margetts, A.J., Scotney, K.H., Thorpe, D.J., and Williams, H.O., 2000. 'The changing estuarine environment in relation to Holocene sea-level and the archaeological implications', *Archaeol. in the Severn Estuary* **11**, 35–53.

Healy, F., 2004. 'Hambledon Hill and its implications', in R. Cleal and J. Pollard (eds.) 2004, 15–38.

Hearne, C.M., and Adam, N., 1999. 'Excavation of an extensive late Bronze-Age settlement at Shorncote Quarry, near Cirencester, 1995–6', *Trans. BGAS* **117**, 35–76.

Hearne, C.M., and Heaton, M., 1994. 'Excavations at a Late Bronze Age settlement in the upper Thames Valley at Shorncote Quarry near Cirencester, 1992', *Trans. BGAS* **112**, 17–58.

Heighway, C., Darvill, T., Saville, A., Ireland, C., and Timby, J., 1988. 'Excavations at King's Stanley, Gloucestershire: sites next to St George's Church. An archive report compiled by Carolyn Heighway and the Crickley Hill Trust from excavations carried out by P Griffin and D Evans' (King's Stanley, Past Historic report).

Hicks, D., 2000. 'Cirencester, The Whiteway', in J. Wills (ed.), 'Archaeol. Review 24', *Trans. BGAS* **118**, 222.

Hoad, S., 2002. 'Kempsford, R.A.F. Fairford', in J. Wills (ed.), 'Archaeol. Review 26', *Trans. BGAS* **120**, 248–9.

Hodder, I., 1984. 'Archaeology in 1984', *Antiquity* **58**, 25–32.

Hodder, I. (ed.), 1991. *Archaeological theory in Europe. The last three decades* (London, Routledge).

Hodder, I., Isaac, G., and Hammond, N. (eds.), 1981. *Pattern of the past. Studies in honour of David Clarke* (Cambridge University Press).

Holbrook, N., 2000. 'The Anglo-Saxon cemetery at Lower Farm, Bishop's Cleeve: excavations directed by Kenneth Brown 1969', *Trans. BGAS* **118**, 61–92.

Holgate, R., 1988. *Neolithic settlement of the Thames Basin* (BAR Brit. Series **194**, Oxford).

Howell, R.J., 1980. 'Tytherington, Stidcot Farm', in B. Rawes (ed.), 'Archaeol. Review 4', *Trans. BGAS* **98**, 185.

Hughes. J., 2004. 'Stone me ... French Flintstone was here', *Western Daily Press* 22 November 2004.

Hunter, J., and Ralston, I. (eds.), 1999 *The archaeology of Britain. An introduction from the upper Palaeolithic to the Industrial revolution* (London, Routledge).

Hutton, D., and Hutton, M., 1994. 'Town Farm, Newent', *Dean Archaeol.* **7**, 5–7.

Hutton, D., and Hutton, M., 1995. 'Newent, Town Farm', in B. Rawes (ed.), 'Archaeol. Review 19', *Trans. BGAS* **113**, 200–1.

Iles, R., 1980. 'Acton Turville', in B. Rawes (ed.), 'Archaeol. Review 4', *Trans. BGAS* **98**, 178.

Iles, R., and White, H., 1986. 'Avon archaeology 1985', *Bristol Avon Archaeol.* **5**, 51–5.

Insole, P., 1997. 'Avonmouth, Seabank', in J. Rawes and J. Wills (eds.), 'Archaeol. Review 21', *Trans. BGAS* **115**, 278.

Jacobi, R.M., and Petit, P.B., 2000. 'An Aurignacian point from Uphill Quarry (Somerset) and the earliest settlement of Britain by *Homo sapiens sapiens*', *Antiquity* **74**, 513–18.

James, T., and Walters, B., 1988. 'Some recent prehistoric finds in Dean', *Dean Archaeol.* **1**, 39–44.

Jennings, D., Muir, J., Palmer, S., and Smith, A., 2004. *Thornhill Farm, Fairford, Gloucestershire: An Iron Age and Roman pastoral site in the Upper Thames Valley* (Oxford Archaeol. Thames Valley Landscapes Monograph **23**).

Johns, B., 1990. 'Cup stones and arrow stones', *New Regard of the Forest of Dean* **6**, 19–25.

Johns, B., 1992. 'Dowsing for trackways in Blakeney Hill woodlands and district', *New Regard of the Forest of Dean* **8**, 36–45.

Johns, B., 1993. 'Some recent archaeological finds', *New Regard of the Forest of Dean* **9**, 39–41.

Jones, A., and MacGregor, G. (eds.), 2002. *Colouring the past. The significance of colour in archaeological research* (Oxford, Berg).

Keeley, H.C.M. (ed.), 1984. *Environmental Archaeology: a regional review* (Directorate of Ancient Monuments and Historic Buildings Occasional Paper **6**, London, Department of the Environment).

Kelly, S., and Laws, G., 2002. 'Siddington, Dryleaze Farm', in J. Wills (ed.), 'Archaeol. Review 26', *Trans. BGAS* **120**, 253.

Kilminster, G., 1990. 'Bishop's Cleeve, Oakfield Road', in B. Rawes (ed.), 'Archaeol. Review 14', *Trans. BGAS* **108**, 193.

Kilminster, G., 1995. 'Bishop's Cleeve, Oakfield Road', in B. Rawes (ed.), 'Archaeol. Review 19', *Trans. BGAS* **113**, 185.

Lambrick, G., 1988. *The Rollright Stones: megaliths, monuments, and settlement in the prehistoric landscape* (Historic Buildings and Monuments Commission for England Archaeological Rep. **6**, London, English Heritage).

Lamdin-Whymark, H., 2003. 'Fairford, Horcott Pit', in J. Wills, 'Archaeol. Review 27', *Trans. BGAS* **121**, 277.

Lankstead, D., 2004. 'Ebrington, Home Farm', in J. Wills (ed.), 'Archaeol. Review 28', *Trans. BGAS* **122**, 182.

Laws, G., 2002. 'Somerford Keynes, Cotswold Community', in J. Wills (ed.), 'Archaeol. Review 26', *Trans. BGAS* **120**, 253.

Lawson, A., 1979. 'A late middle Bronze Age Hoard from Hunstanton, Norfolk', in C. Burgess and D. Coombs (eds.) 1979, 43–92.

Leah, M., and Young, C., 2001. 'A Bronze-Age Burnt Mound at Sandy Lane, Charlton Kings, Gloucestershire: excavations in 1971', *Trans. BGAS* **119**, 59–82.

Leech, R., 1981. *Historic towns of Gloucestershire* (CRAAGS Surv. **3**, Bristol).

Lewis, S.G., and Maddy, D. (eds.), 1997. *The Quaternary of the South Midlands and the Welsh Marches. Field Guide* (London, Quaternary Research Assoc.).

Locock, M., 1999a. 'Buried soils of the Wentlooge Formation', *Archaeol. in the Severn Estuary* **10**, 1–10.

Locock, M., 1999b. 'Cabot Park, Avonmouth, Bristol: Excavation on later Bronze Age and medieval sites at Kites Corner and Moorend Farm, 1999', *Archaeol. in the Severn Estuary* **10**, 125–8.

Locock, M., 2001. 'A later Bronze Age landscape on the Avon Levels: settlement, shelters and saltmarsh at Cabot Park', in J. Brück (ed.) 2001, 121–8.

Locock, M., and Lawler, M., 2000. 'Moated enclosures on the North Avon Level: survey and excavation at Rockingham Farm, Avonmouth, 1993–7', *Trans. BGAS* **118**, 93–122.

Locock, M., Robinson, S., and Yates, A., 1998. 'Late Bronze Age sites at Cabot Park, Avonmouth', *Archaeol. in the Severn Estuary* **9**, 31–6.

Longman, T., 1999. 'Bristol, Canon's Marsh', in J. Wills and J. Rawes (eds.), 'Archaeol. Review 23', *Trans. BGAS* **117**, 170.

Longman, T., 2001. 'Lechlade, Lechlade Manor', in J. Wills (ed.), 'Archaeol. Review 25', *Trans. BGAS* **119**, 201–2.

Marshall, A., 1978. 'Material from Iron Age sites in the northern Cotswolds', *Trans. BGAS* **96**, 17–26.

Marshall, A., 1985. 'Neolithic and earlier Bronze Age settlement in the northern Cotswolds: a preliminary outline based on the distribution of surface scatters and funerary areas', *Trans. BGAS* **103**, 23–54.

Marshall, A., 1986. 'Cup-marked stones from the Gloucestershire Cotswolds', *Trans. BGAS* **106**, 220–5.

Marshall, A., 1989. 'Excavation of ring-ditch type cropmarks at Guiting Power, Gloucestershire', *Trans. BGAS* **107**, 193–6.

Marshall, A., 1992a. 'Guiting Power 3 Round Barrow SP 0956 2454', *Glevensis* **26**, 29–30.

Marshall, A., 1992b. 'Chedworth, Wickwell', in B. Rawes (ed.), 'Archaeol. Review 16', *Trans. BGAS* **110**, 215.

Marshall, A., 1992c. 'Hampnett, Middle Down', in ibid. 223.

Marshall, A., 1992d. 'Rendcomb, Shawswell', in ibid. 225.

Marshall, A., 1992e. 'Withington, Gulf Scrubs', in ibid. 227.

Marshall, A., 1993. 'Guiting Power, Guiting Power 1 Round Barrow', in B. Rawes (ed.), 'Archaeol. Review 17', *Trans. BGAS* **111**, 225.

Marshall, A., 1994. 'Guiting Power, Guiting Power 3 Round Barrow', in B. Rawes (ed.), 'Archaeol. Review 18', *Trans. BGAS* **112**, 203.

Marshall, A., 1995a. 'Bourton-on-the-Water, Salmonsbury', in B. Rawes (ed.), 'Archaeol. Review 19', *Trans. BGAS* **113**, 185–6.

Marshall, A., 1995b. 'Condicote, Round Barrow 2', in ibid. 192.

Marshall, A., 1995c. 'Hawling, Round Barrow 2', in ibid. 198.

Marshall, A., 1995d. 'Temple Guiting', in ibid. 203–5.

Marshall, A., 1995e. 'Upper Slaughter, Round Barrow 1', in ibid. 206.

Marshall A., 1996a. 'Bourton-on-the-Water, Salmonsbury', in J. Rawes and J. Wills (eds.), 'Archaeol. Review 20', *Trans. BGAS* **114**, 165–6.

Marshall, A., 1996b. 'Chedworth, Chedworth 1 Long Barrow', in ibid. 170–1.

Marshall A., 1996c. 'Farmington, Farmington 1 Long Barrow', in ibid. 172–3.

Marshall A., 1996d. 'Hazleton, Hazleton 1 Long Barrow', in ibid. 178–9.

Marshall A., 1996e. 'Northleach with Eastington, Northleach 1 Long Barrow', in ibid. 181.

Marshall A., 1996f. 'Rendcomb, Rendcomb 1 ?Barrow', in ibid. 182.

Marshall, A., 1996 g. 'Temple Guiting, Temple Guiting 2 Long Barrow', in ibid. 183.

Marshall, A., 1997a. 'Chedworth, Chedworth 1 Long Barrow', in J. Rawes and J. Wills (eds.), 'Archaeol. Review 21', *Trans. BGAS* **115**, 279.

Marshall, A., 1997b. 'Guiting Power, Guiting Power 1 Round Barrow', in ibid. 285–7.

Marshall, A., 1997c. 'Hazleton, Hazleton 3 Round Barrow', in ibid. 288.

Marshall, A., 1998. 'Neolithic long barrows: use of integrated remote sensing at high resolution to establish general layout and detect foreground structure', *Archaeol. Prospection* **5**, 101–16.

Marshall, A., 2003. 'Sudeley, Belas Knap Area', in J. Wills (ed.), 'Archaeol. Review 27', *Trans. BGAS* **121**, 285.

Marshall, A., and Allen, M., 1998. 'Guiting Power Area', in J. Rawes and J. Wills (eds.), 'Archaeol. Review 22', *Trans. BGAS* **116**, 203–4.

Martin, C., and Phipps, R., 2004. 'Research framework for the archaeology of Wales' (web-based documents available at http://www.cpat.org.uk/research/ [accessed on 08/03/2005]).

Mercer, R., 1988. 'Hambledon Hill, Dorset, England', in P. Topping *et al.* (eds.) 1988, 89–106.

Miles, D., 2002. 'Portable Antiquities Scheme extended', *Conservation Bulletin* **43**, 32–3.

MLA (Museums, Libraries and Archives Council) 2005. *Portable Antiquities Scheme Annual Report 2004/05* (Museums, Libraries and Archives Council, London).

Moore, C., Allen, M.J., and Scaife, R., 2002. 'An archaeological evaluation at Western Approach Business Park, Severnside, South Gloucestershire', *Archaeol. in the Severn Estuary* **13**, 159–62.

Moore, J., 2002. 'Lechlade, Leaze Farm', in J. Wills (ed.), 'Archaeol. Review 26', *Trans. BGAS* **120**, 249.

Morris, R.W.B., and Marshall, A., 1983. 'A cup- and ring-marked stone from Nottingham Hill, Gotherington', *Trans. BGAS* **101**, 171–3.

Morton, R., 1993. 'Rissington, Great Rissington Sewer', in B. Rawes (ed.), 'Archaeol. Review 17', *Trans. BGAS* **111**, 229.

Mudd, A., Williams, R.J., and Lupton, A., 1999. *Excavations alongside Roman Ermin Street, Gloucestershire and Wiltshire: the archaeology of the A419/A417 Swindon to Gloucester Road Scheme* (Oxford Archaeol. Unit: 2 volumes).

Needham, S., 1979. 'The extent of foreign influence on early Bronze Age axe development in southern Britain', in M. Ryan (ed.) 1979, 265–93.

Needham, S., Cowie, T., and Hook, D., 1996. 'A flat axehead from Viney Hill, Blakeney, Gloucestershire', *Dean Archaeol.* **9**, 13–14.

Needham, S., and Saville, A., 1981. 'Two early Bronze Age flat bronze axeheads from Oddington', *Trans. BGAS* **99**, 15–20.

Nichols, P., 1999. 'Walton Cardiff, The Wheatlieces', in J. Wills and J. Rawes, 'Archaeol. Review 23', *Trans. BGAS* **117**, 185.

Nichols, P., 2001. 'Bourton-on-the-Water, Primary School', in J. Wills, 'Archaeol. Review 25', *Trans. BGAS* **119**, 187.

Nichols, P., 2002. 'Kemble, Station Road', in J. Wills, 'Archaeol. Review 26', *Trans. BGAS* **120**, 248.

Oakey, N. (ed.), 2000. *Three medieval sites in Gloucestershire* (Cotswold Archaeol. Trust Occasional Paper 1).

O'Neil, H.E., 1967. 'Bevan's Quarry round barrow, Temple Guiting', *Trans. BGAS* **86**, 16–41.

O'Neil, H.E., and Grinsell, L.V., 1960. 'Gloucestershire barrows', *Trans. BGAS* **79.1**, 5–148.

Oswald, A., Dyer, C., and Barber, M., 2001. *The creation of monuments. Neolithic causewayed enclosures in the British Isles* (London, English Heritage).

Parker, A.J., 1984. 'A Roman settlement at Lawrence Weston', *Bristol Avon Archaeol.* **3**, 27–35.

Parry, A., 2000. 'Beverstone, Babdown Farm', in J. Wills (ed.), 'Archaeol. Review 24', *Trans. BGAS* **118**, 214.

Parry, A., 2001. 'Bradley Stoke, Bradley Stoke Way', in J. Wills (ed.), 'Archaeol. Review 25', *Trans. BGAS* **119**, 188.

Parry, C., 1998. 'Excavations near Birdlip, Cowley, Gloucestershire, 1987–8', *Trans. BGAS* **116**, 25–92.

Parry, C., 1999. 'Excavations at Camp Gardens, Stow-on-the-Wold, Gloucestershire', *Trans. BGAS* **117**, 75–88.

Parry, C., and Cook, S., 1995. 'Badgeworth, Round barrow west of Hunt Court', in B. Rawes (ed.), 'Archaeol. Review 19', *Trans. BGAS* **113**, 184.

Parsons, J., 2003. 'Finders keepers, losers weepers: Treasure and the portable antiquities recording scheme', *Glevensis* **36**, 43–6.

Phillips, R., 1979. 'Fairford', in B. Rawes (ed.), 'Archaeol. Review 3', *Trans. BGAS* **97**, 127.

Piggott, S., 1928. 'Neolithic pottery and other remains from Pangbourne, Berks., and Caversham, Oxon.', *Proc. Prehist. Soc. East Anglia* **6** (1928–31), 30–9.

Pine, J., and Preston, S., 2004. *Iron Age and Roman settlement and landscape at Totterdown Lane, Horcott near Fairford, Gloucestershire* (Thames Valley Archaeological Service Monograph 6, Reading).

Price, A., 1991. 'A smithing hearth from east Dean', *New Regard of the Forest of Dean* **7**, 51–3.

Price, E., 2000a. *Frocester. A Romano-British settlement and its antecedents and successors. Volume 1 – The sites* (Stonehouse, Gloucester and District Archaeol. Research Group).

Price, E., 2000b. *Frocester. A Romano-British settlement and its antecedents and successors. Volume 2 – The finds* (Stonehouse, Gloucester and District Archaeol. Research Group).

Price, E., 2004a. 'A Neolithic axehead', *Glevensis* **37**, 45.

Price, E., 2004b. 'Uley', in J. Wills (ed.), 'Archaeol. Review 28', *Trans. BGAS* **122**, 191.

Price, W., 2001. 'A flint adze from the Wye at English Bicknor', *Glevensis* **34**, 72–3.

Pryor, F., 1976. 'A Neolithic multiple burial from Fengate, Peterborough', *Antiquity* **50**, 232–3.

Pryor, F., 1984. *Excavation at Fengate, Peterborough, England: the fourth report* (Northamptonshire Archaeol. Soc. Monograph 2 and Royal Ontario Museum Archaeol. Monograph 7, Northampton).

Rawes, B. (ed.), 1981. 'Archaeol. Review 5', *Trans. BGAS* **99**, 172–9.

Rawes, B., 1984. 'Archaeological discoveries from the Northleach bypass', *Glevensis* **18**, 25–42.

Rawes, B., 1986. 'The Romano-British settlement at Haymes, Cleeve Hill, near Cheltenham', *Trans. BGAS* **104**, 61–93.

Rawes, B., 1991. 'A prehistoric and Romano-British settlement at Vineyards Farm, Charlton Kings, Gloucestershire', *Trans. BGAS* **109**, 25–90.

Rawes, B., and Rawes, B., 1984. 'Northleach, Bypass', in B. Rawes (ed.), 'Archaeol. Review 8', *Trans. BGAS* **102**, 231.

Roe, D., 1981. *The lower and middle Palaeolithic periods in Britain* (London, Routledge).

Roe, F., 1985. 'Two prehistoric implements found near Tytherington, Avon', *Trans. BGAS* **103**, 220–2.

Russett, V., 1993. 'Stoke Gifford, Bradley Stoke Way', in B. Rawes (ed.), 'Archaeol. Review 17', *Trans. BGAS* **111**, 230.

Ryan, M. (ed.), 1979. *The origins of metallurgy in Atlantic Europe: proceedings of the fifth Atlantic Colloquium* (The Stationery Office, Dublin).

Samuel, J., 1997. 'Stoke Gifford, Harry Stoke Lane', in J. Rawes and J. Wills (eds.), 'Archaeol. Review 21', *Trans. BGAS* **115**, 293.

Samuel, J., 2002a. 'Bradley Stoke, Bradley Stoke Way', in J. Wills (ed.), 'Archaeol. Review 26', *Trans. BGAS* **120**, 235.

Samuel, J., 2002b. 'Westerleigh, Kendleshire Golf Club', in ibid. 255.

Savage, R., 1986. 'Badgeworth/Coberley, Crickley Hill', in B. Rawes (ed.), 'Archaeol. Review 10', *Trans. BGAS* **104**, 231.

Saville, A., 1980. *Archaeological sites in the Avon and Gloucestershire Cotswolds* (CRAAGS Surv. 5, Bristol).

Saville, A., 1983. 'Excavations at Condicote Henge Monument, Gloucestershire, 1977', *Trans. BGAS* **101**, 21–48.

Saville, A. (ed.), 1984. *Archaeology in Gloucestershire* (Cheltenham Art Gallery and Museums and the BGAS).

Saville, A., 1984a. 'Paleolithic and Mesolithic evidence from Gloucestershire', in A. Saville (ed.) 1984, 60–79.

Saville, A., 1984b. 'A Palaeolith presumed to be from Charlton Abbots, Glos.', *Trans. BGAS* **102**, 219–22.

Saville, A., 1986a. 'A Bronze Age palstave from near Cinderford, Glos.', *Trans. BGAS* **104**, 226–7.

Saville, A., 1986b. 'Mesolithic finds from west Gloucestershire', *Trans. BGAS* **104**, 228–30.

Saville, A., 1986c. 'Bronze Age arrowhead from Kilkenny, Dowdeswell', *Glevensis* **20**, 53.

Saville, A., 1986d. 'Flint Artefacts', in B. Rawes 1986, 90–2.

Saville, A., 1987. 'A Neolithic polished stone axehead from Oxenhall, near Newent', *Glevensis* **21**, 51.

Saville, A., 1989a. 'Rodmarton long barrow, Gloucestershire, 1988', *Trans. BGAS* **107**, 189–92.

Saville, A., 1989b. 'A Neolithic polished stone axehead from Broadwell, near Stow-on-the-Wold', *Glevensis* **23**, 46–7.

Saville, A., 1990a. *Hazleton North. The excavation of a Neolithic long cairn of the Cotswold-Severn group* (HBMCE Archaeological Rep. **13**, London, English Heritage).

Saville, A., 1990b. 'Broadwell, The Gables', in B. Rawes (ed.), 'Archaeol. Review 14', *Trans. BGAS* **108**, 194.

Saville, A., and Roe, F., 1984. 'A stone battle-axe from Wotton-under-Edge, and a review of battle-axe and macehead finds from Gloucestershire', *Trans. BGAS* **102**, 17–22.

Schulting, R.J., and Wysocki, M., 2002. 'Cranial trauma in the British earlier Neolithic', *Past* **41**, 4–6.

Shotton Project 2005 'The Shotton Project: a Midlands Palaeolithic network' (website at www.arch-ant.bham.ac.uk/shottonproject/ [accessed on 28:06:2005]).

Smith, G.H., 1989. 'Evaluation work at the Druid Stoke megalithic monument, Stoke Bishop, Bristol, 1983', *Trans. BGAS* **107**, 27–38.

Smith, M.J., and Brickley, M.B., 2004. 'Analysis and interpretation of flint toolmarks found on bones from West Tump long barrow, Gloucestershire', *International J. Osteoarchaeol.* **14**, 18–33.

Smith, R., 1986a. 'Dumbleton', in B. Rawes (ed.), 'Archaeol. Review 10', *Trans. BGAS* **104**, 234.

Smith, R., 1986b.'Toddington, East of The Warren' and 'Tanworth/Hampnett', in ibid. 245, 247.

Smith, R., and Cox, P., 1986. *The past in the pipeline. Archaeology of the Esso Midline* (Salisbury, Trust for Wessex Archaeol.).

Snashall, N., 2002. 'The idea of residence in the Neolithic Cotswolds' (University of Sheffield Ph.D. thesis).

Stait, A., 1990. 'Prehistoric flint artefacts from English Bicknor', *Dean Archaeol.* **3**, 47–9.

SWARF 2005. 'South West Archaeological Research Framework' (web-based documents available at http://www.so,erset.gov.uk/somerset/cultureheritage/heritage/swarf/ [accessed on 08/03/2005]).

Tavener, N., 1996. 'Avonmouth, Stup Pill', in J. Rawes and J. Wills (eds.), 'Archaeol. Review 20', *Trans. BGAS* **114**, 163–4.

Thomas, A., Holbrook, N., and Bateman, C., 2003. *Later prehistoric and Romano-British burial and settlement at Hucclecote, Gloucestershire* (Bristol and Gloucestershire Archaeol. Rep. **2**, Cirencester, Cotswold Archaeol.).

Thomas, J., 1999. *Understanding the Neolithic* (London, Routledge).

Timberlake, S., and Switsur, R., 1988. 'An archaeological investigation of early mine workings on Copa Hill, Cymystwyth: new evidence for prehistoric mining', *Proc. Prehist. Soc.* **54**, 329–33.

Topping, P., Mordant, C., and Maddison, M. (eds.), 1988. *Enclosures and defences in the Neolithic of Western Europe* (BAR International Series **403**, Oxford: two volumes).

Townsend, A., 2002. 'Mangotsfield, Land at Emersons Green', in J. Wills (ed.), Archaeol. Review 26', *Trans. BGAS* **120**, 250.

Trow, S., 1985. 'An interrupted-ditch enclosure at Southmore Grove, Rendcomb, Gloucestershire', *Trans. BGAS* **103**, 17–22.

Walker, G., 1991. 'Awre, Blakeney Hill Woods', in B. Rawes (ed.), 'Archaeol. Review 15', *Trans. BGAS* **109**, 223.

Walker, G., Thomas, A., and Bateman, C., 2004. 'Bronze-Age and Romano-British sites south-east of Tewkesbury: evaluations and excavations 1991–7', *Trans. BGAS* **122**, 29–94.

Walrond, L.F.J., 1986. 'Nailsworth', in B. Rawes (ed.), 'Archaeol. Review 10', *Trans. BGAS* **104**, 242.

Walters, B., 1985. 'Archaeological notes', *New Regard of the Forest of Dean* **1**, 21–9.

Walters, B., 1988. 'The distribution of prehistoric flint artefacts in Dean', *Dean Archaeol.* **1**, 36–8.

Walters, B., 1989. 'A survey of prehistory in Dean c.12,000 BC to AD 43', *Dean Archaeol.* **2**, 9–22.

Walters, B., 1990. 'Newland', in B. Rawes (ed.), 'Archaeol. Review 14', *Trans. BGAS* 108, **197**.

Walters, B. (ed.), 1991. 'Summary observations and additions to the archaeological record', *Dean Archaeol.* **4**, 38–46.

Walters, B, 1992. *The archaeology and history of ancient Dean and the Wye Valley* (Thornhill Press).

Walters, B., 1993. 'Coleford, The Common, Sling', in B. Rawes (ed.), 'Archaeol. Review 17', *Trans. BGAS* **111**, 220.

WAT 1985. 'Western Archaeological Trust Eleventh Annual Report 1984–85' (Bristol, Western Archaeol. Trust report).

Watkins, M., 1982a. 'Badgeworth, Hunt Court Farm', in B. Rawes (ed.), 'Archaeol. Review 6', *Trans. BGAS* **100**, 258.

Watkins, M., 1982b. 'Standish', in ibid. 265.

Weaver, S., 2004. 'Somerford Keynes, Shorncote, Cotswold Community', in J. Wills, (ed.), 'Archaeol. Review 28', *Trans. BGAS* **122**, 187–8.

Whitehead, P.F., 1979. 'An Acheulian handaxe from South Cerney', *Trans. BGAS* **97**, 117–19.

Whittle, A., Pollard, J., and Grigson, C., 1999. *The harmony of symbols. The Windmill Hill causewayed enclosure, Wiltshire* (Oxford, Oxbow Books/Cardiff Studies in Archaeol.).

Wilkinson, K.N., 1994. 'Great Rissington / Bourton Link Sewerage Scheme: A study of Late Devensian and Early to Middle Flandrian environments from material recovered during the watching brief' (London, report for Thames Water and Cotswold Archaeol. Trust).

WMRRF 2004. 'West Midlands Regional Research Framework for Archaeology' (web-based documents available at: http://www.arch-ant.bham.ac.uk/wmrrfa/intro.htm [accessed on 08/03/2005]).

Woodward, A., and Leach, P., 1993. *The Uley Shrines. Excavation of a ritual complex on West Hill, Uley, Gloucestershire: 1977–9* (HBMCE Archaeol. Rep. **17**, London, English Heritage).

Wymer, J.J., 1996. 'The English Rivers Palaeolithic survey', in C. Gamble and A. Lawson (eds.) 1996, 7–23.

The Iron Age

Tom Moore

INTRODUCTION

In the twenty years since Alan Saville's (1984) review of the Iron Age in Gloucestershire much has happened in Iron-Age archaeology, both in the region and beyond.[1] Saville's paper marked an important point in Iron-Age studies in Gloucestershire and was matched by an increasing level of research both regionally and nationally. The mid 1980s saw a number of discussions of the Iron Age in the county, including those by Cunliffe (1984b) and Darvill (1987), whilst reviews were conducted for Avon (Burrow 1987) and Somerset (Cunliffe 1982). At the same time significant advances and developments in British Iron-Age studies as a whole had a direct impact on how the period was viewed in the region. Richard Hingley's (1984) examination of the Iron-Age landscapes of Oxfordshire suggested a division between more integrated unenclosed communities in the Upper Thames Valley and isolated enclosure communities on the Cotswold uplands, arguing for very different social systems in the two areas. In contrast, Barry Cunliffe's model (1984a; 1991), based on his work at Danebury, Hampshire, suggested a hierarchical Iron-Age society centred on hillforts directly influencing how hillforts and social organisation in the Cotswolds have been understood (Darvill 1987; Saville 1984). Together these studies have set the agenda for how the 1st millennium BC in the region is regarded and their influence can be felt in more recent syntheses (e.g. Clarke 1993).

Since 1984, however, our perception of Iron-Age societies has been radically altered. In particular, the role of hillforts as central places at the top of a hierarchical settlement pattern has been substantially challenged (Hill 1996). Despite developments in Iron-Age studies in and beyond the region, Saville's paper remains one of the few detailed reviews of the period for the county. Considering the past influence of such models on interpretation of the Iron Age in the county, it seems timely to review the new Iron-Age material now available and suggest to what extent long-held models of Iron-Age society in the region, such as those proposed by Saville (1984), Darvill (1987) and Marshall (1978), can now be reviewed or challenged. This review is based on a fuller discussion (Moore forthcoming) of the Iron Age in the wider region of the Severn-Cotswolds. It incorporates some information from sites beyond the county boundary in an attempt to avoid some of the dangers in conducting county-based surveys of prehistoric material (see Bradley 1988).

THE ARCHAEOLOGICAL RESOURCE SINCE 1984

One of the most significant developments in archaeology since 1984 has been the implementation of Planning Policy Guidance note (PPG) 16. Although rescue archaeology took place prior to this date, it has only been since 1990 that such work has become a widespread pre-requisite of the planning process, leading to a marked increase in archaeological investigations and subsequent information. Figure 1 shows the number of archaeological investigations, including excavations, evaluations and geophysical surveys, producing Iron-Age material in the Severn-Cotswolds (Moore forthcoming). There has been a dramatic increase in Iron-Age sites examined since 1990, most as a result of PPG 16, with significant numbers in Gloucestershire. Subsequently, there is a range of new information on Iron-Age sites, although much of this work remains unpublished or is only

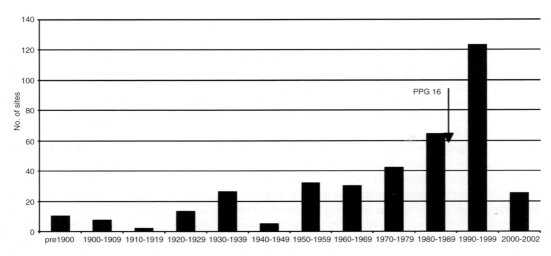

Fig. 1:   Number of Iron Age sites investigated (by decade) from the Severn-Cotswolds.

available in interim reports. To this material can be added publication of many investigations in adjoining counties which have important implications for our understanding of the Iron Age in Gloucestershire, for example Groundwell West near Swindon (Walker *et al.* 2001), Thornwell Farm near Chepstow (Hughes 1996), and various sites in southern Worcestershire (e.g. Edwards and Hurst 2000; Napthan *et al.* 1997). In addition to the wealth of new material provided by developer-funded archaeology a number of significant research projects have since come to fruition. These include the important excavations at Frocester (Price 2000), the first volume from Crickley Hill (Dixon 1994) and Conderton Camp (Thomas 2005). Recent reviews of the period in Warwickshire (e.g. Hingley 1989; 1996), Oxfordshire (Miles 1997) and the Welsh Marches (D. Jackson 1999; Wigley 2002) also allow the region to be placed in a wider context. It should however be noted that at the present time more Iron-Age sites and information are coming to light. For many such sites only interim statements are currently available and questions over chronology and interpretation will undoubtedly change or require revision. Discussion of these sites therefore must be regarded as provisional. However, the incorporation of this information remains important, particularly as much of it may significantly alter our perceptions of Iron-Age societies.

One of the major impacts of PPG 16 on the archaeology of the 1st millennium BC has been to shift the geographic focus of archaeological investigation. Throughout the 20th century Iron-Age archaeology in the region was predominantly focused on hillforts, reflecting a wider perception of these as the focus of Iron-Age settlement and social organisation. Although this resulted in substantial research on these monuments (e.g. Champion 1976; Dixon 1976; 1994; Dunning 1976; Hencken 1938) there was far less investigation of lowland sites and is reflected in Saville's limited discussion (1984, 149) of non-hillfort settlement. Since 1990 the development of many areas of lowland Gloucestershire, for example around the city of Gloucester, and gravel extraction in the Upper Thames Valley have led to increased archaeological investigation in these areas. As a result we have a far better knowledge of non-hillfort settlement than in 1984.

CHRONOLOGY

Traditionally the Iron Age has been divided in to three phases: early, middle and late (Cunliffe 1991; Saville 1984). Recent reassessment of the chronological evidence suggests this model may not be entirely appropriate for the region and should be slightly revised (Moore forthcoming). However, the chronology of the 1st millennium BC is far from straightforward and in many instances variations in the adoption and use of material culture and settlement patterns alongside landscape differences mean that chronological boundaries are likely to vary from region to region and even site to site.

Determining the transition from the Bronze Age to the Iron Age is more difficult than might first appear to be the case. Recent reviews suggest the late Bronze Age ended *c*.800 BC with an 'earliest' Iron Age from 800 to 600 BC (Needham in press) although in terms of settlement architecture in the region there are seemingly many similarities between the two periods. Plain ware pottery at sites like Shorncote and, further south, Potterne (Wiltshire) suggests that those sites end around 9th–8th centuries BC (Lawson 2000; Morris 1994a) although late Bronze-Age/early Iron-Age finger-impressed pottery may have had a longer period of use than is often suggested, possibly even as late as the 5th century BC (Moore forthcoming). Whilst dating of metalwork (Needham in press) may provide more refinement and a clearer end to the Bronze Age, such dates may be less helpful in dating changes in settlement patterns. It is not the place of this paper to discuss the detailed arguments involved in these chronological debates and for this reason the settlement and landscape evidence of the late Bronze Age and early Iron Age will be discussed in relatively broad terms with possible areas of transition and change outlined.

The dating of the transition from the early to the later Iron Age is also in need of modification. Assessment of radiocarbon dates associated with pottery of 'middle Iron-Age' form from the Severn-Cotswolds indicates the traditional date of *c*.400–450 BC for the transition may be too early and that a date around the mid 4th century BC is more realistic (Moore in press a). Limited dating evidence suggests other aspects of settlement and material culture also changed in this period with the appearance of the smaller enclosed settlements, storage pits and new settlement types. To this we might also add the emergence of new hilltop enclosures and the apparent decline of earlier hillforts. All mark a potentially widespread change in society around the 4th century BC. This modification of the chronology reflects a redefining of the beginning of the middle Iron Age in other parts of southern Britain (e.g. Cunliffe 1995).

The period from the 4th century BC to the 1st century AD is referred to here as the 'later' Iron Age rather than the middle Iron Age, identifying the 'late' Iron Age only as a specific, cultural element of the 1st centuries BC and AD. The reason for this is the continued use of middle Iron-Age handmade pottery forms into the late 1st century AD in many areas of the county and the limited presence of traditionally late Iron-Age attributes, such as imports. For many communities in the county, the transition from 'middle Iron-Age' ways of life to a 'late Age' may not have been particularly apparent (and is therefore difficult to recognise archaeologically) with only certain communities/groups obtaining and using late Iron-Age material. The late Iron Age therefore was in many ways a cultural phenomenon restricted to only a selection of communities as much as a chronological shift.

SETTLEMENT PATTERNS AND LANDSCAPES

The Late Bronze Age and the Earlier Iron Age (c.10th–4th century BC) (Fig. 2)

In general, the earlier 1st millennium BC is harder to recognise archaeologically than the later Iron Age. Recent investigations in advance of the upgrading of the A419/417 road, for example,

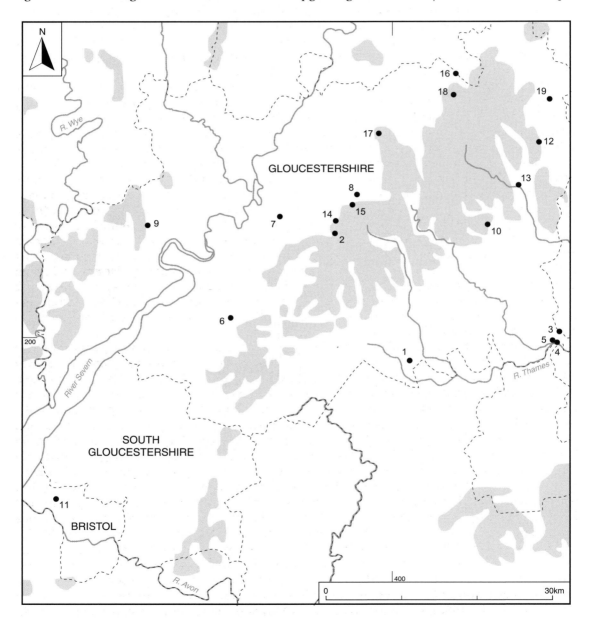

Fig. 2: Late Bronze-Age and early Iron-Age sites mentioned in the text.

produced no early Iron-Age or late Bronze-Age finds despite uncovering evidence of a number of later Iron-Age sites (Mudd *et al.* 1999). The reasons for this are likely to be varied, not least the nature of earlier 1st-millennium BC archaeology which appears to be made up of more ephemeral, less artefact-rich settlements, that are less susceptible to detection through traditional archaeological approaches (see Moore in press a). Additional problems are raised by the potentially long use of pottery types in the late Bronze Age–early Iron Age and difficulty in defining distinctly early Iron-Age material on some sites. The plateau in the radiocarbon calibration curve in this period creates further problems and entails that dates from early 1st-millennium BC sites are often relatively broad, spanning many centuries and making definition of occupation periods difficult, as was the case at Hucclecote discussed below.

Until relatively recently our understanding of non-hillfort settlement evidence in the county was extremely poor. However, a number of recent excavations have produced sites of early 1st-millennium BC date and, whilst we still do not have a great corpus, some observations can be made. The Upper Thames Valley has seen the greatest amount of excavation with large-scale stripping for gravel extraction enabling unenclosed settlements and late Bronze-Age/early Iron-Age landscapes to be examined. Unenclosed settlements of early Iron-Age date exist around Lechlade at Roughground Farm (Fig. 2, no. 3; Allen *et al.* 1993), Butler's Field (Fig. 2, no. 4; Boyle *et al.* 1998), Sherborne House (Bateman *et al.* 2003) and the Loders (Fig. 2, no. 5; Darvill *et al.* 1986), in many cases associated with pit alignments and ditches. These sites comprise single roundhouses (most commonly post-built) in landscapes of field systems (Fig. 3). This contrasts with the large spread of unenclosed late Bronze-Age roundhouses revealed at Shorncote (Fig. 2, no. 1; Hearne and Adam 1999; Hearne and Heaton 1994). Shorncote comprises around 26 houses representing either periodically shifting households, with only four or five houses contemporary (Hearne and Adam 1999, 70), or a larger 'village' like agglomeration. If the latter is the case, there may be a divergence between larger agglomerations of households in the late Bronze Age (before *c.*800 BC) and smaller settlements in the early Iron Age, potentially representing a shift from communal settlements to smaller (household scale?) settlements in the early Iron Age.

In a number of areas the early Iron-Age landscapes of the Upper Thames Valley appear to have been divided up by pit alignments, with examples excavated at Ashton Keynes/Shorncote (Hey 2000) and around Lechlade at Butler's Field (Boyle *et al.* 1998), Memorial Hall (Thomas and Holbrook 1998) and Roughground Farm (Allen *et al.* 1993). In some cases these pit alignments and other land boundaries combined to form larger landscape divisions, cutting off spurs in the river (Boyle *et al.* 1998). A similar use of pit alignments to divide up the gravel terraces and floodplains and delineate river bends has been noted both in the Upper Severn and north Avon Valleys (Wigley in press; Hingley 1996). Evidence from the Thames Valley suggests that in a number of cases linears were formed by ditches on higher ground and pit alignments in low-lying areas. One possibility is that pit alignments were used to define territories on the floodplains, where ditches were less necessary, perhaps allowing cattle to pass through common pasture and being intentionally designed to retain water (Rylatt and Bevan in press). Overall, the picture is of a highly structured landscape in the Thames Valley in the early 1st millennium BC (Yates 1999).

In the Severn Valley, excavation at Hucclecote has revealed post-built roundhouses in an unenclosed settlement, with radiocarbon dates ranging between the 8th and 4th centuries cal. BC (Fig. 2, no. 2; Thomas *et al* 2003, 30). In addition, there are fragmentary hints of early Iron-Age occupation at Frocester (Fig. 2, no. 6; Moore in press a; Price 2000), Saintbridge (Fig. 2, no. 7; Darvill and Timby 1986), Gloucester (Dunning 1933) and Dumbleton (Coleman and Hancocks forthcoming; Coleman *et al.* 2003). In the late Bronze Age it seems many areas of the valley were

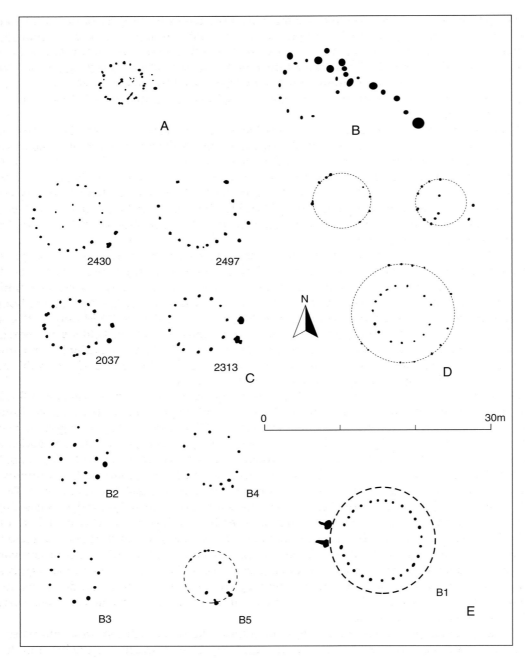

Fig. 3: *Late Bronze-Age and early Iron-Age roundhouses from Gloucestershire. A: Roughground Farm (after Allen et al. 1993); B: Butler's Field (after Boyle et al. 1998); C: Shorncote (after Hearne and Adam 1999); D: Hucclecote (after Thomas et al. 2003); E: Crickley Hill (after Dixon 1973).*

divided up by long linear ditches with an example from Frocester stretching for hundreds of metres across the gravel terraces (Price 2000 and pers. comm.); similar examples are known from south Worcestershire at Beckford (Britnell 1974) and Wyre Piddle (Napthan *et al.* 1997). Alongside evidence of increased alluvium in the Warwickshire Avon between 1300 and 600 BC (Shotton 1978) and maximum terrace clearance around Tewkesbury between 1200 and 800 BC (Brown 1982, 102), the impression is of a relatively intensively farmed, predominantly pastoral, Severn Valley by the end of the Bronze Age.

Although the evidence is limited, it seems likely that settlement in these landscapes was similar to that at Hucclecote and those in the Upper Thames Valley; predominantly unenclosed, post-built roundhouses located on the gravel terraces. Elsewhere in the Severn Valley, a late Bronze-Age burnt mound and early Iron-Age pottery have been recorded at Sandy Lane, Charlton Kings (Fig. 2, no. 8; Elsdon 1994; Leah and Young 2001). Such features have been suggested elsewhere as feasting areas or sweat huts (Barfield and Hodder 1987) and examples in the Thames Valley have been shown to be associated with unenclosed settlements (Brossler 2001). Sandy Lane may represent a similar situation.

On the western side of the Severn our understanding of the early Iron Age is poorer. Excavations just beyond the county at Thornwell Farm (Hughes 1996) revealed early Iron-Age post-built roundhouses in an apparently unenclosed settlement, potentially suggesting a similar emphasis on unenclosed settlement here too. Further south, rectangular late Bronze-Age houses have been uncovered on the Gwent Levels at Redcliff (Bell *et al.* 2000). At Welshbury earthworks beneath the rampart have been suggested as representing a later Bronze-Age field system, possibly indicating the early 1st-millennium BC use of these landscapes (Fig. 2, no. 9; McOmish and Smith 1996). These investigations stress not the lack of earlier 1st-millennium BC land use in this area but the variety and complexity of evidence that awaits discovery.

Our knowledge of late Bronze-Age and early Iron-Age settlement on the Cotswolds still relies primarily on hilltop sites with limited knowledge of non-hillfort settlement. The large enclosures at Norbury (Fig. 2, no. 10; Saville 1983) and Bathampton (Wainwright 1967) are suggested as late Bronze Age or earliest Iron Age (Cunliffe 1991; Saville 1983). To this group might be added the large enclosure at Nottingham Hill, which has produced late Bronze-Age metalwork (Fig. 2, no. 17; Hall and Gingell 1974), and Little Solsbury (Solisbury), which has produced finger-impressed pottery (Falconer and Adams Bryan 1935). The smaller enclosure at King's Weston, Bristol (Fig. 2, no. 11; Rahtz 1956), is of early Iron-Age date, and the associated, undated cross dyke, enclosing a larger area, may represent an earlier phase, similar to early 1st-millennium BC cross dykes in the Welsh Marches (Wigley 2002). The large enclosures have been suggested as storage centres and the rectilinear structures from Norbury may be granaries. However, these buildings can be compared to domestic rectangular structures at Crickley suggesting some sites may have also had significant occupation (Moore 2003). There has been some suggestion that these enclosures developed from late Bronze-Age unenclosed settlements, for instance at Bathampton (Marshall 1978; Wainwright 1967), but the evidence is inconclusive.

Probably contemporary with these larger enclosures were smaller hilltop sites, with potential examples beneath Stow-on-the-Wold (Fig. 2, no. 12; Parry 1999a), which has produced middle–late Bronze-Age ramparts, and Malmesbury (Wiltshire), where a radiocarbon date from the ramparts suggests a late Bronze-Age or early Iron-Age date.[2] Further investigation is clearly required but the possibility of more smaller hilltop enclosures in the county, similar to that at Rams Hill in Berkshire (Needham and Ambers 1994), should be considered.

Other early settlement on the Cotswolds consists of possibly unenclosed sites at Stables Quarry and Kings Beeches (Gray and Brewer 1904; RCHME 1976, 107). The Park at Guiting Power has also produced a radiocarbon date which may imply an early Iron-Age date (Marshall 1995) although other dating evidence suggests a later Iron-Age date. An ill-defined late Bronze-Age or early Iron-Age enclosure at Moreton-in-Marsh (Fig. 2, no. 19; Cotswold Archaeology 2004; see fig 10 in Darvill this volume) represents the only early enclosed settlement in the county and has some similarities with later Bronze-Age enclosures at Reading Business Park (Moore and Jennings 1992), examples from Dorset (Barrett *et al.* 1991, 209) and the early Iron-Age enclosure at Groundwell (Walker *et al.* 2001). Recent excavations of an apparently unenclosed early–middle Iron-Age settlement at Bourton-on-the-Water (Fig. 2, no. 13; Barber and Leah 1998; Nichols 1999; Piper and Catchpole 1996) in contrast emphasise the unenclosed nature of most non-hillfort settlement in the region. The location of the Bourton site reflects those in the Thames and Severn Valleys, situated on a gravel terrace above the floodplain of the river Windrush.

Around the 8th–6th century BC a number of small hillforts appeared with pottery similar to Cunliffe's All Canning Cross style (Cunliffe 1991; Elsdon 1994) although the chronological sequence is far from clear-cut. These include the enclosures at Shenberrow (Fig. 2, no. 18; Fell 1961), Cleeve Cloud, Crickley Hill (Fig. 2, no. 14; Dixon 1994) and Leckhampton (Fig. 2, no. 15; Champion 1976). More recently, early Iron-Age pottery has been recorded outside the ramparts at Burhill (Fig. 2, no. 16; Marshall 1989), indicating extramural settlement or an unenclosed settlement prior to the hillfort. The traditional model of larger, late Bronze-Age enclosures replaced by smaller, early Iron-Age hillforts still fits much of the evidence but assuming from similarity of morphology that many of the unexcavated hillforts are of the same date (Darvill 1987, 128) may be too simplistic. Examination of hillforts in Hampshire (e.g. Cunliffe 2000) and Berkshire (e.g. Gosden and Lock 1998) has indicated the variation and complex histories of these monuments and reinforces the notion that no simple model should be applied. Clearly, a similar campaign of investigation through geophysical surveys and limited excavation is required for the hillforts of the Cotswolds.

Early Iron-Age Society

To summarise, the evidence of earlier 1st-millennium BC settlement patterns in the county suggests non-hillfort settlement was predominantly unenclosed with generally little evidence for the kind of enclosed sites seen to the south at Groundwell West (Walker *et al.* 2001) and Longbridge Deverill (Hawkes 1994). There appear to have been a variety of hilltop enclosures with possibly the smaller sites dating to the early Iron Age.

We need to be cautious however as investigation strategies may have heavily influenced our knowledge of this period and in particular under-represented earlier 1st-millennium BC settlement. The suggestion that the Cotswolds themselves were not densely settled in the early Iron Age (Saville 1979) might be supported by current evidence but it more likely reflects a poverty of recent data as archaeological investigation has concentrated on the lowlands. Similarly, the lack of evidence for dense early Iron-Age settlement in the Severn Valley might imply some form of nucleation to hilltop sites in this period but evidence from the Thames Valley and recent discoveries at Hucclecote cautions against such an interpretation. It seems more likely that early Iron-Age settlement merely remains undetected. However, the evidence from some excavations of a lack of settlement (and possibly exploitation) on the heavy clay soils in the early Iron Age, after use in the Bronze Age as seen at Tewkesbury (Walker *et al.* 2004), should not be overlooked. The possibility that there was a short-lived nucleation of settlement to hillforts, like Crickley Hill, in the early Iron Age, increasingly being postulated elsewhere (Haselgrove and Pope in press), should be explored. Current chronologies of the early 1st millennium BC clearly need to be refined in order to do this.

The Later Iron Age (4th century BC–1st century AD) (Fig. 4)

Through excavation, cropmarks and fieldwalking we now have a picture of a densely settled region in the later Iron Age. Small, household-sized enclosures (less than 1 ha in area), usually rectilinear in shape, became increasingly common and are found throughout the region, particularly on the north Cotswolds and in the Severn Valley (Fig. 5; e.g. Marshall 2001). A number of such enclosures have seen investigation most extensively at Frocester (Fig. 4, no. 1; Price 2000), Birdlip (Fig. 4, no. 2; Parry 1998a), Guiting Power (Fig. 4, no. 3; Saville 1979), The Bowsings (Fig. 4, no. 4; Marshall 1995) and Preston (Fig. 4, no. 9; Mudd *et al.* 1999), whilst other forms of enclosure are known from Highgate and Ermin Farm (Fig. 4, no. 32; ibid.). Dating evidence from these sites and comparison with similar enclosures in southern Worcestershire (Moore in press a) suggest they appeared from the 4th century BC onward with many occupied into the 1st century AD, some such as Frocester continuing into the Roman period. In some areas these enclosures appear to form distinct clusters, for example near Birdlip and in the Temple Guiting area, stressing that many of them were part of larger communities or that they occasionally shifted across the landscape (Moore forthcoming) rather than the isolated communities envisaged by Hingley (1984).

The evidence from the Upper Thames Valley also indicates a densely settled and intensively farmed landscape predominantly comprising unenclosed settlements known from cropmarks (Hingley and Miles 1984). Excavated examples include Cleveland Farm, Ashton Keynes (Coe *et al.* 1991); Warrens Field-Claydon Pike (Fig. 4, no. 7; Anon. 2005; Hingley and Miles 1984); Stubbs Farm, Kempsford (Cromarty *et al.* n.d.); and Thornhill Farm, Fairford (Fig. 4, no. 8; Jennings *et al.* 2004; Palmer and Hey 1989). Even on these unenclosed sites there appears to have been an emphasis on bounding the household community with large, visibly impressive enclosure ditches around a number of houses, for example at Claydon Pike and Thornhill Farm (Allen *et al.* 1984; Anon. 2005; Hingley and Miles 1984) (Fig. 6B and A). Excavations and cropmarks around Preston have also revealed segmented boundary ditches associated with a polygonal enclosure dating to the 4th–2nd centuries BC, one of which forms a long boundary feature possibly using Bronze-Age barrows as landscape markers (Mudd *et al.* 1999, 40). These segmented ditches appear peculiar to the region and seem to form enclosures further south at Shorncote (Brossler *et al.* 2002) (Fig. 6D) and around Lechlade (Bateman *et al.* 2003; Boyle *et al.* 1998). The role of these ditches is unclear, some replacing earlier pit alignments, and they may mark changing agricultural needs but also reflect the increasing emphasis on enclosure in the later Iron Age.

Our knowledge of settlement patterns in the Severn Valley has developed considerably since 1984 through widespread but small-scale investigations. This is particularly true to the north of the county around Bredon Hill, with later Iron-Age pottery and features recorded at Dumbleton (Coleman and Hancocks forthcoming; Coleman *et al.* 2003; Marshall 1990b; Saville 1984), Alstone (Cox 1985), Wormington Grange, Stanton (Marshall 1990b), and Aston Somerville (Brett and Coleman 2000). Elsewhere, agglomerated settlements of smaller enclosures and trackways exist at Hailes-Stanway, which has yielded later Iron-Age pottery (Clifford 1944; Webster and Hobley 1964), and dense clusters of probably later Iron-Age enclosures exist at Broadway (Worcestershire) (Moore forthcoming; Smith 1946). Alongside cropmark evidence and excavations elsewhere in this area (e.g. Dinn and Evans 1990; Webster and Hobley 1964) the evidence

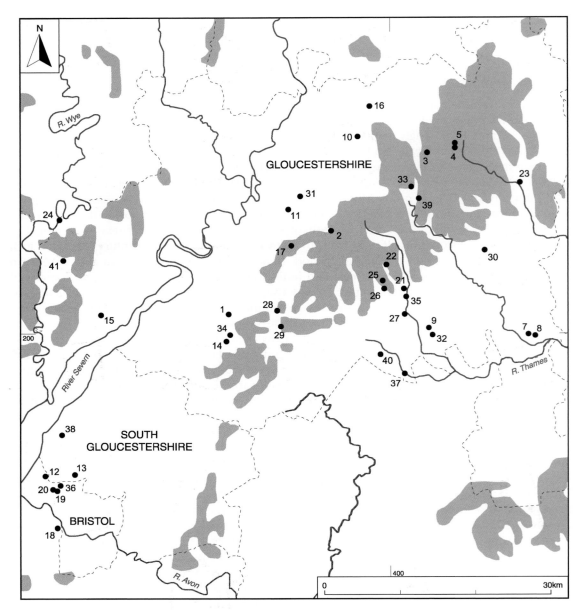

Fig. 4:   Later Iron-Age sites mentioned in the text.

indicates a densely occupied landscape by the later Iron Age and a picture of enclosures integrated into complex field systems made up of field boundaries, trackways and pit alignments.

Settlement further south in the Severn Valley may have been similar but the evidence is not as widespread. Frocester (Price 2000) indicates the type of settlement which may have been

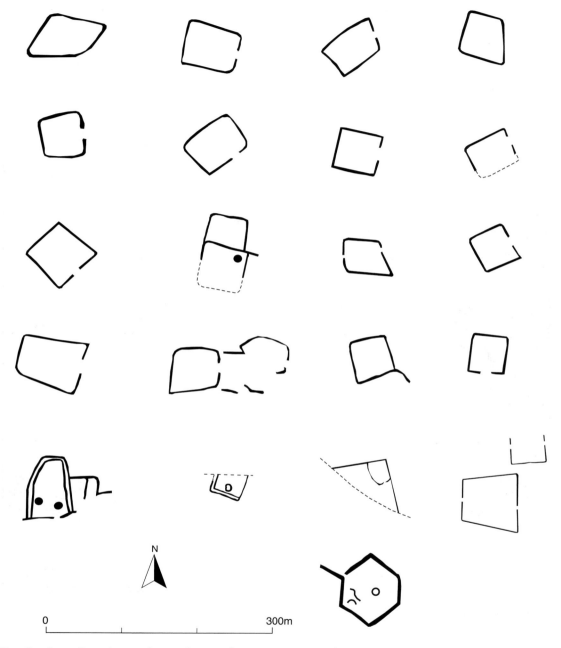

Fig. 5: Later Iron-Age enclosures known from excavation and cropmarks.

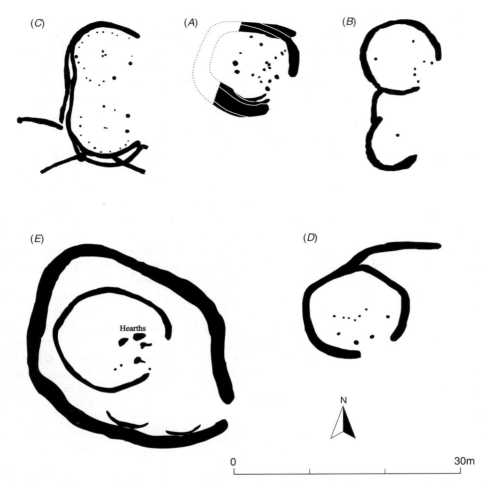

Fig. 6:   Later Iron Age 'enclosed' roundhouses. A: Thornhill (after Jennings et al. 2004); B: Claydon Pike (after Allen et al. 1984); C: Salmonsbury (after Dunning 1976); D: Shorncote 1997–8 (after Brossler et al. 2002); E: Claydon Pike (after Allen et al. 1984).

common; a single ditched enclosure later embellished with multiple ditches, possibly representing the increasing status of the inhabitants. Other possible Iron-Age enclosures exist at Longford near Gloucester (Moore forthcoming) with examples of roundhouses within smaller enclosures at Abbeymead (Fig. 4, no. 11; Atkin 1987) and a less well defined spreading, later Iron-Age, settlement at Gilder's Paddock (Fig. 4, no. 10; Parry 1999b). The overall impression is that later Iron-Age occupation was as dense in this area as that around Bredon Hill.

From the 4th/3rd century BC we also see expansion into areas of the landscape that had previously been under utilised. Throughout the region the wet marshy landscapes of the Avon, Gwent and Somerset Levels saw increasing activity in the later Iron Age with evidence of more permanent settlement not seen previously. Excavations at Hallen (Fig. 4, no. 12; Gardiner *et al.* 2002) have revealed an unenclosed, probably permanently occupied, but short-lived, settlement in the Avon Levels dating to the 3rd/2nd century BC, matching the appearance of the lake villages at Glastonbury and Meare in the Somerset Levels (Coles 1987; Coles and Minnit 1995). It seems likely that the Avon Levels were utilised in early periods, with evidence for example of late Bronze-Age trackways from the Somerset, Gwent and Avon Levels, but that occupation was predominantly seasonal (Bell *et al.* 2000; Gardiner *et al.* 2002, 22; Locock 2001). The reasons for an expansion into these previously marginal areas in the later Iron Age are not entirely clear but it almost undoubtedly marks a population increase and possibly the development of specialised, industrial or farming communities as seen at Glastonbury (Coles and Minnit 1995).

Our knowledge of other later Iron-Age settlement in the Bristol area is limited. Excavations have revealed a conjoined enclosure at Cribb's Causeway apparently located in a field system (Fig. 4, no. 13; King 1998) which may indicate the types of settlement that existed in this area. In form it appears somewhat similar to sites like Abbeymead and may represent an agglomeration of enclosures fulfilling a variety of functions but a lack of publication makes it difficult to comment further. Elsewhere, possible evidence for later Iron-Age activity has been found in the form of residual pottery at Inns Court (R. Jackson 1999) and Lawrence Weston (Fig. 4, no. 20; Boore 1999) with stray finds from elsewhere in the city (Portway-Dobson 1933; Tratman 1946) but with little indication of the nature of occupation in these areas.

The later Iron Age also sees the appearance of new hilltop enclosures after some of the early sites are abandoned, some possibly violently. Crickley Hill was abandoned by the 5th century BC after a final act of destruction (Dixon 1994, 107, 220) with Leckhampton also seemingly finally burnt. Around the 4th century BC new hilltop sites emerged at Uley Bury (Fig. 4, no. 14; Saville 1983), Bredon Hill (Hencken 1938) and Conderton, possibly in the 5th or 4th century BC (Thomas 2005). It seems likely that a number of other elaborate hillforts were also occupied at this time, including Painswick (Fig. 4, no. 17) and Beckbury. Stray pottery finds from Oxenton Hill indicate later, and possibly some early, Iron-Age activity (Fig. 4, no. 16; Watson 2002). In general, few hillforts seem to display evidence of the continuity from the early to later Iron Age seen at some sites in Wessex, possibly implying a major realignment of social systems around this time. In southern Gloucestershire, hillforts occupied in this period occur at Stokeleigh (Fig. 4, no. 18; Haldane 1975) and Blaise Castle (Fig. 4, no. 19; Rahtz and Clevedon-Brown 1959) although little can be said about the nature of occupation. Of the many hillforts known on the west side of the Severn in the Forest of Dean few have seen investigation although excavation at Lydney indicates occupation in the later Iron Age (Fig. 4, no. 15; Wheeler and Wheeler 1932). Earthwork survey at Welshbury (McOmish and Smith 1996) suggests some affinity with the smaller, elaborate later Iron-Age enclosures to the west in Wales. This may indicate a somewhat different social organisation in this area with smaller communities placing greater emphasis on defining their social space in elaborate enclosures.

Later Iron-Age Society

The belief that hillforts acted as the top of a settlement and social hierarchy in the middle Iron Age (Saville 1984, 147) has been widely critiqued elsewhere in Britain (e.g. Hill 1996). The evidence from Gloucestershire is in many ways too patchy to lend much to the debate. However, Elaine Morris's (1994b) assessment of the distribution of Malvern pottery in the region suggests there was no distinction between hillfort and non-hillforts in the amounts of decorated wares consumed. This may imply there was no social distinction between these communities, thereby possibly concurring with Hill's argument (1996) that Wessex hillforts have less evidence for social and economic differences or occupation by élites than non-hillfort settlements. The evidence from Uley Bury may support this; there the smaller enclosures inside the hillfort might suggest it performed a similar role to the larger unenclosed settlement as an agglomeration of settlement. On Bredon Hill it appears at least two 'hillforts' were contemporary with one another and with the field systems in the valley but there is no evidence that they controlled or dominated the lowland communities. The size and features of Conderton Camp suggest that some communities in the smaller hilltop enclosures were not vastly different from those in the valley, such as Frocester, and were not necessarily of any higher status. The evidence from excavated hillforts in the county suggests that they served a variety of functions varying from site to site and over time and generalisations about these monuments are unhelpful.

A major change in the nature of settlement and landscape organisation between the earlier and later Iron Ages appears to be marked by the increasing 'enclosure' of smaller communities. The appearance of enclosures across the landscape suggests that household-sized communities felt the need from the 4th century BC onward to demarcate their social space more overtly. This is seen not just at widespread small, enclosed settlements but also at sites like Claydon Pike where roundhouses are increasingly demarcated by large enclosure ditches. The size of ditches encompassing particular houses, such as the example from Claydon Pike (Fig. 6B), implies these are unlikely to be for drainage alone. The lack of such ditches at other houses near by and around early Iron Age houses in the Thames Valley suggests these ditches are as much about demarcating social space as about functional considerations. In addition, the presence of smaller enclosures within the hillfort at Uley Bury not only signifies dense settlement (Saville 1984, 147) but also the need to define social spaces even within these larger enclosures. Evidence from Frocester also indicates that later Iron-Age communities were placing more emphasis on defining their place in the landscape. Around the 4th century BC the enclosure was built over a junction between late Bronze-Age and early Iron-Age land boundaries. This appears to represent an existing community, which may have been unenclosed, marking itself more prominently in the landscape and perhaps making a more overt claim to the land by positioning itself on this important node in the earlier field system (Moore in press a).

The increasing emphasis on defining household communities may relate to an increasing population in the later Iron Age and the subsequent need to mark landownership and boundaries more overtly than was required previously. With increasing population and possibly the emergence of larger social units, there was a greater need for communities to mark their permanence, sense of place and ownership of the landscape. Hingley (1984) has claimed in his assessment of Iron-Age Oxfordshire that the development of enclosure boundaries around sites on the Cotswolds marked their social and economic isolation from each other. The picture from much of the Cotswolds and the Severn Valley in contrast suggests in these areas many enclosures clustered in large communities integrated into wider field systems (Moore forthcoming). Far from being isolated, these communities were probably part of an intensively settled and heavily negotiated landscape and part of much wider social networks and communities.

The Late Iron Age: Land of the Dobunni? (1st century BC–1st century AD)

It seems increasingly clear that the division between the Middle and Late Iron Age cannot be defined as a clear-cut boundary. The continued use of essentially 'middle Iron-Age', handmade pottery forms as late as the 1st century AD suggests there was not a widespread, single chronological or cultural shift.[3] In many cases only certain communities adopted, or had access to, late Iron-Age wheel-thrown wares or imported material. In some cases the lack of chronological refinement caused by these pottery forms may suggest that some sites argued as being 'middle Iron Age' continued into the 1st century AD (Moore in press b) but merely do not have late Iron-Age pottery. In addition, the presence of late Iron-Age pottery forms (previously frequently referred to as 'Belgic') does not just indicate late Iron-Age activity but signifies the adoption or consumption of new food stuffs and new eating habits, as platters and cups appear, marking a radical change from 'middle' Iron-Age ways of life. There is also increasing evidence that early Severn Valley wares were in use prior to the conquest (Timby 1990;1999a and b) with important implications for the dating of a number of late Iron-Age sites. These changes in pottery therefore should be considered as marking changes in eating habits, food consumption, exchange systems and social relations as much as reflecting a new chronological phase.

The late Iron Age sees major changes in settlement patterns. There appears to be a general abandonment of hillforts between the 2nd and 1st century BC, with Conderton Camp, for example, abandoned in the 2nd century and little evidence for late Iron-Age activity at Uley Bury. In some instances this may merely denote a lack of pottery finds resulting from the small nature of some investigations (e.g. Uley Bury). Elsewhere, small-scale excavations at Symonds Yat revealed late Iron-Age pottery (Fig. 4, no. 24; Parry 1994) and there is some evidence for limited late Iron-Age re-use of Crickley Hill (Dixon 1994, 194) indicating activity on some hillforts in the county in the 1st century AD. Such evidence may represent a variety of types of activity, with small-scale re-occupation possible at some hillforts, or mark early Roman use, possibly even temples similar to that seen at Uley-West Hill (Woodward and Leach 1993). It is perhaps misleading to argue that Ditches represents continued occupation of a 'hillfort' (Cunliffe 2005); the enclosure has a distinct morphology and its chronology cannot be pushed much earlier than the 1st century BC.

The abandonment of some hillforts does not appear to be matched necessarily by changes elsewhere. Some field systems show signs of continuity into the late Iron Age, for example around Dumbleton, with early Severn Valley wares present and possible re-cutting of later Iron-Age trackways and ditches (e.g. Coleman et al. 2003; Coleman and Hancocks forthcoming). Others at Aston Mill (Worcestershire) may be abandoned or reconfigured (Dinn and Evans 1990). Some enclosures in this area, such as those at Beckford appear to have been occupied in the 1st century AD (Oswald 1974; Jan Wills pers. comm.) whilst others appear to have been abandoned. Evidence from Tewkesbury indicates the appearance of a possible enclosure, probably in the early 1st century AD (Hannan 1993), with other enclosures like that at Bushley Green also possibly appearing around this time (Moore-Scott 1997). Further south, Frocester continued to be occupied, presumably with its associated land organisation, into the Romano-British period. At Birdlip, the enclosure appears to have shifted slightly and there may have been a short hiatus between middle Iron-Age and 1st-century AD occupation (Parry 1998a). At the Bowsings the enclosure appears to have been abandoned at some point in the 1st century AD (Marshall 1995), although it is unclear if the inhabitants moved to a new settlement nearby for there is certainly Roman material from the vicinity. The indication is that some communities moved around the landscape but stayed generally in the same location with perhaps a strong sense of landownership. Overall, the picture may be varied with some reorganisation of the landscape and changes in settlement in the 1st century BC/AD in certain areas whilst they continued relatively unchanged in others.

Emergence of 'Oppida'

The most dramatic development of the late Iron Age is the appearance of a range of new monuments, the so-called 'oppida'. Salmonsbury, apparently the earliest of these new sites, was probably occupied as early as the 1st century BC and continued into the 1st century AD (Fig. 4, no. 23; Haselgrove 1997, 61). It consists of a low-lying, large enclosure encompassing some 23 ha with antenna ditches marking possible stock corralling areas. The enclosure was intensively occupied; it included conjoined roundhouses and smaller enclosures (see Fig. 6C; Dunning 1976).[4] The intensive occupation is similar to Dyke Hills in Oxfordshire (Cunliffe 2005, 403) and Uley Bury and suggests that Salmonsbury was a focus of occupation and permanent settlement. It might even represent the kind of nucleation of communities into one larger enclosure seen on a number of sites in northern France around this time (Moore forthcoming).

Bagendon represents the most impressive of the late Iron-Age sites. A large dyke system encompassed an area of between 80 and 200 ha and represents a 'territorial oppidum' similar to those at Colchester and Verulamium (Fig. 4, no. 21; Cunliffe 2005, 191). Bagendon was constructed somewhat later than Salmonsbury; the dyke system was dug probably in the 1st century AD with a flourish of activity in the immediate post-conquest period. Although there appears to have been activity at the site in the early–mid 1st century AD suggestions that the site is entirely post-conquest (Swan 1975) seem unlikely. The nearby enclosure at Ditches emerged first in the 2nd or 1st century BC (Fig. 4, no. 22; Trow 1988) and together the Bagendon dyke system and Ditches enclosure represent part of a wider complex (Fig. 7). Only limited investigation has taken place in the interior (Clifford 1961; Trow 1982; Trow et al. forthcoming b) and has revealed an industrial area at the entrance including coin minting. Both sites indicate high-status occupation in the early 1st century AD, with imported Gallo-Belgic and samian pottery. The subsequent building of an exceptionally early villa at Ditches in the late 1st century AD (Trow et al. forthcoming a) further indicates the inhabitants' high status and rapid adoption of Romanized lifestyles. The excavation of contemporary sites at Middle Duntisbourne and Duntisbourne Abbots (Fig. 4, nos. 25 and 26; Mudd et al. 1999) and recent finds of late Iron-Age pottery near Stratton (Fig. 4, no. 27; Wymark 2003) reveal a cluster of possibly similar sites in this area representing a focus of high-status late Iron-Age communities engaged in exchange with the kingdoms and oppida of South-East England.

The role of the Bagendon complex is not entirely understood. Claiming sites like Bagendon as 'urban' (Cunliffe 1991, 173) is clearly incorrect as most of the interior appears not to have been intensively occupied. Instead the evidence represents a more scattered set of activities rather than one single centre. The apparent high-status nature of the finds from the site has led it to be variously regarded as a royal centre or 'park' (Darvill 1987, 168; Reece 1990, 27). However, it seems likely that Bagendon performed a variety of roles as well as possibly being the centre for new élites. Its focus around a low-lying well watered valley is similar to other sites in Britain, such as Verulamium and Stanwick (Haselgrove 1995), and might suggest, as seems to be the case elsewhere, that it acted as a ritual place. Coinage deposition at wet locations was a common feature of many such sites in the late Iron Age. The location of Bagendon around a valley and the presence of large antenna ditches at sites like Ditches and Salmonsbury also indicate an emphasis on controlling stock, probably cattle or horses. It has been suggested that horses in particular were valuable commodities in the late Iron Age (Creighton 2000) and the apparent importance of stock corralling may explain the importance of horse imagery on 'Dobunnic' coinage.

A common feature of Bagendon and Salmonsbury fundamental to their development is their location on route nodes; Salmonsbury on the confluence of the Windrush and Dikler and Bagendon on the river Churn. Both are also located on the interface of topographic zones; between the 'upland' Cotswolds and the Thames Valley and between potentially different 'cultural' and

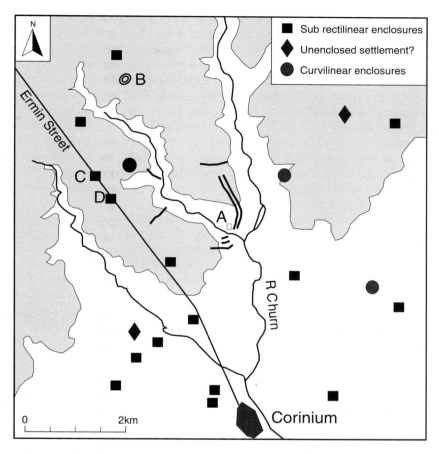

Fig. 7: Bagendon complex. A: 'Industrial' area (1956 and 1980 excavations: Clifford 1961; Trow 1982); B: Ditches enclosure; C: Duntisbourne Grove; D: Middle Duntisbourne.

economic zones. These sites may to some extent have acted as emporia between the more 'Romanised' kingdoms of the South-East and the Iron-Age communities to the west.

The variety of ditches and banks at Minchinhampton have also been argued as representing a late Iron-Age territorial oppidum (Fig. 4, no. 29; Clifford 1937; RCHME 1976). Parry (1996) instead argues convincingly that many of the earthworks are of medieval date, probably wood enclosure boundaries. The presence of late Iron-Age/early Roman settlement in the Minchinhampton and Rodborough area does seem likely however on the basis of finds of late Iron-Age metalwork and pottery (Clifford 1937; Parry 1996). The rectilinear enclosure has recently been argued to be late Iron Age (Fig. 4, no. 28; Ecclestone 2004) whilst some of the banks and ditches at Minchinhampton probably represent elements of a later prehistoric field system.

These may not be the only such sites to appear in the late Iron Age. There is some suggestion that some of the large complexes of banjo-shaped enclosures known through cropmarks across the eastern Cotswolds may have served similar roles. Their form also appears to indicate an emphasis on controlling and corralling livestock. Such complexes occur at Ashton Keynes, Eastleach Turville,

Barnsley and Northleach-Broadfield, all of which possess a variety of enclosures and trackways (Darvill and Hingley 1982; Moore forthcoming). At Northleach (Fig. 4, no. 30) a number of banjo enclosures cluster with other enclosures and linear ditches, the similarities between them suggesting they form a larger settlement unit. The clustering of banjo and other enclosures on the interface between the Cotswold uplands and Upper Thames Valley perhaps indicates either a cultural restriction or a particular subsistence role. There has been no investigation of these enclosure complexes and they require further fieldwork. They have affinities with similar complexes in Dorset (Barrett *et al.* 1991) and Hampshire (Corney 1989) which have produced late Iron-Age pottery and coinage. The possible presence of a banjo-shaped enclosure within the dyke system at Bagendon may further suggest a similarity between these complexes and late Iron-Age sites such as the Ditches-Bagendon complex. Other enclosures which may also be of late Iron-Age date include that at Frampton Mansell which has yielded both Dobunnic and Corisolite coins (de Jersey 1994; 1997; RCHME 1976).

Some of these late Iron-Age enclosures saw the development of early Roman villas. Examples include Ditches (Trow 1988; Trow *et al.* forthcoming a) and possibly Waltham near Whittington (Hirst n.d.), and cropmark evidence suggests a number of the banjo enclosures have a similar relationship. A banjo enclosure in Rodmarton (Darvill and Locke 1988), for example, appears to be situated in the vicinity of Hocberry villa. The latter was partly excavated in the 19th century and may have produced early imported pottery potentially indicative of late Iron-Age and early Roman activity (Clifford 1961, 211). A similar relationship between early Roman villas and late Iron-Age complexes has been noted in Dorset and Hampshire (Corney 2002) further supporting the impression that many of these enclosures represent high-status, late Iron-Age communities that rapidly adopted Roman lifestyles.

A range of evidence for later Iron-Age activity is known from the Gloucester area at Kingsholm (Hurst 2005; Timby 1999b), Hucclecote (Clifford 1933; Sermon 1998), Churchdown (Fig. 4, no. 31; Hurst 1977), possibly Barnwood (Clifford 1930), Abbeymead and Saintbridge (Atkin 1987). There has been a suggestion that the material from Kingsholm indicates the existence of a pre-Roman centre prior to the fortress, perhaps helping to explain its location, and there is an indication that some late Iron-Age occupation may have been of high status, for example the possible currency bars from Hucclecote (Sermon 1997). However, the variety of evidence and its wide distribution suggest instead a range of Iron-Age settlement existing in the area when the Roman fortress at Kingsholm was constructed and the sites at Abbeymead and Saintbridge appear to be no more than farmsteads.

Coinage

It is in the late Iron Age that we see the emergence of coinage in the region. Occasional Gallo-Belgic coins are known from the county, for example at Uley Bury, and Potin coins from The Park, Guiting Power (Fig. 4, no. 6; Marshall 1990a), and Shipton Oliffe (Timby 1998) date to the 2nd century BC. By the 1st century BC/AD we see the emergence of so-called 'Dobunnic' coinage (Van Arsdell 1994) which was exchanged over a wide area centred on Gloucestershire. The Portable Antiquities Scheme has added an increasing number of find spots from the region in recent years (Cunliffe 2005, 190; de Jersey 1994). It has been argued this coinage was minted by new kings that emerged in the latest Iron Age at centres like Bagendon. Some issues have the names of individuals and there is evidence of coin minting at Bagendon and Ditches. However, a possible coin mould from Wycomb (Fig. 4, no. 33; Timby 1998) makes the picture potentially more complicated, indicating that coin minting may also have taken place at other locations.

Defining this coinage as 'tribal' is also problematic. There is somewhat a circular argument in defining Dobunnic coinage as 'Dobunnic' on the basis of its occurrence in Dobunnic territory and then defining that territory as Dobunnic on the basis of coin finds (Moore and Reece 2001). In addition, the majority of coin finds from the wider region do not come from late Iron-Age sites or pre-conquest contexts but instead from Roman contexts, a large number from temples which cannot be securely dated prior to the conquest, such as Bath (Moore forthcoming). It seems increasingly likely that the majority of these coins were deposited after the Roman conquest and their deposition reflects their use in the early Roman period rather than necessarily reflecting Iron-Age practices. It is also increasingly clear that late Iron-Age coinage was used in expressing a range of social obligations and in religious contexts (e.g. Creighton 2000) and that its distribution does not necessarily reflect ethnicity but a range of social ties and ritual relationships. It is hoped that current studies of the archaeological context of Dobunnic coinage will reveal more about the roles and relationships of coinage in the late Iron Age and early Roman period (Haselgrove et al forthcoming).

Social Organisation in the Latest Iron Age

The appearance of the Bagendon complex has been argued as marking the emergence of an élite, tribal capital in the late Iron Age (Cunliffe 1991, 173; Millett 1990, 26). However, the nature of activity at Bagendon and its location in the landscape suggest the picture was more complex. One of the most striking aspects of the Bagedon complex is the limited evidence of early or middle Iron-Age activity at its sites or in the surrounding area, possibly implying a somewhat limited level of occupation in the centuries preceding the 1st century AD. All of the sites in the complex date little earlier than the mid 1st century BC, with Bagendon and the Duntisbourne sites no earlier than the 1st century AD. In addition, despite apparently favourable cropmark conditions, the number of enclosures in the immediate vicinity of Bagendon is less than in many areas on the Cotswolds. Bagendon, therefore, may have emerged in a landscape not occupied by the dense clusters of later Iron-Age settlement discussed above. This is not to argue that later Iron-Age settlements did not exist nearby or that this area of the landscape was completely unutilised, but that the intensity of land use now apparent for other areas is not evident. This may suggest that the complex was deliberately constructed in an area where previous settlement density was low, at least compared to parts of the northern Cotswolds, the Lower Severn, the northern part of the Avon Valley and the Upper Thames. Such areas were not necessarily 'empty' in the preceding centuries, but potentially had other functions, perhaps, for example, used seasonally or for ritual purposes.

The emergence of 'oppida' in areas where earlier activity and settlement is less apparent is not restricted to the county and has been suggested for other British oppida, such as Verulamium in Hertfordshire (Haselgrove and Millett 1997; Hill 1995a). The reasons for this expansion into new areas may represent the emergence of new groups in areas away from existing social groups. This might be the case in the county with Bagendon emerging discreet from the dense settlement in the Severn and Thames Valleys and north Cotswolds. It might also be significant that Bagendon is located on the fringes of the exchange networks of regional potteries from the Malverns (Fig. 8). It is possible that Bagendon was located away from existing social groups to act as a meeting place and centre of exchange beyond existing social networks, as has been suggested for the lake villages (Moore in press b; Sharples 1991). This may mark the emergence of a new élite, constructing a centre away from existing power centres, or represent a new community developing away from the constraints of existing social systems and landscapes. Seeing Bagendon in this way has major implications for our understanding of the nature of tribal identity in the region in the late Iron Age.

It is increasingly difficult to see the existence of a unified tribal entity known as the Dobunni. Instead, the peripheral location of Bagendon from communities to the west and the increasing evidence for fragmented ideas of identity, seen for example in the varied burial rites of the late Iron Age, may suggest a complex society where power was far more fluid than we have previously imagined.

PRODUCTION, EXCHANGE AND IDENTITY

Our knowledge of Iron-Age production and exchange in the region has increased markedly since 1984. This informs us not just about technology and subsistence patterns but also about changes in social organisation and community relationships in the 1st millennium BC. Pottery production appears to have been predominantly local in the early 1st millennium BC with the fabric of pottery from the late Bronze-Age site at Shorncote, for example, indicating the use of temper from the immediate vicinity (Morris 1994b).[5] From the 4th century BC onwards, radical changes take place with the increasing importance of regional potteries produced from fabrics in the Malvern Hills area (Morris 1983; 1994b; Peacock 1968) and near Martley (Worcestershire) (Morris 1983) to the north of the county and in areas of the Mendips to the south (Peacock 1969). Between the 4th century BC and the 1st century AD this material was exchanged as far as 40 km from these sources (Fig. 8). During the later Iron Age Malvern wares in particular became an increasingly important component of pottery assemblages, with an increasing dominance of regional over locally manufactured pottery at sites such as Birdlip and Gilder's Paddock (Hancocks 1999; Parry 1998b) matched by similar sites in southern Worcestershire. Glastonbury ware pottery was predominantly exchanged to the south of the county but examples have been found in Gloucestershire at Hallen (Laidlaw 2002) and as far north as Abbeymead, Gloucester, the distribution suggesting occasional exchange of this material via the river Severn (Fig. 8). The increasing emphasis on Malvern pottery in many assemblages over the later Iron Age and its continued use in the early Roman period may indicate the emergence of more specialised communities (or locations) focused perhaps on particular industries such as pottery.

Recent work on quern stones in the county also indicates that particular sources dominated by the later Iron Age and were exchanged over long distances (Fig. 9). Fiona Roe has demonstrated that querns from May Hill were traded at sites as far away as the Thames Valley (cf. Moore forthcoming; e.g. Roe 1999). The increasing focus on pottery from the Malvern area and querns from May Hill suggests consumption and production were closely related to highly visible, impressive landscape features in the region. The potential importance of these hills suggests the obtaining of these materials and their use by Iron-Age communities related to symbolic properties in addition to any perceived functional benefits (Moore in press b). In addition, the use of these materials indicates greater social and economic relationships between communities in the Severn Valley and north Cotswolds as pottery and other material goods were exchanged and groups negotiated over land rights in these densely occupied landscapes. As noted above, it must surely be significant that Bagendon emerges on the edge of these distribution networks and on the periphery of such social and economic ties.

In the early and later Iron Age salt containers (briquetage) from Droitwich and rarer examples from Cheshire were exchanged over increasingly long distances and occur at a number of Iron-Age sites in the county (Fig. 10; Morris 1985; 1994b). Their distribution again stresses the role of the Severn in long-distance exchange. Currency bars found at a number of sites in the county and beyond (e.g. Uley Bury and Ditches: Hingley 1990) also indicate the importance by the later Iron

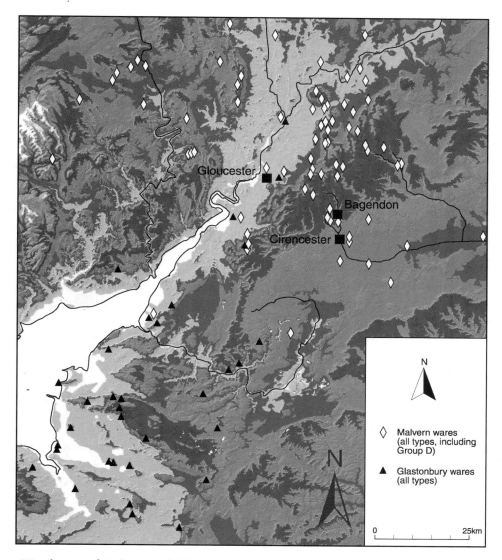

Fig. 8: Distribution of Malvern and Glastonbury ware pottery.

Age of the exchange of iron, much of it probably produced in the Forest of Dean. Unfortunately, we still know remarkably little about pre-Roman iron production in the Forest despite work on Roman manufacturing sites, although it was clearly a major centre of iron production that was quickly taken over by the Romans (Jackson forthcoming; Walters 1992). There is evidence for iron working from a number of sites in the county, including Uley Bury, Preston, Frocester, Duntisbourne Grove, Ditches and Bagendon. Bronze working is also known from Ditches, Bagendon, Frocester and Uley Bury.[6] The range of sites, enhanced by more examples from beyond

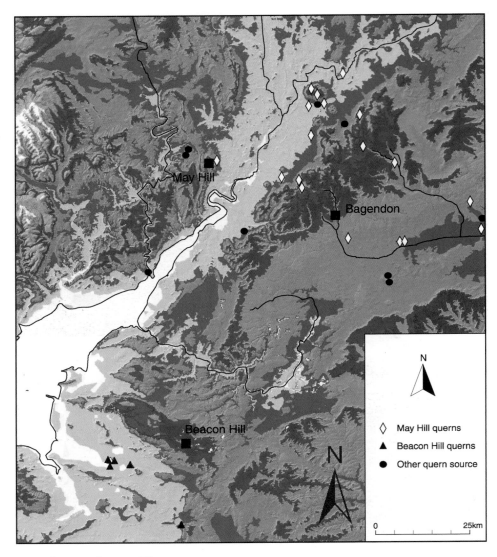

Fig. 9:   Distribution of May Hill querns.

the county (Moore forthcoming), supports evidence from elsewhere in southern Britain that local metal working was undertaken on a range of sites and not restricted to hillforts.

Occasional rare finds in the county also hint at the existence of longer-distance exchange using the Severn Estuary to reach wider Atlantic trade networks. The figurine from Aust appears to have Iberian parallels (Cunliffe 2005, 474) and, despite its provenance being questioned (Stead 1984), the possibility that exotic finds like it represent a more widespread west coast sea-borne exchange has been suggested elsewhere (Matthews 1999). In addition, occasional late Iron-Age exotic coins

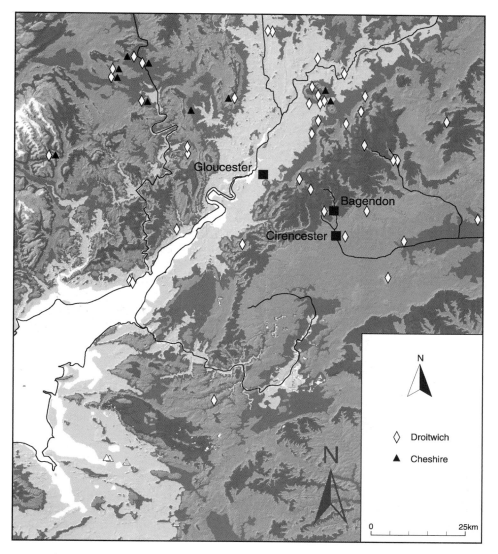

Fig. 10:   Distribution of briquetage.

in the region, including examples from Brittany, further indicate links between north-western France and the Severn Estuary (Moore forthcoming).

The agricultural subsistence on which Iron-Age communities in the county were based has only recently started to become clearer. There is some indication from the environmental remains from late Bronze-Age communities, such as those at Shorncote, that they practised predominantly pastoral farming although the picture remains limited (Allen and Montague 1994; Symmons 1999; Yates 1999, 165). By the Iron Age most communities undertook mixed farming with a range of crops including barley, emmer and spelt wheat as seen at Birdlip (Dobney and Jaques 1998).

Grain storage pits are known from a number of sites. Sheep, cattle and pig were exploited at most sites with variation depending on local agricultural regimes. The environmental and faunal remains from later Iron-Age Claydon Pike and Thornhill Farm, for example, appear to stress the role of cattle (and possibly also horse) husbandry in the Thames Valley (Levine 2004; Robinson n.d.; Sykes n.d.). There is some indication from Birdlip and Ditches that cattle became increasingly important in the late Iron Age, possibly representing an increasingly 'Romanised' diet in the 1st century AD (Hambleton 1998).

Recent work by Stevens (1996) has argued that crops were in some cases exchanged over relatively long distances. For example, seed assemblages from the enclosure at Rollright, on the Oxfordshire border, suggest that crops grown on damper soils, presumably in the Thames Valley, were brought to the site. The implication is that later Iron-Age communities may have been more integrated in agricultural production than is often suggested (e.g. Hingley 1984) and that in some cases crops were brought in from elsewhere. Stevens's discussion rests on only a handful of assemblages and further study is clearly required. However, it reminds us of the potential complexity of exchange and social systems in which later Iron-Age communities were engaged.

Evidence from the later Iron-Age sites at Hallen and Northwick (Fig. 4, no. 38; Gardiner et al. 2002) indicates that the Avon Levels were used seasonally for cattle pasture with little indication of arable crop production. More exceptionally, a radiocarbon date from a fish trap at Oldbury-on-Severn provided a later Iron-Age date (Allen and Rippon 1997). This latter find is surprising considering the limited evidence for the exploitation of fish resources from both Hallen and from Iron-Age Britain in general (Dobney and Ervynck in press) and suggests that communities such as that at Oldbury may have been practising relatively unusual subsistence strategies.

The evidence of production and exchange indicates the extent to which communities were engaged by the later Iron Age in a variety of long-distance exchanges of material, emphasising not their isolation but their involvement in various economic and social relationships. The apparent increasing dependence on regional pottery and long-distance exchange stresses the move from the 4th century BC to more specialised sites and communities, possibly as populations increased and people were engaged in wider social and economic networks.

BELIEF SYSTEMS AND TREATMENT OF THE DEAD

Saville (1984, 160) was able to dedicate only half a page to discussion of Iron-Age burial and suggested that most was down to "casual disposal". We can now think of treatment of the dead in the Iron Age in more complex terms. It is clear that the majority of the Iron-Age population was treated in a way after death that predominantly left few remains, usually regarded as some form of excarnation (Carr and Knusel 1997; Cunliffe 1991, 507; Whimster 1981). However, there has been increasing evidence throughout southern Britain and from this region of more widespread inhumation rites for certain members of the population and of variation in how the dead were treated. Recent excavation, for example, has revealed a crouched inhumation of later Iron-Age date from Lynches near Baunton (Fig. 4, no. 35; Mudd et al 1999; Fig. 11A). That burial was only recognised as Iron Age on the basis of radiocarbon dates.[7] Isolated crouched inhumations such as that from the ramparts at Uley Bury (Saville 1983, 12; Fig. 11B) and examples from Norbury (Saville 1983, 42) and Shipton Oliffe (Fig. 4, no. 39; Timby 1998) are probably Iron Age and represent a more widespread burial rite in the region. Other crouched inhumations are known from Roughground Farm (Allen et al. 1993), Bourton-on-the-Water (Nicholls 2001; 2004), Frocester and Salmonsbury and from storage pits at Guiting Power (Gascoigne 1973). Three examples

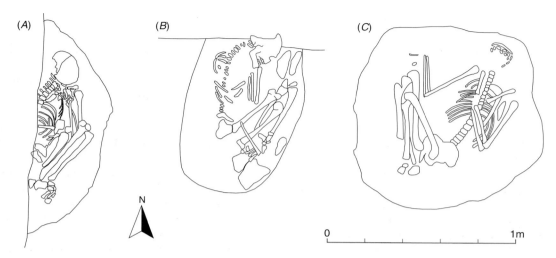

Fig. 11: Iron-Age crouched inhumations. A: *Lynches (after Mudd* et al. *1999); B: Uley Bury (after Saville 1983); C: Kemble (after King* et al. *1996).*

possibly represent a 'cemetery' at Kemble (Fig. 4, no. 40; King *et al.* 1996; see Fig. 11C). To these can now be added the apparent cemetery of crouched inhumations at Henbury near Bristol dating to the late Iron Age. One of those burials is associated with some form of post structure (Fig. 4, no. 36; Cotswold Archaeology 2005).

The longevity of the tradition of placing inhumations in pits and its potential importance may be exhibited by the early Iron-Age crouched inhumation with broken legs in a pit alignment at Ashton Keynes/Shorncote (Hey 2000, 4) and by the continuance of crouched inhumation as a regional burial tradition into the 1st and 2nd centuries AD with examples from Hucclecote (Thomas *et al.* 2003, 20) and elsewhere (Holbrook this volume). Suggestions that the cist burials at Naunton, Nympsfield (Staelens 1982, 29) and Hailes (Clifford 1944) are Iron-Age remain uncertain and have not been added to. These could mark high-status burials similar to those at Birdlip (Saville 1984, 160; Staelens 1982) but the limited information makes it difficult to say more.

In addition to rare inhumations, disarticulated human remains have been found on a variety of sites in the county, including Frocester, Salmonsbury, Ditches (Trow 1988; Trow *et al.* forthcoming a), Bagendon (Clifford 1961; Rees 1932, 24) and Little Solsbury (Falconer and Adams Bryan 1935). Animal remains were also frequently treated and deposited in special ways, such as the articulated horse leg placed in a pit at Sherborne House, Lechlade (Bateman *et al.* 2003, 38). In some instances human remains were associated with animal remains and other artefacts, such as a skull at Salmonsbury associated with a goat skull and lower jaw of a pike (Dunning 1976). At Ditches, skull fragments were found in a late Iron-Age storage pit associated with a quern stone (Trow *et al.* forthcoming a). Such deposits match those elsewhere in Britain of the deliberate placement of human and animal remains with artefacts indicating them as not mere rubbish disposal but as special, structured deposits (Hill 1995b). The choice of body parts may also have been significant. That skulls show greater representation, with examples from Bagendon, Ditches, Little Solsbury and Shorncote, may mark some form of ancestor head cult. The fact that in many instances these are skull fragments possibly indicates that they were given to individuals or communities as acts of social linkage to the deceased. Alternatively, evidence of sword cuts on some human remains, such as those from Ditches (Brothwell 1988), suggests some were the victims of violence although whether these represent warfare, sacrifice or ritualized killing is open to debate.

The location of these human remains sheds further light on the meaning of such deposits and suggests they were far from casual disposals. Deposition of human remains in some locations may have been regarded in a similar symbolic light to the pit burials, as ways into the earth or as offerings to 'chthonic deities' (Cunliffe 1992). This might be true of the human remains found in the swallow hole at Alveston[8] and in the late Bronze-Age waterhole at Shorncote (Brossler et al. 2002). There also appears to have been an emphasis placed on deposition in boundary features. This includes remains in the entranceways at Bredon Hill and Salmonsbury; in enclosure ditches and house gullies at Frocester and sites just beyond the region, such as Groundwell West (Walker et al. 2001) and Beckford (Oswald 1974); and in postholes and floor levels at Bredon Hill (Hencken 1938; Moore forthcoming). This is matched by the deposition of other artefacts, such as currency bars (Hingley 1990) and quern stones (Moore forthcoming) which show a similar tendency to be deposited in boundary features. This seems to mark the cultural importance of boundaries in Iron-Age societies and the emphasis on defining households and communities symbolically, as well as physically, in the landscape.

Other evidence also emphasises that Iron-Age communities structured their world in symbolic ways. Assessment of the orientation of enclosure and hillfort entrances indicates a tendency to face south-east/east (Moore forthcoming) and the orientation of roundhouse doorways from the Severn-Cotswolds shows a similar emphasis (Moore forthcoming). These patterns reflect other parts of Britain (Hill 1996; Oswald 1997) where Iron-Age communities oriented their enclosures and houses in reference to cosmological references such as the midwinter sunrise. The overall impression is that Iron-Age societies constructed and deposited material around their settlements and houses in reference to complex belief systems as well as to any functional necessities.

The late Iron Age saw some individuals being treated in new ways after death which may have important implications for understanding the wider social changes taking place. At Birdlip a group of individuals was inhumed with grave goods, the most impressive being a female burial with bronze mirror and brooches (Staelens 1982). At High Nash, Coleford, a sword and shield boss appear to represent the remnants of a warrior burial, probably dating to the 1st century AD (Fig. 4, no. 41; Webster 1989; 1990). The region does not see the widespread adoption of cremation burial seen in South-East England in the 1st centuries BC/AD, although there is some evidence of possible late Iron-Age cremation burials from Barnwood (Clifford 1934) and Bagendon (Rees 1932, 28; Staelens 1982, 29) and there is some evidence of a possible late Iron-Age bucket burial from Rodborough (Parry 1996). Even at sites like Bagendon, however, there is clear evidence that communities at high-status, late Iron-Age sites continued practices of an earlier, Iron-Age tradition with disarticulated human remains found at both Bagendon and Ditches in 1st-century AD contexts. It is clear that burials like those at Birdlip were the preserve of only certain members of the community with little indication of a widespread change in burial practices.

It is also at this time that we see the emergence of designated 'shrines' in the Iron Age. The most fully understood of these is Uley-West Hill where a small enclosure preceded a large Roman temple complex (Fig. 4, no. 34; Woodward and Leach 1993). Finds of late Iron-Age pottery and coins suggest similar shrines may also have existed as precursors to Roman temples at Wycomb (Timby 1998) and Hailey Wood (Moore 2001) and another shrine might be implied by the unusual coins from Neigh Bridge, Somerford Keynes (Fig. 4, no. 37; King 2005). The appearance of designated ritual shrines marks a departure from the earlier symbolic practices discussed above (Hill 1995b, 120) and together with the emergence of some new burial rites seems to indicate an increasingly fracturing society with some members, presumably members of a new, more visible élite, adopting new ritual practices whilst other members of society continued to observe traditional ways.

CONCLUSIONS AND FUTURE PROSPECTS

Increasing evidence from the county enables a more detailed picture of Iron-Age societies to be constructed. A number of major social shifts took place over the 1st millennium BC, the most dramatic potentially being between the earlier and later Iron Age (around the 4th century BC) when settlement expanded across the landscape and communities increasingly demarcated their living space through enclosure. The transition from the late Bronze Age to the early Iron Age is harder to define archaeologically but to what extent this means that it was less dramatic than has previously been suggested is unclear. Increasingly, by the later Iron Age societies appear to have been embedded in an array of social and exchange networks and existed in milieus in which cosmology and symbolism were important in all aspects of life from exchange to the structuring of social spaces. By the final centuries of the period new monuments associated with potentially new élites and new social relationships emerged which we might now regard as indicating an increasingly fracturing society immediately prior to the Roman conquest rather than a unified tribal entity.

Despite this increasing wealth of material there are still problems with our knowledge of the Iron Age in the region. Much of the material relating to developer-funded investigations is fragmentary and only available in interim reports making assessment of these sites and their full impact on our understanding of the period difficult. There is a need for much of this material to be published to allow for a fuller assessment and understanding of its impact in reappraisals of the region.

Saville's recognition (1984, 140) that the Iron Age in the Forest of Dean and west of the county was poorly understood still remains largely true. Despite increased archaeological investigation and research in many areas of Gloucestershire, the west of the Severn still remains somewhat of a 'black hole' in terms of Iron-Age information. What excavation has taken place in this area has been of a fragmentary and poorly understood nature (e.g. Anon. 1994; Anon. 1996; Walters 1992; Walters and Walters 1989) yet it hints at the exceptional and rich information that exists and which has been lost through a lack of excavation or poor recording. The hillforts of this region, for example, offer tantalising hints of varied and complex histories (e.g. Parry 1994) that would benefit further research whilst elsewhere High Nash has produced a rare 'warrior burial' from the region (Webster 1989; 1990). Current research by Gloucestershire County Council Archaeology Service will hopefully go some way to rectifying this and the area must become a priority in examination for Iron-Age evidence of all types.

A number of other areas of the region are also poorly represented despite increased levels of investigation, for example Bristol and its environs. Publication of recent work in these areas, such as the unusual site at Cribb's Causeway (King 1998), should be a priority alongside a focused understanding of why Iron-Age material appears to be absent from much of the development that has taken place in this area in the last 20 years. The important and dramatic results of work at

Hallen, and more recently at Henbury, suggest that Iron-Age material is prevalent in this area, that it is potentially fundamentally different from that elsewhere and that it may provide a radically new perspective on the Iron Age in the South West.

A shift from major field research projects on hillforts and other larger sites has meant there has been little reassessment of these monuments. This is a particularly disappointing development considering the new research questions that are being raised in Iron-Age studies regarding hillforts (e.g. Hamilton and Manley 2001; Hill 1996) and the extent of work being undertaken in regions nearby (e.g. Cunliffe 2000; Gosden and Lock 1998). We need to remember that long-term research projects on individual sites and landscapes are still essential in placing much of the developer-funded archaeology in a broader context. Less satisfactory is the continued lack of publication of a number of the major excavations discussed by Saville in 1984 although many are now seeing renewed focus on post-excavation (e.g. Beckford, Ditches, Bagendon) and will soon be published.

Many fundamental questions on the nature of Iron-Age societies in the county still require considerably more investigation. For example, greater research on the nature and location of non-hillfort earlier Iron-Age settlement and an examination of the possibility of nucleation in the early Iron Age are required. These relate to a wider need to refine our chronological frameworks, a matter in which a more systematic use of radiocarbon dating in relation to key pottery types may prove useful. In addition, we know little of the date and role of many of the major Iron-Age features including the banjo enclosure clusters noted above and the role of sites like oppida and their relation to the wider settlement patterns. In many cases targeted geophysical surveys and excavation in association with developer-funded archaeology may provide some initial answers to many of these questions.

ACKNOWLEDGEMENTS

Much of the information and ideas discussed here are based on a wider survey of the material from the Severn-Cotswolds (Moore forthcoming) to which readers should refer for more detailed discussion. I thank Neil Holbrook for asking me to contribute to this volume, all at Cotswold Archaeology, particularly Annette Hancocks, Simon Cox, Ed McSloy and Gail Stoten, for their help and information on a number of projects prior to publication, and Fiona Roe for discussing quern stone sources in the region. I would also like to thank the staff at Gloucestershire, South Gloucestershire, Worcestershire and Bath and North-East Somerset SMRs for assistance in searches of their archives and Paul Nichols at Gloucester County Council Archaeological Services for information on the burials at Bourton-on-the-Water. Discussions with many people, but in particular J.D. Hill, Mark Bowden, Richard Reece and Henry Hurst, have helped refine many of the ideas presented here and I am grateful for their comments. Any errors or omissions of course remain my own.

NOTES

1. For the purposes of this paper, 'Gloucestershire' is taken to include the modern unitary authorities of South Gloucestershire and Bristol.
2. Archaeology Data Service (http://ads.ahds.ac.uk: hereafter referred to as ADS), record EHNMR 1337480.
3. Seen for example at Cirencester (Rigby 1982) and Ditches (Trow et al. forthcoming a; Trow 1988).
4. Also indicated by a recent geophysical survey by GSB for Cotswold Archaeology (see above, Darvill, fig. 5).
5. Although there is some indication that Bronze-Age pottery from Sandy Lane contains temper from the Malverns (Timby 2001).

6. See Moore forthcoming for more details and full references.
7. Four radiocarbon dates from the same body give dates at 2 sigma of 390–110 BC; 340–70 BC; 340–40 BC; and 300–80 BC (data from Mudd *et al.* 1999 recalibrated using OxCal 3.3; see Moore forthcoming).
8. South Gloucestershire SMR reference SG8181.

BIBLIOGRAPHY

Allen, J., and Rippon, S., 1997. 'A Romano-British Shaft of Dressed Stone and the Settlement at Oldbury-on-Severn, South Gloucestershire', *Trans. BGAS* **115**, 19–28.

Allen, M.J, and Montague, R., 1994. 'Animal remains', in Hearne and Heaton 1994, 47.

Allen, T.G., Darvill, T.C., Green, L.S., and Jones, M.U., 1993. *Excavations at Roughground Farm, Lechlade, Gloucestershire: a prehistoric and Roman Landscape* (Oxford Archaeol. Unit Thames Valley Landscapes: the Cotswold Water Park **1**).

Allen, T., Miles, D., and Palmer, S., 1984. 'Iron Age buildings in the Upper Thames region', in B. Cunliffe and D. Miles (eds.), *Aspects of the Iron Age in central southern Britain* (Oxford University Committee for Archaeol. Monograph **2**), 89–101.

Anonymous 1994, 'Dean Archaeology 1994. Town Farm, Newent', *Dean Archaeol.* **7**, 5.

Anonymous 1996. 'Dean Archaeology 1996. Rodmore Farm', *Dean Archaeol.* **10**, 7.

Anonymous 2005. 'The middle Iron Age settlement at Warrens Field' (Oxford Archaeol. http://www.oxfordarch.co.uk/cotswoldweb/text/warrens_field_strat.pdf).

Atkin, M., 1987. 'Excavations in Gloucester – An interim Report', *Glevensis* **21**, 7–17.

Barber, A., and Leah, M., 1998. 'Prehistoric and Romano-British activity at Bourton-on-the-Water Primary school, Gloucestershire. Excavations 1998' (Cotswold Archaeol. Trust report GSMR 16943).

Barfield, L., and Hodder, M., 1987. 'Burnt mounds as saunas, and the prehistory of bathing', *Antiquity* **61**, 370–9.

Barrett, J., Bradley, R., and Green, M., 1991. *Landscape, monuments and society.* (Cambridge University Press).

Bateman, C., Enright, D., and Oakey, N., 2003. 'Prehistoric and Anglo-Saxon Settlements to the rear of Sherborne House, Lechlade: excavations in 1997', *Trans. BGAS* **121**, 23–96.

Bell, M., Caseldine, A., and Neumann, H., 2000. *Prehistoric intertidal archaeology in the Welsh Severn Estuary* (CBA Research Rep. **120**, Cardiff).

Boore, E., 1999. 'A Romano-British site at Lawrence Weston, Bristol, 1995', *Bristol Avon Archaeol.* **16**, 1–48.

Boyle, A., Jennings, D., Miles, D., and Palmer, S. (eds.), 1998. *The Anglo-Saxon cemetery at Butlers Field, Lechlade, Gloucestershire. Vol. 1: Prehistoric and Roman activity and Anglo-Saxon grave catalogue* (Oxford Archaeol. Unit Thames Valley Landscapes Monograph **10**).

Bradley, R., 1988. 'Review' of T. Darvill, *Prehistoric Gloucestershire*, in *Trans. BGAS* **106**, 230–1.

Brett, M., and Coleman, L., 2000. 'Aston Somerville' (Cotswold Archaeol. Trust report).

Britnell, W., 1974. 'Beckford', *Current Archaeol.* **4**, 293–7.

Brossler, A., 2001. 'Reading Business Park: the results of phases 1 and 2', in J. Bruck (ed.), *Bronze Age Landscapes. Tradition and Transformation* (Oxford Oxbow), 129–38.

Brossler, A., Gocher, M., Laws, G., and Roberts, M., 2002. 'Shorncote Quarry: excavations of a late Prehistoric Landscape in the Upper Thames Valley, 1997 and 1998', *Trans. BGAS* **120**, 37–88.

Brothwell, D.R., 1988. 'Human bone from the inner enclosure ditch', in Trow 1988, 77.

Brown, A., 1982. 'Human impact on the former floodplain woodlands of the Severn', in M. Bell and S. Limbrey (eds), *Archaeological aspects of Woodland Ecology* (BAR International Series **146**), 93–105.

Burrow, I., 1987. 'Hillforts and the Iron Age', in M. Aston and R. Iles (eds.), *The Archaeol. of Avon* (Bristol, Avon County Council), 43–51.

Carr, G., and Knusel, C., 1997. 'The ritual framework of excarnation by exposure as the mortuary practice of the early and middle Iron Ages of central southern Britain', in A. Gwilt and C. Haselgrove (eds.), *Reconstructing Iron Age societies* (Oxbow Monograph **71**, Oxford), 167–73.

Champion, S., 1976. 'Leckhampton Hill, Gloucestershire, 1925 and 1970', in D.W. Harding (ed.), *Hillforts. Later prehistoric earthworks in Britain and Ireland* (London, Academic Press), 177–81.

Clarke, S., 1993. 'Settlement patterns in the Cotswold-Severn Region 700BC–AD700' (Bradford University Ph.D. thesis).

Clifford, E., 1930. 'A prehistoric and Roman site at Barnwood, near Gloucester', *Trans. BGAS* **52**, 201–54.

Clifford, E., 1933. 'The Roman villa, Hucclecote', *Trans. BGAS* **55**, 323–76.

Clifford, E., 1934. 'An early Iron Age site at Barnwood, Gloucester', *Trans. BGAS* **56**, 227–36.

Clifford, E., 1937. 'The earthworks at Rodborough, Amberley and Minchinhampton, Gloucestershire', *Trans. BGAS* **59**, 287–307.

Clifford, E., 1944. 'Graves found at Hailes-Stanway, Gloucestershire', *Trans. BGAS* **65**, 187–98.

Clifford, E., 1961. *Bagendon: A Belgic Oppidum* (Cambridge, Heffer and Sons).

Coe, D., Jenkins, V., and Richards, J., 1991. 'Cleveland Farm, Ashton Keynes. Second Interim report on excavation in 1989', *Wilts. Archaeol. Natural Hist. Mag.* **84**, 40–50.

Coleman, L., and Hancocks, A. F., forthcoming. 'Excavations on the Wormington to Tirley Pipeline, 2000: Prehistoric, Romano-British and Anglo-Saxon activity at five sites by the Carrant Brook and River Ishbourne, Gloucestershire and Worcestershire' (Cotswold Archaeol. Occasional Paper **2**).

Coleman, L., Watts, M., and McIlroy, E., 2003. 'Wormington to Tirley Gas Pipeline Gloucesterhsire/Worcesterhsire. Post Excavation Assessment' (Cotswold Archaeol. Trust report 03017).

Coles, J., 1987. *Meare Village East. The excavations of A.Bulleid and H.St George Gray 1932–1956* (Somerset Levels Papers **13**).

Coles, J., and Minnit, S., 1995. *Industrious and fairly civilized: the Glastonbury Lake Village.* (Taunton, Somerset Levels Project and Somerset County Council museums service).

Corney, M., 1989. 'Multiple ditch systems and late Iron Age settlement in Wessex', in M. Bowden, D. Mackay and P. Topping (eds.), *From Cornwall to Caithness: some aspects of British Field Archaeology* (BAR Brit. Series **209**), 111–21.

Corney, M., 2002, 'Late Iron Age in Wessex' (Lecture at the Later Iron Age Conference, Durham, 2002).

Cotswold Archaeology 2004. 'Blenheim Farm, Moreton-in-Marsh, Gloucestershire. Post Excavation Assessment and updated project design' (unpublished report 04107, Cirencester).

Cotswold Archaeology 2005. 'Henbury Secondary School, Bristol: post-excavation assessment and updated project design' (unpublished report 04157, Cirencester).

Cox, P.C., 1985. *The past in the pipeline. Archaeology of the Esso Midline* (Salisbury, Trust for Wessex Archaeol./Esso).

Creighton, J., 2000. *Coins and power in late Iron Age Britain* (Cambridge University Press).

Cromarty, A., Roberts, M., and Smith, A., n.d. 'Archaeological investigations at Kempsford, Stubbs Farm, Gloucestershire. 1991–1995' (Oxford Archaeol.).

Cunliffe, B., 1982. 'Iron Age settlement and pottery 650 BC–60 AD', in M. Aston and I. Burrow (eds.), *The Archaeol. of Somerset* (Taunton, Somerset County Council), 53–61.

Cunliffe, B., 1984a. *Danebury. An Iron Age hillfort in Hampshire. Volume 1. The Excavations 1969–78: the site* (CBA Research Rep. **52**, London).

Cunliffe, B., 1984b. 'The Iron Age in Gloucestershire', *Trans. BGAS* **102**, 2–9.

Cunliffe, B., 1991. *Iron Age communities in Britain* (3rd edn., London, Routledge).

Cunliffe, B., 1992. 'Pits, preconceptions and propitiation in the British Iron Age', *Oxford J. Archaeol.* **11.1**, 69–84.

Cunliffe, B., 1995. *Danebury. Volume 6: a hillfort community in perspective* (CBA Research Rep. **102**, York).

Cunliffe, B., 2000. *The Danebury environs programme: the prehistory of a Wessex landscape. Vol. 1* (Oxford University Committee for Archaeol. and English Heritage Monograph **48**).

Cunliffe, B., 2005. *Iron Age Communities in Britain* (4th edn., London, Routledge).

Darvill, T., 1987. *Prehistoric Gloucestershire* (Gloucester, Gloucestershire County Library and Alan Sutton).

Darvill, T., and Hingley, R., 1982. 'A Banjo enclosure at Northleach', *Trans. BGAS* **100**, 249–50.

Darvill, T., Hingley, R., Jones, M., and Timby, J., 1986. 'A Neolithic and Iron Age site at the Loders, Lechlade, Gloucestershire', *Trans. BGAS* **104**, 27–48.

Darvill, T., and Locke, R., 1988. 'Aerial photography in the Upper Thames Valley and East Cotswolds', *Trans. BGAS* **106**, 192–8.

Darvill, T., and Timby, J., 1986. 'Excavations at Saintbridge, Gloucester 1981', *Trans. BGAS* **104**, 49–60.

de Jersey, P., 1994. 'Gazeteer of Dobunni coinage', in Van Arsdell 1994.

de Jersey, P., 1997. *Armorica and Britain: the numismatic evidence* (Oxford University Committee for Archaeol. Monograph **45**).

Dinn, J., and Evans, J., 1990. 'Aston Mill Farm, Kemerton: excavation of a ring ditch, middle Iron Age enclosure and a grubenhaus', *Trans. Worcs. Archaeol. Soc.* 3rd series **12**, 5–66.

Dixon, P., 1976. 'Crickley Hill, 1969–1972', in D.W. Harding (ed.), *Hillforts, Later Prehistoric Earthworks in Britain and Ireland* (London, Academic Press), 162–75.

Dixon, P., 1994. *Crickley Hill Volume 1: the hillfort defences* (Crickley Hill Trust and the Department of Archaeol., University of Nottingham).

Dobney, K., and Ervynck, A., in press. 'To fish or not to fish? Evidence for the possible avoidance of fish consumption during the Iron Age around the North Sea', in C. Haselgrove and T. Moore (eds.), *Later Iron Age Britain and Beyond* (Oxford, Oxbow).

Dobney, K., and Jaques, D., 1998. 'The Animal bones', in Parry 1998a, 80–4.

Dunning, G.C., 1933. 'Report on pottery found in the Crypt Grammar school grounds, Gloucester during excavations 1931–32', *Trans. BGAS* **55**, 277–91.

Dunning, G.C., 1976. 'Salmonsbury, Bourton on the Water', in D.W. Harding (ed.), *Hillforts. Later prehistoric earthworks in Britain and Ireland* (London, Academic Press), 76–118.

Ecclestone, M., 2004. 'A restivity survey of the Rodborough Earthwork', *Glevensis* **37**, 9–14.

Edwards, R., and Hurst, D., 2000. 'Iron Age settlement and a medieval and later farmstead: excavation at 93–97 High Street, Evesham', *Trans. Worcs. Archaeol. Soc.* 3rd series **17**, 73–111.

Elsdon, S., 1994. 'The Iron Age pottery', in Dixon 1994, 213–41.

Falconer, J.P.E., and Adams Bryan, S., 1935. 'Recent finds at Solisbury Hill Camp, near Bath. A Hallstatt-Early La Tène site', *Proc. University Bristol Spelaeological Soc.* **4.3**, 183–211.

Fell, C.I., 1961. 'Shenberrow Hill Camp, Stanton, Gloucestershire', *Trans. BGAS* **80**, 16–41.

Gardiner, J., Allen, M., Hamilton-Dyer, S., Laidlaw, M., and Scaife, R., 2002. 'Making the most of it: Late prehistoric pastoralism in the Avon levels, Severn Estuary', *Proc. Prehistoric Soc.* **68**, 1–40.

Gascoigne, P., 1973. 'An Iron Age pit at Wood House, Guiting Power', *Trans. BGAS* **92**, 204–7.

Gosden, C., and Lock, G., 1998. 'Prehistoric histories', *World Archaeol.* **30**, 2–12.

Gray, J.W., and Brewer, G.W.S., 1904. 'Evidence of ancient occupation on Cleeve Hill: Stables quarry and Kings Beeches', *Proc. Cotteswold Naturalist Field Club* **15.1**, 49–67.

Haldane, J.W., 1975. 'The excavations at Stokeleigh Camp, Avon', *Proc. Bristol Spelaeological Soc.* **14.1**, 29–63.

Hall, M., and Gingell, C., 1974. 'Nottingham Hill, Gloucestershire, 1972', *Antiquity* **48**, 306–9.

Hambleton, E., 1998. *Animal husbandry regimes in Iron Age Britain: A comparative Study of Faunal Assemblages from British Iron Age sites* (BAR Brit. Series **282**, Oxford).

Hamilton, S., and Manley, J., 2001. 'Hillforts, monumentality and place: a chronological and topographic review of First Millennium BC hillforts of south-east England', *European J. Archaeol.* **4**, 7–42.

Hancocks, A., 1999. 'The Pottery', in C. Parry 1999b, 104–9.

Hannan, A., 1993. 'Excavations at Tewkesbury 1972–74', *Trans. BGAS* **111**, 21–76.

Haselgrove, C., 1995. 'Late Iron Age society in Britain and North East Europe: structural transformation or superficial change', in B. Arnold and D. Blair-Gibson (eds.), *Celtic Chiefdom, Celtic State* (Cambridge University Press), 81–7.

Haselgrove, C., 1997. 'Iron Age brooch deposition and chronology', in A. Gwilt and C. Haselgrove (eds.), *Reconstructing Iron Age societies* (Oxbow Monograph **71**, Oxford), 51–72.

Haselgrove, C., and Millett, M., 1997. 'Verlamion reconsidered', in A. Gwilt and C. Haselgrove (eds.), *Reconstructing Iron Age societies* (Oxbow Monograph **71**, Oxford), 282–97.

Haselgrove, C., and Pope, R., in press. 'Characterising the earlier Iron Age', in C. Haselgrove and R. Pope (eds.), *The Earlier Iron Age in Britain and the near Continent* (Oxford, Oxbow).

Haselgrove, C., Leins, I., and Moore, T. forthcoming. 'Don't mention the Dobunni! An archaeological study of the late Iron Age coinage of the Severn-Cotswolds', in P. Guest and J. Williams (eds.), *Coins and an Archaeologist: A symposium for Richard Reece*.

Hawkes, S., 1994. 'Longbridge-Deverill Cow Down, Wiltshire, House 3: a major roundhouse of the Early Iron Age', *Oxford J. Archaeol.* **13**, 49–69.

Hearne, C., and Adam, N., 1999. 'Excavation of an extensive Late Bronze Age settlement at Shorncote Quarry, near Cirencester, 1995–6', *Trans. BGAS* **117**, 35–73.

Hearne, C.M., and Heaton, J., 1994. 'Excavations at a Late Bronze Age Settlement in the Upper Thames Valley at Shorncote Quarry near Cirencester, 1992', *Trans. BGAS* **112**, 17–58.

Hencken, T.C., 1938. 'The excavation of the Iron Age camp on Bredon Hill, Glos.,1935–1937', *Archaeol. J.* **95**, 1–111.

Hey, G., 2000. 'Cotswold Community at Ashton Keynes' (Oxford Archaeol. Unit unpublished interim report).

Hill, J.D., 1995a. 'The Pre Roman Iron Age in Britain and Ireland: An overview', *J. World Prehistory* **9**, 47–98.

Hill, J.D., 1995b. *Ritual and Rubbish in the Iron Age of Wessex* (BAR Brit. Series **242**).

Hill, J.D., 1996. 'Hillforts and the Iron Age of Wessex', in T. Champion and J. Collis (eds.), *The Iron Age in Britain and Ireland Recent trends* (Sheffield University Press), 95–116.

Hingley, R., 1984. 'Towards a social analysis in archaeology: Celtic society in the Iron Age of the Upper Thames valley', in B. Cunliffe and D. Miles (eds.), *Aspects of the Iron Age in central southern Britain* (Oxford University Committee for Archaeol. Monograph **2**), 72–88.

Hingley, R., 1989. 'Iron Age settlement and society in central and southern Warwickshire: directions for future research', in A. Gibson (ed.), *Midlands Prehistory: some recent and current researches into the prehistory of central England* (BAR Brit. Series **204**), 122–56.

Hingley, R., 1990. 'Iron Age currency bars: the archaeological and social context', *Archaeol. J.* **147**, 91–117.

Hingley, R., 1996. 'Prehistoric Warwickshire: a review of the evidence', *Birmingham Warwickshire Archaeol. Soc. Trans.* **100**, 1–24.

Hingley, R., and Miles, D., 1984. 'Aspects of the Iron age in the Upper Thames Valley', in B. Cunliffe and D. Miles (eds.), *Aspects of the Iron Age in central southern Britain* (Oxford University Committee for Archaeol. Monograph **2**), 51–71.

Hirst, K., n.d. 'An evaluation of archaeological remains at Waltham Roman villa, Gloucestershire' (Time Team unpublished report).

Hughes, G., 1996. *The excavation of a later Prehistoric and Romano-British settlement at Thornwell Farm, Chepstow, Gwent 1992* (BAR Brit. Series **244**, Oxford).

Hurst, H., 1977. 'The prehistoric occupation on Churchdown Hill', *Trans. BGAS* **95**, 5–10.

Hurst, H., 2005. 'Roman Cirencester and Gloucester compared', *Oxford J. Archaeol.* **24(3)**, 293–305.

Jackson, D., 1999. 'Settlement and society in the Welsh Marches during the 1st millennium BC' (University of Durham Ph.D. thesis).

Jackson, R., 1999. 'An interim report on the excavations at Inns Court, Bristol, 1997–1999', *Bristol Avon Archaeol.* **16**, 51–60.

Jackson, R., forthcoming. 'The Roman settlement of Ariconium, near Weston-under-Penyard, Herefordshire: an assessment and synthesis of the evidence' (CBA research report).

Jennings, D., Muir, J., Palmer, S., and Smith, A., 2004. *Thornhill Farm, Fairford, Gloucestershire: an Iron Age and Roman pastoral site in the Upper Thames Valley* (Oxford Archaeol. Thames Valley Landscapes Monograph **23**).

King, C., 2005. 'The coins from Somerford Keynes, Neigh Bridge' (Oxford Archaeol. draft report).

King, R., 1998. 'Land at Cribbs Causeway, Filton, Archaeological evaluation and excavation' (Foundations Archaeol. unpublished report in South Gloucestershire SMR 11360).

King, R., Barber, A., and Timby, J., 1996. 'Excavations at West Lane, Kemble: an Iron-Age, Roman and Saxon burial site and a medieval building', *Trans. BGAS* **114**, 15–24.

Laidlaw, M., 2002. 'Pottery fabrics, form and decoration', in J. Gardiner *et al.*, 'Making the most of it: Late prehistoric pastoralism in the Avon levels, Severn Estuary', *Proc. Prehistoric Soc.* **68**, 35–9.

Lawson, A., 2000. *Potterne 1982–5: Animal husbandry in Later Prehistoric Wiltshire* (Wessex Archaeol. Report **17**).

Leah, M., and Young, C., 2001. 'A Bronze-Age Burnt Mound at Sandy Lane, Charlton Kings, Gloucestershire: excavations in 1971', *Trans. BGAS* **119**, 59–82.

Levine, M., 2004. 'The faunal remains', in Jennings *et al.* 2004, 109–2.

Locock, M., 2001. 'A later Bronze Age landscape on the Avon levels: settlement, shelters and saltmarsh at Cabot Park', in J. Bruck (ed.), *Bronze Age landscapes: tradition and transformation* (Oxford, Oxbow) 121–8.

Marshall, A., 1978. 'The pre-Belgic Iron Age in the Northern Cotswolds', *Trans. BGAS* **96**, 9–16.

Marshall, A., 1989. 'The hillfort at Burhill, Buckland, Gloucestershire: evidence for occupation during the earliest phase of the Iron Age', *Trans. BGAS* **107**, 197–203.

Marshall, A., 1990a. *A pit based enclosure of mid Iron Age date at the Park, Guiting Power* (Cotswold Archaeol. Research Group Research Rep. 5).

Marshall, A., 1990b. 'Stanton, Wormington Grange,' and 'Stanway', in B. Rawes (ed.), 'Archaeol. Review 14', *Trans. BGAS* **108**, 197–8.

Marshall, A., 1995. 'From Iron Age to Roman: The Park and Bowsings sites at Guiting Power', *Glevensis* **28**, 13–19.

Marshall, A., 2001. 'Functional analysis of settlement areas: Prospection over a defended enclosure of Iron Age date at the Bowsings, Guiting Power, Gloucestershire', *Archaeol. Prospection* **8.2**, 79–106.

Matthews, K., 1999. 'The Iron Age of North-west England and Irish sea trade', in Bevan (ed.), *Northern Exposure: interpretative devolution and the Iron Age in Britain* (Leicester Monograph 4), 173–96.

McOmish, D., and Smith, N., 1996. 'Welshbury Hillfort' *Trans. BGAS* **114**, 55–64.

Miles, D., 1997. 'Conflict and complexity: the later prehistory of the Oxford region', *Oxoniensia* **62**, 1–19.

Millett, M., 1990. *The Romanization of Britain* (Cambridge University Press).

Moore, J., and Jennings, D., 1992. *Reading Business Park: a Bronze Age landscape* (Oxford Archaeol. Unit Thames Valley Landscapes: The Kennet Valley 1).

Moore, T., 2001. 'Hailey Wood Camp: a Roman Temple complex in the Cotswolds?', *Trans. BGAS* **119**, 83–93.

Moore, T., 2003. 'Rectangular Houses in the British Iron Age: Squaring the Circle', in J. Humphrey (ed.), *Re-searching the Iron Age* (Leicester University Monograph 11), 47–58.

Moore, T., forthcoming. 'Iron Age societies in the Severn-Cotswolds: developing narratives of social and landscape change' (BAR Brit. Series).

Moore, T., in press a. 'The early to later Iron Age transition in the south west Midlands: from communal to household?', in C. Haselgrove and R. Pope (eds.), *The Earlier Iron Age in Britain and the near Continent* (Oxford, Oxbow).

Moore, T., in press b. 'Exchange, settlement and identity in the later Iron Age of the Severn-Cotswolds', in C. Haselgrove and T. Moore (eds.), *Later Iron Age Britain and Beyond* (Oxford, Oxbow).

Moore, T., and Reece, R., 2001. 'The Dobunni', *Glevensis* **34**, 17–26.

Moore-Scott, T., 1997. 'Bushley Green', *Glevensis* **30**, 7–8.

Morris, E., 1983. *Salt and Ceramic exchange in Western Britain during the First Millennium BC* (Department of Archaeol., University of Southampton).

Morris, E., 1985. 'Prehistoric salt distributions: two case studies from Western Britain', *Bull. Board of Celtic Studies* **12**, 336–79.

Morris, E., 1994a. 'Pottery', in Hearne and Heaton 1994, 34–43.

Morris, E., 1994b. 'Production and distribution of pottery and salt in Iron Age Britain: a review', *Proc. Prehistoric Soc.* **60**, 371–93.

Mudd, A., Williams, R.J., and Lupton, A., 1999. *Excavations alongside Roman Ermin Street, Gloucestershire and Wiltshire: The Archaeology of the A419/A417 Swindon to Gloucester Road Scheme* (Oxford Archaeol. Unit: 2 volumes).

Napthan, M., Hancocks, A., Pearson, E., and Ratkai, S., 1997. 'Evaluation of proposed Wyre Piddle Bypass' (County Archaeological Services: Hereford and Worcester County Council).

Needham, S., in press. '800 BC, the great divide', in C. Haselgrove and R. Pope (eds.), *The Earlier Iron Age in Britain and the near Continent* (Oxford, Oxbow).

Needham, S., and Ambers, J., 1994. 'Redating Rams Hill and reconsidering Bronze Age enclosure', *Proc. Prehistoric Soc.* **60**, 225–43.

Nichols, P., 1999. 'An archaeological evaluation at Bourton-on-the-water, Primary school, Gloucestershire' (Gloucestershire County Council Archaeol. Service typescript report: Gloucestershire SMR 16943 source 5204).

Nichols, P., 2001. 'Bourton on the Water, Primary school', in J. Wills (ed.), 'Archaeol. Review 25', *Trans. BGAS* **119**, 187.

Nichols, P. 2004. 'Bourton on the Water. Primary school', in J. Wills (ed.) 'Archaeol. Review 28' *Trans. BGAS* **122**, 175.

Oswald, A., 1974. 'Excavations at Beckford', *Trans. Worcs. Archaeol. Society* 3rd series **3** (1970–1972), 7–54.

Oswald, A., 1997. 'A doorway on the past: practical and mystic concerns in the orientation of roundhouse doorways', in A. Gwilt and C. Haselgrove (eds.), *Reconstructing Iron Age societies* (Oxbow Monograph **71**, Oxford), 87–95.

Palmer, S., and Hey, G., 1989. 'Thornhill Farm, Fairford', *Glevensis* **23**, 43–6.

Parry, C., 1994. 'Symonds Yat Promontory fort, English Bicknor, Gloucestershire: Excavations 1990–91', *Trans. BGAS* **112**, 59–72.

Parry, C., 1996. 'An earthwork on Rodborough Common, Gloucstershire. A review of the evidence', *Trans. BGAS* **114**, 143–62.

Parry, C., 1998a. 'Excavations near Birdlip, Cowley, Gloucestershire, 1987–8', *Trans. BGAS* **116**, 25–92.

Parry, C., 1998b. 'Iron-Age and Roman Coarse Pottery', in Parry 1998a, 68–76.

Parry, C., 1999a. 'Excavations at Camp Gardens, Stow-on-the-Wold, Gloucestershire', *Trans. BGAS* **117**, 75–88.

Parry, C., 1999b. 'Iron Age, Romano-British and Medieval Occupation at Bishop's Cleeve, Gloucestershire: excavations at Gilder's Paddock 1989 and 1990–1', *Trans. BGAS* **117**, 89–118.

Peacock, D.P.S., 1968. 'A petrological study of certain Iron Age pottery from Western England', *Proc. Prehistoric Soc.* **34**, 414–27.

Peacock, D.P.S., 1969. 'A contribution to the study of Glastonbury Ware', *Antiq. J.* **49**, 41–61.

Piper, P.J., and Catchpole, T., 1996. 'Bourton-on-the-Water Primary school excavation', *Glevensis* **29**, 24–6.

Portway-Dobson, D., 1933. 'A Celtic weaving comb from Bristol', *Proc. University Bristol Spelaeological Soc.* **4**, 155.

Price, E.G., 2000. *Frocester, A Romano-British settlement, its antecedents and successors. Volume 1: The Sites* (Stonehouse, Gloucester and District Archaeol. Research Group).

Rahtz, P., 1956. 'Kings Weston Down Camp, Bristol, 1956', *Proc. University Bristol Spelaeological Soc.* **8.1**, 30–9.

Rahtz, P., and Clevedon-Brown, J., 1959. 'Blaise Castle Hill Bristol 1957', *Proc. University Bristol Spelaeological Soc.* **8.3**, 147–71.

RCHME 1976. *Iron Age and Romano-British monuments in the Gloucestershire Cotswolds* (Royal Com. on Hist. Monuments England, HMSO).

Reece, R., 1990. *Cotswold Studies II. Excavations, survey and records around Cirencester* (Cirencester).

Rees, G.E., 1932. *The History of Bagendon.* (Cirencester, privately published).

Rigby, V., 1982. 'The Coarse Pottery', in J.S. Wacher and A.D. McWhirr (eds.), *Early Roman occupation at Cirencester* (Cirencester Excavations **1**, Cirencester Excavation Committee), 153–203.

Robinson, M., n.d. *The invertebrate and waterlogged plant remains from Claydon Pike* (Oxford Archaeol.).

Roe, F., 1999. 'The Worked Stone', in Mudd *et al.* 1999, vol. 2, 414–21.

Rylatt, J., and Bevan, B., in press. 'Realigning the world: pit alignments and their landscape context', in C. Haselgrove and T. Moore (eds.), *Later Iron Age Britain and Beyond* (Oxford, Oxbow).

Saville, A., 1979. *Excavations at Guiting Power, Gloucestershire 1974* (CRAAGS Occasional Paper **7**, Bristol).

Saville, A., 1983. *Uley Bury & Norbury Hillforts. Rescue excavations at two Gloucestershire Iron Age sites* (Bristol, Western Archaeol. Trust Excavation Monograph **5**).

Saville, A., 1984. 'The Iron Age', in A. Saville (ed.), *Archaeology in Gloucestershire* (Cheltenham Art Gallery and Museums and the BGAS), 140–78.

Sermon, R., 1997. 'Gloucester Archaeol. Unit Annual report 1996', *Glevensis* **30**, 41.

Sharples, N., 1991. 'Late Iron Age society and continental trade in Dorset', in A. Duval (ed.), *Les Gaulois d'Amorique. La Fin de l'age du Fer en Europe Tempérée. Actes du XII colloque AFEAF. Quimper 1988* (Paris, AFEAF), 299–304.

Shotton, F.W., 1978. 'Archaeological inferences from the study of alluvium in the lower Severn-Avon valleys', in S. Limbrey and J. Evans (eds.), *The effect of man on the landscape: the Lowland Zone* (CBA Research Rep. **21**), 27–31.

Smith, C.N.S., 1946. 'A prehistoric and Roman site at Broadway', *Trans. Worcs. Archaeol. Soc.* new series **23**, 57–71.

Staelens, Y., 1982. 'The Birdlip Cemetery', *Trans. BGAS* **100**, 20–31.

Stead, I., 1984. 'Imported metalwork in Iron Age Britain', in S. Macready and F. Thompson (eds.), *Cross channel Trade between Gaul and Britain in the Pre-Roman Iron Age* (London, Society of Antiquaries), 43–65.

Stevens, C., 1996. 'Iron Age and Roman agriculture in the upper Thames Valley: archaeological and social perspectives' (University of Cambridge Ph.D. thesis).

Swan, V., 1975. 'Oare reconsidered and the origins of Savernake ware', *Britannia* **6**, 37–61.

Sykes, N., n.d. 'Draft Animal bone report for Warrens Field and Longdoles Field' (Oxford Archaeol.).

Symmons, R., 1999. 'Faunal remains', in Hearne and Adam 1999, 67.

Thomas, A., and Holbrook, N., 1998. 'Excavations at the Memorial Hall, Lechlade, 1995', in Boyle *et al.* (eds.) 1998, 286–92.

Thomas, A., Holbrook, N., and Bateman, C., 2003. *Late prehistoric and Romano-British burial and settlement at Hucclecote, Gloucestershire* (Bristol and Gloucestershire Archaeol. Rep. **2**, Cirencester, Cotswold Archaeol.).

Thomas, N., 2005. *Conderton Camp, Worcestershire: a middle Iron Age hillfort on Bredon Hill* (CBA Research Rep. **143**, London).

Timby, J., 1990. 'Severn valley ware: a reassessment', *Britannia* **21**, 243–51.

Timby, J., 1998. *Excavations at Kingscote and Wycomb, Gloucestershire* (Cirencester, Cotswold Archaeol. Trust).

Timby, J., 1999a. 'Later Prehistoric and Roman pottery', in Mudd *et al.* 1999, vol. 2, 320–38.

Timby, J., 1999b. 'Pottery supply to Gloucester colonia', in H. Hurst (ed.), *The Coloniae of Roman Britain* (Journal of Roman Archaeol. Supplementary Series **36**, Portsmouth, Rhode Island), 37–44.

Timby, J., 2001. 'The Pottery', in Leah and Young 2001, 67–70.

Tratman, E.K., 1946. 'Prehistoric Bristol', *Proc. University Bristol Spelaeological Soc.* **5.3**, 162–82.

Trow, S., 1982. 'The Bagendon Project 1981–82: A brief interim report', *Glevensis* **1**, 26–9.

Trow, S., 1988. 'Excavations at Ditches hillfort, North Cerney, Gloucestershire. 1982–3', *Trans. BGAS* **106**, 19–86.

Trow, S., James, S., and Moore, T., forthcoming a. 'Excavations at Ditches 'hillfort' and Romano-British villa, North Cerney, Gloucestershire, 1984–5', *Antiq. J.*

Trow, S., Moore, T., and Reece, R., forthcoming b. 'Excavations at Bagendon, Gloucestershire, 1979–1981'.

Van Arsdell, R.D., 1994. *The Coinage of the Dobunni* (Oxford University Committee for Archaeol. Monograph **38**).

Wainwright, G., 1967. 'The excavation of an Iron Age hillfort on Bathampton Down, Somerset', *Trans. BGAS* **86**, 42–59.

Walker, G., Langton, B., and Oakey, N., 2001. *An Iron Age site at Groundwell West, Wiltshire 1996* (Cirencester, Cotswold Archaeol. Trust and Swindon Borough Council).

Walker, G., Thomas, A., and Bateman, C., 2004. 'Bronze-Age and Romano-British Sites south east of Tewkesbury: evaluations and excavations 1991–7', *Trans. BGAS* **122**, 29–94.

Walters, B., 1992. *Archaeology and history of ancient Dean* (Cheltenham, Thornwell Press).

Walters, B., and Walters, M., 1989. 'Ariconium Military site', *Dean Archaeol.* **2**, 32–45.

Watson, B., 2002. 'Recent Iron Age finds from Oxenton Hill', *Glevensis* **35**, 37–8.

Webster, G., 1989. 'Part of a late Celtic Sword-belt found at Coleford, Gloucestershire, in 1987', *Dean Archaeol.* **2**, 30–1.

Webster, G., 1990. 'A late Celtic sword with a ring and button found at Coleford, Gloucestershire', *Britannia* **21**, 294–5.

Webster, G., and Hobley, B., 1964. 'Aerial Reconnaissance over the Warwickshire Avon', *Archaeol. J.* **71**, 1–22.

Wheeler, R.E.M., and Wheeler, T.V., 1932. *Report on the excavation of the Prehistoric, Roman and Post-Roman site in Lydney Park, Gloucestershire* (Reports Research Committee Soc. Antiq. London 9, Oxford).

Whimster, R., 1981. *Burial practices in Iron Age Britain* (BAR Brit. Series **90**, Oxford).

Wigley, A., 2002. 'Building Monuments, Constructing Communities: Landscapes of the First Millennium BC in the Central Welsh Marches' (University of Sheffield Ph.D. thesis).

Wigley, A., in press. 'Pitted histories: early first millennium BC pit alignments in the central Welsh Marches', in C. Haselgrove and R. Pope (eds.), *The Earlier Iron Age in Britain and the near Continent* (Oxford, Oxbow).

Woodward, A., and Leach, P., 1993. *The Uley shrines. Excavation of a ritual complex on West Hill, Uley, Gloucestershire: 1977–9* (English Heritage Archaeol. Rep. **17**, London).

Wymark, C., 2003. 'Thames Water repairs to public sewers, Cirencester, Gloucestershire. Programme of archaeological recording' (Cotswold Archaeol. unpublished report CA 03140).

Yates, D.T., 1999. 'Bronze Age field systems in the Thames valley', *Oxford J. Archaeol.* **18.2**, 157–70.

The Roman Period

Neil Holbrook

The Roman period was well covered in *Archaeology of Gloucestershire* (Saville 1984), with papers on the Cotswolds (Richard Reece), the Thames Valley (David Miles) and cities and large rural settlements (Alan McWhirr). McWhirr's *Roman Gloucestershire* published in 1981 remains the best general account, and there is much still to be gained from reading it. In some areas, however, new discoveries and approaches to Romano-British archaeology now point to somewhat different conclusions to those presented more than two decades ago. It is these topics that form the subject of this paper. Inevitably the pace of progress has not been even. While major advances have been made in our understanding of rural settlement, and this will be discussed in some detail, elsewhere we are little further forward in our knowledge of, for example, the Roman military conquest. No new military sites have been recognised and the conclusion that the territory of the Dobunni was not intensively garrisoned in the aftermath of the Roman invasion is inescapable. The fort at Cirencester now appears anomalous, and I favour the view that it was established as a demonstration of support for a pro-Roman Dobunnic leader based at Bagendon during the unsettled period of the early Welsh campaigns, rather than as part of a scheme of territorial subjugation (Darvill and Holbrook 1994, 53–5).

Figure 1 presents my version of a map of Roman Gloucestershire. All such exercises are necessarily selective and dependent upon the scale of study. The elements common to almost all maps which seek to depict our area on a single page (e.g. McWhirr 1981; Fulford 2003, fig. 2) are the towns (Gloucester and Cirencester as well as the smaller centres) and roads. It is rural settlement which causes the most problems simply because the large number of sites, combined with difficulties in classification, does not lend itself to mapping at this scale.

ROADS AND SETTLEMENTS

Roads

The relationship of Cirencester to its surrounding road system is a puzzle that has taxed several generations of scholars, although significant progress has been made in the last decade. Gerald Hargreaves' (1998) detailed survey work led him to propose that the Fosse Way was originally conceived as a through route to which the siting of the fort at Cirencester and the subsequent town was irrelevant. Developing the theme, Richard Reece (2003) has observed the irrationality of the course adopted by Ermin Street in the vicinity of the town. The strategic objective of Ermin Street was to achieve the easiest route to the edge of the Cotswold escarpment and thereafter down to the crossing of the Severn at Kingsholm. But the road did not follow the logical course to achieve this aim in the vicinity of Cirencester where it adopted a marked deviation to the south-west to enter the Churn valley on the site later adopted for the Roman town. This must have been a conscious decision by the surveyors which Reece suggests was prompted by a desire to avoid an existing ceremonial area associated with Tar Barrows. This is an intriguing theory that could easily be tested by fieldwork. Subsequent reorganisation of the road system around Cirencester was doubtless prompted by the process of laying out the new town of *Corinium Dobunnorum*. This involved the diversion of both the Fosse Way and Akeman Street to provide a new joint route that fixed the approximate line of the *decumanus maximus* of the town.[1] The Whiteway (Margary

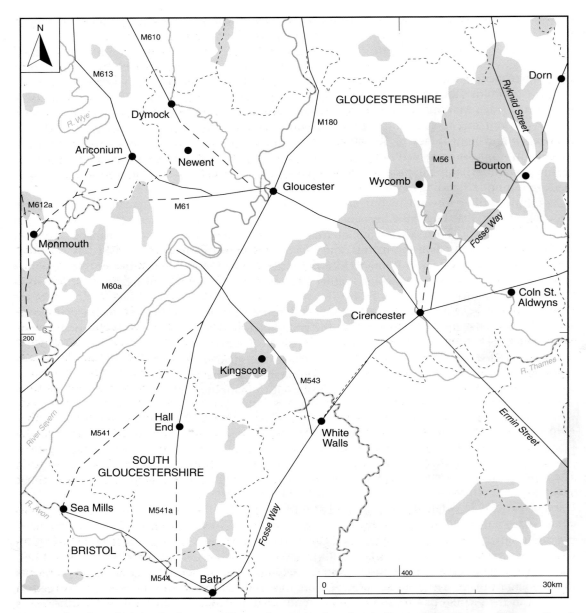

Fig. 1: Roads and Major Settlements. The roads are numbered according to I.V. Margary, Roman Roads in Britain *(1967).*

route 56) is another road whose Roman origin has been disputed, but the case for its existence is strong, even if the details of its final approach into Cirencester remain to be determined.[2]

At other locations in the county confirmatory evidence has been recovered in recent years for some other long suspected routes. Examples include Margary route 543 that branched off from the Fosse Way at Easton Grey and crossed the southern Cotswolds as it made for a ferry crossing of the Severn at Arlingham. This road is surprisingly omitted from a number of maps, but cropmarks which are likely to mark its roadside ditches have been observed at Kingscote and possible traces of metalling have been excavated at Frocester (Timby 1998, 7–8; Price and Price 1992). The existence of the road which departed from the Gloucester to Sea Mills road to head for a crossing of the Avon at Bitton (Margary 541a) has been confirmed by the discovery of a substantial roadside settlement at Hall End, Wickwar (see below). A 1st- or early 2nd-century AD date for the piles of a timber bridge across the Wye at Chepstow on the Newnham to Caerleon road (Margary 60a) was determined by radiocarbon dating in 2003.[3] While these various strands of evidence confirm the existence of some routes, the so-called Dean Road (Margary 614) should be removed from the map until evidence is produced to counter the serious doubt that has been cast upon its Roman origin (Standing 1988).

Cirencester and Gloucester

The last intensive campaign of urban excavation had ceased in Cirencester by 1979, and the great achievement of the last 25 years has been the publication of four substantial monographs on various aspects of the Roman town (Wacher and McWhirr 1982; McWhirr *et al.* 1982; McWhirr 1986; Holbrook 1998). Work in Cirencester over the last couple of decades has tended to be on a fairly small scale in advance of individual developments. It has, however, incrementally added new data and thrown up the occasional surprise. The instigation of extensive geophysical survey has produced stunning results at a number of Romano-British urban sites (Wroxeter in particular stands out: Gaffney *et al.* 2000; White and Gaffney 2003). It might be expected that similar results would be achieved in the undeveloped parts of Cirencester but such surveys have been somewhat less successful as work in St Michael's Field (*insula* IX: GSB 1999) and to the rear of Querns Lane (*insula* III: Barker 1998) demonstrates. While major long-lived elements of the town plan such as streets can be detected, the complex palimpsest of structures in the centre of the town, further complicated by differential patterns of post-Roman stone robbing, does not lend itself to the production of readily understandable plots comparable to those at Wroxeter. Perhaps greater success would be achieved on the periphery of the town (such as the playing fields of Victoria Road School and parts of the Abbey Grounds) where a shallower stratigraphic sequence might be expected.

The pattern of archaeological work in Gloucester has been somewhat different. Like Cirencester considerable excavation occurred in the 1960s and 1970s, some of which has been published (Heighway 1983; Heighway and Garrod 1980; Garrod and Heighway 1984; Hurst 1985 and 1986). Unlike Cirencester, however, excavation continued on a sizeable scale after 1979, much of it utilising labour from the Manpower Services Commission. Gloucester is by no means alone in that the considerable amount of effort put into these excavations has not resulted in publications of appropriate detail. To understand what has gone on in the last decades one is reliant upon the interim accounts in the *Transactions* and *Glevensis*. These are sufficient to demonstrate that the excavations were of good quality and yielded significant results, especially concerning the extramural areas. As Carolyn Heighway reviews what has been learnt about the archaeology of Gloucester in all periods elsewhere in this volume, I will concentrate on one aspect of new thinking rather than new discoveries.

Rebuilding of the fortress defences and internal buildings in stone at Gloucester in the Flavian period had originally been interpreted as works associated with the construction of the *colonia*.

In 1988 Hurst revised his earlier interpretation and proposed that these developments related to a reoccupation of the fortress by a new legionary garrison. This reinterpretation has not met with general acceptance, however, and most commentators prefer the sequence as originally proposed. Doubt has also now been cast on the traditional date for the foundation of the *colonia* during the reign of Nerva (AD 96–8). This is based upon the evidence of a tombstone of a veteran born in Gloucester which gives the *colonia* the title of *Ner(via* or *viana)*. Hassall (1999, 183–4) has suggested that it is more likely on general grounds that the *colonia* would have been founded in the late 80s during the reign of Domitian and that it was granted the emperor's title of *Domitiana*. Upon the death of Domitian, and the damning of his memory by Nerva, *Nerviana* would have been substituted for its original name.

Smaller Towns

Nomenclature and classification of the nucleated settlements of Roman Britain have been a major theme of the last couple of decades, with terms such as small town, roadside community, village, and market centre variously invoked. This approach has had the tendency to group seemingly heterogeneous settlements into one category or another simply because they do not fit into other easily defined groups (Millett 1995). More recent discussions have focused on defining site function and economy ahead of a classification based solely upon morphology. In a local context the publication in 1998 of a report on excavations at Kingscote (1973–80) and Wycomb (1973–7) provided an opportunity to review what was also known of the other Cotswold small towns of Bourton-on-the-Water and Dorn (Timby 1998). A wealth of data was presented in this volume, and the heterogeneous nature of the sites is apparent. For instance Kingscote is reasonably interpreted as a rural estate centre, while Dorn appears to be a late Roman official installation. All of these sites have been known for some decades, but an important new discovery has been recently made at Hall End, Wickwar, on the road to Bitton. Geophysical survey and trial excavation have revealed a settlement covering 10 ha which contained a variety of stone-built structures (Young 2003).[4] Hall End is the largest known settlement in the Vale of Berkeley, lying 34 km south-west of Gloucester and 20 km north-east of Sea Mills. It is likely that other roadside settlements would produce similarly exciting results to those recovered from Hall End if they too were subjected to detailed geophysical survey. Coln St Aldwyns/Quenington, on Akeman Street 12 km to the east of Cirencester, would be a good candidate for study; surface scatters extend for almost one kilometre along the road (RCHME 1976, 36, 96–7). Elsewhere we need to be careful not to assume that all settlements which lay on roads were 'small towns' of one kind or another rather than just rural settlements which happen to lie close to a passing road. Settlement remains have been found at Hanham on the anticipated line of the Bath to Sea Mills road, but on current evidence there is nothing to suggest that this is anything other than a rural farmstead and iron-making site. A similar interpretation is also favoured for the site at Birdlip Quarry on Ermin Street. Both of these sites are discussed further below. Elsewhere too little is known of some settlements to say much of their character, as for example in the west of the county at Dymock on the road from Gloucester to Stretton Grandison (Gethyn-Jones 1991) and at The Moat to the south of Newent. At the latter iron-making slag and pottery have been recovered over an area of 47 ha, although the actual area of settlement and industry may have been much smaller than this. The site lies off the known road network and it is most likely to be a large rural settlement (Walters 1999, 81–4). Some previously postulated 'small towns' have not so far lived up to their billing. A settlement near Bitton, close to a road crossing of the Avon and junction with the Bath–Sea Mills road has been supposed, although remains of it are proving elusive.[5] At Birdlip there was clearly a well-appointed building (a *mansio* where horses could be changed after the gruelling climb up the Cotswold escarpment is an attractive interpretation) but a series of evaluations demonstrates that there was no extensive settlement there.[6]

THE COUNTRYSIDE

In this section I discuss advances in our understanding of the agricultural landscape, and in particular the distribution, sequence and economy of rural settlements. There will be frequent references to villas. By this I mean a rural establishment, independent of settlement, normally of stone-built rectangular plan. Hypocausts, mosaics, baths and architectural ornamentation are characteristic. For structures that do not display any of these attributes I have generally adopted the term farmstead. Previous studies have tended to focus on villas to the detriment of farmsteads, but work over the last 25 years has gone some way to redressing the balance. Recent estimates suggest that between 50–70,000 late Iron-Age and Romano-British rural sites are known in England, compared to somewhere between 500 and 2,500 villas. Thus villas represent only about 3–4% of known rural settlements in the country (Mattingly 2004, 14).

The Upper Thames Valley

There is little value in studying the Upper Thames Valley in Gloucestershire as an entity. The vagaries of medieval and later political geography divide between Gloucestershire and Wiltshire an area of common landscape character on either bank of the Thames, while work further down-stream as far as Reading has much to contribute to the understanding of our area. In 1984 David Miles reported upon the recently completed excavations at Claydon Pike and Thornhill Farm near Lechade. The results were exciting and fresh, and by combining this new evidence with that recovered from investigations undertaken in the preceding decade in Oxfordshire he was able to sketch a preliminary model of Romano-British settlement and agriculture in the Upper Thames Valley of Gloucestershire (Miles 1984). Twenty years on Thornhill Farm has just been published (Jennings *et al.* 2004), and Claydon Pike will shortly follow in a volume also covering excavations by the Oxford Archaeological Unit at Kempsford and Somerford Keynes (Miles *et al.* forthcoming). Margaret Jones' excavation at Roughground Farm, Lechlade, has also been reported (Allen *et al.* 1993). In the last 20 years excavation on a truly extensive scale in advance of gravel extraction has occurred in two principal zones, one continuing previous work in the parishes of Lechlade, Fairford and Kempsford, the other in the heart of the Cotswold Water Park around Latton (Wiltshire), Somerford Keynes and Ashton Keynes (Wiltshire). To what degree has the full analysis of the older sites, combined with new discoveries, affected the picture sketched by Miles?

In many respects Miles' model still has currency, although some of his ideas have been significantly developed by George Lambrick in an important paper (1992) covering the whole of the Upper Thames Valley. Lambrick suggests that the increase in floodplain alluvium visible on a number of sites was the result of an intensification of arable agriculture on the valley sides in the late Iron-Age and Romano-British periods. He sees this expansion of arable onto traditional grazing lands on the Cotswold slopes leading to pressure on pasture that resulted in the creation of intensive cattle ranching sites. The type-site in Gloucestershire is Thornhill Farm where numerous ditched enclosures which do not seem to be domestic in character are interpreted as cattle breeding pens. Environmental evidence suggests that the site was surrounded by grassland, with no evidence of arable production at this time (Jennings *et al.* 2004). Continuity of settlement and agricultural practice either side of AD 43 is evident in the Upper Thames Valley, a major episode of settlement dislocation not occurring, as with so much of Britain, until the early 2nd century. In Oxfordshire for instance sites terminating in the first half of the 2nd century are more numerous than those occupied throughout the Roman period in the Valley (Henig and Booth 2000, 106).

In Gloucestershire the pattern is equally clear. At Claydon Pike a centralised agricultural estate concerned with the production of animal fodder developed, while at Thornhill Farm the ranching settlement was replaced by trackways and hay meadows (Jennings *et al.* 2004, 158). Other 2nd-century developments include the construction of a villa at Roughground Farm and farmsteads at Whelford Bowmoor and Kempsford Stubbs Farm. Perhaps the aspect of this sequence that has come into clearest relief in the last 20 years is the sheer extent of Romano-British land management. Cropmarks and excavations show that vast expanses of the flat gravel terraces were turned over to a managed agricultural landscape. In virtually every case where excavation has occurred on any scale ditched trackways and field systems have come to light, and where these can be traced over a distance they may have linked settlements, as with the track between Claydon Pike and Kempsford Bowmoor (ibid. 159). The persistent discovery at various sites of evidence for the reorganisation of the agricultural landscape in the 2nd century points to the operation of an external political, economic or cultural force that entailed considerable capital investment (Lambrick 1992, 105). Miles (1984, 208) originally sought an explanation involving state (army) intervention, although in line with contemporary fashion it would appear that the forthcoming report on Claydon Pike will not stress this as a factor. That villas are much less prevalent in the Upper Thames Valley than the Cotswolds has led some commentators to interpret the field archaeology as evidence of multiple estates centred on Cotswold villas, tenants working the agriculturally productive farms on the river gravels (eg. Salway 1993, 420). It is important to remember, however, that these agricultural developments in the valley pre-date the heyday of Cotswold villas by at least a century. One could just as easily argue for the opposite interpretation that agricultural intensification in the Upper Thames Valley in the later 2nd and early 3rd century created the wealth to finance the construction of Cotswold villas from the mid 3rd century onwards. In either case the question of where the capital came from lies beyond the reach of archaeology.

In the later Roman period differing site histories have been revealed through excavation. At Claydon Pike a modest 4th-century villa was involved in mixed agriculture (the extensive trackways seem no longer to have been in use). Elsewhere some settlements were abandoned completely, such as Whelford Bowmoor and Kempsford Stubbs Farm where flooding occurred, while others such as Cleveland Farm, Ashton Keynes, reveal occupation into the 5th century or later to judge from the recovery of grass-tempered pottery (Jennings *et al.* 2004, 159; Coe *et al.* 1991, 47). Whatever the sequence at individual sites the persistent influence that the system of Romano-British fields and tracks had on the later landscape can be gauged by the fact that some of them have survived as land boundaries into modern times.[7]

The basis of the agricultural economy of the Upper Thames Valley is still not fully understood, and the evidence from the Lechlade area suggests that it was not constant throughout the Roman period. Claydon Pike demonstrates the importance of haymaking, while the tracks testify to the need to move large herds of cattle and sheep around the countryside to exploit grazing. Flax has been found at a number of sites in the Valley, including Claydon Pike, as well as in an old ground surface underlying the later town of Cirencester (Wild 2002, 6–7; Wacher and McWhirr 1982, 228). Horse breeding has sometime been evoked as a significant activity, but the evidence remains inconclusive. Animal bones from Horcott near Fairford have been used to suggest specialist horse rearing (Reilly 2004), while at Thornhill Farm the horse remains are interpreted as those of work animals for the farm (Charles 2004, 132–3).

The Cotswolds

We still do not possess the complete plan of a rural settlement in the Cotswolds that did not develop into a villa. The best evidence we have is that recovered from the settlement next to Ermin Street at Birdlip Quarry, Cowley (Mudd *et al.* 1999). Surface remains suggest a settlement covering *c.*1 ha, of which a fair sample was excavated in advance of improvements to the A417 road. While it would be perverse to argue that the existence of Ermin Street did not have a significant effect on the daily life of the settlement, Birdlip Quarry is clearly not a typical roadside community with strip buildings fronting the road. Rather it appears to be a farmstead formed from a series of rectangular, partly ditched, enclosures containing one or more scattered buildings. Occupation commenced *c.*AD 160/80 and included a stake-built timber roundhouse (the entrance faced away from the road) alongside probable rectangular structures. The roundhouse was rebuilt in the later 3rd century with a timber or cob superstructure resting upon a 12-sided dry-stone foundation.[8] Further timber and stone-founded round and rectangular houses were built before the settlement was abandoned *c.*AD 370/80. The picture gained from Birdlip Quarry is of a farm composed of a number of different social (most probably family) groups involved in mixed agriculture. Wheat was cultivated and cattle, sheep and horses reared. Another unpretentious farmstead has been partially examined at Haymes near Southam on the lower slopes of Cleeve Hill (Rawes 1986). The presence there of an altar is no more than a reflection of everyday religious observance in what was surely an essentially secular farming settlement.

While these sites did not subsequently develop into villas, we can trace the sequence of pre-villa occupation at two other Cotswold sites. Excavation at Barnsley Park came to an end in 1979, but J.T. Smith (1985) has since published a telling re-interpretation of the findings (Fig. 2). Smith is surely correct in believing that the numerous circular structures described in the reports as animal pens were in fact roundhouses. He accordingly considers Barnsley Park as a settlement composed of three farmyards, each with its own house or houses of either circular and rectangular plan, the three families working the surrounding land in joint proprietorship. The farm was occupied from the mid 2nd century AD until *c.*360 when the first villa house was constructed. Smith detects evidence in the plan of the villa house for the persistence of a social structure based around multiple family units. At Marshfield occupation commenced in the late Iron Age with one or more timber roundhouses (Blockley 1985). The roundhouse was rebuilt with stone foundations in the second half of the 1st century AD (it is surely a house rather than a shrine as Blockley maintained), and a villa house was added in the last quarter of the 3rd century. Once again Smith (1987) has attempted a reinterpretation of the published evidence. He believes that analysis of the villa plan indicates that it was initially designed to house two or, more likely, four households, and that this is evidence for the growth and transformation of a social organisation which dates back to the late Iron-Age settlement.

These last two sites bring us neatly to a consideration of Cotswold villas. There are clearly a number of large well-appointed villas that still await discovery. While it might be thought that the visibility of these structures, both through cropmarks and an abundance of artefacts, combined with the systematic survey work of the former Royal Commission on Historical Monuments England would tend towards a reasonably complete set of data, recent discoveries suggest otherwise. Large previously unknown villas have been found at Turkdean and Badminton,

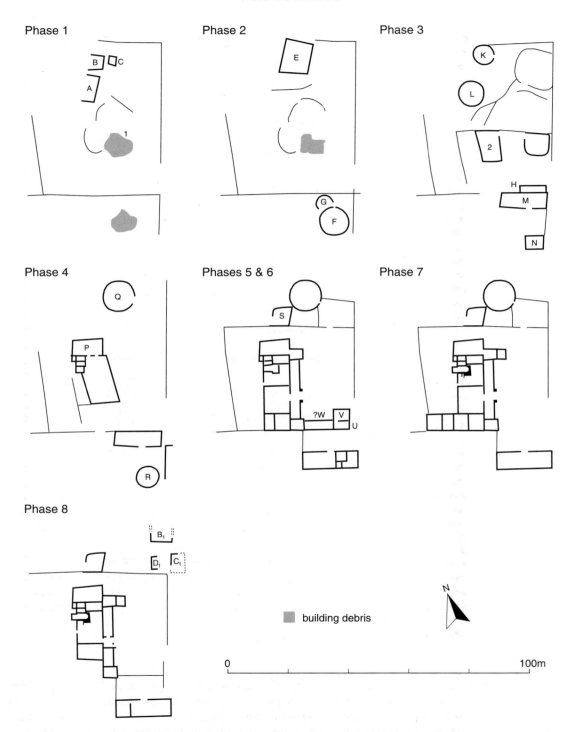

Fig. 2: *The development of Barnsley Park according to J.T. Smith (1985).*

Fig. 3: Turkdean villa: composite plan of parchmarks and geophysical survey results for the main courtyard house.

the latter complete with a fine mosaic (Holbrook 2004a; Osgood 2004) (Figs. 3–5). Smaller villas have come to light at The Ditches near Cirencester; Vineyards Farm in Charlton Kings; and Marshfield and Wortley in the southern Cotswolds, with another just over the Wiltshire border near Malmesbury (Trow and James 1988; Rawes 1991a; Blockley 1985; Wilson 1996; Hart *et al.*

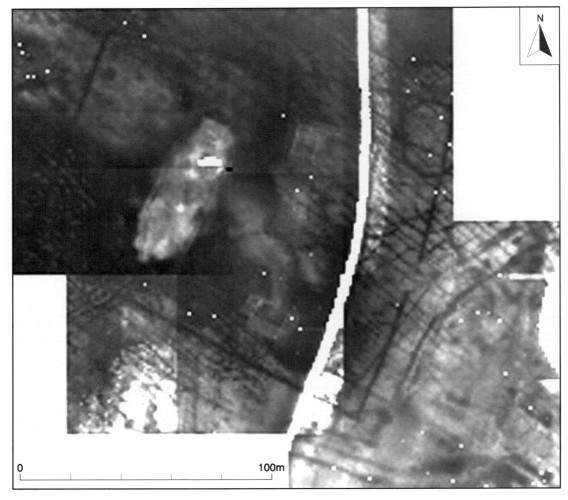

Fig. 4:   Badminton villa: resistance survey results (© Sagascan, M.H. Martin, J. Martin and A.W. Jackson). The main villa building lies to the left of centre, with the apse containing the mosaic visible at the north-east end of the building. Two subsidiary buildings lie to the east of the main building, the whole complex being contained within a trapezoidal enclosure.

2005). Some villas known only from antiquarian investigations were also undoubtedly larger than the often incomplete plans indicate, as has been shown at Great Witcombe (Holbrook 2003a).

It is orthodoxy that the floruit of Cotswold villas occurred in the late Roman period, but recent investigations have shown that some villas were constructed in the 1st or early 2nd century. A small corridor villa was built in the pre-Flavian period at The Ditches within an Iron-Age enclosure which lay just to the north of the main Bagendon complex. The location and early date of this villa strongly suggest that it was the residence of a member of the native aristocracy who quickly assimilated Roman fashions. The villa was abandoned before the end of the 3rd century

Fig. 5:   Badminton villa: mosaic excavated in 2003 (photograph © Richard Osgood). The scales measure two metres. This exceptionally large and well-preserved mosaic has an unusual geometric design and probably dates to the mid 4th century.

(Trow and James 1988). In Waltham Field, Whittington, a site discovered by Wilfred Cox (1979) was further examined for the *Time Team* television programme in 2000 (Hirst no date). The earliest feature examined was a ditch defining a rectilinear enclosure. This probably dates to the late Iron Age as the site produced pottery that can be dated to the period from the 1st century BC to the 1st century AD. The enclosure probably went out of use in the 1st century AD when at least three stone buildings were constructed just outside the ditch. One contained *opus signinum* floors, and demolition material included painted wall plaster, tesserae and hypocaust tile. Occupation of the buildings had ceased by the end of the 3rd century at latest.[9] The similarity with The Ditches is readily apparent. Another possible example is the villa at Rodmarton examined by Samuel Lysons in 1800 (RCHME 1976, 98). The villa has produced pottery and stamped tiles dating from the 2nd century onwards, while aerial photography has detected a polygonal ditched enclosure 200 m to the north (Darvill and Locke 1988, 192). The enclosure is undated but a later prehistoric date is most likely. Wortley is another villa where early activity is suggested by pottery, although fuller publication is required before we can determine whether the villa house itself dates from the 1st century (Wilson 1996, 7). It would be wrong, however, to assume that most Cotswold villas had early origins as it has been shown at other sites which have been investigated to modern standards that the late date traditionally applied is correct. Examples include Barnsley Park (*c.*360), Farmington (early 4th century), Marshfield (late 3rd century) and probably Turkdean (Webster and Smith 1982, 65–7; Gascoigne 1969; Blockley 1985; Holbrook 2004a, 54–5). Arguments that the late date applied to many villas is simply a product of a failure to adequately investigate the earliest levels cannot be maintained in these cases.

It has long been recognised that the Cotswolds in the density and wealth of its villas is at odds with neighbouring areas, although explanations for this phenomenon differ. It is possible to regard the burgeoning of these sites in the 3rd and 4th centuries as a reflection of the intrinsic vitality of the Cotswold economy in the 1st and 2nd centuries. Accumulated profits provided the capital, and the social system the desire, to express status through domestic architecture. Sites with a long history of pre-villa activity such as Barnsley Park and Frocester Court might lend some weight to this idea, although other explanations are possible (new owners buying existing farms and building villas on them). Elsewhere villas, sometimes of considerable scale, appear to have been built on virgin sites. On sites such as Turkdean deep accumulations of stratigraphy or plentiful artefactual evidence of late Iron-Age occupation, so apparent in the Upper Thames Valley, simply do not occur. The counter argument to the creation of indigenous wealth in the Cotswolds is the belief that there was a 'flight of capital' from the areas of Gaul and Germany troubled by barbarian invasions to the relative security of the west country of England in the late 3rd century. Various strands of evidence have been advanced as support for this theory, such as alleged similarities in the plans of villas in western Britain and the north-west provinces, most of which has been dismissed by J.T. Smith in a powerful critique (Branigan 1973; Smith 1983). Whilst it is conceivable that investment did move into western Britain from elsewhere in the province, or indeed the empire, there is no evidence. Indeed it is difficult to see what evidence could be found as the origin and extent of land tenure cannot be determined by archaeology alone.[10]

Other explanations are equally difficult to test, such as the supposition that the pleasing upland valleys of the Cotswolds, combined with good hunting, made this an attractive place to live, then as now (Salway 1993, 419–20). Instead it will be better to concentrate on those areas where archaeology can make a contribution: what was being grown, made, and eaten at these sites? Some commentators have considered that the late Roman agricultural economy of the Cotswolds was founded predominately on sheep or horse rearing. To judge from animal bones recovered some farms doubtless had specialised economies. Barnsley Park, for instance, seems to have been heavily involved in wool production (Noddle 1985; King 1988, 58–9). Elsewhere cattle and sheep often seem to have been kept in roughly equal numbers, pigs to a lesser extent, while horse bones are rarely abundant as site finds (Ayres and Clark 1999, 460–2). Few assemblages of charred or waterlogged plant remains have been published from rural sites in the Cotswolds. One exception is Birdlip Quarry where the cereal assemblage was dominated by spelt wheat as at most Romano-British sites in southern England (Pelling 1999, 479–90). Mixed farming must have been the norm.

The Severn Vale

In reviewing the work done in Gloucestershire in advance of the construction of the M5 motorway Peter Fowler boldly stated that 'Between the early months of 1969 and the end of 1970 the field archaeology of lowland Gloucestershire was more or less created'. Some 24 Romano-British sites were found along the 41 miles of motorway, a surprisingly high tally which led Fowler to wonder whether the density was influenced by the presence of the Roman road from Sea Mills to

Gloucester which ran parallel to the line of the later motorway. Given the absence of late Iron-Age sites he suggested that some form of plantation of settlement may have occurred in the 1st and 2nd centuries AD (Fowler 1977, 40–1). This picture has changed dramatically over the last 25 years due to the expansion of archaeological work in advance of major housing developments and to the landmark publication in 2000 of the results of 40 years of work at Frocester Court (Price 2000). That report allows us to understand in telling detail a continuum of occupation that stretched from the late Iron Age to the post-Roman period. The late Iron-Age farmstead continued little altered until the 2nd century when rectangular wooden structures replaced roundhouses. The ditched enclosure that had been a common aspect of the site since the middle Iron Age was swept away c. AD 275 for the construction of a masonry villa.

Another important facet of Frocester is its location on a spread of fan gravel surrounded by the heavy damp lias clays typical of much of the Severn Vale. It is now apparent that villas, while by no means as numerous as those on the limestone of the Cotswolds, tend to cluster on these intermittent islands of sand and gravel in the Vale, as at Whitminster/Eastington; Cheltenham (where the main settlement awaits discovery); and Bishop's Cleeve (Holbrook 2004b, 87–8).[11] Bishop's Cleeve is a triumph of development-led archaeology. Numerous evaluations and excavations have taken place since 1989 in response to the rapid expansion of the village, if such it can still be called. Remains of virtually all periods between the Bronze Age and the 18th century AD have been revealed (Parry 1999, 99–102). Yet Bishop's Cleeve also exemplifies some of the problems inherent in the post-1990 world of PPG 16. Investigations have been conducted by at least five different organisations on adjacent sites, which exacerbates further an already fragmented picture. Despite these constraints enough is known to suggest that Bishop's Cleeve was surely of similar character to Frocester, with a late Iron-Age and early Roman farmstead receiving a masonry villa in the 3rd or 4th century. Sadly the villa house itself remains unexamined.

It would be incorrect to believe that Romano-British settlement was largely restricted to the gravel spreads of the Vale for many farmsteads are recorded on the lias clays. This was one of the main findings of the work for the M5, yet the salvage conditions under which that project was conducted prevented a clear understanding of the form and development of the identified settlements. This is a deficiency that has been remedied by more recent work.

Romano-British sites can be hard to detect on lias clay as this geology does not lend itself to the production of cropmarks, in contrast to the gravels of the Upper Thames Valley. Fieldwalking and geophysics have, however, proved successful prospecting techniques, the latter yielding parti-cularly good results. A good case study is the investigations undertaken by Cotswold Archaeology to the south-east of Tewkesbury since 1991 (Walker et al. 2004). Two settlements, less than 400 m apart, were sited on a low ridge between the Tirle Brook and river Swilgate, a good location to exploit seasonally flooded pasture. One farmstead (Site II) displays a very complex sequence of development involving numerous alterations to compounds and closes (Fig. 6C). The farm was established in the late Iron Age or early Roman period and continued in use until the first half of the 4th century. Pottery and other finds suggest that people lived there with their animals although no trace of any domestic structure could be found. Houses must have been built from cob or turf that leaves few sub-surface remains. Ephemeral traces of such structures have been found elsewhere in the Vale (Holbrook 2003b, 63). The second Tewkesbury site (Site I) comprised an almost square enclosure containing pits and other traces of occupation, but once again no structures could be made out (Fig. 6A). It dates to the 2nd–early 3rd centuries and bears comparison with the farmstead excavated by Bernard Rawes (1981) at Brockworth, where a similar-sized ditched enclosure contained roundhouses (Fig. 6B).

The initial campaign, associated with the construction of the Tewkesbury Eastern Relief Road, has been supplemented by further work in 2004 and 2005 at Walton Cardiff. There a similar rectilinear enclosure (Fig. 6D) appears to have been occupied from the later Iron Age until the 4th century. Closes for the herding of stock were found, and a corn drier testifies to the processing of crops. These sites are the basic farmsteads from which the Vale was farmed, and the work around Tewkesbury and to the east of Gloucester clearly shows that at least some areas of the Vale were intensively exploited (Thomas *et al.* 2003, 67, fig. 1). Artefacts are not particularly common at these enclosures, especially compared to Cotswold sites such as Birdlip Quarry and Haymes. Whether these small farms were owner-occupied or were the residences for workers on larger estates can only be guessed. They do, however, have the potential to tell us how the Vale was farmed in Roman times.

Recent work in the Vale of Berkeley and the Bristol conurbation has greatly expanded our understanding of rural settlement in those areas. There it seems to have been of a somewhat different character to that around Gloucester and Tewkesbury. Villas were traditionally thought to be rare in this area, but new work is finding more examples to add to the three long-known sites of Kingsweston, Cromhall and Tockington Park. At Lower Woods, Hawkesbury, geophysics and excavation have revealed two rectangular buildings either side of a courtyard (Fig. 7). To judge from the plentiful smelting and smithing slag recovered, the establishment was involved in iron making. One room in the southern range was furnished with painted wall plaster and a 2nd-century mosaic that bears a rare, but sadly incomplete, inscription in the border reading REG[. In the late Roman period the room was given over to iron smithing (Ireland 2005). A second villa has been found 3 km to the south at Springfield Farm, Horton, while architectural fragments suggest another building of status, probably a villa, in Pucklechurch (*South Gloucestershire Archaeology* 4 (2002), 5; Samuel 2000, 12–14).

Aside from these individual sites an area of landscape covering several square kilometres at Bradley Stoke has been examined from the late 1980s onwards by a combination of salvage recording, stray finds and PPG 16-prompted fieldwork. Much of this work has not been adequately published, but a few conclusions are possible from what is so far available (Samuel 2003, 45). Several foci of activity have been located. At Savage's Wood Road a possible stone building of probable 2nd- to 4th-century date is known. One kilometre to the south-east there was another farmstead at Bailey's Court Farm/Webbs Farm where dry-stone walls demarcated fields and paddocks either side of a trackway, and a rectangular building with rounded corners had dry-stone footings.[12] The absence of tiles or slates suggests a thatch or shingle roof. A pottery flagon set into the floor of the building as a foundation deposit contained an unworn coin of AD 305 while pottery suggests occupation on the site from the 2nd until at least the mid 4th century (Russell 1989). A third site is known 1.4 km to the south-west at Stoke Gifford. This was examined under salvage conditions, and only interim notes have so far been published (Parker 1978; Grew 1980, 385; Rankov 1982, 381). A circular stone-built structure, 5.7 m in external diameter with a pitched stone floor, was found. It may be a house, although it is very small.[13] Further rectangular structures were exposed in building work. Numerous hearths and ovens were found, and iron ore, iron slag and evidence for the casting of bronze from scrap were recovered. It is regrettable that we can't currently say much more about the Romano-British settlement of this area, other than to observe the existence of three sites within 1.0–1.5 km of each other and traces of field systems between. The greater use of dry-stone construction than at sites further north in the Vale can be noted, and the presence of occasional inhumation burials seems typical.

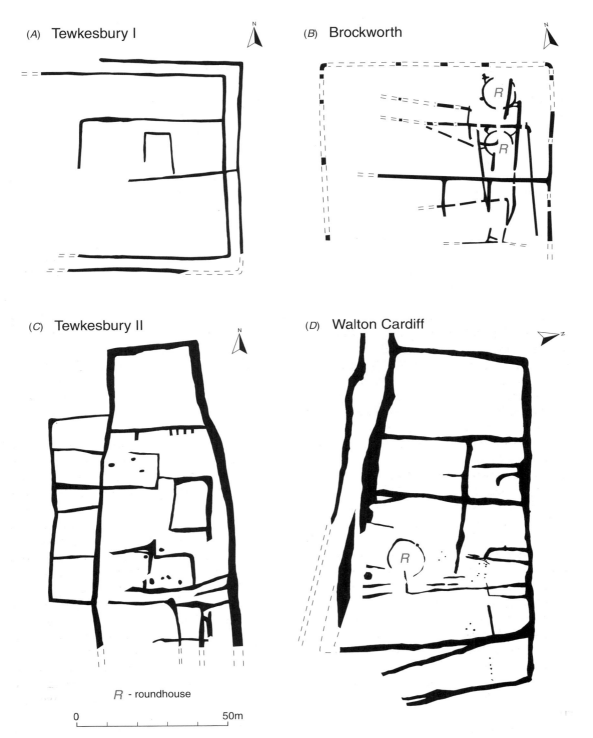

(A) Tewkesbury I

(B) Brockworth

(C) Tewkesbury II

(D) Walton Cardiff

R - roundhouse

0   50m

Fig. 6: *Farmstead enclosures in the Severn valley. A: Tewkesbury I (after Walker et al. 2004); B: Brockworth (after Rawes 1981); C: Tewkesbury II, sub-phase 3c (after Walker et al. 2004); D: Walton Cardiff (plan supplied by Cotswold Archaeology).*

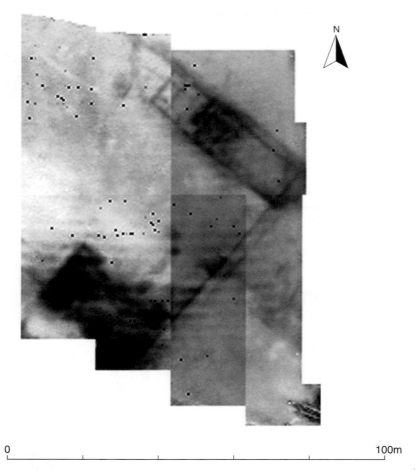

0   100m

Fig. 7:   Lower Woods, Hawkesbury: resistance survey results (© Sagascan, M.H. Martin, J. Martin and A.W. Jackson). The wing to the left was a residential building that contained the mosaic with the inscription REG. The wing to the right appears to have been of a more industrial or agricultural character. The two buildings were joined by a compound wall in which a possible entrance structure can be seen.

The exploitation of iron-ore deposits which occur within the coal measures of the north Bristol coalfield and the contribution of iron making to the rural economy of the Vale of Berkeley are themes which recent work has elucidated. Seams of iron ore occur alongside outcrops of coal around Kingswood and Mangotsfield where sites have been investigated at Stonehill, Hanham, and Rodway Hill, Mangotsfield, in advance of the construction of the Avon Ring Road. Hanham lies on the supposed course of the Roman road from Bath to Sea Mills, and it is possible that we are dealing with a roadside settlement although nothing in the evidence so far suggests typical ribbon development. A horseshoe-shaped structure with a heavily burnt internal surface which seems to have been used in iron making was partially enclosed within a semi-circular ditch. It dated to the early 4th century, and was replaced by a stone-built aisled building with an internal drain against one wall (Fig. 8). An agricultural function is likely for this building, although

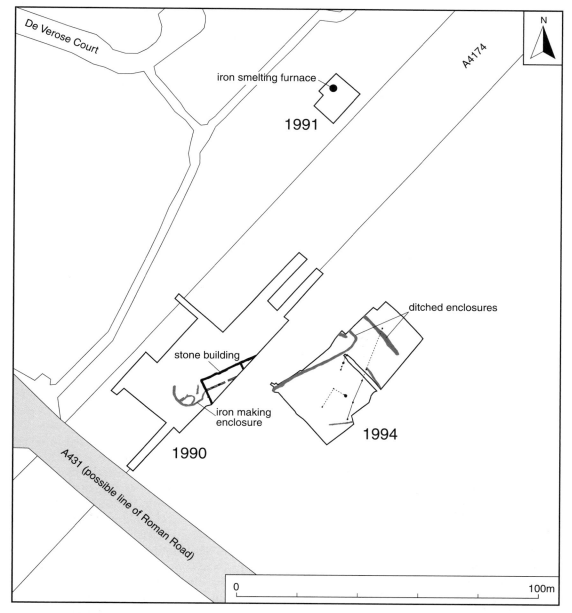

Fig. 8: Hanham: plan of the agricultural and iron-making settlement (after Stiles et al. *1992; Russett 1993; and Yorkston and Piper 1994/5).*

domestic rooms may have lain within an area that was largely unexcavated (Russett 1993).[14] An iron-smelting shaft-furnace with associated cobbled yard was found 70 m to north-east (Stiles *et al.* 1992), while further excavations to the east of the structures revealed a series of ditched enclosures which date from the later 2nd century. In the late 3rd or early 4th century the ditches were backfilled with large quantities of iron-smelting slag, and it is likely that small post-pad structures were associated with iron making. New enclosures were dug in the 4th century, one of which may have contained the aisled building, and, to judge from the absence of slag, iron smelting may have ceased by this date (Yorkston and Piper 1994/5). At Rodway Hill, 4 km north of Hanham, an agricultural and iron-making settlement was discovered during archaeological work covering 150 ha associated with the Emerson's Green urban development. Timber and stone structures involved in iron smelting and smithing and accompanied by field systems and scattered burials have been found. Locally won coal from exposed seams and charcoal fuelled the iron making, while lead-working residues and crucibles are suggestive of the extraction of silver from lead through cupellation (Parry 1998; Erskine 2001).

The Forest of Dean

Previous accounts of the Romano-British archaeology of the Forest of Dean have largely concentrated on the evidence for iron production. A discussion of rural settlement is pertinent, however, as by a quirk of geography the main urban centres involved in iron making lie beyond the border of the modern county (*Ariconium* in Weston-under-Penyard, Monmouth and Worcester). Only Dymock might fall into the category of a roadside settlement involved in iron making (see above). Twenty-five years ago discussions of the Dean iron industry still relied heavily on the work at Lydney Park in 1928–9 (Wheeler and Wheeler 1932). Significant excavations of the last two decades include The Chesters villa in Woolaston (Fulford and Allen 1992), *Ariconium* (Jackson forthcoming) and Worcester (Dalwood and Edwards 2004), and a wealth of information is contained in Bryan Walters' thesis on the Roman iron industry (Walters 1999; see also Walters 1992, 62–108). A major archaeological survey of Dean by Gloucestershire County Council is currently under way; the results are eagerly awaited. These publications allow us to sketch the development of the iron industry and assess how it influenced the economy and settlement pattern of Dean. In the late Iron Age and 1st century AD iron making may have been on a relatively small scale, and there is no good evidence for a military involvement at this, or indeed a later, date.[15] To judge from excavations at *Ariconium*, Monmouth and Worcester production increased in the late 1st and 2nd centuries. Pottery recovered in association with iron-smelting debris at The Moat, Newent, also dates to this period (Walters 1999, 81–4). Production continued at the major centres through the 3rd century, sometimes involving a slight shift in focus (at *Ariconium* the northern industrial area fell into disuse c.AD 230/50, while at Monmouth production moved to Overmonnow on the opposite bank of the Monnow). In this period we can detect the growth of a number of villas whose economies were based on iron making as well as agriculture. A similar story is doubtless true at the still poorly known farmsteads. The number of sites producing iron seems to increase in the 3rd century. Whether this was a cause or effect of the collapse of the Wealden industry around the middle of the century is unclear, although this is another example of the shift to the west of economic activity and prosperity in the later Roman period. Dean was probably the pre-eminent supplier of British iron between the mid 3rd and mid 4th century.[16] Production at *Ariconium* and Overmonnow went into decline in the 4th century, and production may have ceased by the middle of the century. Whether rural production continued after this is unclear.

Much iron making occurred in small rural settlements, but our knowledge of their form, chronology and economy is still very limited. Few farmsteads have been investigated, and we do not have a clear picture of the full layout and economy of a single one of these sites. In some cases continuity of settlement from the late Iron Age can be demonstrated. A series of small rectilinear ditched enclosures (c.50–70 m across) are known at The Great Woulding, 1 km to the north of the centre of *Ariconium*. Some date to the late Iron Age and were associated with iron working, while a later enclosure involved in the same activity was not abandoned until the end of the 1st century AD (Jackson forthcoming; *contra* Walters 1992, 69–72). Similar late Iron-Age and Romano-British ditched enclosures are common in Herefordshire and Wales but were not, as we have seen, a major component of rural settlement east of the Severn. At the southern end of Dean a late prehistoric and Romano-British farm was excavated in 1992 at Thornwell Farm near Chepstow (Monmouth-shire). There occupation seems to have spanned from the late Bronze Age to the later Roman period. The late Iron-Age and Romano-British settlement consisted of a series of timber roundhouses set within closes and discontinuous enclosures defined by dry-stone walls and rubble banks. The settlement practised mixed agriculture (sheep/goat outnumbered cattle), while iron smelting and smithing took place on a small scale (Hughes 1996).

Activity at other sites seems to have begun in the 2nd and 3rd centuries, although few are known in any detail. Excavation by the Dean Archaeological Group since 1993 at Rodmore Farm near St Briavels has revealed a stone-built rectangular building, 17.0 m long by 6.4 m wide, with flagged and cobble floors (Fig. 9C). Some 60 m distant lay a trapezoidal enclosure defined by lines of slag c.2 m wide, on one side infilling a ditch but elsewhere lying on natural clay. These might be foundations for cob walls. Within the enclosure there was at least one iron-smelting shaft furnace, with associated waste pits and dumps of charcoal. Pottery recovered is largely of 2nd–3rd-century date (James 1997; Blake 2003). Elsewhere such sites are poorly known. At Lydney Park the original interpretation of a 3rd-century iron-workers' settlement has not withstood re-examination in 1980–1; the rectangular dry-stone structure under the tail of the rampart may have been accommodation for people making a living from the shrine (Wheeler and Wheeler 1932, 17–18; Casey and Hoffmann 1999, 114). The potential for the discovery of new settlements in Dean has been recently demonstrated by archaeological evaluation of almost 120 ha on the eastern side of Lydney. Trial trenching there has defined two previously unrecorded sites, one seemingly not associated with iron making, the other (1 km distant) yielding plentiful iron-smelting slag associated with later 3rd- and 4th-century pottery (Wessex Archaeology 2003; Cotswold Archaeology 2004).

From the 2nd century stone-built villas are known in Dean, although they were never plentiful and were of modest proportions compared to Cotswold buildings (Fig. 9). Too little work has occurred to chart their origins accurately, although some form of continuity is suggested at Huntsham (Herefordshire), where the villa stood in close juxtaposition to a late Iron-Age enclosure (Taylor 1995). Where examined many of the villas proved to be involved with iron making, the evidence being best explored at The Chesters, Woolaston (Fulford and Allen 1992). The location of villas within Dean is also instructive as they cluster on the banks of the Severn and Wye, doubtless testimony to the importance of these rivers in the distribution of iron.[17] No major iron-making sites are known on or close to the sources of ore, and Stock Farm is the only villa situated on the outcrops (Atkinson 1986). It is thus clear that the ore was mined and then transported to secondary centres where it was smelted into blooms and bars. This has led Fulford and Allen (1992, 204) to wonder whether the temple of Nodens at Lydney Park may have exercised some form of control over the extraction and distribution of iron ore from central Dean as a means of providing revenues for the sanctuary.

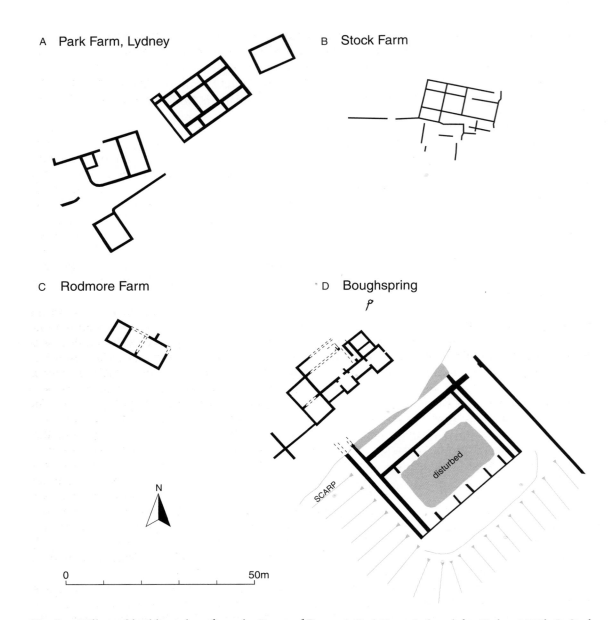

Fig. 9: *Villa and building plans from the Forest of Dean. A: Park Farm, Lydney (after Fitchett 1986); B: Stock Farm, Clearwell (from parchmarks after Atkinson 1986 and Blake 2004); C: Rodmore Farm, St Briavels (after Blake 2003); D: Boughspring, Tidenham (after Pullinger 1990 and Neal and Walker 1988).*

WETLAND RECLAMATION

One of the great achievements of the last 25 years has been the recognition that the tidal mudflats on both sides of the Severn estuary north of Bristol were deliberately reclaimed in the Roman period. This idea simply did not figure in mainstream archaeological consciousness 25 years ago, and there is not a single mention of wetland reclamation in either of the main texts on Roman Gloucestershire. Romano-British reclamation of the north Somerset Levels and the Wentlooge and Caldicot Levels of South Wales had received periodic airings in the archaeological literature of the 1960s and 70s, but little systematic attention had been given to the inner estuary north of Bristol until the work of Allen and Fulford in the 1980s.

On the Avonmouth Levels a number of farmsteads are now known. Some start in the 1st or 2nd century and were abandoned by the later 3rd century. A few others have yielded later Roman material. At Crook's Marsh snails recovered from a ditch were typical of an open dryland environment, and artefacts indicate one or more substantive buildings occupied into the late Roman period. Rippon (1997, 109) uses this evidence to suggest that some 45 km^2 of salt-marsh were reclaimed by the construction of 15 km of sea defences. Gardiner et al. (2002, 31–2) have more recently stressed the evidence for the abandonment of Romano-British field systems by the early 3rd century, presumably due to the rising groundwater levels, and suggest that there was retreat to fen-edge locations in the later Roman period. They are unconvinced that there is sufficient evidence for organised widespread reclamation in the Roman period, although their model does not adequately explain the evidence from Crook's Marsh which sits well out in the Levels. Greater understanding of this important site is a priority.

Higher up the estuary our knowledge of the process of reclamation is dependent upon the work of Allen and Fulford. While their pioneering study urgently needs to be expanded and refined, its broad conclusions are likely to be correct. In one case study they identified Romano-British sites through fieldwalking on alluvium near Elmore, thus indicating that reclamation had occurred by this date. An earthen bank with flanking ditch known locally as the Great Wall extends out across the alluvium and this impressive monument can reasonably be claimed to be a surviving example of a Romano-British flood defence (Allen and Fulford 1990a) (Fig. 10). The long-term trend in relative sea levels in the South-West has been upward, although not at a constant rate or without short-term reversions. Allen and Fulford (1990b) accordingly argue that the lower the height of a reclamation above Ordnance Datum, the earlier the process is likely to have occurred. Application of this model suggests that the pattern of reclamation was not consistent on either side of the inner estuary. On the left Cotswold bank 80% of extant reclaimed wetlands seem to date to the Romano-British period, an area of some 1400 ha. Surprisingly there is little or no evidence for reclamation at this date in the immediate hinterland of Gloucester. It is conceivable that some reclamation may have started in the late prehistoric period, and that around Whitminster is possibly of early Roman date. The bulk of reclamation, however, apparently occurred in the 3rd and 4th centuries. In contrast, on the Dean bank 80% of visible reclamations appear to be of medieval or later date.

It may be telling that no villas are known from the reclaimed areas, unless Oldbury is one. Rather, to judge from the few sites examined, the Levels were populated by farmsteads. On the Avonmouth Levels these seem to have been devoted solely to farming, probably pastoralism, while in the inner estuary the presence of smelting slag in surface scatters indicates that they were also engaged in iron making.[18] Oldbury is the only site that has been examined on any scale, and it is unfortunate that it remains unpublished in detail save for a summary account (Allen and Rippon 1997). The settlement was adjacent to a former tidal stream channel and surface debris spreads over an area of at least 20 ha. Excavation has revealed ditched paddocks and field systems, an area given over to iron making (non-ferrous metal working also took place), timber and stone structures (finds of box tile suggest at least one building of status), and a small cemetery containing

Fig. 10: Elmore: the Great Wall, a probable Romano-British flood defence bank (photograph © Cotswold Archaeology).

at least six burials. Pottery suggests that the settlement expanded in the later Roman period from a 1st- or 2nd-century core on the banks of the stream channel. Plant macrofossils testify to the processing of arable crops, and bones to the presence of cattle (Rippon 1997, 118). A remarkable dressed sandstone pillar found on the river bank has been interpreted as an architectural feature from a building, although James Russell (pers. comm.) pertinently suggests that it may have served as a boundary marker on a sea defence, perhaps in the manner of the famous Goldcliff inscription from South Wales.

The lack of 1st- or 2nd-century reclamation around the *colonia* of Gloucester, where it might be supposed that this would have been a convenient method of making land available to veterans, strongly suggests that there was little or no official involvement in the process. In this case what was the motive behind the reclamations further down the estuary, especially on the Cotswold bank? While the physical environment of the estuary made reclamation possible, the incentive presumably lay in a vibrant late Roman rural economy that generated a rising rural population and a consequent pressure on land. It is also conceivable that over-intensive farming led to soil degeneration further stimulating the desire to create new fertile pastures. The availability of capital and labour provided the means to construct ditches and sea banks several kilometres long in places such as Elmore and Longney. Allen and Fulford (1990b) suggest that the work was funded and organised from the villa estates that lay under the Cotswold scarp (such as Frocester Court) to supplement their land holdings. On the Dean bank a different process was at work. Perhaps the relative lack of reclamation there can be related to the growing importance of the iron industry and the need to maintain large expanses of coppiced woodland to provide the charcoal essential for smelting?

It is important to observe that while expanses of estuarine alluvium are not exclusive to the Severn, there is little evidence at present for reclamation of (for instance) the Thames marshes of Kent and Essex. Even in the Fens, where there was extensive local enclosure and drainage, sea walls do not occur (Rippon 2000, 136–7). There cannot have been the pressure on land to justify the investment of resources in reclamation in the South-East of England, unlike the Severn estuary. Reclamation in this form seems unique in Roman Britain, and is testimony to the economic vitality of this part of Gloucestershire in the later Roman period.[19]

Much is still to be learnt about wetland reclamation along the Severn estuary. The proposed chronology needs to be tested by further fieldwork for it is likely to be an oversimplification of a complex, piecemeal, process. The dichotomy between wet salt-marsh and reclaimed dry land is also perhaps too stark. Palaeoenvironmental analyses could determine whether sites lay on a high tidal salt-marsh or in a fresh-water reclaimed environment. The form, history and economy of sites on the alluvium are also poorly understood. Geophysical survey and sample excavation of sites in the inner estuary which were not subsequently covered by alluvium from post-Roman inundation could tell us much.

PATTERNS OF TRADE AND CONSUMPTION

It has long been recognised that the archaeological study of artefacts and materials permits the reconstruction of the dynamics of trade and patterns of consumption. Alan McWhirr outlined much of the available evidence in 1981, since when further advances have been made, especially concerning products of the Forest of Dean (Reece 1999). The difficulty in determining whether iron objects and waste slags derive from Dean ores or some other source has already been mentioned (see note 16). Greater success has been obtained with coal which is found on many Romano-British sites and can be identified as to source through chemical and/or microscopical methods (Smith 1996; 1997).[20] Coal seams are exposed in several places in the Forest and that between Coleford and English Bicknor on the eastern bank of the Wye appears to have been exploited in the Roman period. While Dean coal was transported as far as Caerwent and possibly Llantwit Major in South Wales (a distance of up to 80 km), it has mostly been found to the east. It is known from sites in the Cotswolds as far eastwards as Chedworth and possibly Roughground Farm, Lechlade. This may be close to the eastern limit of the distribution as coal from Shakenoak villa in western Oxfordshire came from the nearer Warwickshire coalfield (Smith 1996, 383–4; 1997, site no. 39). Coal was also collected from the Bristol (Coalpit Heath) coalfield and samples that are likely to derive from this source have been found at Frocester and Chedworth. Whilst Dean coal seems not to have been traded much beyond 50 km from its source, other Dean products such as Old Red Sandstone roofing slates, flagstones and quernstones travelled much further (Shaffrey 2003, who cites an unpublished 1998 doctoral thesis by Ruth Saunders). Roofing slates and quernstones occur widely in Gloucestershire and neighbouring counties, the distribution extending as far eastwards as Berkshire from the 2nd century onwards. Fulford (2003) notes the economic irrationality of this distribution as Dean products displaced more local ones, and concludes that non-market forces must have operated. He suggests State involvement, perhaps through contracts, in the market.

Detailed study of the sources of coarse pottery found in our area, combined with widespread quantification of the products of each source from a variety of sites, has been one of the major developments of the last couple of decades.[21] These painstaking studies provide us with insights into local trading networks that were simply not available 25 years ago. Work to date serves to highlight once again the heterogeneous character of Gloucestershire. Initially a simple pattern seemed evident with the Cotswold escarpment serving as a 'ceramic watershed'. The North Wiltshire industries based around Swindon were a major source of pottery and ceramic tiles to Cirencester and other Cotswold sites in the 2nd and 3rd centuries, while sites in the Vale were characterised by an abundance of Severn Valley ware. Recent work now suggests a more complex pattern, with interesting differences that cannot be explained solely by geography. For instance Uley temple has more Severn Valley ware than neighbouring Kingscote, and the same fabric is also better represented at Birdlip Quarry on top of the escarpment than might be expected if the ceramic watershed was dominant.[22] Reece (1999, 83) believes that when a distribution cannot be explained by natural boundaries some form of human, political, social or cultural constraint must be at work and in this case may assist in defining the boundary between the political spheres of Cirencester and Gloucester. There is less published data from sites in the Forest of Dean, although both Severn Valley ware and micaceous greyware occur and black-burnished ware from South-East Dorset appears more prevalent than at sites on the Cotswold bank (Allen and Fulford 1996, 245). The importance of coastal trade in the distribution of black-burnished ware is now well understood, and the quantities found in the Forest might be a reflection of cargoes riding on the back of the distribution of iron.[23] The Fosse Way was also an important route in the distribution of black-burnished ware, thus accounting for its greater abundance at Cirencester than Gloucester.

Study of the production and distribution of metalwork has been another area of fruitful research, although the patterning is on a broader geographical scale than the fine grain often detectable in pottery.[24] The distribution of one class of dress accessory can be picked out as being of more than specialist interest. The identification of a class of late 4th-century bronze belt buckle decorated with outward-facing horse-heads was first made by Hawkes and Dunning in 1961. They christened it type IB, and showed that the buckle was worn with long thin belt plates and similarly decorated strap-ends (of the so-called Tortworth type). They showed that this material was undoubtedly of British manufacture, noted that most examples came from the South-West and Midlands, and proposed that they were items of military dress (Hawkes and Dunning 1961, 27–33). This much has long been known, but recently Mark Corney and Nicholas Griffiths have been working on a new study of the distribution of type IB metalwork. The results of this important research are not as yet fully published, although Swift (2000, 2, 185) has summarised some of its key conclusions. Corney and Griffiths have considerably enhanced the original distribution map and show that over 70% of all finds are from the Cotswolds and Wessex, a distribution seemingly centred upon Cirencester. They suggest that production was limited to the province of *Britannia Prima*, of which Cirencester was probably the capital, and that there was military or official regulation of production and distribution. Whether such accoutrements were solely the preserve of soldiers is open to debate, but if so Swift (2000, 213) believes that they must be considered the dress of a provincial rather than specifically Roman army as they do not occur outside Britain. The fresh study of these outwardly familiar artefacts is providing valuable new insights on the nature of State control in the latter half of the 4th century in our area.

BURIAL AND RELIGION

There was a distinctive burial tradition in the Severn Valley in the early Roman period. Excavations in 1998 in advance of the construction of a new road in Hucclecote examined a farmstead which originated in the 1st century AD – whether just before or after the Roman invasion cannot be determined (Thomas *et al.* 2003). Amongst the paddocks and enclosures typical of this kind of site was a small cemetery containing 12 burials dating to the first half of the 2nd century. This cemetery is noteworthy in a number of respects, its association with a rural farmstead, its composition of adults over the age of 15 who were predominately female, and the 2nd-century date for the burial rite of inhumation, in some cases accompanied by grave goods. The burials can confidently be termed a cemetery as they occupy a discrete area and show evidence for organisation. Rural cemeteries are comparatively rare in Britain, if a distinction is drawn with individual or small groups of burials scattered across settlement sites, often within or close to features such as ditches or corn driers (Pearce 1999). The Hucclecote cemetery is clearly unusual. One possibility is that landowners might maintain a cemetery as a statement of their right to a property, while tenant workers and slaves would not have been buried on land to which they had no lasting attachment (Philpott and Reece 1993, 422). If that were so it raises the question of the curious demographic composition of the Hucclecote cemetery (nine females, two males, two unsexed, no children). This suggests that it was not a family group, but rather that the burial population was selected. It is conceivable that there were other cemeteries, or scattered burials, within the unexcavated parts of the settlement containing the missing males, but equally they could have been disposed of in the archaeologically invisible way that was the norm before the advent of widespread inhumation in the 3rd century.

In the late Iron Age there was a localised tradition of burial by inhumation, often crouched, in the Cotswold area. The Birdlip burial is the richest and best known example, and there are also examples in the Severn Valley (Holbrook 2003b, 65). Crouched inhumation burials occur sporadically in the urban cemeteries of Gloucester, which Heighway (1980, 57) considered to represent a survival of native tradition, whilst extended burial is more typical of later Roman practice. Some burials at Hucclecote were accompanied by grave goods (for instance one had a brooch, another a casket, a third an uncooked leg of lamb), a tradition mirrored in other burials in the Gloucester area.

At Frocester Court 60 burials have been found, of which 37 were young infants and 23 children or adults (Price 2000). There were two or three possible late Iron-Age or early Roman crouched inhumations, three mid 3rd-century cremations, the remaining inhumations dating to the late Roman period. Reece (2000) suggests that the burial of infants at Frocester was a constant custom, with adults being disposed of in a way that left no trace until the mid 3rd century when the burial custom changed and adults enter the archaeological record. That the tradition of early inhumation detected at Hucclecote extended southwards down the Severn Valley is demonstrated by work at Henbury on the north-west outskirts of Bristol. Six burials were recorded under salvage conditions in 1982 (Russell 1983), but more extensive excavation in 2004 has uncovered a further 18 crouched inhumations adjacent to an enclosure that dates to the 1st century AD. One of the burials possessed a 1st-century finger ring (Cotswold Archaeology 2005) (Fig. 11). Henbury demonstrates continuity of late Iron-Age traditions of settlement and burial, and the continued use of this burial rite helps to define the distinctiveness of the Severn Valley in the early Roman period.

Fig. 11: Henbury, Bristol: a crouched inhumation burial (photograph © Cotswold Archaeology).

Turning to the world of religion more generally, most of the advances over the last 25 years have been in the publication of earlier discoveries rather than new finds.[25] Henig's (1993) corpus of sculpture from the Cotswold region, much of it religious, now provides a firm basis for future discussion, while the publication of the excavations undertaken at Uley temple between 1977 and 1979 was an important event (Woodward and Leach 1993).[26] Special note should be made of Roger Tomlin's careful (and on-going) decipherment of the 87 lead curse tablets from Uley that cast a light onto the everyday religious thoughts of worshippers at the shrine to Mercury. Many of the curse tablets are complaints of theft addressed to a god, an epigraphic obsession peculiar to Britain (Tomlin 1993; Mattingly 2004, 19–20). At another great Gloucestershire temple, Lydney Park, excavations in 1980 and 1981 have revised Wheeler's 'late' chronology. Casey and Hoffmann (1999) now show that the complex was constructed in the second half of the 3rd century, and was in serious decline after the middle of the 4th century. Also of significance has been the reinterpretation of the famous inscription on the mosaic pavement from the temple (*RIB* 2448.3), which had been considered by Mommsen and Collingwood to be a dedication by an officer in charge of the supply depot of the fleet (Wheeler and Wheeler 1932, 102–4). Mark Hassall's (1980, 82) more plausible restoration 'To the god Mars Nodens, Titus Flavius Senilis, superintendent of the cult, from the offerings had this laid, with the assistance of Victorinus, interpreter (of dreams)' is now commonly accepted. Boon (1989, 212–15) also commented perceptively on the nature of Nodens and his cult. While this multi-faceted god had hunting and healing aspects, Boon saw him as essentially the god of the estuary who rode the Severn Bore in his horse-drawn chariot.

THE FIFTH CENTURY

The preceding pages have highlighted many areas of progress in the last 25 years, but it is pertinent to conclude with some comments on the 5th century. Despite all efforts our knowledge of this period in Gloucestershire is still very weak, and few startling discoveries have been made in recent years. Sub-Roman activity remains elusive, although the number of Roman sites that have yielded grass-tempered pottery from their uppermost levels has grown.[27] We are little further forward, however, in refining the date of this pottery, although it is surely significant that despite frequent, careful, examination of dark earth deposits in Cirencester, not a single sherd has been recovered from within the walls of the Roman town. The two sites most often quoted as examples of 'continuity' in our area are now fully published, although a third crucial one is not.

At Frocester Court the villa house was destroyed by fire. Subsequent occupation within the former courtyard and the shell of the ruined house was associated with grass-tempered pottery, and an animal bone found on the floor of a timber building yielded a calibrated radiocarbon date of 430–660 cal AD.[28] As the excavator is at pains at point out, the occupation that followed the fire need not represent immediate continuity (Price 2000, vol. 1, 111–18). At Uley there was a sequence of buildings on the site of the demolished temple to Mercury that might be Christian churches, although this interpretation is not assured (Woodward and Leach 1993, 66–79; Heighway 2003, 59). Sadly the evidence for the re-use of Crickley Hill Iron-Age hillfort in the late Roman/sub-Roman period remains unpublished in detail (Salway 1993, 330 provides a plan). There a palisaded enclosure that contained substantial timber buildings including a granary was constructed within the defences of the former hillfort. To the east stood an apparently contemporary collection of timber houses. The re-use of hillforts in the early post-Roman period can be demonstrated at a number of sites in Somerset, the implication being that these once again became 'central places' (Burrow 1981; Rahtz 2003). Crickley Hill currently stands alone in Gloucestershire, although Blaise Castle may be another example (Rahtz and Clevedon-Brown 1959).

As more sites are excavated new sequences which clearly stretch into the 5th century and beyond will doubtless be found. However the problems of dating structures and artefacts in the 5th and 6th centuries, and then defining what continuity actually means, will not be easily overcome. If we can at least make some advances in the next 25 years on this topic, that really will be progress.

ACKNOWLEDGEMENTS

I am grateful to the following people who have allowed me to make use of their discoveries in advance of full publication: Richard Osgood and Mike Martin (Badminton); Rebecca Ireland and Mike Martin (Lower Woods, Hawkesbury) and my colleagues at Cotswold Archaeology Simon Cox and Jon Hart (Henbury and Walton Cardiff). The illustrations were produced by Peter Moore and Liz Hargreaves. Richard Reece, who has been a constant source of encouragement during my 15 years in Gloucestershire, and James Russell kindly commented on an earlier version of this paper, but naturally all mistakes remain my own.

NOTES

1. Akeman Street must have been in existence earlier as further east in Oxfordshire sites such as the Alchester fortress and roadside settlement at Wilcote originated in the Claudian period (Sauer 2000, 14). It is conceivable, however, that the road may not have been metalled until the last quarter of the

1st century AD, or even later, as there are now clear indications from excavation that metalling could lag several decades behind the laying out of a route in the wake of military advance (for examples see Holbrook 1996, 121).

2. Excavations preceding the construction of the Cirencester bypass road found no trace of Roman road metalling on either the modern course of the road or an alternative alignment (Mudd *et al.* 1999, vol. 1, 142–3, 280–1).

3. The investigation was carried out as part of the Channel 4 television programme *Extreme Archaeology*. The piles appear to be part of a wooden pier *c.*9 m long and 3 m wide with cutwaters at either end first uncovered in 1911 (Walters 1971, 89; Hart 1967, 37, pl. 17). A sample from one of the piles yielded a date (Wk-14039) of 1981±37 BP which calibrates at 2 sigma (95.4% probability) using the Oxcal version 3.9 programme to 60 cal BC–90 cal AD, 100 cal AD–130 cal AD. The bridge was therefore in existence before 130 cal AD (data from www.channel4.com/history/microsites/E/extremearchaeology).

4. Limited evidence of structures and ditches was found at this site in 1984, but the scale of the settlement was not apparent (Iles and White 1985, 60). A report in *The Times* on 17 August 2004 suggests that the site was defended by a ditch and contained public buildings. Further detail is required before these statements can be accepted uncritically.

5. The evidence is briefly discussed by Russell (1997, 17). Whether the suspected settlement is *Traiectus* listed in *iter* XIV of the Antonine Itinerary is open to question as that name may be the product of an erroneous transcription (Rivet and Smith 1979, 177–8).

6. For the possible *mansio* see RCHME 1976, 40 where it is suggested that the building lay to the west of the Royal George Hotel. Cobbled surfaces and walls dating to the 4th century have been found near the hotel buildings themselves (Guy 1986; Hemingway 1991) while evaluations to the north and east have produced negative results.

7. As at Manor Farm, Kempsford (Miles 1992, 224).

8. At Portway, near Upton St Leonards, Rawes (1984) interpreted a wooden octagonal structure as a shrine, but as polygonal domestic structures existed at Birdlip Quarry there seems no reason why Portway should not be considered a farmstead.

9. Details of this site derive from the televison programme itself, the associated web site (www. channel4.com/history/timeteam/archive/2001wal.htm#stumble) and an archive report (Hirst no date).

10. Richard Reece reminds me that of all the places from which investment could have come, North Gaul and Germany are amongst the least likely. Rural land values there in the aftermath of the barbarian invasions of the AD 250s and after are likely to have been decimated, thus seriously reducing the capital available for investment.

11. Another villa has recently been found at Childswickham near Broadway in the Vale of Evesham, just over the border in Worcestershire. It too lies on a small island of sand and gravel (*Worcestershire Archaeol.* 5 (March 2002); Fitzpatrick 2002, 311).

12. Similar buildings have been excavated at Kingscote (Timby 1998, 68). The rounded corners suggest a turf or cob superstructure above dry-stone foundations.

13. A survey of Romano-British stone-built roundhouses in Oxfordshire and Northamptonshire showed the buildings to range in external diameter from 6 to *c.*16 m (Keevill and Booth 1997, 37).

14. The building is similar to one excavated at Kingscote (building VIII, phase 4.1–4.3: Timby 1998).

15. Jackson (forthcoming) is at pains to stress the late Iron-Age origins of *Ariconium* and the evidence for continuity of occupation and iron making. The supposed fortlets at The Great Woulding are now better interpreted as farmsteads. Manning's (1981, 37–8) belief that a pre-Flavian military base existed around *Ariconium* still awaits confirmation. There is no need to invoke a direct military or imperial involvement in the Dean iron industry as rights to extract and work minerals were granted by the State to private entrepreneurs (Davies 1935). The high-status, late 1st-century stone building at Blakeney is unusual, and may have been the residence of either a State official or licensee concerned with the industry (Walters 1991; 1993; Barber and Holbrook 2000, 57). The reinterpretation of the mosaic inscription from Lydney Park temple (see above) has removed the evidence sometimes advanced for the involvement of the Roman navy in the Forest.

16. Iron-making sites are known on the banks of the Severn from Cardiff to Worcester. It is a vexed question whether all these sites utilized Dean ore. Metallurgical analysis of slags from Worcester was not able to demonstrate this point conclusively, and it is conceivable that the ore derived from now totally exhausted outcrops of a narrow band of iron bearing rock that ran from Kidderminster southwards towards Gloucester (McDonnell and Swiss 2004, 376–8). Indeed these same analyses cast doubt on whether Dean ore was the source of iron represented by smelting slags at some sites on the Cotswold bank of the Severn estuary (cf. Allen and Fulford 1987). Some support for an origin outside the Forest of Dean for the ore smelted in Worcester is suggested by the observation that if Dean ore was transported up the Severn, it is surprising that no evidence of extensive iron making has come from either the suburbs of Gloucester or the settlement at Tewkesbury. Artefacts from Beckford, Worcestershire, also demonstrated an increasing use of non-Dean phosphoritic ores (Salter 2000, 56).

17. A new villa, or just possibly a temple, was discovered in 1996 at Porthcasseg on the west bank of the Wye in Monmouthshire (*Archaeol. in Wales* 36 (1996), 77–8).

18. Allen and Fulford (1987) considered, not unnaturally, that they utilized Dean ore that had been transported across the river, although see above, note 16.

19. Evidence for the economic vitality of the Gloucestershire region in the late Roman period is supported by the numismatic evidence. Ryan (1988, 88–93) has examined finds of 4th-century coins in southern Britain and has shown that, amongst rural sites, coinage of the second half of the 4th century is particularly concentrated on sites in the Gloucestershire–Oxfordshire area. Reece (1993) has demonstrated that Cirencester, Gloucester and Caerwent have an unusually high proportion of coinage of the later 4th century compared to towns further east.

20. Dearne and Branigan (1995) record coal from 20 sites in our area, some 10% of the total from the whole country. More recent finds include Bishop's Cleeve (Barber and Walker 1998, 132); Haymes (Rawes 1986, 90); Lower Woods, Hawkesbury (Ireland 2005); and Rodway Hill, Mangotsfield (Erskine 2001).

21. There have been many useful reports examining patterns of pottery supply. Cooper (1998) and Timby (1999a) chart the changing patterns of supply to Cirencester and Gloucester respectively. Timby (1999b, 353–7) usefully compares the supply to Birdlip, Kingscote, Uley and Frocester Court. Much of Timby's research in and around Gloucester is as yet unpublished. Work in the Forest has been less prevalent, but the main reports are Fulford and Allen 1992; Allen and Fulford 1996; and Timby 2000.

22. Sites on the Cotswolds to the south-west of Cirencester also drew heavily upon micaceous greywares, hardly known at Gloucester, Birdlip and Cirencester (Timby 1999b, 357). The source of the ware is unknown, although the petrography may indicate an origin in the southern Forest of Dean or around Tortworth (Allen and Fulford 1996, 262). Timby (1999b, 357) suggests production in the vicinity of Kingscote. She also believes that the micaceous greyware found in Gloucester and the Forest of Dean, although visually similar, seems to be of later (3rd- to 4th-century) date and may represent a separate industry. The only Severn Valley ware kiln known in the county is at Alkington, although others are to be expected in the vicinity of Gloucester (Timby 1996, 9).

23. An example of the maritime links of the area is provided by the Cornish stone bowl from Lydney Park temple (Casey and Hoffman 1999, 131, no. 43; Holbrook 2001, 154–5).

24. Swift (2000, 129, fig. 174) has identified a type of 4th-century strip bracelet with a clear distribution focused on the Severn estuary.

25. Newly discovered temple sites have been conjectured at High Nash, Coleford, and Littledean Hall, both in the Forest of Dean, but further details of the relevant excavations are required to confirm this interpretation (Walters 1992, 93–4 and 102–3).

26. Sculptures from Bristol and South Gloucestershire are included in Cunliffe and Fulford 1982.

27. Timby (1995) has added a number of new occurrences to the list of grass-tempered pottery produced by Alan Vince in 1984. Other later findspots include Bishop's Cleeve (Timby in Barber and Walker 1998, 124), Cheltenham (Timby 2002, 93); Chedworth (Holbrook 2004a, 66): and Turkdean (Timby in Holbrook 2004a, 59).

28. The sample is CAR–1475 which produced a date of 1490±60 BP which has been calibrated at 2 sigma (95.4% probability) using the Oxcal version 3.9 programme (Price 2000, vol. 1, 185).

BIBLIOGRAPHY

Allen, J.R.L., and Fulford, M.G., 1987. 'Romano-British settlement and industry on the wetlands of the Severn estuary', *Antiq. J.* **67**, 237–89.

Allen, J.R.L., and Fulford, M.G., 1990a. 'Romano-British and later reclamations on the Severn salt marshes in the Elmore area, Gloucestershire', *Trans. BGAS* **108**, 17–32.

Allen, J.R.L., and Fulford, M.G., 1990b. 'Romano-British wetland reclamations at Longney, Gloucestershire, and the evidence for early settlement of the inner Severn estuary', *Antiq. J.* **70**, 288–326.

Allen, J.R.L., and Fulford, M.G., 1996. 'The distribution of South-East Dorset black burnished ware category 1 pottery in South-West Britain', *Britannia* **27**, 223–81.

Allen, J.R.L., and Rippon, S.J., 1997. 'A Romano-British shaft of dressed stone and the settlement at Oldbury-on-Severn, South Gloucestershire', *Trans. BGAS* **115**, 19–27.

Allen, T.G., Darvill, T.C., Green, S., and Jones, M., 1993. *Excavations at Roughground Farm, Gloucestershire: a prehistoric and Roman landscape* (Oxford Archaeol. Unit Thames Valley Landscapes: the Cotswold Water Park **1**).

Atkinson, H.D., 1986. 'Excavations at Stock Farm, Clearwell, 1985', *New Regard of the Forest of Dean* **2**, 28–35.

Ayres, K., and Clark, K.M., 1999. 'Birdlip Quarry', in Mudd *et al.* 1999, vol. 2, 449–62.

Barber, A.J., and Walker, G.T., 1998. 'Home Farm, Bishop's Cleeve. Excavation of a Romano-British occupation site 1993–4', *Trans. BGAS* **116**, 117–39.

Barber, A.J., and Holbrook, N., 2000. 'A Roman iron-smelting site at Blakeney, Gloucestershire: excavations at Millend Lane 1997', *Trans. BGAS* **118**, 33–60.

Baker, P., Forcey, C., Jundi, S., and Witcher, R. (eds.), 1999. *TRAC 98: Proceedings of the eighth annual theoretical Roman archaeology conference, Leicester 1998* (Oxford, Oxbow).

Barker, P.P., 1998. 'A report for CAT on a geophysical survey carried out at Querns Lane, Cirencester October 1998 ' (unpublished report, Upton on Severn).

Blake, J., 2003. 'Excavations at Rodmore Farm 2003', *Dean Archaeol.* **16**, 9–17.

Blake, J., 2004. 'Resistivity survey at Stock Farm villa', *Dean Archaeol.* **17**, 14–15.

Blockley, K., 1985. *Marshfield-Ironmongers Piece; an Iron Age and Romano-British settlement in the south Cotswolds* (BAR Brit. Series **141**, Oxford).

Boon, G.C., 1989. 'A Roman sculpture rehabilitated: the Pagans Hill dog', *Britannia* **20**, 201–17.

Branigan, K., 1973. 'Gauls in Gloucestershire?', *Trans. BGAS* **92**, 82–94.

Branigan, K., and Miles, D. (eds.), 1988. *The economies of Romano-British villas* (University of Sheffield).

Brown, A.E. (ed.), 1995. *Roman small towns in eastern England and beyond* (Oxford, Oxbow).

Burrow, I., 1981. *Hillfort and hill-top settlement in Somerset in the first millennium AD* (BAR Brit. Series **91**, Oxford).

Casey, P.J., and Hoffmann, B., 1999. 'Excavations at the Roman temple in Lydney Park, Gloucestershire in 1980 and 1981', *Antiq. J.* **79**, 81–143.

Catchpole, T., 2002. 'Excavations at West Drive, Cheltenham, Gloucestershire 1997–9', *Trans. BGAS* **120**, 89–101.

Charles, B., 2004. 'Discussion', in Jennings *et al.* 2004, 132–3.

Coe, D., Jenkins, V., and Richards, J., 1991. 'Cleveland Farm, Ashton Keynes: Second interim report: Investigations May–August 1989', *Wilts. Archaeol. Natural Hist. Mag.* **84**, 40–50.

Cooper, N., 1998. 'The supply of pottery to Roman Cirencester', in Holbrook (ed.) 1998, 324–50.

Cotswold Archaeology 2004. 'Land east of Federal Mogul, Lydney, Gloucestershire: Archaeological evaluation' (unpublished report 04157, Cirencester).

Cotswold Archaeology 2005. 'Henbury Secondary School, Bristol: Post-excavation assessment and updated project design' (unpublished report 04200, Cirencester).

Cox, W., 1979. 'Exploratory section across a newly discovered Roman villa in Waltham Field (Whittington) SP00802093', *Glevensis* **13**, 47–50.

Cunliffe, B.W., and Fulford, M.G., 1982. *Great Britain, Bath and the rest of Wessex* (Corpus Signorum Imperii Romani **1.2**, Oxford University Press).

Dalwood, H., and Edwards, R., 2004. *Excavations at Deansway, Worcester, 1988–89: Romano-British small town to late medieval city* (CBA Research Rep. **139**, York).

Darvill, T., and Gerrard, C., 1994. *Cirencester town and landscape: An urban archaeological assessment* (Cirencester, Cotswold Archaeol. Trust).

Darvill, T., and Holbrook, N., 1994. 'The Cirencester area in the prehistoric and early Roman periods', in Darvill and Gerrard 1994, 47–56.

Darvill, T., and Locke, R., 1988. 'Aerial photography in the Upper Thames Valley and eastern Cotswolds in 1986', *Trans. B.GA.S.* **106**, 192–8.

Davies, O., 1935. *Roman mines in Europe* (Oxford).

Dearne, M.J., and Branigan, K., 1995. 'The use of coal in Roman Britain', *Antiq. J.* **75**, 71–105.

Ecclestone, M., Gardner, K.S., Holbrook, N., and Smith, A. (eds.), 2003. *The land of the Dobunni* (Oxford).

Erskine, J., 2001. 'Mangotsfield, Rodway Hill', in Wills (ed.) 2001, 203.

Fedière, A. (ed.), 1993. *Monde des morts, monde des vivants en Gaule rurale* (FERACF, Tours).

Fitchett, M., 1986. 'Excavations at Park Farm, Lydney (SO 625018)', *New Regard of the Forest of Dean* **2**, 24–7.

Fitzpatrick, A., 2002. 'Roman Britain in 2001. I. Sites explored, 5. The Midlands', *Britannia* **33**, 308–20.

Fowler, P.J., 1977. 'Archaeology and the M5 motorway. Gloucestershire 1969–75: A summary and assessment', *Trans. BGAS* **95**, 40–6.

Friendship-Taylor, R.M., and Friendship-Taylor, D.E., 1997. *From roundhouse to villa* (Northampton, Upper Nene Archaeol. Soc.).

Fulford, M., 2003. 'The canton of the Dobunni', in Ecclestone *et al.* (eds.) 2003, 12–23.

Fulford, M.G., and Allen, J.R.L., 1992. 'Iron-making at the Chesters villa, Woolaston, Gloucestershire: Survey and excavation 1987–91', *Britannia* **23**, 159–215.

Fulford, M., and Nicholls, E. (eds.), 1992. *Developing landscapes of Lowland Britain: The Archaeology of British gravels: A review* (Soc. Antiq. London Occasional Paper **14**, London).

Gaffney, C.F., Gater, J.A., Linford, P., Gaffney, V.L., and White, R.H., 2000. 'Large-scale systematic fluxgate gradiometery at the Roman city of Wroxeter', *Archaeol. Prospection* **7**, 81–99.

Gardiner, J., Allen, M.J., Hamilton-Dyer, S., Laidlaw, M., and Scaife, R., 2002. 'Making the most of it: late prehistoric pastoralism in the Avon Levels, Severn estuary', *Proc. Prehistoric Soc.* **68**, 1–39.

Garrod, A.P., and Heighway, C., 1984. *Garrod's Gloucester. Archaeological observations 1974–81* (Gloucester, Western Archaeol. Trust).

Gascoigne, P.E., 1969. 'Clear Cupboard villa, Farmington', *Trans. BGAS* **88**, 34–67.

Gethyn-Jones, E., 1991. 'Roman Dymock – a personal record', *Trans. BGAS* **109**, 91–8.

GSB 1999. 'Cirencester. Geophysical survey report 99/65' (unpublished report, Bradford).

Grew, F.,1980. 'Roman Britain in 1979. I. Sites explored', *Britannia* **11**, 346–402.

Guy, C.G., 1986. 'Royal George Hotel, Birdlip', *Glevensis* **20**, 48–9.

Hargreaves, G.H., 1998.'The Roman road network in the vicinity of Cirencester', in Holbrook (ed.) 1998, 11–17.

Hart, C., 1967. *Archaeology in Dean* (Gloucester).

Hart, J., Collard. M., and Holbrook, N., 2005. 'A new Roman villa near Malmesbury', *Wilts. Archaeol. Natural Hist. Mag.* **98**, 297–306.

Hassall, M.W.C., 1980. 'Altars, curses and other epigraphic evidence', in Rodwell (ed.) 1980, 79–89.

Hassall, M.W.C., 1999. 'Soldier and civilian: A debate on the bank of the Severn', in Hurst 1999, 181–5.

Hawkes, S.C., and Dunning, G.C., 1961. 'Soldiers and settlers in Britain, fourth to fifth century', *Medieval Archaeol.* **5**, 1–70.

Heighway, C.M., 1980. 'Roman cemeteries in Gloucester district', *Trans. BGAS* **98**, 57–72.

Heighway, C., 1983. *The East and North Gates of Gloucester* (Western Archaeol. Trust Excavation Monograph **4**, Bristol).

Heighway, C., 2003. 'Not angels but Anglicans – The origin of the Christian church in Gloucestershire', in Ecclestone *et al.* (eds.) 2003, 56–64.

Heighway, C., and Garrod, P., 1980. 'Excavation at Nos. 1 and 30 Westgate Street, Gloucester', *Britannia* **11**, 73–114.

Hemingway, J., 1991. 'Cowley', in Rawes (ed.) 1991b, 227.

Henig, M., 1993. *Roman sculpture from the Cotswold region* (Corpus Signorum Imperii Romani **1.7**, Oxford University Press).

Henig, M., and Booth, P., 2000. *Roman Oxfordshire* (Stroud, Alan Sutton).

Hirst, K., no date. 'An evaluation of archaeological remains at Waltham Roman villa, Gloucestershire' (Time Team unpublished report, London).

Holbrook, N., 1996. 'Roman bridges in Britain', in Johnson (ed.) 1996, 120–32.

Holbrook, N. (ed.), 1998. *Cirencester: The Roman town defences, public buildings and shops* (Cirencester Excavations **5**, Cotswold Archaeol. Trust).

Holbrook, N., 2001. 'Coastal trade around the South-West peninsula of Britain in the later Roman period: A summary of the evidence', *Proc. Devon Archaeol. Soc.* **59**, 149–58.

Holbrook, N., 2003a. 'Great Witcombe Roman villa, Gloucestershire: Field surveys of its fabric and environs, 1999–2000', *Trans. BGAS* **121**, 179–200.

Holbrook, N., 2003b. 'Discussion', in Thomas *et al.* 2003, 62–7.

Holbrook, N., 2004a. 'Turkdean Roman villa, Gloucestershire: archaeological investigations, 1997–1998', *Britannia* **35**, 39–76.

Holbrook, N., 2004b. 'Romano-British', in Walker *et al.* 2004, 87–90.

Hughes, G., 1996. *The excavation of a late prehistoric and Romano-British settlement at Thornwell Farm, Chepstow, Gwent, 1992* (BAR Brit. Series **244**, Oxford).

Hurst, H.R., 1985. *Kingsholm* (Gloucester Archaeol. Rep. **1**, Cambridge).

Hurst, H.R., 1986. *Gloucester, the Roman and later defences* (Gloucester Archaeol. Rep. **2**, Cambridge).

Hurst, H.R., 1988. 'Gloucester (*Glevum*)', in Webster 1988, 48–73.

Hurst, H.R. (ed.), 1999. *The coloniae of Roman Britain: new studies and a review* (J. Roman Archaeol. Suppl. Series **36**, Portsmouth USA).

Iles, R., and White, H., 1985. 'Avon archaeology 1984', *Bristol Avon Archaeol.* **4**, 56–65.

Ireland, R., 2005. 'Archaeology in Lower Woods, South Gloucestershire', *Archaeol. South-West* **14**, 29–32.

Jackson, R., forthcoming. 'Ariconium, Herefordshire: an assessment and synthesis of the evidence' (CBA Research Rep.).

James, T., 1997. 'Rodmore Farm excavations 1996', *Dean Archaeol.* **10**, 4–7.

Jennings, D., Muir, J., Palmer, S., and Smith, A., 2004. *Thornhill Farm, Fairford, Gloucestershire: An Iron Age and Roman pastoral site in the Upper Thames Valley* (Oxford Archaeol. Thames Valley Landscapes Monograph **23**).

Johnson, P. (ed.), 1996. *Architecture in Roman Britain* (CBA Research Rep. **94**, York).

King, A., 1988. 'Villas and animal bones', in Branigan and Miles (eds.) 1988, 51–9.

Keevill, G., and Booth, P., 1997. 'Settlement, sequence and structure: Romano-British stone-built roundhouses at Redlands Farm, Stanwick (Northants) and Alchester (Oxon)', in Friendship-Taylor and Friendship-Taylor 1997, 19–45.

Lambrick, G.H., 1992. 'The development of late prehistoric and Roman farming on the Thames gravels', in Fulford and Nicholls (eds.) 1992, 78–105.

Manning, W.H., 1981. *Report on the excavations at Usk 1965–1976. The fortress excavations 1968–1971* (Cardiff, University of Wales Press).

Margary, I.V., 1967. *Roman roads in Britain* (2nd edn.: London, John Baker).

Mattingly, D., 2004. 'Being Roman: Expressing identity in a provincial setting', *J. Roman Archaeol.* **17**, 5–25.

McDonnell, G., and Swiss, A., 2004. 'Ironworking residues', in Dalwood and Edwards 2004, 368–78.

McWhirr, A., 1981. *Roman Gloucestershire* (Gloucester, Alan Sutton and Gloucestershire County Library).

McWhirr, A., Viner, L., and Wells, C., 1982. *Romano-British cemeteries at Cirencester* (Cirencester Excavations **2**, Cirencester Excavation Committee).

McWhirr, A., 1986. *Houses in Roman Cirencester* (Cirencester Excavations **3**, Cirencester Excavation Committee).

Miles, D., 1984. 'Romano-British settlement in the Gloucestershire Thames Valley', in Saville (ed.) 1984, 191–211.

Miles, D., 1992. 'Kempsford Manor Farm', in Rawes (ed.) 1992, 224.

Miles, D., Palmer, S., Smith, A., and Edgeley Long, G., forthcoming. 'Iron Age and Roman settlement in the Upper Thames Valley: excavations at Claydon Pike and other sites within the Cotswold Water Park' (Oxford Archaeol. Thames Valley Landscapes Monograph).

Millett, M., 1995. 'Strategies for Roman small towns', in Brown (ed.) 1995, 29–37.

Mudd, A., Williams, R.J., and Lupton, A., 1999. *Excavations alongside Roman Ermin Street, Gloucestershire and Wiltshire: The Archaeology of the A419/A417 Swindon to Gloucester Road Scheme* (Oxford Archaeol. Unit: 2 volumes).

Neal, D.S., and Walker, B., 1988. 'A mosaic from Boughspring Roman villa, Tidenham, Gloucestershire', *Britannia* **19**, 191–7.

Noddle, B., 1985. 'The animal bones', in Webster *et al.* 1985, 82–97.

Osgood, R., 2004. 'The Roman mosaic at Badminton', *Archaeol. South-West* **12**, 28–9.

Parker, A.J., 1978. 'Stoke Gifford Roman site', *Bristol Archaeol. Research Group Bull.* **6.6**, 152–5

Parry, A., 1998. 'Mangotsfield, Hamlet XIII', in Rawes and Wills (eds.) 1998, 206.

Parry, C., 1999. 'Iron-Age, Romano-British and medieval occupation at Bishop's Cleeve, Gloucestershire: Excavations at Gilder's Paddock 1989 and 1990–1', *Trans. BGAS* **117**, 89–118.

Pearce, J., 1999. 'The dispersed dead: preliminary observations on burial and settlement space in rural Roman Britain', in Barker *et al.* (eds.) 1999, 151–62.

Pelling, R., 1999. 'Charred and waterlogged plant remains', in Mudd *et al.* 1999, vol. 2, 469–94.

Philpott, R., and Reece, R., 1993. 'Sépultures rurales en Bretagne romaine', in Fedière (ed.) 1993, 417–23.

Pine, J., and Preston, S., 2004. *Iron Age and Roman settlement and landscape at Totterdown Lane, Horcott near Fairford, Gloucestershire* (Thames Valley Archaeol. Services Monograph **6**, Reading).

Price, E.G., 2000. *Frocester. A Romano-British settlement, its antecedents and successors* (Stonehouse, Gloucester and District Archaeol. Research Group: 2 volumes).

Price, E.G., and Price, A.J., 1992. 'A section across a Roman road?', *Glevensis* **26**, 22–7.

Pullinger, J., 1990. 'Excavation report: The Roman villa at Boughspring with a new assessment', *Dean Archaeol.* **3**, 12–25.

Rahtz, P., 2003. 'The Dobunnic area in post-Roman times', in Ecclestone *et al.* (eds.) 2003, 24–31.

Rahtz, P., and Clevedon-Brown, J., 1959. 'Blaise Castle Hill Bristol 1957', *Proc. University Bristol Spelaeological Soc.* **8.3**, 147–71.

Rankov, N.B., 1982. 'Roman Britian in 1981. I. Sites explored', *Britannia* **13**, 328–95.

Rawes, B., 1981. 'The Romano-British site at Brockworth, Gloucestershire', *Britannia* **12**, 45–77.

Rawes, B., 1984. 'The Romano-British site on the Portway, near Gloucester', *Trans. BGAS* **102**, 23–72.

Rawes, B., 1986. 'The Romano-British settlement at Haymes, Cleeve Hill, near Cheltenham', *Trans. BGAS* **104**, 61–93.

Rawes, B., 1991a. 'A prehistoric and Romano-British settlement at Vineyards Farm, Charlton Kings, Gloucestershire', *Trans. BGAS* **109**, 25–89.

Rawes, B. (ed.), 1991b. 'Archaeol. Review 1990', *Trans. BGAS* **109**, 223–38.

Rawes, B. (ed.), 1992. 'Archaeol. Review 1991', *Trans. BGAS* **110**, 213–30.

Rawes, J., and Wills, J. (eds.), 1998. 'Archaeol. Review 1997', *Trans. BGAS* **116**, 191–212.

RCHME 1976. *Iron Age and Romano-British monuments in the Gloucestershire Cotswolds* (Royal Com. on Hist. Monuments England, HMSO).

Reece, R., 1993. 'British sites and their Roman coins', *Antiquity* **67**, 863–9.

Reece, R., 1999. 'Colonia in context: *Glevum* and *civitas Dobunnorum*', in Hurst 1999, 73–85.

Reece, R., 2000. 'The Frocester cemetery and rural burial in Roman Britain', in Price 2000, vol. 2, 205.

Reece, R., 2003. 'The siting of Roman *Corinium*', *Britannia* **34**, 276–80.

Reilly, K., 2004. 'The animal bones', in Pine and Preston 2004, 76–81.

RIB. R.G. Collingwood and R.P. Wright, *The Roman inscriptions of Britain* I (1965), II (1990–1995).

Rippon, S.J., 1997. *The Severn estuary. Landscape evolution and wetland reclamation* (Leicester University Press).

Rippon. S.J., 2000. *The transformation of coastal wetlands. Exploitation and management of marshland landscapes in North-West Europe during the Roman and medieval periods* (Oxford University Press).

Rivet, A.L.F., and Smith, C., 1979. *The place names of Roman Britain* (London, Batsford).

Rodwell, W.J. (ed.), 1980. *Temples, churches and religion in Roman Britain* (BAR Brit. Series **77**, Oxford).

Russell, J., 1983. 'Romano-British burials at Henbury Comprehensive School, Bristol. A preliminary report', *Bristol Avon Archaeol.* **2**, 21–4.

Russell, J., 1989. 'Excavations at Baileys Court Farm, Stoke Gifford, 1990 (a preliminary note)', *Bristol Avon Archaeol.* **8**, 53–4.

Russell, J., 1997. 'Two earthworks in the parish of Bitton', *Bristol Avon Archaeol.* **14**, 17–19.

Russett, V., 1993. 'A Romano-British, medieval and industrial site at Stonehill, Hanham, near Bristol', *Bristol Avon Archaeol.* **11**, 2–17.

Ryan, N.S., 1988. *Fourth-century coin finds from Roman Britain* (BAR Brit. Series **183**, Oxford).

Salter, C., 2000. 'The metal-working debris', in Barber and Holbrook 2000, 54–7.

Salway, P., 1993. *The Oxford illustrated history of Roman Britain* (Oxford University Press).

Samuel, J., 2000. 'Watching brief excavations at Moat Farm, Pucklechurch, South Gloucestershire, 2000', *Bristol Avon Archaeol.* **17**, 1–16.

Samuel, J., 2003. 'Excavations at 'Matford', Bradley Stoke Way, Bradley Stoke, South Gloucestershire, 2001', *Bristol Avon Archaeol.* **18**, 41–100.

Sauer, E., 2000. 'Alchester, a Claudian 'vexillation fortress' near the western boundary of the Cattuvellauni: New light on the Roman invasion of Britain', *Archaeol. J.* **157**, 1–78.

Saunders, R.L., 1998. 'The use of Old Red Sandstone in Roman Britain. A petrographical and archaeological study' (University of Reading Ph.D. thesis).

Saville, A. (ed.), 1984. *Archaeology in Gloucestershire* (Cheltenham Art Gallery and Museums and the BGAS).

Shaffrey, R., 2003. 'The rotary querns from the Society of Antiquaries' excavations at Silchester', *Britannia* **34**, 143–74.

Smith, A.H.V., 1996. 'Provenance of coals from Roman sites in UK counties bordering the river Severn and its estuary and including Wiltshire', *J. Archaeol. Sci.* **23**, 373–89.

Smith, A.H.V., 1997. 'Provenance of coals from Roman sites in England and Wales', *Britannia* **28**, 297–324.

Smith, J.T., 1983. 'Flight of capital or flight of fancy?', *Oxford J. Archaeol.* **2.2**, 239–46.

Smith, J.T., 1985. 'Barnsley Park villa: its interpretation and implications', *Oxford J. Archaeol.* **4.3**, 341–51.

Smith, J.T., 1987. 'The social structure of a Roman villa: Marshfield-Ironmongers Piece', *Oxford J. Archaeol.* **6.2**, 243–55.

Standing, I.J., 1988. 'Dating the Dean Road, Forest of Dean', *New Regard of the Forest of Dean* **4**, 35–43.

Stiles, R., Cornwell, J., and Taylor, E., 1992. 'Romano-British industry at Stonehill, Hanham, Bristol. A preliminary report', *Bristol Ind. Archaeol. Soc. J.* **24**, 7–22.

Swift, E., 2000. *Regionality in dress accessories in the late Roman West* (Monographies Instrumentum **11**, Montagnac).

Taylor, E., 1995. 'Report on the excavation of Huntsham Romano-British villa and Iron Age enclosure 1959–1970', *Trans. Woolhope Naturalist Field Club* **48.2**, 224–86.

Thomas, A., Holbrook, N., and Bateman, C., 2003. *Late prehistoric and Romano-British burial and settlement at Hucclecote, Gloucestershire* (Bristol and Gloucestershire Archaeol. Rep. **2**, Cirencester, Cotswold Archaeol.).

Timby, J.R., 1995. 'Pottery in the Cotswolds AD 400–1000', in Wilkinson *et al.* 1995, 64–70.

Timby, J.R., 1996. ' "Time's wheel runs backwards or stops; potter and clay endure": A Tribute to Bernard Rawes's contribution to Roman pottery studies', *Trans. BGAS* **114**, 7–10.

Timby, J.R., 1998. *Excavations at Kingscote and Wycomb, Gloucestershire* (Cirencester, Cotswold Archaeol. Trust).

Timby, J.R.,1999a. 'Pottery supply to Gloucester *colonia*', in Hurst (ed.) 1999, 37–44.

Timby, J.R., 1999b. 'Roman pottery from Birdlip Quarry, Cowley', in Mudd *et al.* 1999, vol. 2, 339–65.

Timby, J.R., 2000. 'The pottery', in Barber and Holbrook 2000, 41–6.

Timby, J.R., 2002. 'The pottery', in Catchpole 2002, 92–6.

Tomlin, R.S.O., 1993. 'The inscribed lead tablets: an interim report', in Woodward and Leach 1993, 113–30.

Trow, S., and James, S., 1988. 'Ditches villa, North Cerney: an example of locational conservatism in the early Roman Cotswolds', in Branigan and Miles (eds.) 1988, 83–7.

Wacher, J.S., and McWhirr, A.D., 1982. *Early Roman occupation at Cirencester* (Cirencester Excavations **1**, Cirencester Excavation Committee).

Walker, G.T., Thomas, A., and Bateman, C., 2004. 'Bronze-Age and Romano-British sites south-east of Tewkesbury: evaluations and excavations 1991–7', *Trans. BGAS* **122**, 29–94.

Walters, B., 1992. *The archaeology and history of ancient Dean and the Wye Valley* (Cheltenham).

Walters, B., 1999. *The Forest of Dean iron industry 1st–4th centuries AD* (Dean Archaeol. Group Occasional Paper 4, Lydney).

Walters, I., 1971. 'Shakespeare or Bacon?', *Severn Wye Review* **1.4**, 85–90.

Walters, M., 1991. 'Rescue excavations on the Roman occupation site at Legg House, Blakeney', *Dean Archaeol.* **3**, 40–4.

Walters, M., 1993. 'Excavations on the Roman occupation site at Legg House, Blakeney (1991/2)', *Dean Archaeol.* **5**, 4–12.

Webster, G., and Smith, L., 1982. 'The excavation of a Romano-British rural settlement at Barnsley Park: part II', *Trans. BGAS* **100**, 65–189.

Webster, G., Fowler, P., Noddle, B., and Smith, L., 1985. 'The excavation of a Romano-British rural establishment at Barnsley Park, Gloucestershire, 1961–1979: part III', *Trans. BGAS* **103**, 73–100.

Webster, G. (ed.), 1988. *Fortress into city: the consolidation of Roman Britain first century AD* (London, Batsford).

Wessex Archaeology 2003. 'Land east of Lydney, Gloucestershire: Archaeological evaluation' (unpublished report 53846.01, Salisbury).

Wheeler, R.E.M., and Wheeler, T.V., 1932. *Report on the excavation of the Prehistoric, Roman and Post-Roman site in Lydney Park, Gloucestershire* (Reports Research Committee Soc. Antiq. London 9, Oxford).

White, R.H., and Gaffney, V.L., 2003. 'Resolving the paradox: the work of the Wroxeter hinterland project', in Wilson (ed.) 2003, 221–32.

Wild, J.P., 2002. 'The textile industries of Roman Britain', *Britannia* **33**, 1–42.

Wilkinson, K., Prosser, L., and Holbrook, N., 1995. 'The origin, development, decline and persistence of Cotswold settlement, c. AD 250–1200' (Cotswold Archaeol. Trust unpublished report, Cirencester).

Wills, J. (ed.), 2001. 'Archaeol. Review 2000', *Trans. BGAS* **119**, 185–210.

Wills, J. (ed.), 2003. 'Archaeol. Review 2002', *Trans. BGAS* **121**, 267–89.

Wilson, D., 1996. 'Excavation of a Romano-British villa at Wortley Gloucestershire, twelfth interim report' (unpublished report, Wotton-under-Edge).

Wilson, P. (ed.), 2003. *The archaeology of Roman towns* (Oxford, Oxbow).

Woodward, A., and Leach, P., 1993. *The Uley shrines. Excavation of a ritual complex on West Hill, Uley, Gloucestershire: 1977–9* (English Heritage Archaeol. Rep. **17**, London).

Yorkston, D.E., and Piper, P.J., 1994/5. 'Excavation of a Romano-British site at Stonehill, Hanham', *Bristol Avon Archaeol.* **12**, 5–17.

Young, A., 2003. 'Wickwar', in Wills (ed.) 2003, 287.

The Early Medieval Period

Andrew Reynolds

Of the periods considered in this volume after the Mesolithic, the early middle ages remains the most difficult to identify in the archaeological record. Archaeology has revealed a few new but significant sites since the 1980s and the practice of metal detecting continues to augment the material record. While the data remain limited, scholarly thinking in early medieval archaeology has changed significantly since the mid to late 1980s and what is offered here is a narrative that reviews the significance of certain previously known sites, but which explores additional themes such as the chronology and nature of territorial organisation. This paper, therefore, is not intended as a comprehensive guide to the early medieval archaeology of the county, but rather as an attempt to place aspects of the known evidence in relation to new discoveries and in the light of current thinking at a national level. The archaeology of towns and recent work on ecclesiastical sites is only cursorily mentioned. The abbreviation ASC in the text refers to the Anglo-Saxon Chronicle (Swanton 2000).

INTRODUCTION

Gloucestershire was border country during the early middle ages. During the 6th and early 7th centuries, the county lay at the western limit of cemeteries containing burials with Germanic associations, a feature shared with Wiltshire to the south and the Marcher counties, Hereford and Worcester, to the north. Quite what this distribution represents is considered further below. When documents allow a clearer picture of the emergence of the 11th-century shire, it is as the southern part of the province of the Hwicce, a people first mentioned in the second quarter of the 7th century and politically defunct one hundred years later having lost any aspects of semi-independence that they may have possessed to the Mercians (Stenton 1971, 45). By the Norman Conquest, Gloucestershire had emerged as a county and had been divided into the small parcels of land that substantially equate to the modern parishes of the shire, bearing in mind the many minor, and sometimes major, boundary alterations of the 19th and 20th centuries. Similarly, the names and locations of Gloucestershire's villages and towns were largely established during the early medieval period. In summary, close scrutiny of the archaeology and history of the post-Roman centuries provides a case study in the development of a 'complex society' following 'systems collapse' during the late Roman period. Those with an interest in the modern settlement geography of the county will find its 'foundations', and, in many respects, much of its 'superstructure', in the late Anglo-Saxon period if not earlier and this aspect, among others, underscores the fundamental importance of Anglo-Saxon archaeology to our understanding of the modern environment.

The topography of the county is key to understanding both its role in territorial terms and the nature of settlement and its attendant agricultural regimes. Three contrasting bands of terrain define the Gloucestershire landscape; the eastern side of a wooded plain dissected by the river Wye in the west; a central band of marl and sandstone in the Severn Vale and the Cotswolds formed of limestone to the east. This geology provides an excellent range of building materials reflected today in the field boundaries and vernacular buildings of the region.

THE POST-ROMAN VACUUM

With two major centres in the form of Gloucester and Cirencester, and with excellent communications by road and water, the region was heavily Romanized by the late 1st century AD. Dense concentrations of villas surrounded the urban centres with many others in fully rural areas acting as central places for agricultural estates. What happened to the Roman way of life? Were late Roman power structures immediately succeeded by independent local autocracies? What impact did the transition have on levels of population and the exploitation of the countryside? These are key questions about which much has been written.

From Villa Estate to Parish: Questions of Continuity

A model for the end of villa life *within* the post-Roman period is provided by the Frocester excavations, recently published in two impressive volumes (Price 2000). I have highlighted 'within' because the post-Roman sequence is apparently of short duration, yet such evidence is often used to argue for 'continuity' into the middle ages, usually without any attempt to define what is actually meant by the term and to what social phenomena it applies.

Before examining the Frocester evidence and the conclusions drawn by its excavators, a few comments on the 'continuity' issue might usefully be made. Low-level occupation of a villa, perhaps for a generation is intrinsically interesting, yet demonstrates nothing with regard to the emergence of either the medieval parish or medieval village. Many considerations have been made of the villa to village process, yet the notion that the former is somehow the direct ancestor of the latter is surely a tired one, lacking in conclusive evidence and confounded by the fact that we do not know the extent of a single villa estate and that next to nothing is known of the interrelationships between villas and lower-status farms in tenurial terms. While there are treatises relating to the management of Roman estates, these relate to the core of the empire in the earlier part of our period and may bear little or no relation to north-western Europe, especially in the late Roman period. Indeed, one of the principal failures of much scholarship relating to the continuity question has been to view the Roman period as somehow monolithic, unchanging and predictable.

Neil Faulkner (2000, 139) has highlighted the late Roman period as one of 'manorialisation' of the countryside, perhaps comparable to the later 9th, 10th and 11th centuries in England. The lesson to be learned is that substantial changes occurred to the way that the countryside was exploited *throughout* the Roman and succeeding periods. The likelihood that individual land units survived such apparently comprehensive agricultural and settlement reorganisations is extremely slim, especially when we do not know what we are trying to show continuity of in terms of the extent of a given villa's lands. A line of enquiry worth pursuing is to map Roman settlements in relation to parish boundaries. A cursory view of Hampshire and Wiltshire, for example, reveals a series of sites on parish or county boundaries, and in many cases the boundary in question actually runs through a Roman complex rather than around it (Reynolds 2005a, 175), illustrating beyond doubt a tenurial reconfiguration between the late Roman period and the early middle ages.

Indeed, a glance at a map of Gloucestershire parishes at once betrays a complex sequence of development with estates of widely varying morphology and extent. Perhaps a few units are fortuitous Roman survivals where issues of severe topography might naturally delineate a local territory, but the majority are likely to be much later, probably of the middle to late Anglo-Saxon period. A recent study of the Avebury area in north Wiltshire displays a closely comparable view of long-term fission and fragmentation of local land units within the Anglo-Saxon period highlighting the co-existence of small independent farms alongside fully developed village communities (ibid. 178–80). The finding of a few sherds of chaff-tempered pottery in a villa excavation does not represent evidence for continuity as is so-often claimed; here Frocester is different in the range and quality of the evidence for post-Roman occupation which includes buildings as well as material culture.

Excavations at Frocester since 1961 have revealed clear evidence for post-Roman activity in close proximity to the villa there, although the villa building itself seems to have been only partially occupied (Fig. 1). On the basis of coin losses, the latest Roman period occupation appears to have taken place in Rooms 5 and 12, which lay at opposing ends of the villa, about the end of the 4th century (Boon 2000, 17). Fires had been lit directly on the concrete floors of Rooms 2 and 4, whilst the tessellated pavement in Room 6, the main corridor of the villa fronting the courtyard, had been poorly repaired. Post-Roman occupation of the villa itself is limited to Room 6, which was entered via a doorway midway along the corridor leading off the courtyard (Fig. 2). Domestic occupation evidenced by a hearth and sherds of chaff-tempered pottery characterised the north-eastern half of the corridor, and was apparently partitioned off by posts from the rest of the corridor. Access to this space was perhaps through a doorway on the north-western side of the room. The south-western end of the corridor arguably functioned as a byre, its floor make-up badly holed and worn, suggestive of animal activity. A series of evenly spaced postholes along the inside of the north-western wall is interpreted as supports for a wooden manger, although the absence of

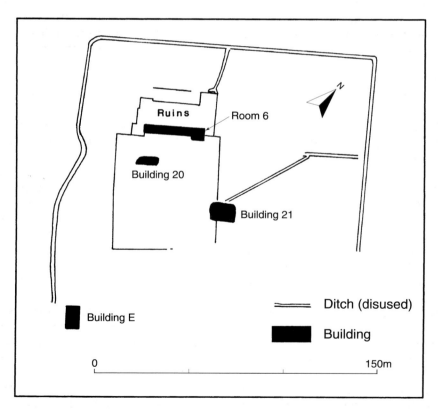

Fig. 1: Frocester Court: plan of the early medieval settlement (after Price 2000).

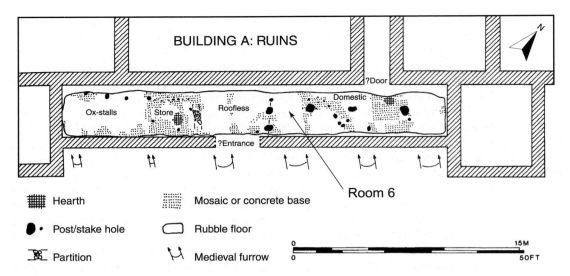

BUILDING A: RUINS

?Door

Domestic

Ox-stalls   Store   Roofless

Room 6

?Entrance

▦ Hearth	▦ Mosaic or concrete base
●· Post/stake hole	⬭ Rubble floor
⬚ Partition	⊔ Medieval furrow

0   15 M
0   50 FT

Fig. 2: Frocester Court: plan of early medieval occupation in Room 6 of the villa (after Price 2000).

a drain is notable given the proximity to apparently domestic occupation. Price (2000, vol. 1, 116) suggests that the tri-partite division of Room 6 is comparable to a medieval longhouse, yet the early dating of the occupation finds few parallels in this respect.

Structural evidence beyond the confines of the villa is represented by three timber buildings (Fig. 1). The earliest is judged to be Building E, some 100 m south-west of the villa. The structure itself is poorly defined, although surviving postholes indicate a building of three bays set on a platform of stone, clay and gravel, probably derived from the ruins of the villa (ibid. 113–14, fig. 6.4). The ephemeral and potentially aisled nature of this building invites comparison with the timber halls at Poundbury, Dorset, which are of a similar date (Sparey Green 1991, 72, fig. 52). The short lengths of stone footings recorded along the line of both the long walls suggest piecemeal underpinning of rotted uprights, a technique otherwise uncommon in the early middle ages before the 8th century. An ox skull placed on the earlier of two floors is potentially a ritual deposit, perhaps associated with the refurbishment of the structure (see also Building 21 below). The two phases of flooring and potential underpinning indicate a relatively long period of occupation, although dating rests on a radiocarbon determination from the ox skull that centres on about AD 590 (CAR 1475), recalibrated by Neil Holbrook (this volume) giving a date at 95% probability of 430–660 cal AD.

Building 20 lay within the courtyard 20 m to the south of the villa but parallel with the corridor (Room 6). As with Building E, structure 20 lay on a platform of re-used building material from the villa and was formed of a timber superstructure. The building had been erected over a large double pit and its floor had been replaced three times due to compaction of the pits' fills and the need to level up the floor. Much chaff-tempered pottery was found in the vicinity of the building and it appears to have remained in use for an extended period (Price 2000, vol. 1, 117).

Building 21 lay c.40 m to the south-east of the north-eastern corner of the villa. Very little chaff-tempered pottery was found in association and it is perhaps the latest in the sequence as it utilises a combination of continuous wall trenches, a feature of 7th-century and later buildings elsewhere, and postholes. The paucity of ceramics, however, may have more to say about the non-domestic, but undetermined, function of the building rather than having a chronological implication. As with Building 20, floor deposits survived slumped into an underlying feature, in this case a timber-lined tank. The presence of ox skulls in the north-west wall trench provides another indication of post-Roman ritual activity, perhaps a foundation deposit.

Dating is a key problem given the nature of the evidence (chaff-tempered pottery), while it is not clear whether the post-Roman occupation represents genuine continuity (ibid. 121) in terms of either the familial or kin group living there either side of the end of Roman rule, or whether the site was re-occupied following a period of abandonment. It does appear, however, that the activity in Room 6 represent a re-occupation of the villa, following a substantial fire. It can be seen therefore, that even when evidence is of a relatively high quality, determining issues of functional or tenurial continuity remain insurmountable in the absence of more accurate dating. Even though chaff-tempered pottery is now accepted as having a much longer date range (5th–early 10th centuries) than previously thought (5th–8th centuries), the recent finding of an annular bead in an occupation deposit immediately outside the north-eastern entrance to Building A and a possible fragment of a glass claw beaker in Room 6 indicate 6th-century activity (ibid. 118; Stamper 2003, 370), as does the radiocarbon determination from Building E. Otherwise, dating either the start or end of the post-Roman phase is fraught with problems, but there is no reason to see the post-Roman activity as anything other than broadly contemporary and representative of a single farmstead of later 6th-century date. The social position of the site is of interest and the presence of glassware in Building A and the finding of a pendant of copper alloy and iron, probably cut from a hanging bowl, in Building E indicate access to high-status objects. One of a group of four post-Roman inhumations from Frocester Court, as yet unpublished, has been radiocarbon dated to at least a century later than the 6th-century occupation (E. Price pers. comm. 2005). Whether these burials relate to the villa occupation or to a widely attested phenomenon of burial at ruined villas in the 7th and 8th centuries remains to be determined.

The nature of the Frocester evidence prompts consideration of a frequently stated misconception about post-Roman/early medieval activity in England; that the use of ground-level sill-beamed buildings and a highly perishable material culture has rendered much of the remains of the period invisible to the archaeologist. While chaff-tempered pottery is rather more fragile than Roman ceramic, this aspect is frequently over-emphasised and used to exaggerate the importance of a small handful of sherds from Roman occupation sites or from fieldwalking surveys. Frocester shows that despite extensive ploughing from the 11th century or earlier, both ceramics in quantity and buildings of immediate post-Roman date survived to be recorded. Beyond Gloucestershire, especially in central and eastern England, where settlement evidence for the early middle ages is better attested, both buildings and objects survive in a non-ephemeral way. It is now time to stop using single sherds of chaff-tempered pottery as markers of continuity and to recognise that early medieval settlement activity has simply not yet been recovered to an extent which is desirable to the archaeologist in western Britain. Indeed, even thirty years ago the known settlement archaeology of the period nationally was scarce to the extent that what might be termed the 'perishable/sill beam argument' was applied on a national scale. We now know rather better and sites like Frocester and Lechlade (see below) demonstrate that early medieval settlements in the region leave unambiguous remains comparable to the better known sites of the period elsewhere in the country.

Sub-Roman Central Places

The re-fortification of hillforts in the sub-Roman period in south-western Britain, Wales and Scotland has long been known. This can be observed in our region at Crickley Hill, but the range of defensible sites apparently re-used by British élites in the region is rather broader with the apparent refortification, or at least re-occupation, of selected Roman towns. Here, the significance of the ASC *s.a.* 577 ought not to be understated. The relevant entry records:

> Here Cuthwine and Ceawlin fought against the Britons and they killed three kings, Coinmagil and Candidan and Farinmagil, in the place which is called Dyrham; and took three cities: Gloucester and Cirencester and Bath.

While caution must be exercised with the reliability of Chronicle entries prior to about AD 850, the AD 577 entry records the (entirely plausible) names of the vanquished British rulers and their arguably most significant power centres. The nature of military conduct in the early part of our period has been much debated (Hawkes 1989). The laws of the West Saxon King Ine were produced AD 688 × 693 and denote an army as a force upwards of thirty men (Attenborough 1925). These early battles no doubt involved small bands of higher-ranking warriors rather than wholesale military conquest by massed forces. Certainly, the Gloucestershire cemetery evidence supports the former view (see below, Germanic Influence). Former Roman centres apparently served as central places well into the 6th century, within a settlement framework of re-used hillforts. The nature of 5th- and 6th-century occupation within the amphitheatre at Cirencester suggests a withdrawal from the town itself, but a continued recognition of the nodal perception of the place in the wider region. Parallels can be drawn, for example with Chester, where sub-Roman activity has been identified within the amphitheatre there (S. Semple pers. comm. 2005). Settlement within the defensible amphitheatre at Cirencester is akin to the re-use of hillforts with timber buildings present, as at Crickley Hill, where occupation of early 5th-century date is attested, although the evidence is problematic with regard to dating. Following re-metalling on two subsequent occasions (dated by coins of 383–7 and 388–402 respectively) the arena entrance was narrowed by a roughly built masonry blocking, further enhanced by a fence or palisade to the north (Holbrook 1998, 174). Following abandonment of the entrance a turf-line developed which contained sherds of chaff-tempered pottery. Part of a substantial timber building at least 7m wide lay within the amphitheatre, although it is poorly dated; a single sherd of 12th century or later pottery from one of the postholes could easily be intrusive given that the features were shallow and just below the modern turfline.

Excavations at Kingsholm about 1 km north of Gloucester city centre revealed important evidence for both sub-Roman and late Anglo-Saxon activity. We will return to the later evidence for a palace, but the late 4th-century cemetery there was also the burial place of a high-ranking individual in the first half of the 5th century (Hurst 1975) (Fig. 3). Excavations on the site of the extramural cemetery revealed a masonry structure originally furnished with a floor of flagstones (thoroughly robbed) set into *opus signinum*. Although only the northern part of the building was exposed, a burial (B1) of an unusual character was found cut through the concrete floor close to the north wall of what is interpreted as a mausoleum re-used for the burial of a high-ranking person (ibid. 274). A male aged 25–35 was buried supine in a well-cut grave within the 'mausoleum'. He was furnished with a fine, and apparently brand-new, silver belt buckle found at the waist, an iron knife with silver fittings by the thigh and one miniature buckle and two

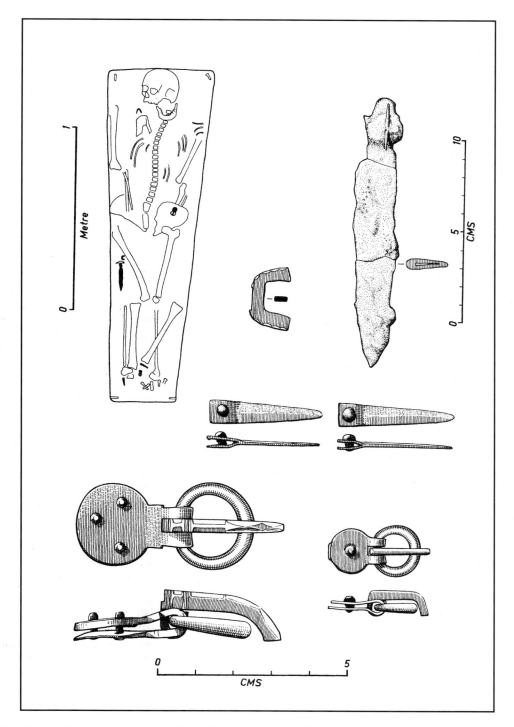

Fig. 3: The early 5th-century burial from Kingsholm, near Gloucester (after Brown 1975).

strap-ends, all of silver, at the feet. A number of iron nails around the edge of the grave indicate a coffined burial. David Brown's assessment of the finds noted parallels in bronze for the belt buckle of later 4th- and 5th-century date, and Frankish and Anglo-Saxon comparisons for the strap-ends of early 5th-century date (Brown 1975, 290–4). The geographical context of the burial, its earlier dating and hybrid nature led Brown to conclude a date of burial between AD 400 and 440 (ibid. 294). This individual is the best candidate so far for the burial of a sub-Roman, or 'British' person of high rank in the region. The objects from the grave, however, find closer parallels with material of 4th- and 5th-century date from south-eastern Europe and south Russia and an eastern Germanic, perhaps Gothic origin has also been proposed for burial B1 from Kingsholm (Hills and Hurst 1989).

While re-used hillforts and other 'market' sites in south-western Britain and south Wales can be identified by the presence of imported Mediterranean amphorae and other wares, there is not a single sherd of so-called Bii amphora, of 5th- to 6th-century date, known from the county. Heighway (1987, 12) has noted that this paucity is surprising if Gloucester was engaged with the trading networks of the late Celtic west; perhaps it was not. Gloucestershire lies on the eastern fringe of the distribution of Mediterranean imported pottery, while the nature of 'British' re-occupation of earlier defensible sites is closely comparable with the style of settlement within the core late Celtic regions. Given that the majority of imported material is derived from coastal sites, the prime importance of sea lanes is clear. Perhaps it was simply not possible for a ship to take a cargo up the Severn as far as Gloucester, owing to militarised control of the route much further down the estuary, perhaps at the point where the fortified aristocratic centres of Dinas Powys and Cadbury Congresbury lay on either side of the river Severn 70 km down river (see Thomas 1990, 13, fig. 4). Overall, little imported material travelled beyond Cornwall and Devon. The presence of a series of 7th- and 8th-century coins in the region reflects trade and exchange with polities to the east by that time (see below).

Before moving on to consider the nature of contact with peoples expressing a Germanic cultural affinity, we must briefly consider West Wansdyke and its role in determining the southern limit of what became the kingdom of the Hwicce and the later county of Gloucestershire. While the earthwork itself lies within the historic county of Somerset, just to the south of Bath and the natural barrier of the Bristol Avon, it requires brief consideration as many have argued for a sub-Roman date in the absence of secure dating evidence (Gardner 1998). There can be little doubt that the earthwork relates to an attempt to define a west–east frontier zone in the early middle ages. A major objection to a sub-Roman date, however, is the nature and scale of military organisation necessary to institute what can only be described as a monumental public work. It is surely contemporary with East Wansdyke, the two sections connected spatially by the *Aquae Sulis–Cunetio* Roman road, an aspect given even more credence by the fact that nationally the two sections of dyke are the only earthworks so named; a detailed consideration of the argument for a 7th- or 8th-century date is not possible here but is provided elsewhere (Reynolds and Langlands in press). While it could be argued that the dyke pre-dates the foundation of the monastery at Bath by Osric, sub-king of the Hwicce, in *c*.675 and that it reflects (from a southern perspective) Hwiccian, ultimately Mercian, control of Bath, viewed on the macro-scale the Wansdyke frontier is much better placed logistically and politically in the period of territorial contest and consolidation between the middle Anglo-Saxon kingdoms of Wessex and Mercia during the 7th, 8th and earlier 9th centuries. It is possible, indeed likely, that sections of both East and West Wansdyke incorporate earlier earthworks, but the named earthworks belong to a later period as a unified frontier.

GERMANIC INFLUENCE

What does the western limit of 'Anglo-Saxon' burials represent? More recently, scholars have considered a much wider range of explanations for the nature and patterning of cemeteries containing burials interred with material culture of a Germanic character. As recently as the 1980s it was common to view such cemeteries as a tide line mapping the influx of Germanic migrants from southern and eastern England westwards. Bearing in mind recent thinking playing down the scale of population movement during the 5th and 6th centuries (see, for example, Lucy 2000), there seems little doubt that eastern England in particular, experienced substantial social augmentation *via* folk movement from both southern Scandinavia and northern Germany from the second quarter of the 5th century, but particularly during the 6th century.

The fact that mainly 6th- and 7th-century burials are found at the western limit of cemetery distribution has led previous commentators to suggest that 'Anglo-Saxons' penetrated the western regions significantly later than their initial settlements in eastern England, although there are burials of likely late 5th-century date at Fairford and Hampnett (Meaney 1964, 90–1), both of which lay just on the Gloucestershire side of the boundary with Oxfordshire, and at Lechlade close to the meeting point of the county boundaries of Gloucestershire, Oxfordshire and Wiltshire. The distribution of cemeteries is shown in Figure 4. Settlement of early 5th-century date is well known in the Upper Thames Valley (Hawkes 1986), while a recent metal-detector find of a spearhead of Swanton's Type L, dated AD 450–550, at Quedgeley (if the findspot is to be believed at all) indicates the potential for early Germanic settlement immediately south of Gloucester (Portable Antiquities Scheme (PAS) website 9 May 2005). Overall, it remains that a persistent Germanic presence in the region dates from the mid 6th century, by which time Cirencester, in contrast to Gloucester, was ringed by cemeteries (Heighway 1996, 32) in a manner identified at many other former Roman towns in Britain, including Dorchester-on-Thames, Oxfordshire, and Salisbury, Wiltshire, to give examples in adjacent counties.

It has been noted that the Cirencester cemeteries pre-date the documented 'Anglo-Saxon' take-over of AD 577 (ibid.) and this provides a clear case study in the ability of archaeology to question the written record. While scholars have long doubted the authenticity of the earlier entries, particularly those relating to the 5th and 6th centuries (Yorke 1993), there is a clear contrast between the two sources and it remains to determine which is the more accurate. A certain degree of leeway, however, should be allowed with regard to dating of both forms of evidence. The 9th-century compilers of the Chronicle may have been drawing on an inaccurate source, or have re-shuffled events according their own designs, which, coupled with the latest possible margins of the burial evidence, still allows for the basic outline chronology to be accepted; but only just.

Given the comparative paucity of early medieval Germanic-style material from Gloucestershire, as in the counties to the north and south, it is perhaps more helpful to explore a wider range of social interpretations for the presence of these 'others' in a 'British' province that survived until the later 7th century. Clearly, material culture of a Germanic nature was travelling well beyond the periphery of the 'Anglo-Saxon' provinces of eastern England. Metalwork from Hod Hill in Dorset represents the south-western limit of such material, while diagnostic finds are known from the re-fortified Iron-Age hillfort at Dinas Powys in south Wales and, indeed, from Scotland (Eagles and Mortimer 1993; Alcock 1963; Proudfoot and Aliaga-Kelly 1996).

Through an examination of place-name and burial evidence, Bruce Eagles has presented a plausible case for the survival of a British territory based on Bath until *c*.675 (Eagles 2003), although how this relates to the AD 577 take over recorded in the ASC is unclear unless the British

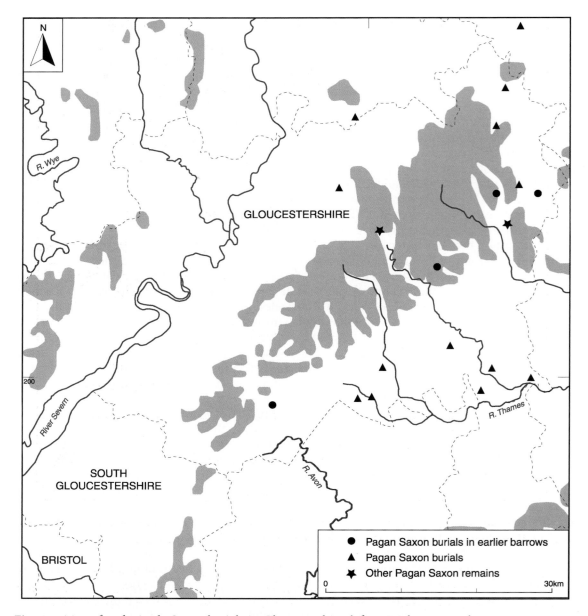

Fig. 4: Map of early Anglo-Saxon burials in Gloucestershire (after Heighway 1987).

regained control of Bath shortly after the West Saxons' Cuthwine and Ceawlin's campaign in the west. What is clear is that, well before the end of the 7th century, much of the territory initially conquered by the (then Thames Valley based) West Saxons was in Mercian hands by AD 628 when the ASC records a settlement between the West Saxon King Cynegils and his son Cwichelm and the pagan Mercian King Penda at Cirencester in favour of the latter (Stenton 1971, 29, 45). Eagles

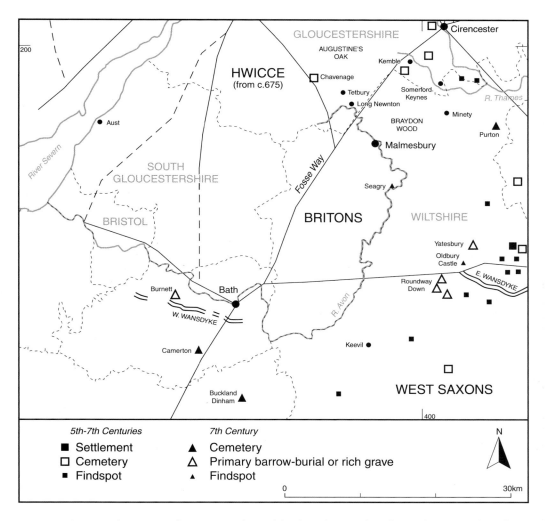

Fig. 5:   Map showing the extent of continuing 'British' political control in the Bath area in the 7th century and the distribution of Germanic influenced material culture (after Eagles 2003).

'British' zone extends westwards into north Somerset and eastwards into north-west Wiltshire as far as Keevil (Fig. 5). When viewed on the regional scale it appears as though the Forest of Braydon in north-west Wiltshire described a boundary zone, as opposed to a fixed line, separating western Britain from the 'Anglo-Saxon' regions to the east. Selwood Forest to the south played exactly such a role from an early period. The ASC, for example, refers to Aldhelm, as the bishop 'west of the woods' *s.a.* 709, and the forest was still significant in the 9th century when in AD 893 King Alfred, in countering the Danes, summoned men 'both west of Selwood and east': Asser, King Alfred's biographer, referred to Selwood as *Coit Maur*, 'great wood' (Stevenson 1904).

Another extensive territory, perhaps that of the *Canningas*, has been proposed adjoining the Bath unit to the east that arguably predates the East Wansdyke, and seeks to emphasise the rapidly changing nature of social definition in the region during the 5th, 6th and 7th centuries (Reynolds 2005a). The liminal nature of the southern boundary of the Hwicce is demonstrated no more clearly than by the meeting of the bishops of the nearest British kingdom (to Kent) and the evangelising St Augustine in AD 603, near Malmesbury, at *Augustinaes Ac...in confinio Huicciorum et Occidentalium Saxonum* (Augustine's Oak, which lies on the border between the Hwiccas and the West Saxons), perhaps at Kemble, in the early 7th century (Eagles 2003). It should be remembered that the frontier is so described in Bede's Ecclesiastical History and thus strictly relates to the border in his day, the early 8th century, rather than in Augustine's.

The most significant burial sites to be published in recent years with regard to the earliest part of our period are the cemeteries at Bishop's Cleeve and at Butler's Field, Lechlade. While other cemeteries and individual burials, sometime in re-used barrows, are known, there is not the space to review them all in detail; in any case this has already been done by Carolyn Heighway (1984, 230, fig. 1; 1987, 22). A few further comments can be made on the nature of the burial evidence in the county before we examine Bishop's Cleeve and Lechlade as case studies, which had not been published at the time of Heighway's review.

As Heighway has noted, early Anglo-Saxon burials in Gloucestershire fall into two major types; groups of inhumations and occasionally cremations as at Burn Ground, Hampnett, and at Lechlade, and secondary burials in barrows. Clearly, this basic division describes contrasting social and political circumstances of each type. The overall distribution of early Anglo-Saxon burials is of interest. There is a series of burial sites roughly following the county boundary with Wiltshire, on an east to west axis, and then turning north following the boundary with Oxfordshire (Fig. 4). While these burials do not all have an explicit relationship with the precise line of the boundary, their distribution does suggest that there was recognition at least of some kind of political frontier reflecting the line of the southern and eastern boundary of the later shire.

The three, or perhaps four, separate cemeteries at Kemble, of 6th- to 7th-century date, for example, lay close to what became the county boundary between Gloucestershire and Wiltshire, in a region that appears to have been contested from the early post-Roman period to the late 19th century when the parish was finally lost to Gloucestershire (Heighway 1996, 34). Indeed, the name Kemble itself might be derived from the Welsh *cyfel* meaning border or boundary (Smith 1964, 75–6). The secondary burials in barrows are part of a broader regional phenomenon of often isolated, frequently high-status burials at prominent points in the landscape, often in frontier territory. Such burials are best read as highly visible markers of a new social and political dominance in the regions where they occur. In Wiltshire, the high-status later 7th-century barrow burials at Roundway Down and Swallowcliffe Down occupy prominent sites on the western limit of Germanic-style burials, while in Buckinghamshire and Oxfordshire a case has been made that certain isolated burials of this kind, albeit far wealthier than the Gloucestershire examples, represent overlordship from afar, from the kingdom of Kent in the case of the outstanding Taplow (Buckinghamshire) burial (Dickinson 1974).

In Gloucestershire, small numbers of inhumations rather than single burials characterise the barrow burials, although it is possible to view them in a similar light as so-called 'sentinel' interments, marking political domination as opposed to wholesale conquest and population influx. Indeed, the finds from Chavenage, and perhaps Oddington, are potentially indicative of such politically motivated burials (Meaney 1964, 60, 62).

At Bishop's Cleeve to the north of Cheltenham, 26 graves, 19 unfurnished, were excavated by Kenneth Brown in 1969, although only recently published (Holbrook 2000). The cemetery provides a complete contrast to the barrow burials and is the only one of Germanic character located in the (Gloucestershire) Severn Vale (Heighway 1996, 32). The cemetery lay *c.*1200 m WSW from the medieval parish church. Graves with datable finds indicate a period of use of about 50 years, probably the second half of the 6th century (Fig. 6). Holbrook, however, notes the presence of worn and re-used objects among the grave finds (see for example Grave 13), while the presence of such a high proportion of unaccompanied burials suggests either that the burial sequence runs into the 7th century, when grave finds become less common nationally, or that a sector of the community was treated somewhat differently at death. Although the grave finds are relatively poor, the fact that the entire burial ground appears to have been excavated is highly significant for, in the absence of contemporary settlement evidence, it provides the only means of assessing the structure of early medieval rural communities in the region. Holbrook quite rightly suggests that a single family used the cemetery, noting the possibility of a community of about 13 burying over a 50-year period or of 9 over a 75-year period. It is essential that cemetery evidence is used to reconstruct living communities in the early Anglo-Saxon period, particularly in western England, and the Bishop's Cleeve community appears to reflect a small settlement, perhaps part of a dispersed settlement pattern, which contrasts with the more sizeable contemporary communities of eastern and northern England.

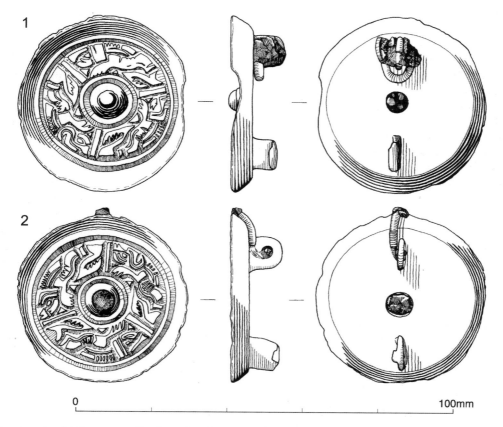

Fig. 6:   *A pair of 6th-century disc brooches from Burial 5 at the Bishop's Cleeve cemetery (after Holbrook 2000).*

Significantly, the Bishop's Cleeve burials indicate a settled community living on the western margin of people who expressed their identity in a Germanic style: they must have been a distinctive group, although the relatively poor grave finds and the absence of swords and, particularly, shields is hardly suggestive of pioneer settlement in a context of Germanic territorial advance. A single prone burial, an unaccompanied female aged 45+ in Grave 6, is an example of the typical superstitious Germanic response to the dead widespread throughout early Anglo-Saxon England. The rite was relatively commonly enacted in the context of otherwise 'normal' community cemeteries. The unsexed individual in Grave 25 was buried only with a large perforated canine tooth found at the neck; a common form of protective amulet during the period. Ultimately, it is difficult to establish whether the Bishop's Cleeve community represents distinctive incomers, a mixture of indigenous people and immigrants, or whether a few members of a family of local origin had adopted a few aspects of eastern English fashion. The lack of beads and weapons other than spears is notable in a 6th-century context, and one wonders whether the latter scenario outlined above might apply in this particular case.

The Butler's Field early Anglo-Saxon cemetery in Lechlade is one of the most important such sites to have been excavated in southern England in recent years. An unexpected discovery, the cemetery yielded a total of 219 inhumation burials and 26 cremation burials with a chronological range from the mid or late 5th to the 7th century. Although not all the cemetery was uncovered, sufficient was exposed to gain a good impression of its full extent and to place it very much within the milieu of cemetery organisation of the Upper Thames Valley. While there is not the space nor desire to review the cemetery in full, a few observations on its social implications are required to emphasise both the differences and similarities with the other Gloucestershire cemeteries.

As the plan of the cemetery shows, the southern extent and parts of the eastern and western limits of the cemetery were established (Fig. 7). A ditch of Roman date perhaps delimited the cemetery area to the south-east, although the mass of burials stops before this feature with only one inhumation, Grave (175), a possible female aged 34–40 buried without finds, located 10 m south-east of the main group and less than 1 m from the boundary. The cemetery also contains several other graves whose contents invite interpretations of a superstitious nature. The most remarkable interment is surely that of the young woman in Grave 18, who had been interred with a wide and unusual range of objects before the grave was packed tightly with stones. She was furnished with a startling array of grave goods including 'normal' objects such as brooches and finger-rings, but also with hundreds of beads, a beaver tooth pendant, probably an amulet, iron, bronze and ivory rings and a fragment of a Roman limestone altar (Boyle *et al.* 1998, 61–3, 196–200).

The grave itself lies on the southern periphery of the cemetery, as do two other unusual burials, Graves 15 and 74, a 40-year old female buried prone with a knife and a few potsherds and a juvenile, also buried prone, with a potsherd and an animal bone. Another juvenile, furnished only with an animal bone, was buried prone in Grave 126 at the western edge of the cemetery. These burials reflect the wider development of liminal burial among early Anglo-Saxon communities nationally from the 6th century (Reynolds forthcoming). While the prone burials perhaps represent those who had transgressed acceptable patterns of social behaviour, the woman in Grave 18 arguably reflects the special role played by certain women in early Anglo-Saxon society. The stone packing of her grave might reflect a desire to prevent her corpse from rising out of the grave and is perhaps a further indication of her perceived supernatural role in life. Presumably, the death of a clever or 'cunning' woman within a given community required a successor who might operate without fear of her predecessor's return.

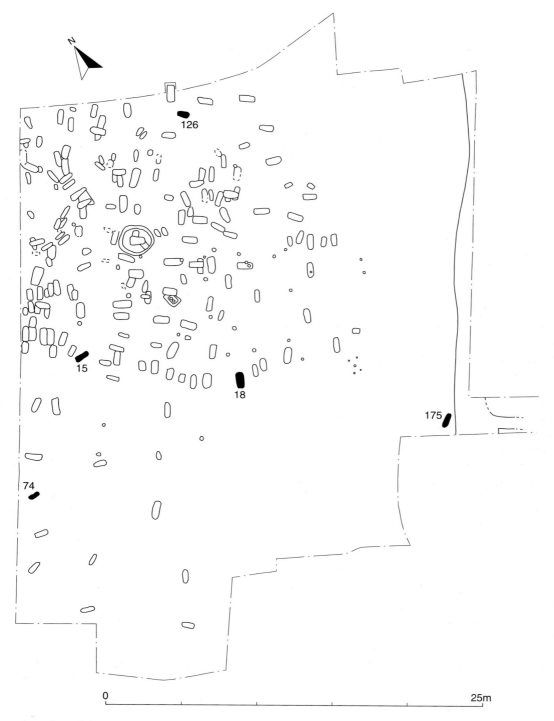

Fig. 7: Plan of the Butler's Field cemetery, Lechlade, showing the location of the 'cunning' woman's grave (18) and other unusual burials (after Boyle et al. 1998).

THE EMERGENCE OF THE HWICCE AND SUPRA-LOCAL TERRITORIAL ORGANISATION

During the 7th century, the consolidation of the middle Saxon kingdoms involved the fusion of a large number of territories or districts, many of which were likely consigned to memory well before others were recorded in the earliest reliable documentary sources. More recently, historians and archaeologists have considered the physical reconstruction of the limits of these early units, although there is little consensus with regard to their role in wider politics and social relations. The so-called 'Tribal Hidage', a tribute list of probable late 7th-century date, records groupings of lands of widely varying extent using an archaic terminology suggestive of the pre-state nature of post-Roman territorial organisation during the 5th to 7th centuries. The extraordinary variation in territorial extent expressed in the list can be read as an assessment of lands made during a period of considerable flux and where the expansionist nature of the larger kingdoms is self evident and where the smallest territories are fortuitously recorded close to the end of their autonomy as 'micro-kingdoms', to use Stephen Bassett's (1989) terminology (although see below).

The rulers of the Hwicce were arguably imposed upon the region by the Mercians, while Gelling has argued for a strong Anglian influence in the place-names of the sub-kingdom (Stenton 1971, 45, n. 1; Gelling 1953, xix). British place-names are also prominent and thus the Hwicce are probably best seen as a people of largely British stock with Anglian elements ruled by a Mercian (ultimately Anglian) dynasty (Hooke 1985, 8–9). By the late 7th century, the emerging kingdom of Wessex lay to the south, while the kingdom of the Hwicce became entirely subsumed within the Mercian kingdom by the late 770s.

Wales lay to the west, but separated from the Hwicce by a territory of comparable size occupied by a group known as the Magonsætan, although, as with the kingdom of the Hwicce, its origins are obscure and contentious (Pretty 1989). Views of early medieval social relationships (effectively concerning conflict and its resolution) across the Mercian/Welsh border can be had as early as the mid 7th century from Welsh poetic sources, and from the 10th-century document known as the Ordinance of the *Dunsæte*; a short legal code seeking to regulate interaction between the English and the Welsh either side of a river, probably the Wye (Kirby 1977; Noble 1983). On the basis of the distribution of 'sæte' (meaning 'dwellers') place-names, Margaret Gelling has highlighted the existence of a series of early administrative units of varying size running south from Oswestry to Hereford (Gelling 1989, 199–201), arguing that they represent administrative reorganisation of the Offa's Dyke frontier in the late 8th century. The kingdom of the Hwicce breaks this naming pattern, although it picks up again south of the Bristol Channel in the names of Somerset and Dorset. Sæte-type names show a strong western distribution marking the cultural ecotone between western and eastern England.

That the kingdom of the Hwicce does not follow the same naming pattern as other major territories in the west is a matter of interest and may reflect an as yet unidentified difference in its origins compared to its neighbours. The Domesday Survey for Gloucestershire betrays a complex web of landholding with several hundreds comprising widely scattered estates of wealthy landowners (Darby and Terrett 1971, 4–5). Accordingly, the hundredal pattern at Domesday is difficult to reconstruct accurately and the origins of individual units require close attention to local circumstances rather than a search for an overarching model. The Gloucestershire Domesday also partly reveals differences between Welsh and English rural economies and social organisation, further emphasising the distinctiveness of the county.

Relationships between western Mercia and Wessex were as often strained as they were along the frontier further to the east. Warfare, apparently between Briton and Saxon, in the 6th century is followed in the 8th and 9th centuries by a series of battles fought between Mercian and West Saxon armies attempting to dominate the frontier between their two kingdoms. The Gloucestershire region, therefore, occupied a unique geographical role within Mercia bordering both Wessex and Wales.

It is equally possible, of course, that the smaller units of 'Bassett' type originated as sub-divisions of larger territories. Such a model should also incorporate the possibility that the origins of hundredal geography, considered by many to be 10th-century, is of the same period as that of the 'micro-kingdoms'. Such a view accords with what is known of the longevity of the Hwicce in the consciousness of early medieval populations. Their identity survived in a vestigial form until after the Norman Conquest. As late as the early 11th century, for example, a charter of Æthelred II records *Leofwine Wicciarum Prouinciarum dux* (Leofwine, ealdorman or regional official of the province of the Hwicce) (Hooke 1985, 20; Sawyer 1968, no. 891).

Indeed, the hundredal pattern in Gloucestershire compares rather better with the ragged and apparently archaic patterns of the Wessex counties than with the Mercian heartlands whose shires and hundreds bear the morphological character of a widespread act of administrative re-organisation; in this case either following the recovery of the Danelaw by Edward the Elder, Æthelflaed and, later, Athelstan or, more likely, later still during the late 10th or early 11th centuries. The county of Gloucestershire itself came into being in the later 10th or 11th centuries, although the first mention of the shire in a contemporary account is in the ASC entry for 1016, which records the movement of King Cnut and his army there after a major battle at Ashingdon, Essex. In the same Chronicle entry the Magonsætan are referred to as fleeing the battlefield with the infamous Ealdorman (and traitor) Eadric Streona, whose political allegiance wavered between the invading Norwegian King Cnut and the English King Edmund. While the broader politics are beyond the remit of this paper, reference to the Magonsætan provides a further illustration of the potential for territorial entities of a much earlier political age to survive in a meaningful way late into the period.

Viking activity in the region is relatively well attested in the ASC where it had rather less success than in other parts of the country and accordingly much less direct impact upon local administrative arrangements compared to regions to the north and east. In AD 845 a Danish raiding fleet was heavily defeated at the mouth of the River Parrett near Bridgwater by the ealdormen of Dorset and Somerset and the men of their respective shires. In 877 King Alfred forced a truce upon them at Exeter, including taking 'prime' hostages, despite the fact that they had holed up in the walled town before he could catch them on their way from Swanage where a storm had destroyed 120 of their ships. Later in the same year, however, the Vikings 'built booths in the streets' of Gloucester according to a translation into Latin of a version of the ASC by Æthelweard, ealdorman of Wessex to the west of Selwood in the late 10th century (Stenton 1971, 461). Heighway (1984, 236) sees this visit to Gloucester as relatively peaceful, a situation perhaps reflected in the ASC entry for 880 when the Vikings 'settled' at Cirencester over the winter of AD 879–80. Although archaeological remains of these visits remain elusive, Heighway's view is supported by the lack of reference to ravaging and burning that characterise so many of the other Chronicle references to the Vikings visiting English towns. Archaeological evidence for Anglo-Scandinavian interaction is, as elsewhere, extremely limited. A finger-ring formed of six platted strands of flattened copper-alloy wire is known from Longford parish (PAS website), north of Gloucester, and is of a type considered to be of Anglo-Scandinavian origin dated to between the 9th and 11th centuries at York and the 11th century at Waterford in southern Ireland (Mainman and Rogers 2000, 2584–6; Tait 1976, 264).

Della Hooke has considered the evidence for Gloucestershire's origins as four groupings of hundreds, based on Bath/Bristol, Cirencester, Gloucester and Winchcombe (Hooke 1985, 76). Although the hundredal groupings in question, such as the seven hundreds of Cirencester, or that of Grumbald's Ash in the south-west of the county, are not mentioned explicitly until after the Norman Conquest, Hooke notes that three of the central places for these territories, Bath, Cirencester and Gloucester, are those mentioned in the ASC entry for 577 as regional power centres of 'tyrant' kings (ibid. 77). The Domesday county, then, is perhaps the product of the amalgamation of a series of districts with seemingly 6th-century, or perhaps earlier, origins based on Roman central places, although the nature of Roman activity at Winchcombe, while evidenced, remains unclear (Saville 1985, 136). The importance of Winchcombe, which was occupied from at least the 8th century and possessed a minster or mother church and a royal manor by AD 821, is self evident in the role that it played as the central place of the short-lived Winchcombeshire which became defunct as an autonomous administrative territory in 1016 or 1017 (Heighway 1987, 152; Whybra 1990, 124).

SETTLEMENT AND LANDSCAPE AT THE LOCAL LEVEL: THE MIDDLE AND LATE ANGLO-SAXON PERIODS

What of the mass of small estates that formed the basis for the parish system crystallised during the 12th century? Debate surrounding the origins of parish units has, oddly, a rather separate historiography from that of the larger units. Whether Domesday manors equate to Roman villa estates remains at the heart of the issue. While many have accepted continuity from the Roman period, I have argued above that continuity of agricultural estates from the Roman period is likely to be absolutely minimal and, indeed, is exemplified by the more extensively excavated sites, notably Frocester (Price 2000).

Reconstructing the territorial units of early medieval communities before the later Anglo-Saxon period is extremely problematic and much rests upon how we understand the nature of territorial organisation before the emergence of the small units that became medieval parishes. The most plausible model is that during the period of kingdom formation in the 6th and 7th centuries, large estates, probably equating broadly to Domesday hundreds (at least in Gloucestershire and the Wessex regions) and with royal manors and minster churches at their centres, administered a multiplicity of farming communities within their bounds. Such units are known variously as 'federative', 'multiple' or 'complex' estates, although their constitution and even their existence is much debated. Parishes (*parochiae*) of minster churches are often observed to be coterminous with the extent of Domesday hundreds (Pitt 1999) and this factor, in combination with place-name evidence suggestive of specialised farms dependant on a central place, supports the general idea. Presumably, when smaller estates were carved out of these large units, as is documented by the granting of small parcels of land by the later Anglo-Saxon kings to private individuals increasingly from the later 9th century, the limits of many of these parcels must surely have followed existing divisions between the components of multiple estates. Support for this view is possibly forthcoming in the location of the 8th-century Lypiatt Cross upon the later medieval boundary between the parishes of Stroud and Bisley, the latter probably a minster church of early origin. Richard Bryant's careful consideration of the location of the cross leaves open the possibility that it stands at its original location, perhaps demarcating Bisley minster's religious jurisdiction (although this is likely to have included the whole of the Domesday hundred of Bisley (Hare 1990, 47)) or sanctuary (Bryant 1990, 46). Ultimately, we cannot trace the origin of the medieval parish back beyond this point.

Archaeological evidence for the 7th to 9th centuries is scarce, as it is elsewhere in western Britain. Early medieval coin finds from the 7th century up to the Norman Conquest are scarce when compared to those from surrounding counties to the east. A search of the Early Medieval Corpus of Coin Finds/Sylloge of Coins in the British Isles website (in May 2005) reveals seven coins of 7th- to mid 8th-century date, including an early shilling, dated AD 620–40, mint and moneyer unknown, from Eastleach Turville just west of Cirencester. The remainder of the early coins fall between AD 710 and 760 and reflect the national pattern of intense coin issue and use during the first half of the 8th century compared to earlier and immediately later (Gannon 2002). Mercian coinage is represented by three issues falling between AD 792 and 821, while a single coin of Edward the Elder (AD 899–924), precedes three coins of Æthelred II, two of Cnut (1016–35) and Harold Harefoot (1035–40) respectively, and three coins of Edward the Confessor (1042–66).

Settlement Sites

The development of rural settlement is particularly hard to characterise during the middle Anglo-Saxon period. It is becoming increasingly clear that the 7th to 9th centuries were characterised by a great complexity of settlement types, although extensively excavated sites are found mainly in central and eastern England. Archaeological evidence for the nature of occupation sites in Gloucestershire is more widespread and of a better quality than that available for study 25 years ago, although much more is required to assess just how representative of the wider scene the known sites are. In our consideration of early medieval settlement, we shall primarily consider Lechlade as an example of persistent occupation throughout our period, and Lower Slaughter, Kingsholm and Tewkesbury as examples of middle and late Anglo-Saxon higher-status settlement.

At Lechlade, excavations at Kent Place and Sherborne House have revealed the first evidence of early Anglo-Saxon settlement since the excavation of a single Sunken Featured Building (SFB) near Bourton-on-the-Water (Dunning 1932). Most importantly, the Lechlade site is probably that whose dead were buried at the Butler's Field cemetery 300 m to the north. The Sherborne House excavation revealed 0.5 ha of a settlement that evidently extended further in all directions and at least 100 m to the south-east as demonstrated by the contemporary evidence from the much smaller intervention at Kent Place (Bateman *et al.* 2003; Kenyon and Collard 2004). The larger excavation established a settlement plan that comprised a series of parallel linear ditches (J, K, L and M) of ephemeral character and an unusual sub-circular enclosure measuring some 25 m across with a rectilinear 'annex' on its north-eastern side (Fig. 8). Six SFBs and parts of three timber 'halls' were recorded along with a limited but nevertheless significant range of objects and other materials. Ditches J and K were only 10 m apart and surely represent a trackway, while ditches K, L and M were 30 m apart and seemingly constitute regular plots within the settlement space; both aspects are common features of middle and late Anglo-Saxon rural settlement elsewhere (Reynolds 2003). Ditch K was cut by several smaller ditches, also of Anglo-Saxon date, while one of these latter ditches was cut by SFB 8 showing that the settlement space was subject to periodic comprehensive re-organisation: similarly, SFB 1 cut ditch M. The three post-built structures are reminiscent of certain of the Frocester buildings, considered above, in terms of their apparently irregular post settings and the possibility that these structures were aisled bears serious consideration. This latter aspect is significant as aisled buildings are common in the Roman period, but not in the early middle ages until the late 9th century when they appear as one of the defining characteristics of late Anglo-Saxon manorial accommodation (ibid.). Similarities with the Poundbury early medieval halls are again apparent and perhaps there are hints here of a western 'style'. A substantial patch of clay and limestone make-up within post-built Building 13 is again reminiscent of those within the Frocester buildings.

The dating of the Sherborne House settlement is problematic. Ceramics were of three fabric types (chaff-tempered, calcareous and sandy) and compare well with those from the Butler's Field cemetery (Timby 2003, 60). While the presence of stamps of 6th-century or perhaps later date on certain of the vessels demonstrates occupation at this time, the overall longevity of the sequence remains difficult to determine. Given the provisos outlined above with regard to the potential date range of organic-tempered wares, we might perhaps allow for a later date of abandonment than the 8th century as suggested by the excavators, especially in view of the degree to which the morphology of the site was altered during our period. An angle-backed knife from Ditch T is dated to between the 5th and mid 8th centuries on the basis of Evison's (1987) Dover Buckland cemetery typology, but her scheme does not take account of the fact that several of her types, including angle-backed knives, continue into the late Anglo-Saxon period (Ottaway 1992). The excavations at Kent Place revealed further occupation, including two ditches (D and F) of 6th- to 9th-century date, that appear to be followed by later alignments of property boundaries up to the present day (Kenyon and Collard 2004, 124). The Lechlade settlement is important in that it illustrates the development of structured and bounded settlement space potentially earlier than elsewhere in England. Although boundary features appear from the late 6th century at sites like Poundbury, they are in the main 7th- and 8th-century features on sites elsewhere (Reynolds 2003).

Minor features from excavations at other sites include a semi-circular arc of postholes $c.4$ m in diameter, dated to between the 7th and 9th centuries on the basis of a single sherd of pottery, from the Stoke Road site at Bishop's Cleeve (Enright and Watts 2002, 11). A further individual posthole from that site is similarly dated, and a copper-alloy strap-end, of typical 9th-century type, recovered from a later medieval context supports the presence of a middle Anglo-Saxon phase. Overall, little more can be said apart from the fact that the posthole structure may not have been a windbreak but perhaps part of a truncated circular building of early medieval date of a newly emerging type recorded elsewhere at Quarrington, Lincolnshire, where two structures of a similar size to that from Bishop's Cleeve were recorded, and Yarnton, Oxfordshire, where a larger circular structure is interpreted as a possible dovecote (Taylor 2003, 239, fig. 7; Hey 2004, 113, fig. 6.9).

Moving into the middle and late Anglo-Saxon periods, recent excavations at Lower Slaughter have revealed a substantial part of a multiple-ditched enclosure dated by three radiocarbon determinations to between the mid 7th century and the end of the 9th century (Kenyon and Watts forthcoming). The ditches probably represent continual redefinition of an ovoid enclosure, perhaps every 17 years on average, measuring $c.100 \times 60$ m wide and partly fossilised in the present plan of the settlement. The ditches themselves were generally 'U'-shaped and shallow; clearly defence was not a motivating factor. The size of the enclosure compares well with those recorded elsewhere surrounding manorial-type accommodation of the late Anglo-Saxon period (Reynolds 2003). Lower Slaughter was clearly a settlement of some standing in the late 10th century when an assembly held there to settle a dispute was presided over by Ealdorman Ælfhere (Blake 1962, 79–80).

In common with many late Anglo-Saxon manorial sites, a church, St Mary's, appears to represent a secondary additon to the complex on its eastern side. Parallels with other early medieval sites with 6th- or 7th-century origins and which became manorial complexes, such as Raunds in Nothamptonshire, are apparent. The only possible trace for Anglo-Saxon activity within the enclosure were two shallow oval pits, although neither contained conclusive dating evidence.

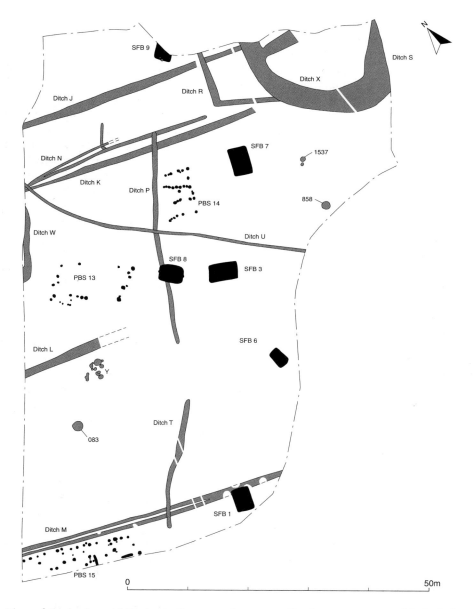

Fig. 8: Plan of the early–middle Anglo-Saxon settlement at Sherborne House, Lechlade (after Bateman et al. 2003).

Outside the enclosure, activity of late Anglo-Saxon date is indicated by the finding of a hooked tag in a shallow ditch to the north of the main enclosure, although the object could feasibly be much earlier; two residual sherds of St Neots-type ware indicate 10th-century activity. One of the more significant aspects of the Lower Slaughter evidence is its persistence as a place of settlement from the 7th century to the present. This aspect compares well with that from Lechlade and suggests stability in the landscape rather than shift during the middle Anglo-Saxon period. Martin Watts's discussion rightly emphasises the significance of the early dating at Lower Slaughter and its implications for settlements studies in the region.

The late Anglo-Saxon archaeology from Kingsholm has been rather neglected in discussions of settlements of the period despite its potential significance. If correctly identified, the Kingsholm evidence provides the only contemporary comparison to the palace at Cheddar, Somerset (Rahtz 1979). A strong case has been made that the parts of timber halls excavated there in the 1970s formed part of the palace recorded in the ASC *s.a.* 1051. The probable late Roman mausoleum containing the high-status early 5th-century burial described above is suggested by the excavators to have remained standing, or at least have been visible, in the late Anglo-Saxon period (Hurst 1985, 20). Certainly, the late Anglo-Saxon timber hall (or part of) there, follows the same alignment (Fig. 9). The construction techniques and dimensions of the most clearly distinguished structure (F69/F72) are consistent with what one might expect at a high-status site of the period with steep-sided continuous foundation trenches describing a building in excess of 10 m long and 6 m wide. The structure may in fact have been 'L'-shaped if the various features, including wall-trench-like slots and postholes to the west of the two parallel wall-trenches, are all part of the same structure. Such buildings are known elsewhere at Catholme, Staffordshire, and North Elmham, Norfolk (Reynolds 2005b).

There is little from the Kingsholm finds assemblage to support a high-status interpretation, although many Anglo-Saxon settlements (including Cheddar) fail to produce substantial numbers of finds either in terms of quantity or range of materials. No 'small-finds' belonged to the late Anglo-Saxon phase, although a shield boss fragment is suggested to be residual and of 6th- or 7th-century date (Hurst 1985, 36–7, fig. 14, 8); perhaps it is late Anglo-Saxon. Although many objects of Roman date were found in early medieval levels, many of the iron objects found, including simple tools, could just as easily relate to the 'palace' phase. Alan Vince's (1985, 94) discussion of the albeit small quantity of ceramics suggests that the 'palace' was supplied in a different way to the city of Gloucester at the time, while he dates the construction of the principal building to the late 10th or early 11th century and its occupation into the later 11th century.

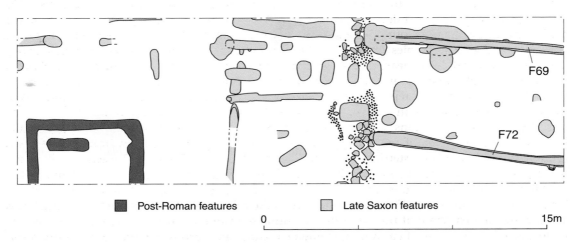

Fig. 9: Plan of the Anglo-Saxon palace at Kingsholm (after Hurst 1985).

Another probable high-status site of the late Anglo-Saxon period was excavated by the late Alan Hannan at Tewkesbury in the mid 1970s, although, again, the evidence there for a substantial hall of late Anglo-Saxon date has been neglected in comparative discussions. The site of Holm Hill lies SSW of the medieval town and abbey of Tewkesbury, where the Domesday Survey records a manorial centre whose regional significance can be identified from at least the early 11th century; it was held by the powerful thegn Brictric Meaw during the reign of Edward the Confessor (Hannan 1997, 84). Holm Hill itself was the location of the residence of the post-Conquest earls of Gloucester and was recorded in Hannan's excavations, while an earlier phase of substantial timber structures very likely represents the accomodation of the earls' Anglo-Saxon predecessors (Fig. 10).

Large post-pits described a complex measuring nearly 40 m in length and between 8 and 12 m in width. As the plan of the site shows, two principal interpretations are possible, both equally plausible. Both suggested layouts centre on two axially aligned timber halls, with a rectangular structure, perhaps a tower, immediately to the south of the easternmost hall. Such alignments are common on middle and late Anglo-Saxon high-status sites, while the possible tower is another feature to be expected at the residence of a thegn.

Beyond the structural evidence, only a loomweight fragment and single sherd of late Anglo-Saxon pottery attest to activity during this period, although the explicit relationship to the suceeding phase and the character and alignment of the timber buildings is entirely consistent with high-status occupation and the site as excavated is best seen as such. As with Kingsholm, the lack of artefacts is not an unusual characteristic of such a site, although Hannan recorded the archaeology under appalling conditions as a rescue exercise during construction work. A further point worthy of note is the geographical separation of high-status residence and population centre exhibited by both Kingsholm/Gloucester and Holm Hill/Tewkesbury.

RURAL ECONOMIES

With regard to the nature of early medieval agriculture and rural economies, there is little evidence from archaeology. The Lechlade settlement excavations, however, have provided indications of the kind of rural economies one might expect in this region. Cattle comprised 56% of the Sherborne Place assemblage, followed by sheep/goat (34%): pig and horse were poorly represented (5% and 4%), while dog and red deer formed less than 1% each overall (Maltby 2003, 73). Domestic fowl, goose and crane were found in small amounts, while fish bones were absent even from sieved soil samples. Four soil samples from SFB 1 were examined for the survival of plant remains. Barley and wheat, flax and Celtic bean were recovered along with high numbers of rush seeds (Stevens 2003, 79). SFB fills, however, are rather problematic and those from Lechlade appear to conform to those elsewhere in that they represent redeposited midden material. The potential for samples taken from SFBs to incorporate non-contemporary elements should thus be borne in mind.

The Frocester excavations also provide important evidence, the earliest of which potentially belongs to the later part of our period and to the era of village formation from the later 9th century, not only in Gloucestershire, but across much of lowland England. The estate of Frocester was a possession of St Peter's Abbey, Gloucester, from the 9th century until the Dissolution. The field in which the villa remains lay was known to Anglo-Saxon farmers as Stanborough, or 'stone-barrow' (Price 2000, vol. 121); surely a reference to the rubble remains of the complex, which was avoided by the first phase of ridge-and-furrow running up to the villa courtyard, but not over it. Unfortunately, this phase of cultivation is undated, although it precedes a pre-13th-century phase of narrower strips that encroached upon the parts of the complex, but not the villa, while the

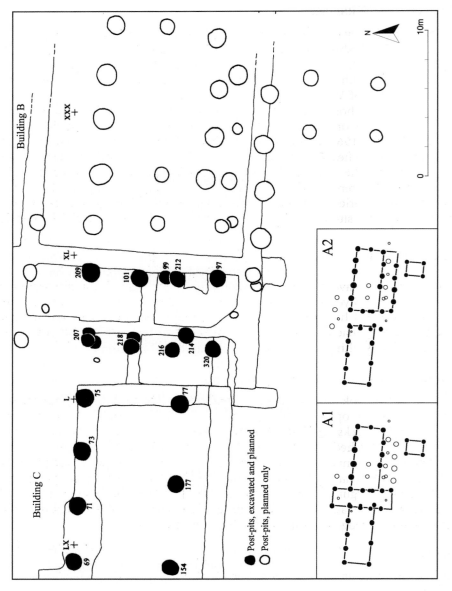

Figure. 10:   Plan of the probable late Anglo-Saxon hall at Holm Hill, Teukesbury (after Hannan 1997).

whole site was ploughed between the 13th and 16th centuries. The naming of the field recalls the *tiggæl beorgae* or 'tile-barrow' recorded in the charter bounds of Exton, Hampshire, of AD 940 that refer to the site of the Meonstoke villa (Sawyer 1968, no. 463; Reynolds 2005, 175).

LATE SAXON GLOUCESTERSHIRE

In 1086 the Domesday Survey records a total of 367 places in the county, including the four towns of Bristol, Gloucester, Tewkesbury and Winchcombe (Darby and Terrett 1971, 6). Territory to the south of the Bristol Avon, the southern fringe of the ancient Hwiccian kingdom, was subsumed within Wessex during the 10th century and the county boundary moved northwards to follow the river rather than the line of West Wansdyke to the south (Reynolds and Langlands in press). Gloucestershire is one of those counties whose ecclesiastical provision is poorly reflected in the Domesday Survey with only ten churches listed against the 14 known through structural survival (Taylor and Taylor 1965; and including St Oswald's in Gloucester). John Blair (1985) has listed secular minster churches in the county, while Peter Sawyer (1983) has considered the county's royal vills within the context of a national overview. Judicial organisation in the county can be reconstructed by reference to charter bounds which record several potential execution sites located on hundred boundaries (Reynolds forthcoming). Hundred meeting places, where judicial courts were held, are little studied in the county and should prove a fruitful topic for future research.

CONCLUSION

In conclusion, I hope to have brought to the fore the more significant discoveries made by archaeologists in the last 25 years and to have set their findings in a broader context. Inevitably, there will be material that I have overlooked, but the one hope is that the next reviewer of the county's early medieval archaeology will be in a position to revise this summary substantially, hopefully armed with a wealth of new data.

ACKNOWLEDGEMENTS

I am grateful to Neil Holbrook for inviting me to speak at the day conference on the archaeology of Gloucestershire and for the opportunity to contribute to the proceedings of that event. Martin Watts and Annette Hancocks of Cotswold Archaeology are thanked for their provision of information about unpublished sites. Eddie Price kindly provided comments on recent finds from Frocester Court and gave permission for the reproduction of previously published plans. Figure 3 is reproduced from the *Antiquaries Journal*, volume 55, by kind permission of the Society of Antiquaries of London. Figures 6–8 are reproduced with kind permission of the Cotswold Archaeological Trust, while all other figures have been redrawn with amendments from the original source as acknowledged in their respective captions.

BIBLIOGRAPHY

Alcock, L., 1963. *Dinas Powys: an Iron Age and early medieval settlement in Glamorgan* (Cardiff, University of Wales Press).

Attenborough, F.L., 1925. *The laws of the earliest English Kings* (Cambridge University Press).

Bassett, S. (ed.), 1989. *The Origins of Anglo-Saxon Kingdoms* (Leicester University Press).

Bateman, C., Enright, D., and Oakey, N., 2003. 'Prehistoric and Anglo-Saxon Settlements to the rear of Sherborne House, Lechlade: excavations in 1997', *Trans. BGAS* **121**, 23–96.

Blair, J., 1985. 'Secular minster churches in Domesday Book', in P. Sawyer (ed.), *Domesday Book: A Reappraisal* (London, Edward Arnold), 104–42.

Blake, E.O., 1962. *Liber Eliensis* (Camden Soc. 3rd series **92**, London, Royal Hist. Soc.).

Boon, G.C., 2000. 'Notes on the coin list by date and type', in Price 2000, vol. 2, 17–18.

Boyle, A., Jennings, D., Miles, D. and Palmer, S. (eds.), 1998. *The Anglo-Saxon cemetery at Butlers Field, Lechlade, Gloucestershire. Vol. 1: Prehistoric and Roman activity and Anglo-Saxon grave catalogue* (Oxford Archaeol. Unit Thames Valley Landscapes Monograph **10**.).

Briggs, G., Cook, J., and Rowley, T. (eds.), 1986. *The Archaeology of the Oxford Region* (Oxford University Committee for Archaeol.).

Brown, D., 1975 'A fifth-century burial at Kingsholm', in Hurst 1975, 290–4.

Bryant, R., 1990. 'The Lypiatt Cross', *Trans. BGAS* **108**, 33–52.

Darby, H.C., and Terrett, I.B., 1971. *The Domesday Geography of Midland England* (2nd edn., Cambridge University Press).

Dickinson, T.M., 1974. *Cuddesdon and Dorchester-on-Thames* (BAR Brit. Series **1**, Oxford).

Dunning, G.C., 1932. 'Bronze Age settlements and a Saxon hut near Bourton on the Water, Gloucestershire', *Antiq. J.* **12**, 279–93.

Eagles, B.N., 2003. 'Augustine's Oak', *Medieval Archaeol.* **47**, 175–8.

Eagles, B.N., and Mortimer, C., 1993. 'Early Anglo-Saxon artefacts from Hod Hill, Dorset', *Antiq. J.* **73**, 132–40.

Enright, D., and Watts, M., 2002. *A Romano-British and medieval settlement site at Stoke Road, Bishop's Cleeve, Gloucestershire* (Bristol and Gloucestershire Archaeol. Rep. **1**, Cirencester, Cotswold Archaeol.).

Evison, V.I., 1987. *Dover: the Buckland Anglo-Saxon cemetery* (Historic Buildings and Monuments Commission for England Archaeol. Rep. **3**, London).

Faulkner, N., 2000. *The decline and fall of Roman Britain* (Stroud and Charleston, South Carolina, Tempus).

Gannon, A., 2002. *The iconography of early Anglo-Saxon coinage* (Oxford University Press).

Gardner, K.S., 1998. 'The Wansdyke Diktat', *Bristol Avon Archaeol.* **15**, 57–65.

Gelling, M., 1953. *The Place-Names of Oxfordshire* (English Place-Name Soc. **23**, Cambridge University Press: 2 volumes).

Gelling, M., 1989. 'The Early History of Western Mercia', in Bassett 1989, 184–201.

Hannan, A., 1997. 'Tewkesbury and the Earl's of Gloucester: excavations at Holm Hill, 1974–5', *Trans. BGAS* **115**, 79–231.

Hare, M., 1990. 'The minster status of Bisley', in Bryant 1990, 46–9.

Hawkes, S.C., 1986. 'The Early Saxon period', in Briggs *et al.* 1986, 64–108.

Hawkes, S.C., 1989. *Weapons and warfare in Anglo-Saxon England* (Oxford University Committee for Archaeol.).

Heighway, C., 1984. 'Anglo-Saxon Gloucestershire', in A. Saville (ed.), *Archaeology in Gloucestershire* (Cheltenham Art Gallery and Museums and the BGAS), 225–47.

Heighway, C., 1987. *Anglo-Saxon Gloucestershire* (Gloucester, Alan Sutton).

Heighway, C., 1996. 'Context of the Kemble burials', in King *et al.* 1996, 32–4.

Hey, G., 2004. *Yarnton: Saxon and medieval settlement and landscape* (Oxford Archaeol. Unit Thames Valley Landscapes Monograph **10**).

Hills, C., and Hurst, H., 1989. 'A Goth at Gloucester?', *Antiq. J.* 69, 154–8.

Holbrook, N., 1998. 'The Amphitheatre: Excavations Directed by J.S. Wacher 1962–3 and A.D. McWhirr 1966', in N. Holbrook (ed.), *Cirencester: The Roman town defences, public buildings and shops* (Cirencester Excavations **5**, Cotswold Archaeol. Trust), 142–75.

Holbrook, N., 2000. 'The Anglo-Saxon cemetery at Lower Farm, Bishop's Cleeve: excavations directed by Kenneth Brown 1969', *Trans. BGAS* **118**, 61–92.

Hooke, D., 1985. *The Anglo-Saxon landscape: the kingdom of the Hwicce* (Manchester University Press).

Hurst, H., 1975. 'Excavations at Gloucester: third interim report: Kingsholm 1966–75', *Antiq. J.* **55**, 267–94.

Hurst, H., 1985. *Kingsholm* (Gloucester Archaeol. Rep. **1**, Cambridge).

Kenyon, D., and Collard, M., 2004. 'Anglo-Saxon and Medieval Remains at Kent Place, Sherborne Street, Lechlade: excavations in 2000', *Trans. BGAS* **122**, 117–26.

Kenyon, D., and Watts, M., forthcoming. 'An Anglo-Saxon enclosure at Church View, Lower Slaughter: excavations in 1999', *Trans. BGAS.* **124.**

King, R., Barber, A., and Timby, J., 1996. 'Excavations at West Lane, Kemble: an Iron Age, Roman and Saxon burial site and a medieval building', *Trans. BGAS* **114**, 15–54.

Kirby, D.P., 1977. 'Welsh Bards and the Border', in A. Dornier (ed.), *Mercian Studies* (Leicester University Press), 31–42.

Lucy, S., 2000. *The Anglo-Saxon way of death* (Stroud, Alan Sutton).

Mainman, A., and Rogers, N., 2000. *Craft, Industry and Everyday Life: Finds from Anglo-Scandinavian York* (CBA for York Archaeol. Trust, The Archaeol. of York **17/14**).

Maltby, M., 2003. 'Animal bone' in Bateman *et al.* 2003, 71–6.

Meaney, A., 1964. *A gazetteer of early Anglo-Saxon burial sites* (London, George Allen and Unwin).

Noble, F., 1983. *Offa's Dyke Reviewed*, ed. M. Gelling (BAR Brit. Series **114**, Oxford).

Ottaway, P., 1992. *Anglo-Scandinavian Ironwork from 16–22 Coppergate* (CBA for York Archaeol. Trust, The Archaeol. of York **17/6**).

Pitt, J., 1999. 'Wiltshire minster parochiae and West Saxon ecclesiastical organisation' (University of Southampton Ph.D. thesis).

Pretty, K. 1989 'Defining the Magonsæte', in Bassett 1989, 171–83.

Price, E.G., 2000. *Frocester. A Romano-British settlement, its antecedents and successors* (Stonehouse, Gloucester and District Archaeol. Research Group: 2 volumes).

Proudfoot, E., and Aliaga-Kelly, C., 1996. 'Towards an Interpretation of Anomalous Finds and Place-Names of Anglian Origin in North and East Scotland', *Anglo-Saxon Studies in Archaeol. and Hist.* **9**, 1–13.

Rahtz, P.A., 1979. *Anglo-Saxon and Medieval Palaces at Cheddar* (BAR Brit. Series **65**, Oxford).

Reynolds, A., 2003. 'Boundaries and settlements in later 6th to 11th century England', in D. Griffiths, A. Reynolds and S. Semple (eds.), *Boundaries in Early medieval Britain* (Anglo-Saxon Studies in Archaeol. and Hist. **12**, Oxford), 98–136.

Reynolds, A., 2005a. 'From *pagus* to parish: territory and settlement in the Avebury region from the late Roman period to the Domesday Survey', in G. Brown, D. Field and D. McOmish (eds.), *The Avebury Landscape: aspects of the field archaeology of the Marlborough Downs* (Oxford, Oxbow), 164–80.

Reynolds, A., 2005b. 'Farmers, traders and kings: the archaeology of social complexity in early medieval north-western Europe', *Early Medieval Europe* **15.1**, 154–71.

Reynolds, A., forthcoming. 'Anglo-Saxon Law in the Landscape' (Oxford University Press).

Reynolds, A., and Langlands, A., in press. 'Social identities on the macro scale: a maximum view of Wansdyke', in W. Davies, G. Halsall and A. Reynolds (eds.), *People and Space in the Early Middle Ages AD 300–1300* (Studies in the Early Middle Ages **15**, Turnhout, Brepols).

Saville, A., 1985 'Salvage recording of Romano-British, Saxon, medieval and post-medieval remains at North Street, Winchcombe, Gloucestershire', *Trans. BGAS* **103**, 101–39.

Sawyer, P., 1968, *Anglo-Saxon Charters: an annotated handlist and bibliography* (London, Royal Hist. Soc.).

Sawyer, P., 1983. 'The Royal Tun in Pre-Conquest England', in P. Wormald with D. Bullough and R. Collins (eds.), *Ideal and Reality in Frankish and Anglo-Saxon Society* (Oxford, Basil Blackwell), 273–99.

Smith, A.H., 1964. *The Place-Names of Gloucestershire Volume 1* (English Place-Name Society **13**, Cambridge University Press).

Sparey Green, C., 1987. *Excavations at Poundbury: volume 1: the settlements* (Dorset Natural Hist. and Archaeol. Soc. Monograph **7**).

Stamper, P., 2003., 'Review' of E.G. Price, *Frocester. A Romano-British settlement, its antecedents and successors* (2000), in *Medieval Archaeol.* **47**, 369–70.

Stenton, F.M., 1971. *Anglo-Saxon England* (3rd edn., Oxford, Clarendon Press).

Stevens, C., 2003. 'The arable economy', in Bateman *et al.* 2003, 76–81.

Stevenson, W.H., 1904. *Asser's Life of King Alfred* (Oxford, Clarendon Press).

Swanton, M., 2000. *The Anglo-Saxon Chronicles* (London, Phoenix Press).

Tait, H., 1976. *Jewellery through 7000 years* (London, British Museum Publications).

Taylor, G., 2003. 'An Early to Middle Anglo-Saxon Settlement at Quarrington, Lincolnshire', *Antiq. J.* **83**, 231–80.

Taylor, H.M., and Taylor, J., 1965. Anglo-Saxon Architecture (Cambridge University Press: 2 volumes).

Thomas, C., 1990, ' "Gallici Nautae de Galliarum Provinciis" - a sixth/seventh century trade with Gaul, reconsidered', *Medieval Archaeol.* **34**, 1–27.

Timby, J., 2003 'Pottery', in Bateman *et al.* 2003, 47–63.

Vince, A., 1985. 'Saxon and medieval pottery', in Hurst 1985, 94–5.

Whybra, J., 1990. *A lost English county: Winchcombeshire in the 10th and 11th centuries* (Studies in Anglo-Saxon Hist. **1**, Woodbridge, The Boydell Press).

Yorke, B.A.E., 1993. 'Fact or fiction? The written evidence for the fifth and sixth centuries AD', *Anglo-Saxon Studies in Archaeol. and Hist.* **6**, 45–50.

East is East and West is Gloucestershire

Richard Reece

Two conferences on the archaeology of a region did exactly what they set out to do – concentrate on Gloucestershire. Yet in doing that they selected mainly the positive and so missed out some elements of the story which can only be seen through the negative. In other words they concentrated on the sites found and the objects recovered at the expense of the sites not found and the objects not recovered.

But this approach creates a problem in that there is a difference in the visibility of archaeological evidence between the eastern and western parts of Britain. In the period between about 100 BC and AD 1000 this seems to have two causes – the connections between the east of Britain and the highly visible material from the other side of the North Sea, and the eastern habit of burying things, whether singly or as groups of objects. Iron-Age torcs, Roman silver plate, and jewellery and ornaments in the Anglo-Saxon style are more immediately obvious and visible than similar objects such as small Iron-Age brooches often made of iron, Roman coarse pottery and the very occasional bronze Dark-Age pin. The former are found in East Anglia, the latter are staple fare in Gloucestershire. Perhaps even more importantly, objects such as torcs and silver plate are particularly well known because they were buried in groups or hoards particularly in East Anglia, more rarely elsewhere, and not at all in Gloucestershire (Hobbs 2006).

There are periods of time when East and West agree on the presence of material, but differ totally in the nature of the material. In the 4th century AD the Cotswolds are a focus for substantial villas with expensive furnishings such as mosaic pavements but they lack any finds of Roman silver plate. East Anglia has a high concentration of hoards of Roman silver plate but very few late villas and almost no expensive mosaics. If we concentrate on one particular type of material such as 4th-century bronze coins then the Cotswolds form a major concentration of both hoards and site finds while East Anglia shows a general small scatter and only a few sites with a concentration of the latest coins (Davies and Gregory 1991).

Moving forward in time to the years around AD 1000 there is a similar disparity in evidence between the two areas. East Anglia has a strong tradition of practical coarse pottery, but only a scatter of surviving pre-Conquest churches. The Cotswolds, and particularly the region around Cirencester, has a scatter of pottery so light that it is invisible, yet it boasts one of the densest concentrations of pre-Conquest churches in Britain. One group is in Daglingworth, Duntisbourne Rouse, Duntisbourne Abbots, Winstone, Miserden, Edgeworth and possibly Syde. Another is in the Ampneys (St Peter, Crucis and St Mary), Bibury and Coln St Dennis (Taylor and Taylor 1965 and personal observation).

If we move to the gap between these two periods, the 5th to 8th century, the differences in visibility become even more important. In the East there are the well known burials, either urned cremations or inhumations furnished with material of the Anglo-Saxon style. These objects are found much less commonly in Gloucestershire and always give the impression of being the westward limits of penetration of the style. Dating a little later in East Anglia there are now many sites on which large amounts of metalwork and early coinage have been found by metal detecting. These sites are now known as Productive Sites but they are unknown, so far, in the West (Pestell and Ulmschneider 2003).

The far west of Britain (Wales, Cornwall, Devon) between AD 400 and 800 has none of the material in Anglo-Saxon style, but some of the sites that have been excavated are usually dated by finds of pottery imported from the Mediterranean – red slip wares and amphorae – and from south-west France – D and E ware. These imports have never been found in Gloucestershire. This leaves us with two mutually exclusive areas as far as visible archaeology and datable finds are concerned, with Gloucestershire sandwiched in between. This is particularly true after the earliest material in Anglo-Saxon style has died out without leaving any visible developments in pottery or metalwork. We need to consider the possible meanings of both presences and absences in the archaeological and material record.

Where material of roughly the same date survives in East and West then it is not enough to comment only on presence; difference must also be considered. This applies to the presence of late Saxon pottery in East Anglia and its rarity in Gloucestershire compared with the groups of pre-Conquest churches in Gloucestershire which cannot easily be paralleled in East Anglia. There are many complications which crowd in upon such generalising, some would say irresponsible, statements. To pick one at random, there may have been just as many churches of the 10th–11th century in East Anglia but they were of wood; the only point which is valid is that the Cotswold churches from an area of good building stone were of stone and so survive. But I think the point I am making is immune to such valid objections. I am not suggesting that the Cotswolds with their surviving pre-Conquest churches were Christian while East Anglia without surviving churches was pagan. I am pointing out that the rarity of 10th- to 11th-century pottery on the Cotswolds, which could be taken to suggest a minimal number of impoverished people has to be set against the counter-indication of an unusual number of churches of the same date.

I have spelled this out in laborious detail because in the period from about AD 400 to 1100 very little pottery indeed has been discovered outside Gloucester itself and the conclusion that some people wish to draw is that where there is no pottery there are no people. A refinement of this would be that a few sites, with a little pottery, are known, so we must accept that evidence, stringently limit the population to those sites and the few that remain undiscovered, and assume a heavy population loss on the Cotswolds in the years after AD 400.

It is possible that such a scenario is true but I doubt it for several reasons. In the first place, if it could be demonstrated such a population loss extending over many centuries would be unique in the history of population studies and would generate great excitement in the demographic world. So far as I know populations simply do not *do* that. Events of major mortality such as the Black Death, the Napoleonic wars, or even the First and Second World Wars cause an immediate drop in population, but, for various reasons, this leads to an increased birth rate and a reasonably quick (150 years or less?) restocking of the population (Scheidel 2002, especially the extensive references in n. 22 at p. 100). It could be that there is a disaster around AD 400, or the dust clouds of AD 540 might be to blame, but the mortality caused ought to have been repaired before AD 700.

The suggestion that there are a few sites which show continuity, and also have a small amount of pottery, has to be taken seriously. Unfortunately a type-site such as Frocester Court Roman villa provides difficulties (Timby 2000, 137–8). Continuity is hoped for because of the grass-tempered pottery found in the last phases of the villa – perhaps associated with its use to shelter animals. Such pottery is not yet well dated. I think the best we can say is that it rarely if ever appears in Roman assemblages of the late 4th century and is certainly not universal in groups of Saxo-Norman (11th-century) date. My impression, which has not been substantiated by detailed search, is that it belongs to the end of the Roman phase rather than the beginning of the Conquest-period phase. It cannot be taken to show continuity over as much as (perhaps) a century, though at sites such as Frocester it can warn us that there is a phase of material occupation, very difficult to study, post-dating the prolific late 4th-century deposits. The other problem with such pottery is its rarity, even on sites on which it is found. As evidence of a discrete phase of unknown duration, perhaps a generation or two, five or ten sherds are acceptable. As evidence spread over five centuries to suggest continuity of occupation and use, I find five or ten sherds unacceptable. Similar problems apply to other types of pottery of roughly similar date, somewhere between AD 400 and 1100.

In summary we therefore have a period of several centuries during which there is good evidence for contact between the far west of Britain and the Atlantic coast of France and the Mediterranean. In the east of Britain there is substantial evidence for contacts across the North Sea with Scandinavia and the Dutch and German coastline. Gloucestershire and the surrounding area has no material evidence of outside contacts at all. It seems likely that contact between the West and points south depended partly on trade – for unless the remaining materials were all gifts, they had to be paid for. The same may well be true in the East. Gloucestershire seems to be an empty wedge between two different trading systems. This Empty Quarter runs from the middle of the modern city of Cardiff to somewhere east of Oxford and I have called it the Cotswold Severn Invisible Culture (Reece 1997, 8–10). It could be that the Cotswolds were producers and if so they could have passed their produce either to the East or the West, but this production and distribution apparently did not lead to the import of any materials into the region in exchange for whatever was produced and 'exported'. We therefore have to consider the possibility that Gloucestershire, and surroundings, did not trade. That is because either there was no one there or the people who were there did not produce a surplus.

Not only can we be quite certain that there were people there, but they must have been quite productive. Gloucestershire is quite well supplied with early charters granting land to people of reasonably high status. To take one example, which has had a lot of attention, an estate at Withington was granted around AD 700 for the foundation of a monastery/nunnery in which daughters of the Establishment could be educated and, if not married, deposited. As Finberg pointed out long ago there is no point in endowing a company of noble women with a wilderness around a swamp. If they are going to settle successfully – and the establishment became successful enough for disputes about its ownership to emerge fairly quickly – the nuns need shelter, food, clothing, servants, and presumably a source of income. Just as you do not endow noble women with a swamp, so you presumably do not bicker over its ownership (Finberg 1959, 34–6). If, on the other hand, the land is ploughed and cropped and the surrounding hills, with gradients too steep for ploughing, are used to grow timber or to feed flocks of wool-producing sheep, then the nuns have sources of income and the ownership of the land becomes worth contesting. Yet, so far as I know, there is virtually no material evidence for that establishment, though there is an earlier pagan burial from Foxcote.

One area in which our ignorance is total is whether the 'estate' had an income and, if it had, how it was generated. If we take a fully 'sustainable' view of the whole land-holding then an income derived from production of a surplus is not strictly necessary. Tied agricultural labourers would not expect monetary wages – they would presumably be pleased if they were given enough time to minister to the shelter, food, and general well-being of their families. Their working time could produce the necessities of life for the ladies of the convent – wood and thatch for buildings and for heating, wool for spinning and weaving, substantial food and drink. But the nuns were perhaps used to more comforts than that, and if they took their educational and religious duties at all seriously they needed manuscripts and materials. Yet they could produce their own writing materials (ink, vellum) and they could engage in exchange with other monastic institutions by copying manuscripts.

The owner of land would be in roughly the same position as the inhabitants of the monastery, but without their religious and educational needs, so he or she could also be more or less self-sufficient. While an income would no doubt be useful for outlandish herbs, spices and medicines, the components of a fairly substantial life-style would all be available from the land. It could be that the rarity in Gloucestershire of foreign objects, whether from East Anglia, Byzantium, or Ireland, supports the idea of a self-sufficient wedge of people between the traders of the East and West. But this may be no more than my longing to demonstrate the re-emergence of a contented pre-lapsarian society in the Cotswolds. This argument has been based on Withington, but Withington is not unique.

The other charters belong to very contrasting areas of the Gloucestershire region. Some are on the high ground of the Wold (e.g. Calmsden, in North Cerney, and Stow-on-the-Wold); others are in the lush, not to say water-logged, lowland (e.g. Somerford Keynes and Ewen). An early date for the charters is supported by a very early church at Somerford Keynes, but again I know of no other material evidence. Following on the reasoning from Withington, there is little point in making the legal fuss of granting these disparate lands, and appearing to bestow great boons, if they were empty wildernesses. Wilderness might be thought an over-statement, but I have always carried with me the sight (about 1966) at Rothamstead Experimental station of an 100-acre field, part of which was left to its own devices in the mid 19th century and part around 1900. The part left alone for 100 years was a substantial wood with some tall trees and thick undergrowth. Unless this actual evidence is for some reason inadmissible for Gloucestershire it means that a landscape left empty by a disaster around AD 450 would have been complete wood and thicket by AD 550, and would so have remained until an intense Saxo-Norman reclamation in time for Domesday. Roads would have disappeared – they did not. Fields would have been totally forgotten and eliminated. The noble women at Withington would have had to make a clearing in the Wild Wood in order to build a wooden shack of branches to meditate out of the rain when they were not gathering nuts, berries and mushrooms in due season. This did not happen.

So what is the pattern of early medieval development in Gloucestershire to compare with the substantial landscape studies elsewhere, and particularly in the East? The answer is that we do not know because, apart from Finberg at Withington, the landscape writers have worked almost completely east of Oxford and have left us out of their pictures. The most recent example is the detailed and provocative study by Tom Williamson (2003) which has received mixed reviews. To me it is particularly provocative in that the study area on which so much attention has been lavished with some excellent results peters out as it reaches the area just east of Oxford.

I am left with my own very vague impressions from a study of the woody species of plant in all the roadside hedgerows in an area within a roughly eight-mile radius of Cirencester. As a result of this work, which needs considerably more attention to detail, I think I can recognise hedges of late 18th–19th-century enclosures and hedges of the 16th century. This leaves a substantial and fairly homogeneous group which ought to be older than the 16th century by three or four hundred years – a post-Norman re-organisation. And beyond that there are a few even richer hedges which seem to belong to an even earlier period. This all seems to come from a long period of use of the countryside which evolved from at least before AD 1000. This agrees with the Domesday record of manors and (thriving?) populations which is remarkably close to our first maps.

And if the hedges were being tended, the fields ploughed, the cows milked and the sheep shorn then the countryside was fully operational and not a desert. That the operators failed to leave us substantial signs of their existence and activities in material derived from excavation is simply a problem to be overcome by the study of other aspects of their life and work.

BIBLIOGRAPHY

Davies, J.A., and Gregory, T., 1991. 'Coinage from a *Civitas*: A survey of the Roman coins found in Norfolk and their contribution to the archaeology of the *Civitas Icenorum*', *Britannia* **22**, 65–101.

Finberg, H.P.R., 1959. *Roman and Saxon Withington* (Department of English Local History Occasional Paper **8**, Leicester University Press).

Hobbs, R., 2006. *Late Roman precious metal deposits AD 200–700: changes over time and space* (BAR Int. Series **1504**, Oxford).

Pestell, T., and Ulmschneider, K. (eds.), 2003. *Markets in early medieval Europe* (Macclesfield).

Price, E.G., 2000. *Frocester. A Romano-British settlement, its antecedents and successors* (Stonehouse, Gloucester and District Archaeol. Research Group: 2 volumes).

Reece, R., 1997. *The future of Roman military archaeology* (Cardiff, Tenth Annual Caerleon Lecture).

Scheidel, W., 2002. 'A model of change in Egypt after the plague of 165', *J. Roman Archaeol.* **15**, 97–114.

Taylor, H.M., and Taylor, J., 1965. *Anglo-Saxon Architecture* (Cambridge).

Timby, J., 2000. 'Pottery' in Price 2000, vol. 2, 125–62.

Williamson, T., 2003. *Shaping Medieval Landscapes* (Macclesfield).

The Medieval Countryside

Mark Bowden

INTRODUCTION

This paper considers the medieval topics that were covered in *Archaeology in Gloucestershire* (Saville 1984) arising out of the 1979 conference – pottery, deserted villages, towns, medieval houses – and some others. I trawled the literature to follow these topics and to see which others had arisen, identifying some of the trends, as I see them, of research in the medieval countryside over the last 20 or so years. One or two very significant themes emerge. Industrial archaeology was also covered in Saville's volume, and as there is no paper in the current volume specifically concerning that subject – in the rural milieu anyway – I have referred to that (briefly at least) and other matters that spill over into the post-medieval period. The locations of the principal places mentioned in the following text are indicated on Figure 1.

During my search of the literature I found two unexpected patterns.

First: there is a healthy tradition in Gloucestershire of professional, amateur and independent earthwork survey. This, I suggest, is contrary to the trend; not many other counties, if any, show such a pattern. Why this should be so is not clear. Gloucestershire has not been covered, for this period, by the national body of archaeological survey, the former Royal Commission on the Historical Monuments of England (RCHME), with the exception of the work at Chipping Campden (Fig. 2) reported by Paul Everson (1989), which relates mainly to the early post-medieval landscape. One should also perhaps note at this point Nicky Smith's (1998) work at Manless Town, Brimpsfield, but this was done as a personal research project in her own time, not as part of her official duties for the RCHME. There have also been two relevant surveys since the RCHME became part of English Heritage, at Minchinhampton Common (Smith 2002a) and at Dyrham Park (Smith 2002b), both for the National Trust. English Heritage Investigators are currently working at Lodge Park, Sherborne, also for the National Trust.

Second: there is a notable concentration on low-status sites at the expense of high-status sites; the county's palaces, castles and abbeys have received comparatively little attention over the past twenty years. This again, I believe, is contrary to the national picture, but it is, arguably, a healthy state of affairs.

TOPICS

Pottery

There is, regrettably, little new to say on this subject. Alan Vince, when asked what advances he thought that there had been, and to what extent the research directions that he had pointed out (1984, 260) had been achieved, mentioned recent excavations at Dursley that have revealed sources of 12th–13th-century pottery that are different from those he knew of, even though it is only a few miles from the major production centre at Haresfield. The excavations at Acton Court (Rodwell and Bell 2004) and other excavations have also provided new assemblages. However, Vince's overall impression is that 'fieldwork in the past 20 years seems to have been mainly going over the same ground as far as pottery is concerned, whilst there are still large parts of the county with no recent fieldwork' (pers. comm.).

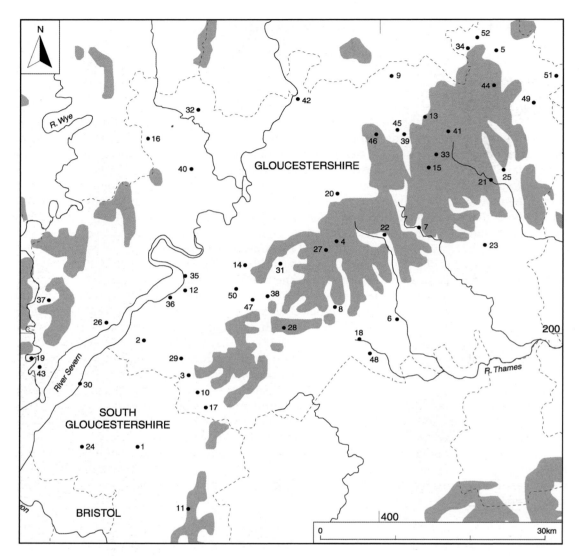

Fig. 1: Map showing principal places mentioned in the text. 1 Acton Court; 2 Berkeley; 3 Bradley; 4 Brimpsfield;
5 Chipping Campden; 6 Cirencester; 7 Compton Abdale; 8 Daneway; 9 Dumbleton; 10 Dursley; 11 Dyrham Park;
12 Frampton on Severn; 13 Hailes; 14 Haresfield; 15 Hawling; 16 Hay Wood; 17 Hillesley; 18 Hullasey; 19 Lancaut;
20 Leckhampton; 21 Little Aston; 22 Little Colesbourne; 23 Lodge Park; 24 Lower Almondsbury; 25 Lower Slaughter;
26 Lydney Level; 27 Manless Town; 28 Minchinhampton Common; 29 Nibley Green; 30 Oldbury-on-Severn;
31 Painswick; 32 Redmarley D'Abitot; 33 Roel; 34 Saintbury; 35 Saul; 36 Slimbridge; 37 St Briavels; 38 Stroud;
39 Sudeley; 40 Taynton Parva; 41 Temple Guiting; 42 Tewkesbury; 43 Tidenham; 44 Upton; 45 Winchcombe; 46 Bishop's
Cleeve; 47 Ebley; 48 Kemble; 49 Moreton-in-Marsh; 50 Stonehouse; 51 Todenham; 52 Weston Subedge.

Fig. 2:   Chipping Campden: site of 17th-century house and surviving earthwork gardens (photograph by Roger Featherstone, November 1986: © Crown copyright. National Monuments Record 3152/17).

Martin Ecclestone's (2000) important work at Haresfield itself has to be excepted from this. Ecclestone used documentary and place-name evidence, supported by aerial photos and experimental work, to locate the probable area of pottery manufacture but found little, if any, field evidence. This research should surely be followed up.

Deserted Villages and Other Rural Settlements

The term 'deserted medieval village' has been applied over-liberally to many sites which are nothing of the kind, a problem noted by Aston and Viner (1984, 281–3). Sites so designated are often no more than farmsteads or hamlets, and are sometimes not even of medieval date.

There have been very few excavations on medieval rural settlements in Gloucestershire since the 1960s; exceptions are Kemble (King 1996), Lower Slaughter (Enright and Kenyon 2000), Ebley, Moreton-in-Marsh and Stonehouse (Oakey 2000) and Bishop's Cleeve (Enright and Watts 2002). Major advances on the topic of medieval settlement and agriculture in Gloucestershire are the work not primarily of archaeologists but of a landscape historian who takes archaeological evidence seriously, Professor Christopher Dyer. He has published a series of papers studying settlement and land use on the Cotswolds; these are extremely valuable in at least providing a substantial body of material to work on. These papers cover villages and smaller, dispersed, settlements – at large and in particular – and the previously unexplored subject of sheepcotes and seasonal settlement on the Cotswolds. Dyer (e.g. 1982; 1987) has thrown much needed new light on village formation, village planning, the causes and process of shrinkage and desertion, and the reasons why some settlements were not deserted. Dyer (1995, 160; 2002, 16) stresses just how extensive arable farming was on the Cotswolds from an early date, something that is being reinforced by the aerial photographic transcription being undertaken in the Cotswolds for the English Heritage National Mapping Programme – ridge-and-furrow is almost ubiquitous on the fringes of the hills. Two Gloucestershire townships, Todenham and Weston Subedge, are included in Hall's gazetteer of areas of Midland ridge-and-furrow of national importance (2001, 70, 71). Caution has to be exercised, first over the dating and secondly over the function of this ridge-and-furrow: is it in fact of medieval date and does it all represent arable agriculture, or is it in some cases an effort to improve the pasture? The answer to the first question is that much of it *is* probably medieval. The answer to the second may be more doubtful but a high level of agricultural activity, at some times and in some places at least, seems to be indicated. Sheep were entirely necessary in fairly large numbers to manure the relatively poor Cotswold soil – as Dyer puts it, the balance between sheep and corn was the key to successful agriculture; each ploughland in Temple Guiting, for example, was accompanied by 300–400 sheep (Dyer 1987, 177). The sheep got their feed from stubbles and fallows and imported hay, rather than from permanent pasture, of which there seems to have been very little (idem 1995, 158, 160). Dyer and his colleagues also find something which is being recognised more and more by landscape archaeologists – boundaries are stable but settlements shift (Aldred and Dyer 1991, 142).

Patterns of medieval settlement are more complex than could have been imagined 25 years ago. Not only are there primary and secondary settlements, or dual-focus settlements, but sometimes a secondary settlement pertaining to one manor can be found physically linked to the primary settlement of an adjacent manor. In their study of Roel and Hawling, Aldred and Dyer (1991, 149–53) suggest that the location of the manor house at Roel, when most of the tenants lived in the more desirable location of Roelside in Hawling, may be due in part at least to the existence of an earlier stock farming centre on the site. However, they do not note (though it is shown on their plan) the existence of an oval enclosure at Roel, apparently pre-dating other features, surrounding the manorial complex. The unusual topographic location suggests that this is not a prehistoric enclosure but it might well be of early medieval date and represent a high-status pre-Conquest focus. This might be analogous to the oval enclosure that underlies Lower Slaughter (Enright and Kenyon 2000), but in that case apparently including a church. Aldred and Dyer (1991, 146–8) count the number of earthwork buildings and crofts at Roel and Roelside and find they coincide approximately with the number of tenants recorded in documents; this is very neat but one should be cautious of such apparently close correlates between archaeological and documentary evidence. Archaeological evidence should not be used just to corroborate the documents but to challenge them.

As with permanent settlements, Dyer studied the documentary and archaeological evidence for sheepcotes. He identified a considerable number of sites in the field (mainly in isolated upland locations), though many more are documented (and of these many were within or adjacent to manorial *curia* – where they are less likely to survive physically). These were long narrow buildings, capable of holding up to 500 sheep, often associated with enclosures and other buildings, as at Compton Abdale (Dyer 2002, 22–6) (Fig. 3). Sheepcotes were used for

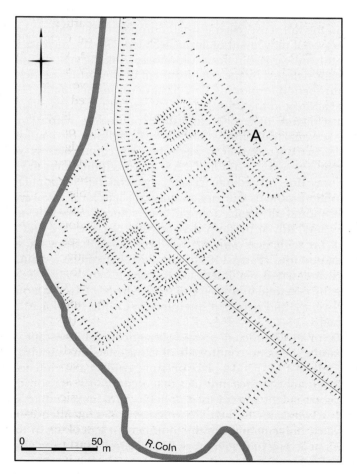

Fig. 3: Compton Abdale: plan of sheepcote (after Dyer 2002, fig. 8). The long, narrow sheephouse itself (A) lies at the north-eastern edge of a series of yards with subsidiary buildings. This is a very substantial complex, though not all the elements are necessarily contemporary. The leat cutting through the site from north-west to south-east is clearly a relatively late feature but its precise relationship to some of the platforms is uncertain.

shelter, for fodder storage, for lambing, for administration and flock management, and as a source of manure (idem 1995, 151–5; 1996, 32). They date from the 12th century and were in use until the 17th century. Dyer (1995, 155–6) stresses a change in historians' views of medieval agriculture (which had previously been very negative) – medieval sheep farming was highly successful because of good management and care for the animals. This is true of peasant farmers as well as the owners of great estates (ibid. 159).

Despite the fact that even 'isolated' sheepcotes were no more than about 2.5 km from the nearest settlement, there is evidence that people dwelt at them temporarily (Dyer 1995, 161; 1996). This would involve shepherds bringing flocks of ewes and lambs to the upland pastures in summer but also dairymaids milking the ewes (idem 1996, 28–9). However, whether these upland sheepcotes represent a fully transhumant pattern of pastoral practice, with all the social implications of that identified by Herring (1996, 35, 39), is perhaps doubtful. Given the small distances involved, the sheepcotes might be seen as outstations of the permanent settlements, rather than shielings in the full sense, even if small numbers of individuals were dwelling in them at certain times. The seasonal movement of flocks declined with the increase in leasing of pastures from the late 14th century onwards, but flocks of wethers could be kept on upland pastures all year round, a practice perhaps reflected by the establishment of sheepcotes on deserted settlement sites from approximately this period, exploiting new pasture on former arable (Dyer 1996, 31).

In his presidential address to the Bristol and Gloucestershire Archaeological Society, Professor Dyer (2002) painted a picture of a well cultivated countryside with a mix of nucleated and dispersed settlement, seasonal variation, a mix too of planning by landlords and assertion of peasant rights and collective organisation. It was a dynamic countryside as well, with villages and other settlements growing between 1100 and 1300 and declining after the troubles of the 14th century. The decline was due to agrarian crises, a general fall in population and to various particular socio-economic problems but not to grasping landlords. However, even this decline brought in its wake economic diversification and new sources of wealth, such as the economic boom in the Stroud valleys, driven by cloth making, that began in the mid 13th century.

Other good work on settlement remains has been done. Earthwork surveys of a possible farmstead at Little Colesbourne (Parry 1989), shrunken settlement remains at Tidenham (Ellis 1984a) and an extensive deserted settlement at Hullasey, Coates (Ellis 1984b; Aston and Viner 1984, fig. 4), illustrate the potential of this type of work. However, much more is required, both in terms of breadth of coverage and depth of interpretation if the full potential of such earthwork remains is to be realised.

The current picture of a well-ordered, prosperous agricultural landscape, however, should not blind us to the fact that the medieval countryside of Gloucestershire was also (sometimes at least) an unhealthy place (Franklin 1983) and a place of crime, conflict and violence. Even Dyer's (1995, 148; 1996, 31) evidence for sheepcotes indicates that security was a factor in the requirement for shepherds or others to be resident and for their doors to have locks and keys – sheep, equipment and sheepskins all being vulnerable to theft. Recorded episodes of violence and lawlessness in the county include aggravated burglary and multiple murders in Painswick in the early 13th century (Baddeley 1907, 71–2); poaching in the Forest of Dean (Birrell 2001) and elsewhere (e.g. Franklin 1989, 157); the battle of Nibley Green in 1470; and, most notoriously, the murder of King Edward II at Berkeley in 1327. The intransigence of individuals could also be an identifiable contributory factor in settlement desertion, as in the case of Richard Miller of Little Aston (Dyer 1987, 174, 177). More widely, archaeological evidence for concerns of rural security also exists in the earthworks surrounding individual tofts (Astill and Grant 1988, 51–4) and in the generous provision of locks and bolts on village sites (e.g. Hurst 1984, 98). Keys, barrel padlock keys, hasps and locks were notable finds at Upton (Hilton and Rahtz 1966, 120–1, fig. 13; Rahtz 1969, 105, 108, fig. 12). Moats, although there is now probably almost universal agreement that they are principally a statement about social standing or pretension, are also about security at some level.

Moats

The term 'moat' is another classification, like 'deserted medieval village', that has turned into a straight-jacket. Supposed moats often turn out to be something unexpected, such as 17th-century water gardens. In extreme cases, such as the curious circular 'moat' at Redmarley D'Abitot (Wootton and Bowden 2002), there may be complete uncertainty as to whether the site is a moat or not.

A few moated sites across the county have been surveyed (e.g. Ellis 1984c). The moat at Bradley, Wotton-under-Edge (Iles and Popplewell 1985), with its associated ponds is an interesting example but like so many moats it raises several questions – is it in fact the documented manorial site, as the authors assume? Its position on a parish boundary should at least cause this question to be asked. Moats could be created by people in quite humble circumstances in relatively peripheral locations, as seems to be the case for many of the moats around the Malvern Hills (Bowden 2005, 40–1). What are the earthworks to the south-west of the Bradley complex that the authors describe as 'amorphous' and 'possibly quite recent'? Apparently amorphous earthworks should always be surveyed – it is the unravelling of such unpromising remains that often gives a vital key to interpretation. The tendency always to classify medieval ponds as 'fishponds' must also be questioned. Iles and Popplewell use this term, while noting that the lower pond at Bradley is exceptionally large – no doubt these ponds were used for raising fish, but they may have had other purposes besides, including ornamental ones (Everson 1998; Taylor 2000).

Towns

Towns were covered by Roger Leech in 1984. He complained that almost no attention had been paid to the smaller towns. (Bristol and Gloucester are covered by separate essays in this volume.) The situation remains much the same today, it seems; very little work has been done recently, outside of the Extensive Urban Survey (EUS) conducted by Gloucestershire County Council Archaeology Service, and some rescue excavations at, for instance, Cirencester, Tewkesbury and Winchcombe (e.g. Leech and McWhirr 1982; Wilkinson and McWhirr 1998; Hannan 1993, 1997; Hoyle 1992; Saville 1985; Ellis 1986; Guy 1986), though much of this work was undertaken before 1979. Cirencester has also been subject to an urban archaeological assessment (Darvill and Gerrard 1994).

Town plan analysis has been undertaken at Tewkesbury (Lilley 1997). St Briavels was covered by the EUS and a development sequence proposed (Douthwaite and Devine 1998a). Recent aerial photographic transcription in the Forest of Dean, part of the English Heritage National Mapping Programme, has, however, shown a more complex picture (Fig. 4), which seems to indicate that there have been episodes of shrinkage as well as growth (Cathy Stoertz and Fiona Small pers. comm.). Painswick (along with Dursley and Tetbury) was identified by Leech (1984, 297) as a town whose plan indicates more than usually complex development, associated with early settlement. Town plan analysis is wanted for such settlements (Fig. 5).

The Archaeology of Standing Buildings

Houses were covered by Lionel Walrond in 1984. There have been a few advances here but most have concentrated on individual buildings or complexes. Kirsty Rodwell's (1991) work at Court

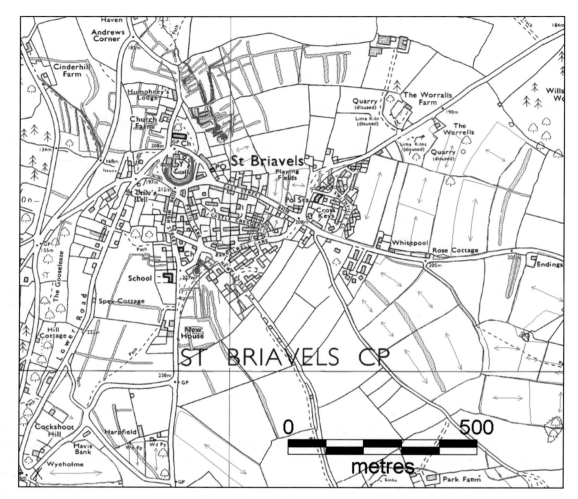

*Fig. 4: St Briavels: an extract from the English Heritage National Mapping Programme aerial photo-
graphic transcription, showing earthwork remains beyond the current extents of the village: based on an
Ordnance Survey map. © Crown copyright. All rights reserved. English Heritage Licence No. 100019088.
2005.*

Farm, Lower Almondsbury, for instance, is a good example, with an excellent analysis of the
standing buildings. She notes that the manorial complex may have been moated but does
not mention that the whole settlement – manor, church and village – appears to sit within an
oval – again, as at Roel, possibly early medieval – enclosure (Fig. 6). Warwick Rodwell's (2000)
work on Daneway – a diminutive hall dated by dendrochronology to *c.*1315 – raises the question
of other diminutive halls of similar date still awaiting detailed study, such as Skinner's Mill Farm in
the Painswick valley. This tiny but well-fenestrated hall indicates social pretension at a fairly low
social level in the 14th century – perhaps on the part of the miller himself.

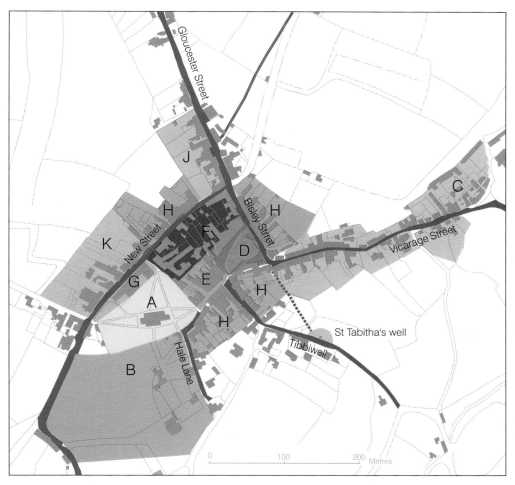

Fig. 5: Painswick: suggested scheme of urban development (based on Leech 1981, map 34, with additions). North is to the top of the page. If we assume that the present church occupies the site of the church inferred by Domesday Book (A), and that the manorial curia occupied the area immediately to the south (B) – though there is as yet no concrete evidence to support either assumption – then it is possible that the 10th–11th-century settlement straggled down the slope to the east and that the properties on either side of Vicarage Street (C) represent the tail of this original settlement. This might explain the awkward dog-leg in the main medieval through-route between Bisley Street, part of the new planned town, and Vicarage Street. However, there were alternative routes to the south-east via Hale Lane and Tibbiwell, or possibly by an extension of Bisley Street to St Tabitha's Well, now blocked. The planned market place, possibly of 12th- or 13th-century date, is usually taken to have occupied the area bounded by Friday Street (D) and now infilled by shops and houses. This area is small, however. It is also detached from the churchyard, whereas the church authorities were generally adept at ensuring themselves a profitable frontage on to any market area. Answering this objection, the authors of the Extended Urban Survey (Douthwaite and Devine 1998b, 151–66) proposed that the market place extended along the whole length of St Mary's Street (D and E). It could be proposed, alternatively, that the entire block south-east of New Street (D, E and F) was the market place. This is a very large area, but no larger than that identified as the original market place at Ludgershall, Wiltshire (Everson et al. 2000), for instance. Of course, the market place might have occupied all these areas at different times, through the effects of infilling and encroachment. However, if the church's property was at any time isolated from the market place, this would give a context for the creation of New Street, at some time before 1421, with the church authorities being main drivers in this development. They would have derived profitable church rents from their frontage on this new commercial street (G). Ironically these strips of land, almost certainly originally church property, were given to the church by generous donors in the 20th century. Burgage plots surrounding the market place (H) and extending along Gloucester Street (J), and later ones on the north-west side of New Street (K), can be identified.

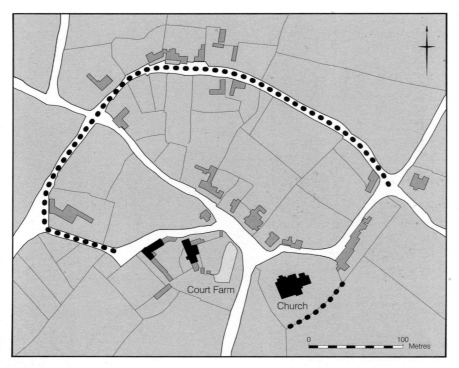

Fig. 6: Almondsbury: plan (after K. Rodwell 1991, fig. 2, with additions). The road pattern suggests the existence of an oval enclosure around manor, church and village core.

More synthetic work on houses is represented only by Linda Hall (1983) on the rural houses of the southern end of the county, Walrond and Powell (1985) on smoke vents and other features of small medieval houses in the Severn Valley and, in the post-medieval period, Kingsley (2001) and, on weavers' houses, Palmer and Neaverson (2003). Issues of building conservation and restoration have been discussed by, for instance, Hill and Birch (1994). Industrial buildings will be mentioned below.

Parish churches are another class of building which has had some attention recently. Excellent papers have covered timbers (Morley 1985; Morley and Miles 2000), wall paintings (e.g. Edwards 1986; 1994), rooms over porches (MacAleer 2002) and general fabric (e.g. Parry 1990). However, there has been little consideration of churches in their landscape context (even Parry makes scant reference to the archaeological surroundings of Lancaut church), though Heighway (1989) has made some interesting reflections on medieval churches and manorial complexes in relation to high-status Romano-British sites.

NEW TOPICS – LANDSCAPE FEATURES

Fields and Woods

Terry Moore-Scott's paper on Leckhampton's fields (2000), using field-name evidence and surviving ridge-and-furrow, attempts a reconstruction of the open fields. More work of this kind is

Fig. 7:   Field system in the Painswick valley (photograph January 2003, © Dr R.H. Bewley). Greenhouse Lane, a route of some antiquity, can be seen cutting diagonally through the fields. The relationship is complex because it suggests that the fields were regarded as being of secondary importance, or were perhaps even abandoned, at the time the road was established and yet their boundaries are, in most cases, still in use today. The fields are small, rectangular and lynchetted, and could well be of prehistoric origin. Plots of ridge-and-furrow are largely confined within these existing fields. The lower slopes were almost entirely under pasture in 1820 (Baker and Fosbrook). The ridge-and-furrow could be later than this but two features suggest an earlier, probably medieval, date. In a square field at the lower extreme right of the picture the ridge-and-furrow is very faint; this is the only field in the area that was under arable in 1820, so earlier cultivation remains might have been ploughed out at this time. In the elongated field immediately to the north (below and left), the ridge-and-furrow lies in two parcels, respecting a previous boundary, which had been removed before 1820; if the field had been ploughed in ridges after that date presumably it would have been ploughed in one parcel.

needed. The English Heritage Aerial Survey National Mapping Programme mapping of ridge-and-furrow has been mentioned above, but Gloucestershire does not have only extensive, classic, open-field systems. In the Painswick valley medieval or early post-medieval ploughlands were fitted into a pre-existing, indeed probably prehistoric, field system, which still survives today (Fig. 7).

Similarly, there has been some pioneering work on woodlands by Tom Heyes (1995; 1996) and others. Bick (1996) on earthworks in or near Hay Wood at Oxenhall in the Forest of Dean describes what may well be the 'haga' that gave its name to the wood – it certainly looks like a deer park on the map. It must not be forgotten that the doyen of historic woodland studies, Oliver Rackham, has had things to say about Gloucestershire. His passing remark (1980, 153) that the Forest of Dean was 'probably the last place approximating to virgin wildwood in England' may be open to question. However, Rackham's statistics on the differing yields of the various forests are instructive and raise questions which, so far as I know, have not been addressed – why was the Forest of Dean such a major supplier of swine compared to other forests, until the mid 13th century at least (ibid. 185)?

One of the most exciting developments, however, has been a series of papers by John Allen and colleagues, opening up an entirely new area of landscape studies in the Severn Valley. The first, in 1986, concerned salt-marsh reclamation around Slimbridge, Frampton on Severn and Saul, as evidenced by documents and, on air photographs and in the field, by seabanks and ridge-and-furrow. These date from at least the 14th century and continued until the 19th century. The story is a localised one of gains and losses to a 'fickle, tidal river' (Allen 1986, 153). On the left bank almost the whole area gained seems to have been ploughed, for a time at least, and farmsteads may even have been established; later, by the 17th century, the fields were enclosed as pasture and settlement shifted eastwards, off the alluvium onto bedrock (idem 1992). This dating, it has to be said, relies heavily on the assumption that 'classic' reverse-S ridge-and-furrow is of high medieval date. On Lydney Level, by contrast, only a little more than half the area enclosed was ever ploughed and settlement was never established (idem 2001, 54). Other uses of the estuary are attested by quays (Fulford *et al.* 1992) and by fish weirs and traps, as at Oldbury-on-Severn (e.g. Riley 1998).

Castles and Abbeys

These more traditional monument classes have been strangely under-studied in Gloucestershire; there may as well have been almost no rural abbeys in the county as far as the archaeological literature of the past 20 years is concerned (though much of the work in small towns, mentioned above, concerns religious houses). This is not entirely a true reflection of the state of affairs – and more work is now under way at Hailes, for instance – but it is indicative of a relatively slight incidence of activity. The more historical literature, however, has had interesting things to say about persons of high status in the county (e.g. Birrell 2001; Vincent 1998; Warmington 1986).

The Bristol and Gloucestershire Archaeological Society presidential address by David Walker in 1991 was on the subject of castles but its approach looks old-fashioned from the standpoint of 2004 – castle studies have advanced by leaps and bounds during the past 15 years through the work of scholars such as Coulson (e.g. 1979; 2003), Creighton (2002), Johnson (2002) and the staff of the former RCHME (e.g. Everson 1996; 1998; Taylor 2000). More positively, in Gloucestershire there have been at least two surveys and some excavation of earthwork castles – Hillesley (Ellis 1984c; B. Williams 1987) and Taynton Parva. At the latter Sarah Williams (1997) notes that the motte fits awkwardly into its ditch and suggests that it started as a ringwork – a useful addition to the literature of such sites (see e.g. Welfare *et al.* 1999); the identification, supported by place-name evidence, of a large pool on the northern edge of the site as a swannery raises interesting questions about the status of this site. Williams refers to the settlement here as a 'village', but the evidence seems to point to a manorial complex in an area of dispersed settlement (as it still is today). Even the more recent discovery of further building platforms (Jasper Blake pers. comm.) does not necessarily suggest that this was ever more than a hamlet.

Dodd and Moss (1991) published a paper about Brimpsfield Castle and the Giffard family, accompanied by a very appealing reconstruction drawing. However, it is not clear from the text what the status of this drawing is – on what evidence is it based? The authors state that their findings are 'mainly conjectural'. A survey is mentioned but the results of the survey are not

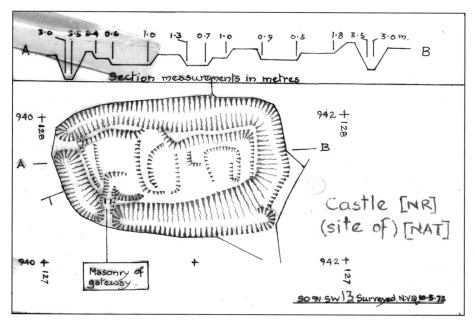

Fig. 8: Brimpsfield Castle: antiquity model prepared by Norman Quinnell for the Ordnance Survey Archaeology Division 1972 (© Crown copyright. National Monuments Record). (Scale 1:2500). North is towards the top of the page. Antiquity models were drawings by OS Archaeology Division Investigators indicating changes to the depiction of antiquities for new editions of OS maps; they were prepared on small extracts cut from old, pre-national grid maps.

presented, nor is the method or level of survey stated. Therefore it is impossible to know how much credence we can give to this drawing. There is, however, a 1972 Ordnance Survey Antiquity Model, reproduced here (Fig. 8). Several major questions about Brimpsfield remain: Dodd and Moss refer to the castle as a 'ringwork' but that is surely erroneous – it is much too big and far from circular. If we use the term 'ringwork' for castles such as this it will lose whatever meaning it has. The castle's plateau-edge location is notable and its surrounding ditch is massive: is it a re-used hillfort? Why is this impressive castle located in this large but not particularly wealthy manor, in an area otherwise devoid of large castles? It is not even central to the Giffards' estates, which were mostly in other parts of the country. What are the (unsurveyed) earthworks in the field to the north of the castle – evidence of shifted village settlement or part of the site of Brimpsfield's medieval priory, or are they more closely related to the castle? What is the date and purpose of the motte in the valley below? What was Brimpsfield's status as a settlement in the medieval period?

Sudeley Castle (Fig. 9) has apparently received no substantial attention recently but it is a site with huge research potential. The house itself may be now, partly at least, a Victorian reconstruction but the surrounding landscape clearly contains remains of the greatest interest. Sudeley was a major palatial house of the mid to late 15th century, of the type now known to be typically surrounded by extensive pleasure gardens and ornamental landscapes (Everson 1998; Taylor 2000), and with symbolic links to other features in the area. Much of what is now visible at Sudeley must relate to later phases, not least the 16th-century visits of Elizabeth I, but we should ask what the present

Fig. 9: Sudeley Castle (photograph by Damian Grady, December 2003, © English Heritage, National Monuments Record 23307/21).

landscape reveals about the 15th-century setting of this great house, and what are the links with Winchcombe town, its church and, perhaps most importantly in this respect, its abbey.

Early Post-Medieval and Industrial Archaeology

The incisive survey of weavers' houses by Palmer and Neaverson (2003) has been mentioned above. Work on Gloucestershire industry, especially but not exclusively the iron industry in the Forest of Dean, continues and is now a mainstream part of archaeological activity, as attested by a number of articles in the journal *Post-Medieval Archaeology* in the later 1980s (e.g. Kemp 1987; Stratton and Trinder 1988; Mullin 1989) and by the attention paid by 'mainstream' archaeologists, such as English Heritage's personnel undertaking the National Mapping Programme in the Forest of Dean. The RCHME's work on textile mills of the Stroud valleys was published by Keith Falconer in 1993, though more work has been done since in the south-west of the county. Quarrying has been somewhat neglected, though mention should be made of Hill and Birch (1994, 21–44), Arthur Price's work (e.g. 1995), King (1996) and Cedric Nielsen's (1999) fieldwork demonstration of a medieval or earlier date for some of the Painswick quarries.

Transport continues to be a major source of interest in all its forms, from the most local to the regional level. The Painswick Local History Society's milestones survey and restoration project (Minall 1999) is an instance. In 1984 David Viner described the Stroudwater Canal as 'a good opportunity for restoration in the future' (Viner 1984, 330) – that restoration is now, though controversial, going ahead (Eaton 2004); Gloucester Docks – 'arguably the county's most pressing problem' for Viner in 1984 (Viner 1984, 333) – are now triumphantly restored. Stroud station, also mentioned by Viner for its Brunel-inspired buildings (ibid. 335), has also been in the news recently – the goods shed received a substantial grant towards its restoration in 2004.

Aside from industry, parks and gardens are the most fashionable topics today for research in medieval and post-medieval archaeology. I have referred already to the RCHME's seminal work at Chipping Campden and more recent work at Dyrham and Lodge Park. An earthwork and resistivity survey of 18th-century gardens at Dumbleton was reported briefly by Maxwell and Mayes in 2003. This was primarily an exercise in testing out new geophysical equipment, but it was also successful in demonstrating that the gardens depicted by Kip had in fact been created. Much more remains to be done in this field.

CURRENT INITIATIVES

There is a healthy amount of fieldwork going on in the county – Gloucester and District Archaeological Research Goup's recent purchase of geophysical equipment, and the considerable efforts of the Dean Archaeological Group and the Gloucestershire Society for Industrial Archaeology are worthy of note. Three closely inter-related professionally-led projects should also be mentioned.

Forest of Dean Survey

This initiative, led by the Gloucestershire Archaeology Service, possibly will not make as much impact for the medieval countryside as for earlier periods, as it is specifically targeted at the pre-afforestation landscape. It is an essential next step nevertheless.

English Heritage Aerial Survey National Mapping Programme Projects in the Forest of Dean and the Cotswolds

Work on St Briavels in the Forest of Dean and on ridge-and-furrow in the Cotswolds has been mentioned above. There is certainly much more to come out of these projects. One example is Saintbury (Fig. 10) on the northern edge of the Cotswolds, an area assessed in the pilot phase of the Cotswolds project (Ed Carpenter pers. comm.). This remarkable parish sits within an area of outstanding earthwork survival, where further landscape studies would prove invaluable. The parish church, which contains some interesting architectural puzzles in its own right, sits within an oval enclosure that also contains, immediately to the west of the church, a rectangular sub-enclosure, probably the manorial *curia*. On the scarp above is the remains of a rabbit warren, with the site of the warrener's lodge possibly identifiable, and a large area of 'humps and bumps', mostly of geological rather than archaeological interest but probably including some of the latter. The present village straggles downslope to the north of the church, to the crossroads at Lower Farm marked by a late medieval cross (Fig. 11). Just without the current boundary of the parish are other significant sites, including the hillfort on Willersey Hill and a motte-and-bailey castle near the edge of Weston Park.

FUTURE RESEARCH

The development of a framework for archaeological research in South-West England is now under way (web address: somerset.gov.uk/somerset/cultureheritage/heritage/swarf). It is important that

Fig. 10:   Saintbury: (photograph by Damian Grady, November 2003, © English Heritage, National Monuments Record 23275/24).

discussion on future research frameworks does not descend immediately into a series of 'wish lists'. The examples mentioned in this paper are just examples, not firm suggestions. There are many issues to be considered but three points will be aired here, in no particular order.

The first is a question: is it more important to fill the gaps or to build on the strengths where good work has already been done? There are some yawning gaps in our understanding of the medieval countryside – environmental archaeology, for instance, is an almost complete blank (though the Forest of Dean Survey will be addressing this issue for that part of the county). Should effort be expended first there or, for instance, on taking another close look at the earthworks cited by Professor Dyer? An independent check on his results would be extremely valuable – does the archaeological evidence really confirm what the documents are saying, or does it challenge it?

The second point is that, whatever the emphasis of future research, it is vital that it is genuinely inter-disciplinary. Study of the medieval countryside (as of any other landscape) must involve geologists and geomorphologists, soils specialists, natural historians, place-name specialists, landscape and architectural historians, and so on, as well as all manner of archaeologists.

The third point is directed primarily at those undertaking earthwork survey, but it is more widely applicable. We must be more robust about earthworks and build on the good work that is already being done. The cup is half full, not half empty; it is not right to say of a well preserved earthwork site, 'there is virtually nothing left . . . except for some earthworks' (Dodd and

Fig. 11: Saintbury: medieval cross (© English Heritage, National Monuments Record). The cross dates from the 14th century and has a mid 19th-century head. Such crosses are often described as 'wayside' or 'preaching' crosses but these terms disguise their focal position in medieval processional liturgical practice (Duffy 1992, 136–9 et passim), which gave them a key place in the structuring of the medieval countryside. The crosses that survive are a tiny proportion of those originally existing.

Moss 1991, 34). The approach should be, rather, that the survival of any earthworks is a matter for rejoicing; earthworks are full of archaeological evidence and are an important part of the beauty and fascination of the landscape. Similarly, there is no reason to apologise for the practice of earthwork survey or landscape analysis. These are not 'second-best' to excavation – they are valid research strategies with their own unique strengths (Bowden 1999, 80–96). It follows that one should not survey the earthworks and then write an interpretation that simply reinforces the received wisdom about the site; it is vital to interrogate the earthworks themselves, to be inquisitive about origins, classifications and functions, about modifications and later re-use. The comments above about inter-disciplinary research notwithstanding, there should be no automatic deference either to excavated evidence or to documentary evidence – the visible physical remains are the primary evidence for what actually happened.

Unfortunately, the earthworks of the county are not secure. This can be illustrated by the gross vandalism at Hillesley, where a very interesting and important (and barely understood) earthwork complex was levelled, as recently as 1979 as it happens, to create a playing field (Ellis 1984c, 206–7; B. Williams 1987, 147). This is not a counsel of despair either; the situation at Hillesley could be mitigated by further research – analysis of the village plan followed by geophysical survey and targeted excavation. But only by making people aware of the value of earthwork remains in their locality can we ensure that the Hillesley disaster does not befall other places in the county.

Finally, it is not enough to call for more field research in the hope that we will somehow one day have 'enough' evidence. Archaeological evidence is, by its nature, fragmentary and incomplete.

Interpretation, developing an understanding of the past from partial, inadequate evidence, is the business of the archaeologist, and we must press on with it.

ACKNOWLEDGEMENTS

I would like to record my thanks to colleagues in English Heritage Aerial Survey, especially Ed Carpenter, Fiona Small and Cathy Stoertz, for discussion of their work in the Forest of Dean and the Cotswolds. I also wish to record my gratitude to my colleagues in Archaeological Investigation, in this case Graham Brown and Nicky Smith in particular, for maintaining their high standards of professionalism and commitment in very trying times as well as for their specific assistance with aspects of this paper. I am, as so often, indebted to Deborah Cunliffe for preparing the illustrations and to Damian Grady and Bob Bewley for their excellent aerial photographs.

BIBLIOGRAPHY

Aldred, D., and Dyer, C., with Bond, J., and Lewis, C., 1991. 'A medieval Cotswold village: Roel, Gloucestershire', *Trans. BGAS* **109**, 139–70.

Allen, J.R.L., 1986. 'A short history of salt-marsh reclamation at Slimbridge Warth and neighbouring areas, Gloucestershire', *Trans. BGAS* **104**, 139–55.

Allen, J.R.L., 1992. 'A reconnaissance map of medieval alluvial ploughlands in the Vale of Berkeley, Gloucestershire and Avon', *Trans. BGAS* **110**, 87–97.

Allen, J.R.L., 2001. 'The landscape archaeology of the Lydney Level, Gloucestershire: natural and human transformations over the last two millennia', *Trans. BGAS* **119**, 27–57.

Astill, G.G., and Grant, A. (eds.), 1988. *The Countryside of Medieval England* (Oxford, Blackwell).

Aston, M., and Viner, L., 1984. 'The study of deserted medieval villages in Gloucestershire', in Saville (ed.) 1984, 276–93.

Baddeley, W.St.C., 1907. *A Cotteswold Manor: being a History of Painswick* (Gloucester, John Bellows).

Baker, C., and Fosbrook, W., 1820. 'Maps and surveys of Painswick': MSS in Gloucestershire Record Office, P 244A/MI 1/1–5.

Bick, D., 1996. 'Earthworks in or near Hay Wood, Oxenhall', *New Regard of the Forest of Dean* **11**, 35–7.

Birrell, J., 2001. 'Aristocratic poachers in the Forest of Dean: their methods, their quarry and their companions', *Trans. BGAS* **119**, 147–54.

Bowden, M.C.B. (ed.), 1999. *Unravelling the Landscape: an inquisitive approach to archaeology* (Stroud, Tempus).

Bowden, M.C.B., 2005. *The Malvern Hills: an ancient landscape* (Swindon, English Heritage).

Coulson, C., 1979. 'Structural symbolism in medieval castle architecture', *J. Brit Archaeol. Assoc.* **132**, 73–90.

Coulson, C., 2003. *Castles in Medieval Society: fortresses in England, France and Ireland in the central Middle Ages* (Oxford University Press).

Creighton, O.H., 2002. *Castles and Landscapes* (London, Continuum).

Darvill, T., and Gerrard, C., 1994. *Cirencester: town and landscape, an urban archaeological assessment* (Cirencester, Cotswold Archaeol Trust).

Dodd, A., and Moss, P., 1991. 'The history of Brimpsfield Castle and the Giffard family', *Glevensis* **25**, 34–7.

Douthwaite, A., and Devine, V., 1998a. 'Gloucestershire Historic Towns Survey: Forest of Dean District' (Gloucester, Gloucestershire County Archaeol. Service).

Douthwaite, A., and Devine, V., 1998b. 'Gloucestershire Historic Towns Survey: Stroud District' (Gloucester, Gloucestershire County Archaeol. Service).

Duffy, E., 1992. *The Stripping of the Altars: traditional religion in England 1400–1580* (Yale University Press).

Dyer, C., 1982. 'Deserted medieval villages in the west midlands', *Econ Hist Rev.* **35.1**, 19–34.

Dyer, C., 1987. 'The rise and fall of a medieval village: Little Aston (in Aston Blank), Gloucestershire', *Trans. BGAS* **105**, 165–81.

Dyer, C., 1995. 'Sheepcotes: evidence for medieval sheep farming', *Med. Archaeol.* **39**, 136–64.

Dyer, C., 1996. 'Seasonal settlement in medieval Gloucestershire: sheepcotes', in H.L.F. Fox (ed.), *Seasonal Settlement* (Vaughan Paper **39**, University of Leicester), 25–34.

Dyer, C., 2002. 'Villages and non-villages in the medieval Cotswolds', *Trans. BGAS* **120**, 11–35.

Eaton, T., 2004. 'Josiah's Dream', *Brit. Archaeol.* **79**, 26–7.

Ecclestone, M., 2000. 'The Haresfield pottery: an investigation', *Glevensis* **33**, 47–55.

Edwards, J., 1986. 'The mural and the morality play: a suggested source for a wall painting at Oddington', *Trans. BGAS* **104**, 187–200.

Edwards, J., 1994. 'Turkdean church wall-paintings: a cautionary tale', *Trans. BGAS* **112**, 105–10.

Ellis, P., 1984a. 'Earthworks at Bishton Farm, Tidenham', *Trans. BGAS* **102**, 204–5.

Ellis, P., 1984b. 'The medieval settlement at Hullasey, Coates', *Trans. BGAS* **102**, 210–12.

Ellis, P., 1984c. 'Earthwork surveys of three sites in Avon', *Trans. BGAS* **102**, 206–10.

Ellis, P., 1986. 'Excavations in Winchcombe, Gloucestershire, 1962–72: a report on excavation and fieldwork by B.K. Davison and J. Hinchliffe at Cowl Lane and Back Lane', *Trans. BGAS* **104**, 95–138.

Enright, D., and Kenyon, D., 2000. 'The origins of a Cotswold village: evidence from recent excavations at Lower Slaughter', *Glevensis* **33**, 56–8.

Enright, D., and Watts, M., 2002. *A Romano-British and medieval settlement site at Stoke Road, Bishop's Cleeve, Gloucestershire* (Bristol and Gloucestershire Archaeol. Rep. **1**, Cirencester, Cotswold Archaeol.).

Everson, P.L., 1989. 'The gardens of Campden House, Chipping Campden, Gloucestershire', *Garden History* **17.2**, 109–21.

Everson, P.L., 1996. 'Bodiam Castle, East Sussex: castle and its designed landscape', *Chateau Gaillard* **17**, 79–84.

Everson, P.L., 1998. '"Delightfully surrounded with woods and ponds": field evidence for medieval gardens in England', in P. Pattison (ed.), *There by design: field archaeology in parks and gardens* (BAR Brit. Series **267**, Oxford), 32–8.

Everson, P.L., Brown, G., and Stocker, D., 2000. 'The castle earthworks and landscape context', in P. Ellis (ed.), *Ludgershall Castle: excavations by Peter Addyman 1964–72* (Wiltshire Archaeol. Natural Hist. Soc. Monograph **2**), 97–119.

Falconer, K.A., 1993. 'Mills of the Stroud valleys', *Ind. Archaeol. Rev.* **16.1**, l62–81.

Franklin, P., 1983. 'Malaria in medieval Gloucestershire: an essay in epidemiology', *Trans. BGAS* **101**, 111–22.

Franklin, P., 1989 'Thornbury woodlands and deer parks, part 1: the earls of Gloucester's parks', *Trans. BGAS* **107**, 149–70.

Fulford, M.G., Rippon, S., Allen, J.R.L., and Hillam, J., 1992. 'The medieval quay at Woolaston Grange, Gloucestershire'. *Trans. BGAS* **110**, 101–27.

Guy, C., 1986. 'Excavations at Back Lane, Winchcombe, 1985', *Trans. BGAS* **104**, 214–20.

Hall, D., 2001. *Turning the Plough: Midland open fields: landscape character and proposals for management* (Northamptonshire County Council/English Heritage).

Hall, L.J., 1983. *The Rural Houses of North Avon and South Gloucestershire, 1400–1720* (City of Bristol Museum & Art Gallery Monograph **6**).

Hannan, A., 1993. 'Excavations at Tewkesbury, 1972–4', *Trans. BGAS* **111**, 21–75.

Hannan, A., 1997. 'Tewkesbury and the Earls of Gloucester: excavations at Holm Hill, 1974–5', *Trans. BGAS* **115**, 79–231.

Heighway, C., 1989. 'Excavations near the site of St Gregory's Church, King's Stanley', *Glevensis* **23**, 33–42.

Herring, P., 1996. 'Transhumance in medieval Cornwall', in H.S.A. Fox (ed.), *Seasonal Settlement* (Vaughan Paper **39**. University of Leicester), 35–44.

Heyes, T., 1995. 'Bowldown Wood', *Glevensis* **28**, 35–40.

Heyes, T., 1996. 'Kemble Wood', *Glevensis* **29**, 51–2.

Hill, M., and Birch, S., 1994. *Cotswold Stone Homes: history, conservation, care* (Stroud, Alan Sutton).

Hilton, R.H., and Rahtz, P.A., 1966. 'Upton, Gloucestershire, 1959–64', *Trans. BGAS* **85**, 70–146.

Hoyle, J., 1992. 'Tewkesbury Abbey Meadow', *Glevensis* **26**, 30–1.

Hurst, J.G., 1984. 'The Wharram research project: results to 1983', *Med. Archaeol.* **28**, 77–111.

Iles, R., and Popplewell, J., 1985. 'Bradley moat and fishponds, Wotton-under-Edge', *Trans. BGAS* **103**, 214–16.

Johnson, M., 2002. *Behind the Castle Gate: from medieval to renaissance* (London, Routledge).

Kemp, R.L., 1987. 'A 17th-century royal forge in the Forest of Dean', *Post-Med. Archaeol.* **21**, 127–46.

King, R, 1996 'The medieval occupation', in R. King, A. Barber and J. Timby 'Excavations at West Lane, Kemble: an Iron Age, Roman and Saxon burial site and a medieval building' *Trans. BGAS* **114**, 15–54.

Kingsley, N., 2001. *The Country Houses of Gloucestershire I, 1500–1660* (2nd edn., Chichester, Phillimore).

Leech, R., 1981. *Historic Towns in Gloucestershire* (CRAAGS Surv. 3, Bristol).

Leech, R., 1984. 'Medieval urban archaeology in Gloucestershire', in Saville (ed.) 1984, 294–303.

Leech, R., and McWhirr, A.D., 1982. 'Excavations at St John's Hospital, Cirencester, 1971 and 1976', *Trans. BGAS* **100**, 191–210.

Lilley, K., 1997 'Historical analysis of the plan form of the town [Tewkesbury]', in Hannan 1997, 88–93.

MacAleer, J.P., 2002. 'The rooms over the porches of Bishop's Cleeve and Bredon parish churches: a question of dating', *Trans. BGAS* **120**, 133–75.

Maxwell, A., and Mayes, D., 2003. '18th-century gardens at Dumbleton', *Glevensis* **36**, 23–7.

Minall, P., 1999. 'Painswick milestones', *Painswick Chronicle* **3**, 18–21.

Moore-Scott, T., 2000. 'Leckhampton's fields', *Glevensis* **33**, 35–42.

Morley, B.M., 1985. 'The nave roof of the Church of St Mary, Kempley, Gloucestershire', *Antiq. J.* **65**, 101–11.

Morley, B.M., and Miles, D.W.H., 2000. 'The nave roof and other timberwork at the Church of St Mary, Kempley, Gloucestershire: dendrochronological dating', *Antiq. J.* **80**, 294–6.

Mullin, D., 1989. 'The archaeology of Camp Mill: a re-assessment', *Post-Med Archaeol.* **23**, 15–20.

Nielsen, C., 1999. 'A possible medieval boundary wall on Painswick Beacon Common', *Glevensis* **32**, 37–40.

Oakey, N. (ed), 2000. *Three Medieval Sites in Gloucestershire* (Cotswold Archaeol. Trust Occasional Paper 1).

Palmer, M., and Neaverson, P., 2003. 'Handloom weaving in Wiltshire and Gloucestershire in the 19th century: the building evidence', *Post-Med. Archaeol.* **37.1**, 126–58.

Parry, C., 1989. 'An earthwork survey at Little Colesbourne, Withington, Gloucestershire', *Trans. BGAS* **107**, 223–8.

Parry, C., 1990. 'A survey of St James's church, Lancaut, Gloucestershire', *Trans. BGAS* **108**, 53–103.

Price, A.J., 1995. 'Traditional stone use in the Cotswolds', *Glevensis* **28**, 12.

Rackham, O., 1980. *Ancient Woodland* (London, Edward Arnold).

Rahtz, P.A., 1969. 'Upton, Gloucestershire, 1964–8: second report', *Trans. BGAS* **88**, 74–126.

Riley, H., 1998. 'Intertidal Palaeoenvironmental and Archaeological Features at Oldbury-on-Severn, South Gloucestershire' (Exeter, RCHME).

Rodwell, K., 1991. 'Court Farm, Lower Almondsbury', *Trans. BGAS* **109**, 179–93.

Rodwell, K., and Bell, R., 2004. *Acton Court: the evolution of an early Tudor courtier's house* (London, English Heritage).

Rodwell, W., 2000. 'Daneway and Lodge Park: the archaeology of two Gloucestershire houses', *Trans. BGAS* **118**, 11–32.

Saville, A. (ed), 1984. *Archaeology in Gloucestershire* (Cheltenham Art Gallery and Museums and the BGAS).

Saville, A., 1985. 'Salvage recording of Romano-British, Saxon, medieval and post-medieval remains at North Street, Winchcombe, Gloucestershire', *Trans. BGAS* **103**, 101–40.

Smith, N.A., 1998. 'Manless Town, Brimpsfield: an archaeological survey', *Glevensis* **31**, 53–8.

Smith, N.A., 2002a. 'Minchinhampton Common, Gloucestershire' (English Heritage Survey Report AI/12/2002, Swindon).

Smith, N.A., 2002b. 'Dyrham Park, South Gloucestershire' (English Heritage Survey Report AI/39/2002, Swindon).

Stratton, M., and Trinder, B., 1988. 'Stanley Mill, Gloucestershire', *Post-Med Archaeol.* **22**, 143–80.

Taylor, C.C., 2000. 'Medieval ornamental landscapes', *Landscapes* **1.1**, 38–55.

Vince, A., 1984. 'Late Saxon and medieval pottery in Gloucestershire', in Saville (ed.) 1984, 248–75.

Vincent, N., 1998. 'The borough of Chipping Sodbury and the fat men of France (1130–1270)', *Trans. BGAS* **116**, 141–59.

Walker, D., 1991. 'Gloucestershire castles', *Trans. BGAS* **109**, 5–23.

Walrond, L.F.J., 1984. 'The medieval houses of rural Gloucestershire', in Saville (ed.) 1984, 304–14.

Walrond, L.F.J., and Powell, C., 1985. 'Medieval smoke vents and low room walls in the Severn plain', *Trans. BGAS* **103**, 163–73.

Warmington, A., 1986. 'Some knights of the household of King John with lands in Gloucestershire', *Trans. BGAS* **104**, 175–82.

Welfare, H.G., Bowden, M.C.B., and Blood, N.K., 1999. 'Fieldwork and the castles of the Anglo-Scottish borders', in P. Pattison, D. Field and S. Ainsworth (eds.), *Patterns of the Past: essays in landscape archaeology for Christopher Taylor* (Oxford, Oxbow Books), 53–60.

Wilkinson, D.J., and McWhirr, A.D., 1998. *Cirencester Anglo-Saxon Church and Medieval Abbey* (Cirencester Excavations 4, Cotswold Archaeol. Trust).

Williams, B., 1987. 'Excavation of a medieval earthwork complex at Hillesley, Hawkesbury, Avon', *Trans. BGAS* **105**, 147–63.

Williams, S., 1997. 'Taynton Parva', *Glevensis* **30**, 27–32.

Wootton, D., and Bowden, M.C.B., 2002. 'A Circular Enclosure at Redmarley d'Abitot', Gloucestershire' (English Heritage Survey Report AI/43/2002, Swindon).

Bristol

Robert H. Jones

INTRODUCTION

Archaeological research in Bristol has a long and distinguished pedigree. It begins with William Worcestre in the late 15th century and continues through antiquarians such as William Barrett and Samuel Seyer into the 19th century with the work of W.R. Barker and especially John Pritchard, the latter paving the way for the practice of modern archaeology in the city. The standard of recording of the latter scholars in particular bears healthy comparison with modern archaeological practice. The impetus provided by the local societies from the late 19th century, especially the Bristol and Gloucestershire Archaeological Society, of which John Pritchard was president from 1918 to 1920, and the Clifton Antiquarian Club, provided the boost which was needed in this period of rapid change in the city's fabric. It also helped to raise the political profile of the city's heritage and, while it did not provide the same sort of protection that we would be used to today, it nevertheless meant that there was a pride in the heritage which undoubtedly helped in the recording efforts of Pritchard, Barker and many others.

The city is currently undergoing a period of rapid and extensive change in its fabric and economy. Ensuring that the city's historic environment is properly conserved and recorded represents a challenge to modern archaeologists working in the city. Such changes are not new. The period from the late 19th century witnessed major development, transforming Bristol from the largely medieval and Georgian town depicted in the wonderful paintings and drawings collected by George Weare Braikenridge to the bustling Victorian and 20th-century city seen on early photographs. Major and catastrophic upheaval occurred in the Second World War when, especially in 1940, Bristol suffered extensive bomb damage, changing the face of the city centre for ever. As with other towns and cities throughout the United Kingdom in the post-war years, major plans were introduced to reconstruct the city centre. Many of these ideas never progressed beyond the drawing board, but major changes still took place: the completion of the inner ring road, the development of Broadmead as the new shopping centre of Bristol, and the construction of high-rise office premises and associated roads.

This paper will present specifically the results of archaeological investigation that has been carried out in the city in the last 25 years, from the end of the 1970s onwards, while acknowledging the contribution of earlier field-workers. By looking at the range of archaeological work that has been taking place over this period, it will attempt to illustrate how new ideas are beginning to emerge relating both to the medieval and later urban core as well as to the historic landscape of the greater Bristol area.

Approximately the first half of the period covered by this paper coincides with the introduction of the government-sponsored Job Creation Schemes as a major source of funds for archaeological work. As a result, extensive excavations were undertaken, from the mid 1970s until the late 1980s, involving large numbers of field-workers and specialists. Unfortunately, there was not the commensurate funding for the essential post-excavation assessment and publication. The completion of the post-excavation work on these sites, some of which have the potential to answer important research questions regarding the city's development, remains a high priority.

During this period, virtually all major archaeological work within the city was undertaken by the city council's own archaeological field unit, set up from the late 1960s onwards by Michael Ponsford, formerly curator of field archaeology at Bristol City Museum, until its demise in 1992. The archaeological unit still survives as Bristol and Region Archaeological Services (BaRAS), now a self-financing arm of the council's museum service, although a considerable amount of field-work is now also carried out by external archaeological units.

From 1990, when PPG 16 was issued and, for Bristol, from 1992 with the appointment of an archaeological officer within the planning division of the city council, archaeology became firmly embedded within the planning process. One consequence of this has been the opportunity to extend the range, both in a geographical and a temporal sense, of archaeological activity. With this has come about a greater realisation that there is much more to the study of archaeology within the borders of Bristol than simply the study of the medieval urban core.

The Bristol Urban Strategy programme, funded by English Heritage, has allowed the creation of an Urban Archaeological Database, a much more comprehensive dataset for the historic core of the city. The second stage of this programme will see the publication of a detailed resource assessment of past archaeological activity. A second draft has been submitted to English Heritage and it is expected that this work, which will be expected to guide future standards and directions for archaeological research, will be published in the near future.

THE PREHISTORIC LANDSCAPE

In recent years, there has been important work in looking at the prehistoric landscapes of the greater Bristol area (Fig. 1). While there has been important work in the past on the major Iron-Age hillforts at Blaise, Kingsweston and to a lesser extent Clifton Camp, and many artefacts dating from the earliest prehistoric periods have been found often in less than ideal conditions, there has been little understanding of the wider landscape of these periods, its development and exploitation.

The Shirehampton area of Bristol, lying on gravel terraces near the confluence of the Avon and Severn, is well known for the casual recovery by collectors over many years of a fine series of Palaeolithic artefacts. Work is currently being carried out to begin to understand the context of the Palaeolithic settlement of the Bristol Avon, especially the sediment sequences which have routinely produced these artefacts, both within Bristol and beyond. In the Shirehampton area, archaeological work within the development control process is now regularly targetting these deposits for study. An initial review of the deposits producing such artefacts has now been completed and a more detailed document setting out the research frameworks for the Palaeolithic in the Bristol Avon has recently been produced. The latter will guide future work in this area, both within Bristol itself and elsewhere along the Bristol Avon (Bates and Wenban-Smith 2005).

The Bronze Age in Bristol has received intermittent attention including work on King's Weston Hill (Tratman, 1925), but there has not been any consistent survey of artefacts and landscapes of this period. Recent work on the Avonmouth Levels, in response to the creation of a business park of over 60 ha known as Cabot Park as well as other developments on the Levels, has provided the opportunity for intensive investigation of these potentially rich archaeological deposits. Extensive field-work in the area has produced evidence for a number of sites, of late Bronze Age or early Iron Age date. They suggest a seasonal settlement pattern in the alluvial floodplain and are seemingly connected to a series of palaeochannels that weave through the Levels, some still surviving in the modern landscape as drainage rhines. These sites are presumably associated with better-known settlements on the higher ground to the east and suggest widespread utilisation of the Levels for

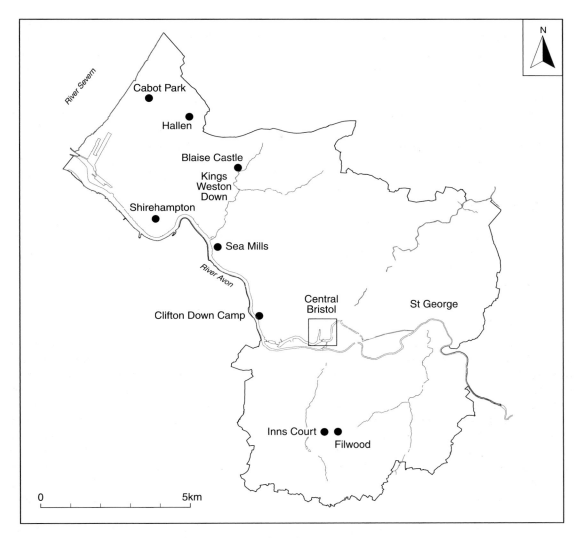

Fig. 1: Greater Bristol: plan of sites mentioned in the text.

a variety of purposes. Such settlements are typically ephemeral in nature and consist of layers of burning, with bone, charcoal, pottery and heat-cracked stone (Locock 2001). There is little in the way of structures although a recent site, examined in difficult conditions, produced evidence for a well-defined ditch, possibly a boundary. Several more sites of this type are known, suggesting a concerted use of the Levels for seasonal activities such as hunting, fishing and possibly salt production.

The evidence for Iron-Age occupation on the Levels comes from the two sites at Northwick, which lie outside the city boundary in South Gloucestershire, and Hallen. The Hallen site was investigated from 1992 in advance of the construction of the M49 motorway. It was dated by the pottery assemblage to the late 2nd to 1st centuries BC and it is one of the few examples so far of

Iron-Age exploitation of this economically important area (Gardiner, *et al.* 2002). However, what has become clear, from the work at Cabot Park and elsewhere on the Levels, is that this is an archaeologically rich area with far more yet to be done. The discovery of stabilised soil horizons over much of the area from the Neolithic period (and possibly earlier in some cases) is significant and has enabled a greater understanding of the complex Holocene sedimentation in this area. The discovery of settlement sites from the later prehistoric period onwards highlights the need to understand the complex interrelationships between these sites and corresponding activity on the higher ground to the east, such as the recorded Bronze-Age barrows on King's Weston Hill.

In the urban core, where relatively little work in investigating possible pre-urban settlement sites has previously been carried out, it has now become routine, using the experience gained on the Avonmouth Levels, to interrogate the deep alluvial sequences upon which much of the modern city is built. Early results are promising. Immediately north of Canon's Marsh, on the edge of the high ground, borehole investigation, accompanying formal archaeological investigation of the later archaeology of the site by Cotswold Archaeology, has suggested the presence of a former river valley, perhaps one of several former channels of the river Frome. The evidence retrieved also suggested that in the early Neolithic there was localised clearance of the lime and oak forest, probably on the higher ground, presumably to allow for agricultural activity and settlement. There is also the possibility that some exploitation of the alluvial floodplain could have occurred during the early and middle Neolithic, although no direct evidence was recovered from this site (Wilkinson 2002).

ROMAN SETTLEMENT IN THE BRISTOL AREA

The Roman landscape of greater Bristol has also received some attention in recent field-work (Fig. 1). The earlier work of George Boon at the Roman town of Sea Mills and at Kingsweston Villa has long been published and is well known (Boon 1945; 1950). However, a number of new sites have come to light and these are reinforcing the view that the Bristol area was fairly densely populated and was economically prosperous. There is also the exciting prospect of a hitherto unknown Roman settlement awaiting discovery somewhere in east Bristol in the St George area, close to the presumed line of the Roman road from Bath. The discovery here in 2002 of a number of burials, radiocarbon dated to the late Roman period (1573±68 BP:Wk-11396) (340–640 cal. AD at 95.4% confidence), close to the site where over 15 burials were found during sewer construction in 1894, suggests a potentially large late Roman cemetery, perhaps at least 2 ha in area (Williams 2004).

Work at Inns Court in south Bristol has uncovered a settlement dating probably from the late Iron Age, with a major stone building constructed in the second half of the 3rd century and surviving at least until the second half of the 4th century (Jackson 1999). It was almost certainly associated economically, and possibly physically with a nearby settlement excavated in 1982 at Filwood Park about 300 m to the east (Williams 1983). The relationship of these settlements to each other has yet to be defined. However, it is possible that here we see an example of interrelated compounds, perhaps forming a small village, as suggested for Catsgore in Somerset (Leech 1982), for example. Whatever is the final answer, it is certainly the case that new evidence like this, as well as other sites such as that recently excavated at Henbury School in north Bristol, is beginning to answer existing questions, as well as pose new ones, about the nature of late Iron-Age and Romano-British settlement and exploitation of the landscape in the Bristol area.

In the central core of the city, despite the occurrence of Romano-British artefacts in residual contexts, much of any physical evidence for Roman settlement is likely to have been severely truncated or removed by overlying construction activities associated with the development of the medieval and later town. However excavations in the 1970s near Upper Maudlin Street, to the north of the city centre, revealed a small Roman settlement, dating from the late 2nd century and continuing in occupation until the 5th century. In 1999, further excavations revealed more of the settlement, although the evidence was ephemeral (no. 1 on Fig. 2). However, there was some evidence recovered for iron working in the form of iron slag, together with the discovery in the 1970s excavation of a probable bowl furnace. This evidence would not be inconsistent with an essentially rural settlement where small-scale iron working was being carried out, as at the nearby sites of Stonehill, Hanham, and Gatcombe, North Somerset (Jackson 2000).

THE URBAN ORIGINS OF BRISTOL

There has been surprisingly little new evidence to complement the work of Philip Rahtz who carried out excavations at Mary-le-Port Street in 1962–3 (no. 2 on Fig. 2) and demonstrated the late Saxon origin of that street (Watts and Rahtz 1985). Further evidence for late Saxon occupation

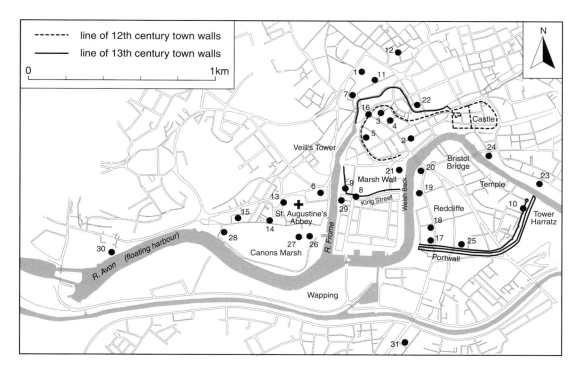

Fig. 2: Central Bristol: location of sites mentioned in the text. Key: 1 Upper Maudlin Street; 2 Mary-le-Port Street; 3 Tower Lane; 4 Newmarket Avenue; 5 Small Street; 6 St Augustine-the-Less; 7 St Bartholomew's Hospital; 8 Marsh Wall; 9 Site of water-gate; 10 Site of water-gate near Tower Harratz; 11 Franciscan Friary, Lewin's Mead; 12 St James's Priory; 13 Bristol Cathedral; 14 College Square; 15 Deanery Road; 16 St John's Church; 17 82–90 Redcliff Street; 18 Canynges House, Redcliff Street; 19 Dundas Wharf, Redcliff Street; 20 Bristol Bridge; 21 Spicer's Hall, Welsh Back; 22 Union Street; 23 Soap Boilers' and Hoopers glasshouses; 24 Cheese Lane glasshouse; 25 Portwall Lane glasshouse; 26 Canon's Marsh excavation 2000; 27 Canon's Marsh excavation 1997; 28 Canon's Marsh gasworks; 29 St Clement's and Aldworth's docks; 30 Excavation at Poole's Wharf; 31 Boot Lane, Bedminster.

was subsequently found on the site of Bristol Castle in the late 1960s and early 1970s. More recently these discoveries have been augmented with evidence for cess pits and postholes producing late 10th- to early 11th-century pottery from excavations at Tower Lane in 1979 (no. 3 on Fig. 2) (Boore 1980) and at Newmarket Avenue in 1990 (no. 4 on Fig. 2) (Williams 1992). Excavations at Small Street in 1990 (no. 5 on Fig. 2) revealed part of an earth bank near Leonard Lane, tentatively interpreted as evidence for the defences of the late Saxon *burh*, but no dating evidence was retrieved to support this hypothesis (ibid. 54). Indeed, the nature and location of the early defences have yet to be properly investigated. The significance of the double ditch on the line of Dolphin Street, excavated by Rahtz in 1962–3 (Watts and Rahtz 1985) has yet to be satisfactorily explained and its possible interpretation as an element of the eastern defensive circuit of the late Saxon town must be questioned. It is hoped that there may be further opportunities for investigation as part of future development proposals for this area.

Similarly, the evidence for the early port can presently only be surmised. Ponsford (1985) has suggested that it may have been located between Welsh Back and the site of Bristol Castle. The placename *rakhyth*, the modern Rackhay, well to the west of Welsh Back, may give a clue to the location of the early port, at this time perhaps merely a gently sloping bank where boats could be pulled ashore, akin to similar examples in London and elsewhere.

The evidence so far retrieved seems to support the traditional view, put forward by Stephenson (1933) and others, of the location of the original settlement, centred upon the Carfax, with at least the beginnings of a gridded network of streets. The scale of this early settlement has yet to be established, although the discovery of late Saxon features under the castle could suggest that it was reasonably extensive. There are clearly many questions to be resolved in furthering our understanding of the late Saxon origins of Bristol, not least the outstanding matters of the precise limits of the town and the date, course and form of its defences.

Late Saxon settlement outside the urban core also seems likely. To the west of the river Frome, in the early medieval manor of Billeswick, within which the abbey of St Augustine (now Bristol Cathedral) was founded by Robert Fitzharding *c.*1140, excavations at the former church of St Augustine-the-Less (no. 6 on Fig. 2) in 1983 recovered inhumations which could be late Saxon (Boore 1985, 25). However, radiocarbon dating of these burials did not demonstrate conclusively the pre-Norman date so this must remain a matter of conjecture. The meagre evidence so far retrieved could substantiate the inference drawn from the Harrowing of Hell relief, discovered in 1831 below the floor of the abbey chapter house (Smith 1976), that a late Saxon religious site was located somewhere in this area of the manor, possibly on the site occupied by the later church of St Augustine-the-Less.

Excavations at the site of St Bartholomew's Hospital on the north bank of the Frome (no. 7 on Fig. 2) produced evidence for possible late Saxon settlement, perhaps adjacent to a small creek (Price with Ponsford 1998). In addition, Roger Leech has suggested the possibility of late Saxon settlement, known as 'Arthur's Acre' around the southern approach to an early Bristol Bridge (Leech 2000a, 10).

THE GROWTH OF THE MEDIEVAL TOWN

The Defences and Castle

There is an increasing body of evidence for the growth, form and functions of the medieval town especially from *c.*1200 onwards. However the data are still piecemeal and hampered by the lack of opportunities for investigation in the most crucial areas, especially in the heart of the historic core of the medieval town. For example, while knowledge of the course of the medieval defensive circuit encircling the town was considerably enhanced by the work of Rahtz, in the 1950s, and others suggesting a construction date in the 12th century for the first stone defences, there are still outstanding questions concerning its form and even its course, especially in the eastern area of the town.

In the first half of the 13th century the walled area of the town was extended to both north and south with the enclosure of the low-lying land north of St John's Church as far as the southern bank of the river Frome, and with the construction of the Marsh Wall to the north of King Street from where it returned northwards along the east side of the river Frome. This north–south length of the Marsh Wall probably terminated at a tower, Viell's Tower. There is currently no evidence that the wall ever continued north of this point, despite the assumption in previously published plans of the medieval town that it met the 12th-century town wall somewhere near St Giles Gate. At roughly the same time the Portwall was constructed, enclosing the suburb of Redcliffe and Temple, probably with a grant of murage made in 1232 (Cronne 1945). These works broadly coincided with the diversion of the river Frome from its original course to the south of the early medieval core to its present course further south. Roger Leech has suggested that the somewhat sinuous course of the Marsh Wall along King Street reflects an original course of the Frome, based on his detailed study of the development of tenement boundaries in this area (Leech 1997). However, verification of these ideas must await the results of more extensive field-work and palaeoenvironmental sampling.

No recent work has been undertaken on the northern extension of the walled circuit and only limited work on the Marsh Wall. A bastion on part of this wall was exposed in 1960 and is now a Scheduled Ancient Monument. In 1995, the base courses of part of the Marsh Wall were exposed (Burchill 1995) (no. 8 on Fig. 2), while in 1979, in a watching brief maintained during construction works to extend the former Bristol and West building, part of the north–south section of this wall was uncovered together with what is likely to have been a water-gate (no. 9 on Fig. 2) through the wall (Price 1991).

In contrast, far more extensive work has been carried out on the Portwall. Excavation in 1983 uncovered a 70-m length of the wall, including an interval tower (Iles 1984, 59). Subsequently, as part of recent comprehensive redevelopment of the eastern part of the Temple suburb for a new complex of office developments, a large proportion of the rest of the Portwall was exposed, including parts of several interval towers. The eastern terminal tower of the Portwall, Tower Harratz, was fully investigated. It was 13 m in diameter and constructed with a clay core that extended out in six 'spines'. It probably was originally situated on the contemporary river bank but the Portwall had been extended beyond it as new land was reclaimed (Jackson 1994). To the south-west of Tower Harratz, a small water-gate (no. 10 on Fig. 2) consisting of two buttresses flanking an arched passage was found. Associated with it was a sally port that possibly gave access to a small jetty (Cox 2000).

Bristol Castle was founded as a motte-and-bailey structure c.1080, possibly, according to Ponsford (1979), replacing a short-lived ringwork constructed in the years immediately following the Norman Conquest. A stone keep was constructed from c.1135 on the site of the motte which was levelled and the motte ditch infilled. Michael Ponsford's unpublished thesis (1979) remains the only detailed and comprehensive account of archaeological works on the castle up to 1970. This work retrieved vital information about the development of this hugely important monument, including what may be remains of the barbican gate and possibly part of the constable's quarters. Ponsford also recovered evidence for the motte ditch and parts of the succeeding stone keep.

Work on the castle keep in 1989 revealed further evidence for this monumental structure and for the underlying motte ditch. The latter appears to have been infilled rapidly prior to and during the construction of the stone keep (Good 1996). A few fragments of dressed fine-grained limestone were found which could have originated from Caen, the reputed source of the building stone for the keep. Further landscaping works from the early 1990s uncovered further sections of the castle, including part of the south and west curtain walls. These have now been preserved and are largely open for public view.

However, only a relatively small proportion of the castle has been examined. It is also the case that while it lies within a public park, managed by the local authority and hence reasonably protected against indiscriminate development, the full extent of the castle's preservation and hence its potential remain uncertain. The 1989 work has been published (Good 1996), but this only covers a specific area in any detail. The landscaping of the 1990s revealed that more of the fabric of the castle remains than was hitherto expected. The great hall, for example, at the eastern end of the precinct, may be well preserved under a modern earth bank. The entrance chamber still stands and is protected as a Scheduled Ancient Monument. Parts of the south and west curtain walls were discovered during these works, necessitating last-minute changes to the landscaping proposals to allow them to be preserved and exposed to public view.

Churches and Religious Houses

Religious houses, churches, chapels, preaching crosses and other religious foundations and institutions were essential elements of everyday life in the medieval and later town. Bristol was almost encircled by the buildings and estates of a variety of religious houses, some wealthy, some impoverished, while almshouses, chapels and preaching crosses, for example, would have been familiar within the medieval street scene (Fig. 3). The publication in 1998 of important excavations at St Bartholomew's Hospital (no. 7 on Fig. 2), carried out between 1976 and 1978, revealed the potential of such sites and highlighted the need for the wider study of urban hospitals and almshouses, as well as other urban religious institutions (Price with Ponsford 1998). Occupying the site of an earlier (late Norman) first-floor hall, a new hospital was founded c.1234 with additions to the north in the late 13th or early 14th century. By the late 14th century, most of the buildings had been reconstructed and a church was built on the site of the former hall. By 1445, and until the end of the 15th century, the hospital provided a home for retired mariners. The hospital closed in 1532, shortly before the Dissolution, and it subsequently housed Bristol Grammar School, the Queen Elizabeth's Hospital School and, latterly, domestic and industrial premises.

The adjacent Franciscan friary in Lewin's Mead (no. 11 on Fig. 2) was excavated in 1973 but remains largely unpublished, although an interim report has been produced (Ponsford n.d.). This work uncovered evidence for part of the church, the chapter house and part of the cloisters. A garderobe to the rear produced a superb range of finds including wooden bowls and leather shoes. Later work, in 1989, revealed what may have been the warden's lodging, or possibly the guest-house of the friary, constructed on a terrace cut into the rock and overlooking the main friary complex (Ponsford et al. 1989, 42–4).

At the neighbouring site of St James's Priory (no. 12 on Fig. 2), founded c.1129, fairly limited excavations in 1989 were complemented by far more extensive work in 1995. Over 200 burials were uncovered, together with traces of the extensively robbed-out remains of the chancel, a possible side chapel and perhaps the north transept of the priory church which was demolished

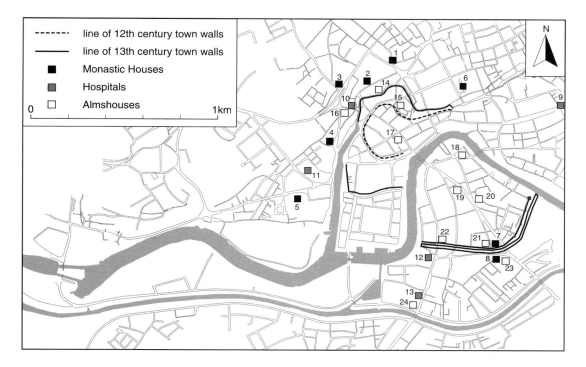

Fig. 3: Bristol: location of medieval religious sites (after Price with Ponsford 1998). Key: Monastic Houses: *1 St James's Priory; 2 Franciscan Friary; 3 St Mary Magdalen Nunnery; 4 Carmelite Friary; 5 St Augustine's Abbey; 6 Dominican Friary; 7 Augustinian Friary; 8 Friars of the Sack.* Hospitals: *9 Holy Trinity; 10 St Bartholomew's; 11 St Mark's; 12 St John's; 13 St Mary Magdalen.* Almshouses: *14 Spencer's; 15 Strange's; 16 Foster's; 17 All Saints'; 18 Fullers'; 19 Burton's; 20 Weaver's; 21 Spicer's; 22 Forster's; 23 Magdalen's; 24 Canynges'.*

in 1540 (Jackson 1997; Jackson 2006; Williams 1996, 85). The western half of the church, including the tower, formed the parish church of St James and it survives. The earliest burials were uniformly contained within head-niche graves and dated from the priory's foundation into the 13th century. Later burials appeared in the main to be coffin burials contained in rectangular or sub-rectangular grave cuts. There was a preponderance of males around the eastern end of the priory church perhaps indicating that this area was reserved for clerics and other priory officials. Towards the eastern end of the burial ground the proportions of the sexes were more balanced, perhaps suggesting that this area was part of the parochial burial ground. The detailed examination of the human remains suggested a population which enjoyed a comfortable social and economic status, perhaps to be expected of a religious house, with low incidence of trauma. To date this remains the only skeletal assemblage of an appreciable size to have been examined in Bristol. Whether it is atypical of contemporary assemblages must remain an open question until comparable work has been carried out on other sites and assemblages of a similar period.

Apart from Bristol Castle, probably the major single medieval building complex is the former abbey of St Augustine (now Bristol Cathedral). Founded *c.*1140 by Robert Fitzharding, there may have been an earlier religious building on the site, as suggested earlier. Whatever is the case, it is perhaps remarkable that there has been so little detailed archaeological study of this complex series of interrelated buildings. This is in contrast to some excellent works of synthesis, especially on the sculptures and iconography, and transcriptions and analyses of the abundant documentary sources (e.g. Rogan 2000; Muñoz de Miguel 1997).

Of the archaeological work that has occurred, the excavation in 1992 at the west end of the cathedral (no. 13 on Fig. 2) in advance of a proposed visitor centre (which has yet to be built) is of particular note (Boore 1992). The earliest building found there, immediately west of the 19th-century west tower, was probably contemporary with the 12th-century foundation of the abbey and may have been the abbot's house and guest-house. In the 13th century another building, possibly a workshop, was constructed to the south. This contained floor levels of oolite chippings and may have been used for stone carving. A bell-casting pit was found to the west. Following demolition of the workshop, a *cellarium* or storehouse was built along the west side of the cloister. In the 15th to 16th century, most of the Norman hall and the *cellarium* were demolished and the so-called Minster House was built. This building survived with many modifications until its demolition in 1884.

In 2001 excavation to the west of College Square, possibly originally the outer cloister of the abbey, revealed evidence for early use of the area (no. 14 on Fig. 2). A fishpond was created, probably soon after the abbey's foundation, and was roughly lined with cobbles. This was backfilled by the late 13th or early 14th century, the fill including a sequence of organic-rich layers containing animal hair and straw. Overlying this was a large aisled building of 13th- or 14th-century date, possibly the main abbey barn. By the end of 17th century this building had been demolished and replaced by a series of tenements (Insole 2003).

The area to the west of the abbey (no. 15 on Fig. 2) was investigated in 2000 (Cox *et al.* 2004). This area became known as the Bishop's Park from the 16th century by which time a series of ponds had been created. These ponds may well have had a medieval origin, possibly serving the needs of the abbey for the supply of fresh fish. A large circular stone-built structure, heavily truncated by later development, was found, with an estimated external diameter of *c.*8 m. Its function remains in some doubt: one possibility is that it was associated in some way with the abbey's water supply which is thought to have run from a spring on the southern slopes of Clifton, terminating at a conduit house in College Square. A more likely interpretation, however, is that it formed the base of a dovecote, probably of medieval date, perhaps similar to another example recorded in a watching brief during the construction of a new classroom block for Bristol Cathedral School in 1979 (Boore 1979).

There has been little work so far at other church sites. There have been a number of surveys of surviving churches, most notably of the crypt of St John's Church (no. 16 on Fig. 2) (Pilkington 1999) and of St James's Church (no. 12 on Fig. 2) (Bryant 1993). Only one church site has been fully excavated, that of St Augustine-the-Less (no. 6 on Fig. 2), and this remains largely unpublished apart from an interim report (Boore 1985) and an important article derived from the study of the coffin furniture and burial practices found on the site (idem 1998). The excavation revealed the very ephemeral traces of a possible 12th-century church, within which were the lower halves of two coarse-ware jars, interpreted as acoustic jars set below the floor. The church had been extensively rebuilt in the late medieval period, removing much of the earlier evidence. The excavation was particularly notable for the number of post-medieval (17th- to 19th-century) burial vaults encountered – 116 brick vaults were found. That evidence can illuminate the only partially studied subject of post-medieval burial practices, as well as enhance our knowledge of the city's population in this later period.

The Port and Waterfronts

Bristol is currently experiencing major development of its waterfront areas as part of the overall regeneration of the city centre. At the beginning of the 1980s several schemes for redeveloping the by then run-down Redcliffe waterfront on the south side of the Avon started to be implemented. A comprehensive series of large-scale excavations that took place over the next seven years in advance of these developments has transformed our understanding of the port of Bristol. The high potential of the waterfront deposits and the way in which the topography of Redcliffe had been altered by the continual striving for new land were clearly demonstrated and important evidence was recovered for the economy and living conditions of its inhabitants.

In 1980 the first of this series of excavations was carried out on the west side of Redcliff Street at its southern end (no. 17 on Fig. 2). The work was complemented in 1999 by further excavation closer to the contemporary waterfront (Williams 1981; Williams and Cox 2000). This work revealed a series of structures dating from the 13th century including a slipway. There was also evidence for dyeing in the form of vat bases as well as the occurrence of dye plants in secondary reclamation contexts.

Major excavations were subsequently carried out (Jones 1986; Good 1991) at the former site of the house of Bristol merchant William Canynges and at nos. 127–129 Redcliff Street (Dundas Wharf) (nos. 18 and 19 on Fig. 2). On both these sites the extensive and rapid reclamation processes were notable, with the waterfront transformed from a muddy bank only a few metres from Redcliff Street in the early 12th century to a well-developed series of stone-revetted waterfronts by the beginning of the 13th century. Over 60 m of new land was reclaimed from the river at the Canynges House site between c.1200 and c.1450. This was the result both of natural sedimentation, which has been estimated to have been as much as 8 to 12 times greater than before occupation of the waterfront (Jones and Watson 1987), and deliberate dumping of industrial and household refuse. There was frequent provision of slipways to ensure access to the water's edge at all levels of the tidal range. Some would have served the many ferry crossings across the harbour. Some, such as that excavated at Dundas Wharf, would have served a number of properties with connecting passages leading into the slipway itself (Fig. 4).

On both the Dundas Wharf and Canynges House excavations, and to an extent on an excavation by Bristol Bridge (no. 20 on Fig. 2) carried out in 1981, as well as on subsequent excavations in this area, palaeoenvironmental sampling programmes were seen as key elements of the project. The first results for the Dundas Wharf site have been published and have revealed good evidence for the presence of dye waste, such as spent madder, dyers greenweed and weld (Jones and Watson 1987). Timber revetments and other structures have provided a good insight into the development of carpentry techniques from the 12th century onwards. Some timber structures will have had specific functions, such as the wooden barrels found at Dundas Wharf which may have been used in the tanning process (Good 1991, 40) and a possible timber latrine attached to the rear of one of the properties. The re-use of former ship and boat fragments was common, seen most notably at the Bristol Bridge site where a series of ships timbers was re-used in the construction of a back-braced revetment (Williams 1982).

However, while there have been overview reports which interpret the evidence retrieved from these waterfront sites (e.g. Jones 1991) there is still a major unprocessed backlog of material from many of these sites. It will be important to examine this in detail for the evidence it can produce for the economy of this area, noted for its cloth-finishing industry, and for the changing environmental conditions and land use of the Redcliffe area as a whole. The concentration on fine sieving of all major deposits has meant also that we could obtain a detailed insight into the diet of the medieval inhabitants of Redcliffe and into the distribution and degree of local consumption of foodstuffs such as imported fish and fruit.

Despite the lack of an overall synthesis from these sites, the picture that is emerging from the work in Redcliffe is one of rapid but relatively unplanned development of the waterfront from the early 12th century onwards, with the possible exception of earlier settlement around the southern bridgehead as suggested above. Settlement may well have extended southwards from the area close to the bridge from at least as early as *c*.1120, based on dendrochronological evidence (Nicholson and Hillam 1987, 141), with the whole of Redcliff Street built up by the end of the 12th century. The substantial stone or timber revetments built following plot expansion into the river formed essentially *private* quays for the mooring of individual owners' boats, in marked contrast to the *public* quays across the river at Welsh Back and along the Frome.

Relatively little work has been carried out along the main public quays on Welsh Back and the Frome. Excavation took place in 1995 at the north end of Welsh Back, on the former site of the 14th-century Spicer's Hall (no. 21 on Fig. 2), which was given to the town in 1377 and was subsequently used for the storage of strangers' goods before their release on the market (Blockley 1996). The excavation demonstrated that prior to the diversion of the river Frome in the mid 13th century the area had been marginal land, probably marshland subjected to frequent flooding although there was evidence for settlement and for the dumping of rubbish. From the second half of the 13th century the area was levelled up, presumably to counteract the threat of flooding, and timber- and subsequently stone-founded buildings were constructed. Flooding seemed to have been a continual problem and flood silts containing large numbers of fish bones were found over the floor of one of the 14th-century buildings. While the contemporary waterfront and street were not examined, it is presumably from the second half of the 13th century that the quay and Welsh Back were formally laid out with associated properties on their western sides.

Even less work has been carried out on the upper reaches of the Frome and Avon rivers, away from the economic activity associated with the main quays. These are nevertheless important areas for archaeological study given the likely preservation quality of the prevailing waterlogged conditions and their ability to provide key evidence for the local economy and environment. However, in 2000, development in Union Street on the north side of the Frome, immediately outside the medieval town, provided the opportunity to examine in detail a site (no. 22 on Fig. 2) thought to have been developed from the late 12th or early 13th century. It was found that an earlier course of the river had been diverted by the construction of a river wall, possibly serving as a quay. An industrial complex was established in the late 12th century with stone hearths and a circular furnace structure, possibly a dye vat base. In the late 13th or early 14th century this complex was replaced by a stone building constructed of yellow Lias and roofed in slate. It must have been an imposing building, sited on a bend in the river, across the river from the castle. It may have been the house of the Wilcocks family, first mentioned in 1394 and described in 1546 as a 'mansion and brewhouse' (Williams 2000, 143–4). The house had been demolished by the late 17th century and replaced by a complex of buildings known as 'New Buildings'. The main road running past the site, Union Street, was laid out in 1771 and buildings were constructed alongside it. From the 1840s the Frys' chocolate factory occupied the site.

As part of the investigations of 2000 a comprehensive programme of palaeoenvironmental and geoarchaeological sampling was carried out. The final results are expected to be published in the near future, but preliminary assessment suggests that the botanical and insect remains survive well from the waterlogged samples and will provide good evidence for diet and local environment.

Fig. 4:   Dundas Wharf, Redcliffe: medieval slipway (photograph Bristol City Museum).

For example, the fill of one pit, contemporary with the earliest phase of settlement, produced remains of bran and fruit and of fly pupae and beetles and cess material. The assemblage of mammal and fish bone suggested the high status of the inhabitants of the medieval house, with the presence of expensive cuts of meat as well as a possible hunting trophy recovered from a later medieval context.

THE DEVELOPMENT OF THE EARLY MODERN CITY

Much of the work over the last 25 years and more has concentrated upon the examination of the medieval historic core of the city. There has, until fairly recently, been relatively little archaeological study of the equally important physical, social and economic development of the city in the early modern and post-medieval period. There are notable exceptions: the work of Reg Jackson and Roger Price in establishing a chronology for the important Bristol clay pipe industry still stands as an important reference work (Jackson and Price 1974). The same authors, together with Philomena Jackson, also produced an important study of Bristol potteries from the beginning of the 17th century (Jackson *et al.* 1982). However, these studies of particular artefact types and their production have stood largely unmatched by parallel studies into the development of Bristol's urban landscape and its economy, especially in the period following the Restoration when Bristol once again regained much of its importance on the world stage. This is in contrast to the works of historical synthesis which have done much to answer important questions about the city's industrial and economic heritage from the 17th century onwards.

The balance is now being redressed. Roger Leech's ongoing work on town houses and his recognition of the survival of the second houses of the urban élite, the so-called summer houses or garden houses, does much to enhance our understanding of the role and influence of the social élite in the city of this period. It also helps us to understand just how the suburban hinterland immediately surrounding the medieval city came to be developed. His analysis, for example, of the historic landscape of the St Michael's Hill precinct of the University of Bristol, the aim of which was 'to provide an understanding of the historical archaeology contained within the St Michael's Hill precinct', has shown how the area changed from a largely rural setting in the medieval period to become, after the Civil War, an area favoured by the wealthy as the location of their second homes (Leech 2000b). The picture depicted by Millerd in 1673 can now be looked at in the context of this gradual retreat from the centre and the colonisation of the slopes surrounding the now crowded medieval core (Fig. 5).

The development of new industries in Bristol has also been recognised as of paramount importance in establishing the city's powerful position in the late 17th and 18th centuries. Joan Day's work on the development of the brass industry in Bristol is pioneering in this respect (Day, 1973).

Recently, following many years of documentary research into the development of the equally important glass-working industry, it has been possible to examine archaeologically a few key sites and there is the likelihood that there will be further opportunities in the near future. The Soap Boilers' glasshouse in St Philips was established in 1715 by a consortium of soap makers in Cheese Lane (now Avon Street) making bottle glass. A second glasshouse was soon constructed alongside for the manufacture of crown glass. In 1720 the Hoopers glasshouse was founded by a consortium including hoopers and a barber surgeon as well as a glass maker, several merchants and a soap maker. In 1853 the earlier of the soap boilers' glasshouses amalgamated with the Hoopers glasshouse, then Powell's glasshouse, and in the 1860s the company began using the Siemen's

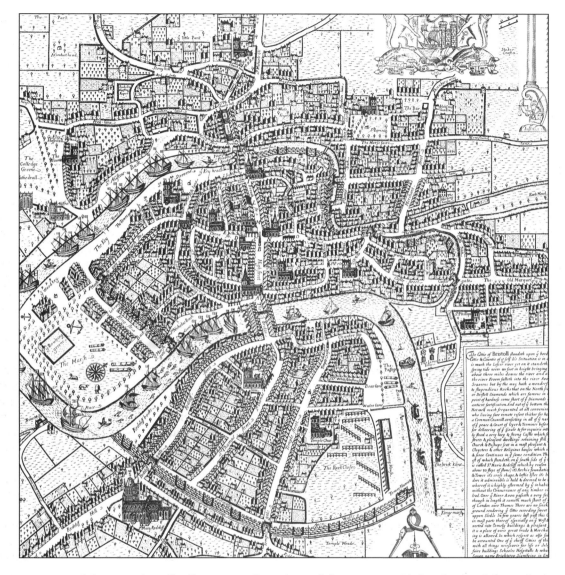

Fig. 5:   Detail from Jacob Millerd's Exact Delineation of the Famous Cittie of Bristol *(1673).*

regenerative furnace, a revolutionary new technique in glass production. Limited archaeological works in 1988–9 revealed the excellent survival of the main elements of these manufacturing sites, including a series of three or four annealing ovens and possible elements of the Siemen's furnace (no. 23 on Fig. 2). Quantities of stamped bricks, glass bottle waste, plaster moulds and cullet were also recovered (Egan 1989, 61). Unfortunately this initial work was not fully published and one of the glasshouses was destroyed during the construction of a major office development. However, more recent evaluation of the rest of the site as part of a planned comprehensive redevelopment

203

scheme for this area has shown that much of the remaining glasshouses survives intact (Dawkes 2002). More comprehensive archaeological works are therefore planned to recover the full extent of the surviving glasshouses and to investigate the development of the glass-working process as far as it has survived the continual rebuilding and modification that characterise historic glasshouses.

Work in 2001 on one of the earliest glasshouses in Bristol revealed traces of a possibly late 17th-century glassworks, with fragmentary traces of a glass cone of this period (no. 24 on Fig. 2). By 1736 it had been taken over by Sir Abraham Elton, one of the foremost of the merchant élite of the time, showing how profitable this industry had become (Fig. 6). Contemporary newspaper reports indicated that the cone had collapsed during repair. Detailed analysis of the glass-working waste suggested a change in technology between the earlier and later periods of glass production (Jackson 2005). The glassworks survived until the early 19th century when the glass cone was demolished. From the mid 19th century the site was used for the manufacture of lead sheet and pipe. The lead works survived until 1994 and the construction and modification of these works had caused considerable damage to the underlying archaeology.

Initial evaluation has been carried out of a glass-working site at Portwall Lane, immediately inside the line of the medieval Portwall (no. 25 on Fig. 2). Little is known of this glasshouse. Cartographic evidence suggests that a glassworks existed by 1786, later augmented by a second glass cone by 1797. The preliminary work has suggested that these glassworks are likely to survive

Fig. 6:   General view of Cheese Lane glassworks during excavation in 2001 (photograph Bristol and Region Archaeological Services).

in a good state of preservation and further work is planned for this site (Townsend 2002). Similarly, further archaeological work is anticipated at the site of possibly Bristol's earliest glasshouse at Redcliff Wharf, where earlier limited works had uncovered a small part of Vigor and Steven's glasshouse, possibly in existence as early as 1673 (Ponsford *et al.* 1989, 44).

The enormous changes to the landscape of the area known as Canon's Marsh have been the subject of considerable archaeological study in recent years, in advance of current regeneration. This area, which lay within the estate of the abbey of St Augustine and afterwards was part of the dean and chapter lands, was primarily in agricultural use throughout the medieval period, crops of hay being recorded in the abbey records for 1491–2, for example (Beachcroft and Sabin 1938, 276–7). Major changes to this landscape were taking place from the late 17th century. A dock, Limekiln Dock, was constructed at the western end of Canon's Marsh by 1693 while further docks had been constructed along the river Frome at the eastern end of the marsh by 1742. Excavation in 2000 in the eastern part of the marsh revealed part of a formal garden, probably of the late 17th or early 18th century and recorded by Jean Rocque in 1742 (no. 26 on Fig. 2). Later 18th- and 19th-century buildings were also investigated, some of which were certainly industrial in character, possibly used in the processing of timber (Parry 2001). Further excavation to the west (no. 27 on Fig. 2) revealed part of a ropewalk and other features that may have been part of the rope-making process (Williams 1997, 82). At the western end of the marsh the Bristol and Clifton Oil Gas Company was founded in 1823, manufacturing gas from whale oil (no. 28 on Fig. 2). From 1836 the process was altered to accommodate the use of coal, after the use of whale oil became uneconomic. Before and during the necessary decontamination of the gasworks site, a comprehensive archaeological study was carried out, including analysis of the many records relating to the works and a detailed survey of the surviving elements (Croft 2000 37–48). The very nature of gas production meant that the works were heavily modified and expanded over time and six phases of construction and modification were identified.

Further work is planned in the Canon's Marsh area, to elucidate in particular previously identified medieval structures and features towards the northern end of the marsh. However, the picture is now emerging of an area subject to seasonal flooding throughout the medieval period, but probably protected from the worst excesses of the tide by river banks and further provided with drainage ditches. By the late 17th or early 18th century, encroachment on the marsh seems to have begun with the construction of some housing and industrial premises, including a ropewalk, and at least one formal garden. Further industrialisation occurred throughout the 19th century, probably on a fairly piecemeal basis until the improvement in port facilities in the late 19th century and the establishment of a rail access to the marsh in 1906.

From the end of the 17th century, it became increasingly clear to the Bristol city corporation and the merchants that the old port, centred upon the quay and Welsh Back, was becoming increasingly outmoded. The formerly advantageous factors of extreme tidal range and the distance of the port from the mouth of the Severn were now becoming impediments to the efficient operation of the port as ships became larger and the risks of running aground on the banks of the Avon became greater. Even before this, in the 16th and 17th centuries, the area of the working port was being expanded with the construction in the 16th century of St Clement's Dock on the east bank of the Frome, immediately to the south of the Marsh Wall. This appears to have been abandoned soon after the launch in 1581 of the *Minion*, the last ship to be built there. Immediately to the north was Robert Aldworth's Dock, built *c.*1625 and infilled *c.*1687. These docks lay in an area noted for its shipbuilding activities from at least the late medieval period onwards. Archaeological observation during construction works in the 1950s recorded large numbers of ships timbers. Formal excavation in 1978–9 (Good 1987) recovered evidence for both Aldworth's Dock and St Clement's Dock with the ribs of a carvel-built boat resting at the base of the former (no. 29 on Fig. 2).

Throughout the 18th century and later attempts were made to arrest the slow decline of the port by expanding the area of the working port to the south and west: as we have seen, new docks were built on the west side of the Frome at Canon's Marsh. Docks were also created on the south bank, in the area known as Wapping, a previously marshy area, notably Albion Dock constructed in 1820 and the Great Western Dock, home of the S.S. *Great Britain*, constructed from 1839. Most radical was the construction in 1712, by Joshua Franklyn, of a wet dock within the old Roman port at Sea Mills. This venture failed because of its remote location *c.*5 km from the old docks. New docks were created in Hotwells, on the north bank of the Avon, such as the wet dock created by the industrialist William Champion between 1762 and 1768. While this dock was not an initial success, it was bought by the Society of Merchant Venturers who renamed it Merchants Dock. Evidently they made it a successful base for shipbuilding and repair, especially of naval vessels. Excavation to the east of this dock (no. 30 on Fig. 2) investigated a number of buildings, some with intact wooden floors and box drains, dated to the late 18th and 19th centuries (Erskine and Prosser 1997). Some of these may have been used for the housing of livestock while the name Deal Yard, which lay within the site, suggests that the processing or treating of timber was also being carried out here.

Complementing Roger Leech's work on urban housing is the need to augment our existing knowledge of the material culture of the poorest classes in relation to the often inadequately recorded slum or artisan housing of the urban poor in the early modern and post-medieval periods. Their lives and living conditions are rarely mentioned in documentary sources, or only through the eyes of those with an obvious bias in their reporting. For instance, it would be interesting to examine the living conditions of the immigrant communities who swelled Bristol's population during the late 18th and 19th centuries.

It has been estimated that the population of Bedminster increased twenty-five fold in the course of the 19th century. Archaeological work in 2002 in the north end of the suburb (no. 31 on Fig. 2) has provided an insight into the lives of the inhabitants of the small one-room cottages which lined Boot Lane, a small lane off the main thoroughfare, from the end of the 18th century. There a hitherto unsuspected small pottery kiln was found, established by 1780, possibly under the auspices of Nathaniel Ireson of Wincanton. Ireson, the owner of the Wincanton delft and red ware pottery, also owned property on the opposite side of Boot Lane. It may well be that the excavated housing was provided to cater for the workforce of this pottery. The housing consisted of single rooms on the ground floor, presumably with others above. Space was limited and privies were communal, provided at each end of the common courtyard (Parry 2004). It will be interesting when all the specialist studies have been fully assessed to look at the material culture of a section of society which only marginally exists in the documentary record.

CONCLUSION

This paper has attempted to set out the huge breadth of work that has taken place in the 25 and more years that have been its focus. A number of major issues stand out, not least of which is the absence of major assessment and synthesis of some of the most important excavations carried out in that period. Without these it is difficult to formulate research frameworks to build upon and challenge some of the accepted ideas to date. Also it is hoped that a move away from a below-ground bias in the medieval city centre has been demonstrated, although this is still of huge importance, to a wider examination of its hinterland as well as to a study of the standing buildings, from the ordinary to the most grand. The antecedents of Bristol and the understanding of the landscape from the earliest prehistoric periods onwards are equally deserving of our research. There is much which has been done and much still to do to place medieval and later Bristol, a mere 1000 years of time, into the context of human settlement which encompasses many millennia of human activity in the area.

BIBLIOGRAPHY

Unless otherwise stated, copies of all unpublished reports listed below are held in the Bristol Historic Environment Record where they can be viewed by prior appointment.

Bates, M.R., and Wenban-Smith, F.F., 2005. 'Palaeolithic Research Framework for the Bristol Avon Basin' (unpublished report for Bristol City Council).

Beachcroft, G., and Sabin, A., 1938. *Two Compotus Rolls of Saint Augustine's Abbey* (Bristol Rec. Soc. 9).

Blockley, K., 1996. 'Spicer's Hall, Bristol: excavation of a medieval merchant's house, 1995' (BaRAS unpublished report).

Boon, G.C., 1945. 'The Roman site at Sea Mills, 1945–46', *Trans. BGAS* **66**, 258–95.

Boon, G.C., 1950. 'The Roman villa in Kingsweston Park (Lawrence Weston Estate) Gloucestershire', *Trans. BGAS* **69**, 5–58.

Boore, E.J., 1979. 'Bristol Cathedral School classroom extension', *Bristol Archaeol. Research Group Bull.* **6(8)**, 198–200.

Boore, E.J., 1980. 'A summary report of excavations at Tower Lane, Bristol, 1979–80', *Bristol Archaeol. Research Group Review* **1**, 18–26.

Boore, E.J., 1985. 'Excavations at St. Augustine the Less, Bristol, 1983–84', *Bristol Avon Archaeol.* **4**, 21–33.

Boore, E.J., 1992. 'The Minster House at Bristol cathedral – Excavations in 1992', *Bristol Avon Archaeol.* **10**, 42–50.

Boore, E.J., 1998. 'Burial vaults and coffin furniture in the West Country', in M. Cox (ed.), *Grave concerns: death and burial in England 1700–1800* (CBA Research Rep. 113, York), 67–84.

Bryant, J., 1993. 'Architectural recording at St. James' Priory, Bristol', *Bristol and Avon Archaeol.* **11**, 18–34.

Burchill, R., 1995. 'Archaeological excavation at Olivetti House, King Street/Marsh Street, Bristol, Avon' (BaRAS unpublished report).

Cox, S., 2000. 'Archaeological excavation of a medieval watergate at Temple Quay, Bristol, 2000' (BaRAS unpublished report).

Cox, S., Barber, A., and Collard, M., 2004. 'The archaeology and history of the former Bryan Brothers garage site, Deanery Road, Bristol: the evolution of an urban landscape' (Cotswold Archaeol. unpublished report, Cirencester).

Croft, R., 2000. 'Canon's Marsh Gas Works, Bristol: development, recording and archaeological assessment', *Bristol Ind. Archaeol. Soc. J.* **33**, 37–48.

Cronne, H.A., 1945. *Bristol Charters 1378–1499* (Bristol Rec. Soc. 11).

Dawkes, G., 2002. 'Land to the Rear of Avon Street, Bristol. Report on an Archaeological Evaluation' (AOC Archaeol. unpublished report).

Day, J., 1973. *Bristol Brass: a history of the industry* (Newton Abbot, David & Charles).

Egan, G., 1989. 'Post-medieval Britain and Ireland in 1988', *Post-Med. Archaeol.* **23**, 25–67.

Erskine, J.G.P., and Prosser, L., 1997. 'Poole's Wharf, Hotwells, Bristol. Archaeological excavation prior to redevelopment' (Avon Archaeol. Unit unpublished report).

Gardiner, J., Allen, M.J., Hamilton-Dyer, S., Laidlaw, M., and Scaife, R.G., 2002. 'Making the most of it: late prehistoric pastoralism in the Avon Levels, Severn Estuary', *Proc. Prehist. Soc.* **68**, 1–39.

Good, G.L., 1987. 'The excavation of two docks at Narrow Quay, Bristol, 1978–9', *Post-Med. Archaeol.* **21**, 25–126.

Good, G.L., 1991. 'Some aspects of the development of the Redcliffe waterfront in the light of excavation at Dundas Wharf', *Bristol Avon Archaeol.* **9**, 29–42.

Good, G.L., 1996. 'Bristol Castle keep – a reappraisal of the evidence and report on the excavations in 1989', *Bristol Avon Archaeol.* **13**, 11–45.

Iles, R., 1984. 'Avon archaeology 1983', *Bristol Avon Archaeol.* **3**, 54–65.

Insole, P., 2003. 'Archaeological Excavation of land at College Square, Bristol' (BaRAS unpublished report).

Jackson, R.G., 1994. 'Archaeological evaluation and excavation at Quay Point, Temple Meads, Bristol' (BaRAS unpublished report).

Jackson, R.G., 1997. 'Excavations at St. James Priory in 1989 and 1995' (BaRAS unpublished report).

Jackson, R.G., 1999. 'An interim report on the excavations at Inns Court, Bristol, 1997–1999', *Bristol Avon Archaeol.* **16**, 51–60.

Jackson, R.G., 2000. 'Archaeological excavations at Upper Maudlin Street, Bristol, in 1973, 1976 & 1999', *Bristol Avon Archaeol.* **17**, 29–110.

Jackson, R.G., 2005. 'Excavations on the site of Sir Abraham Elton's Glassworks, Cheese Lane, Bristol', *Post-Med. Archaeol.* **39.1**, 95–133.

Jackson, R.G., 2006. *Excavations at St James's Priory* (Oxbow Books, Oxford).

Jackson, R.G., and Price, R.H., 1974. *Bristol clay pipes: a study of makers and their marks* (City of Bristol Museum and Art Gallery).

Jackson, R.G., Jackson, P., and Price, R., 1982. *Bristol Potters and Potteries, 1600–1800* (Stoke-on-Trent City Museums).

Jones, J., and Watson, N., 1987. 'The early medieval waterfront at Redcliffe, Bristol', in N.D. Balaam, B. Levitan and V. Straker (eds.), *Studies in palaeoeconomy and environment in South West England* (BAR Brit. Series **181**, Oxford), 135–62.

Jones, R.H., 1986. *Excavations in Redcliffe 1983–5: survey and excavation at 95–97 Redcliff Street* (City of Bristol Museum and Art Gallery).

Jones, R.H., 1991. 'Industry and Environment in medieval Bristol', in G.L.Good, R.H. Jones and M.W. Ponsford (eds.), *Waterfront Archaeology: Proc. Third International Conference, Bristol, 1988* (CBA Research Rep. **74**, London), 19–26.

Leech, R.H., 1982. *Excavations at Catsgore 1970–1973. A Romano-British Village* (Western Archaeol. Trust Excavation Monograph **2**, Bristol).

Leech, R.H., 1997. 'The medieval defences of Bristol revisited', in L. Keen (ed.), *"Almost the richest city": Bristol in the Middle Ages* (London, Brit. Archaeol. Assoc.), 18–30.

Leech, R.H., 2000a. 'A Desk Top Evaluation of the Counterslip Brewery Site, Bristol' (Cultural Heritage Services unpublished report).

Leech, R.H., 2000b. *The St. Michael's Hill Precinct of the University of Bristol* (Bristol Rec. Soc. **52**).

Locock, M., 2001. 'A later Bronze Age landscape on the Avon Levels: settlement, shelters and saltmarsh at Cabot Park', in J. Brück (ed.), *Bronze Age landscapes: traditions and transformations* (Oxford, Oxbow), 121–8.

Muñoz de Miguel, M., 1997. 'The iconography of Christ *Victor* in Anglo-Saxon art: a new approach to the study of the "Harrowing of Hell" relief in Bristol Cathedral', in L. Keen (ed.), *"Almost the richest city": Bristol in the Middle Ages* (London, Brit. Archaeol. Assoc.), 75–80.

Nicholson, R.A., and Hillam, J., 1987. 'A dendrochronological analysis of oak timbers from the early medieval site at Dundas Wharf, Bristol', *Trans. BGAS* **105**, 133–45.

Parry, A., 2001. 'Archaeological excavation on the site of the South Building, Canon's Marsh' (BaRAS unpublished report).

Parry, A., 2004. 'Archaeological excavation of land at Squire's Court, Bedminster Parade, Bedminster, Bristol' (BaRAS unpublished report).

Pilkington, J., 1999. 'Archaeological recording during conservation work at St John the Baptist Church crypt, Bristol, 1998', *Bristol Avon Archaeol.* **16**, 61–71.

Ponsford, M.W., n.d. *Excavations at Greyfriars, Bristol* (City of Bristol Museum and Art Gallery).

Ponsford, M.W., 1979. 'Bristol Castle: archaeology and the history of a royal fortress' (University of Bristol M.Litt. thesis).

Ponsford, M.W., 1985. 'Bristol's medieval waterfront: "the Redcliffe Project" ', in A. Herteig (ed.), *Conference on waterfront archaeology in north European towns No. 2* (Historisk Museum Bergen), 112–21.

Ponsford, M.W., *et al.* 1989. 'Archaeology in Bristol 1989', *Bristol Avon Archaeol.* **8**, 41–5.

Price, R.H., 1991. 'An excavation at Broad Quay (Watergate), Bristol, 1979', *Bristol Avon Archaeol.* **9**, 24–8.

Price, R.H., with Ponsford, M.W., 1998. *St. Bartholomew's Hospital, Bristol. The excavation of a medieval hospital: 1976–8* (CBA Research Rep. **110**, York).

Rogan, J. (ed.), 2000. *Bristol Cathedral; History & Architecture* (Stroud, Tempus Publishing Ltd.).

Smith, M.Q., 1976. 'The Harrowing of Hell relief in Bristol Cathedral', *Trans. BGAS* 94, 101–6.

Stephenson, C., 1933. *Borough and town: a study of urban origins in England* (Cambridge, Mass., The Medieval Academy of America).

Townsend, A., 2002. 'Archaeological evaluation of land at Dick Lovett site, Portwall Lane, Bristol' (BaRAS unpublished report).

Tratman, E.K., 1925. 'Second report on King's Weston Hill, Bristol', *Proc. University Bristol Spelaeological Soc.* **2**, 238–43.

Watts, L., and Rahtz, P., 1985. *Mary-le-Port, Bristol: excavations, 1962–1963* (City of Bristol Museum and Art Gallery).

Wilkinson, K., 2002. 'Land at Anchor Road/Deanery Road, Bristol: stratigraphy and palaeoenvironment' (Cotswold Archaeol. unpublished report, Cirencester).

Williams, B., 1981. *Excavations in the Medieval Suburb of Redcliffe, Bristol, 1980* (City of Bristol Museum and Art Gallery).

Williams, B., 1982. 'Excavations at Bristol Bridge, 1981', *Bristol Avon Archaeol.* **1**, 12–14.

Williams, B., 1992. 'Archaeology in Bristol 1990–92', *Bristol Avon Archaeol.* **10**, 53–4.

Williams, B. (ed.), 1996. 'Review of archaeology 1995–1996', *Bristol Avon Archaeol.* **13**, 79–91.

Williams, B. (ed.), 1997. 'Review of archaeology 1996–1997', *Bristol Avon Archaeol.* **14**, 75–89.

Williams, B. (ed.), 2000. 'Review of archaeology 1999–2000', *Bristol Avon Archaeol.* **17**, 139–51.

Williams, B. (ed.), 2004. 'Review of archaeology 2001–2002', *Bristol Avon Archaeol.* **19**, 99–116.

Williams, B., and Cox, S., 2000. 'Excavations at 82–90 Redcliff Street, Bristol 1980 and 1999: the development of the medieval waterfront' (BaRAS unpublished report).

Williams, R.J.G., 1983. 'Romano-British settlement at Filwood Park, Bristol', *Bristol Avon Archaeol.* **2**, 12–20.

Gloucester

Carolyn Heighway

Had a person of judgment been present when these things were discovered, many curious particulars might have been preserved

Samuel Rudder, *New History of Gloucestershire* (Cirencester, 1779).

I hope that whoever has the task of updating this historical survey after the next phase of excavation in some 10 years time will feel that we have done justice within our own lights and limitations to the 2000 years and more of human development that is Gloucester

Malcolm Atkin, 'Gloucester Archaeology 1900–1990: An Historical Review', *Trans. BGAS* **110** (1992).

THE ORGANISATION OF ARCHAEOLOGY IN GLOUCESTER

The history of archaeological research in Gloucester was surveyed about ten years ago by Malcolm Atkin (1992a) and need not be retold here. In summary, key events were the creation of the Gloucester Roman Research Committee in the 1930s, the appointment of a Museum Archaeological Assistant from 1951, the formation of the Gloucester and District Archaeological Research Group (GADARG) in 1967; and the appointment of a Field Archaeologist, Henry Hurst, in 1968. The building boom of the late 60s occasioned seven years of unremitting excavation. Those 'Rescue' years, 1967–1974, with all their problems (underfunding, lack of time, inadequate premises) gained an unprecedented amount of new information about the past of Gloucester.

In 1973 an Excavation Unit was set up with a staff of four. One of the Unit's first creations was a policy document (Heighway 1974). By then one quarter of the walled city had already been developed. Impending redevelopment, by contrast, involved a comparatively modest area – indeed some of these sites are still not developed 30 years later. In a sense the Unit was created too late.

Nevertheless, there was plenty to do. The city was spreading outwards, and in the last 25 years hundreds of sites have been investigated in the suburbs and still further out in the city district (Atkin 1992a, 29; e.g. Sermon 1996, 12). The historic hunterland is now better understood: the number of known Iron-Age sites has greatly increased, and there seems to have been a ring of villas about 1 km from the *colonia* (Atkin 1986). The search for 'centuriation' has had negative results – but there is some evidence that after the Roman conquest, the countryside was re-organised to serve the Roman town (Thomas *et al.* 2003) and must have been exploited differently after the town fell into disuse (Atkin 1992a, 29–30).

The archaeologists with responsibility for Gloucester spanned the whole range of historic interests, and in the right order. Henry Hurst, a Romanist, was followed by myself (1974–81), with an interest in the Anglo-Saxon and medieval period. After a few years when archaeology was managed from Bristol by Western Archaeological Trust, the Unit was re-created in 1985 with the appointment of Malcolm Atkin, a post-medievalist (Atkin 1988b). Malcolm also began marketing archaeology to developers (e.g. Atkin 1988a) with the aim of encouraging developer funding – a principle which with PPG 16 became part of the planning process in November 1990. Since 1995 Malcolm's successor Richard Sermon has been consolidating the mass of information accumulated by his predecessors and has set up the Urban Archaeological Database.

In 2004 archaeology in Gloucester was again re-organised. Most projects are now contracted to outside agencies, and a reduced staff, now the Heritage and Museums Service Historic

Environment Team, is responsible for planning advice and education. The Urban Database, or Historic Environment Record (HER), is maintained by Phil Greatorix as Historic Environment Record Officer (HERO).

The Urban Database (Historic Environment Record)

The database originated as a card index in the 1950s; it was augmented and mapped by Yvette Staelens *c.*1980 and is now entered into a GIS system. Archaeological data can be retrieved from the system in a number of ways, and there are associated maps including the principal 19th-century historic maps of the city. Eventually the database will include overlays of original excavation site plans in their actual locations; all this information can be displayed and printed. Records from adjacent sites can be combined or compared (Sermon 1999, 25).

Watching Briefs

Archaeological watching briefs in the last 25 years have usually been done by Patrick Garrod, in various guises (as a volunteer, as the Unit's field archaeologist, and now again as a volunteer). Patrick knows buried Gloucester better than most of us know it today, and he has contributed an enormous amount of information over the years (see Fig. 1). Many of the so-called 'Minor Sites' were published in 1984 (Garrod and Heighway 1984); others have been reported as summaries in the annual reports in *Glevensis* and the *Transactions of the Bristol and Gloucestershire Archaeological Society*.

Fig. 1: Archaeological watching brief: street levels from 1st to 20th century in a sewer shaft in Northgate Street (photograph Patrick Garrod 1976).

Archaeological watching briefs in Gloucester have been a success. They have contributed greatly to the stock of information; they are numerous and they are cheap. Their disadvantage is that they deal with exceptionally small segments of information and so are difficult both to interpret and to publish coherently, and the text summaries which are usually the only published record seldom include the very eloquent drawings, particularly sections, which constitute the most important part of the field record. A paramount value of the Urban Database will be to provide a mode of access to the dataset of small sites and so to enable full use of these.

Buildings

The last 15 years have seen much recording work at Gloucester Cathedral, where archaeological recording always precedes maintenance and stone repair. Though the archaeology has to follow the repair programme and so is inevitably piecemeal, a picture is building up of how the great Romanesque church was adapted into a gothic one. There is also a good deal of information about medieval building technique including stone use and quarry extraction methods (e.g. Bagshaw, Heighway and Price 2004). Reports on the archaeological work are deposited in the cathedral and city libraries and also with the Urban Database. An overall assessment of the whole cathedral precinct (which forms an integral part of the Urban Database) is also available in these libraries (Heighway 2001). Recently the cathedral dean and chapter produced a conservation plan which includes a re-assessment by Richard Morris of all the precinct buildings (Morris 2003). The precinct contains an outstanding collection of medieval and late medieval buildings which mostly remain unrecorded.[1]

The archaeology of the standing buildings of the town has never achieved the same attention from archaeologists as the below-ground work, in spite of PPG 15. Much of Gloucester's historic building stock is hidden from view, which can mean a valuable historical resource is neglected until too late. In the early 1980s the then curator of the Folk Museum, Stuart Davies, started a register and archive of Gloucester's historic buildings. This is not currently maintained, but remains a useful if incomplete archive of historic buildings (the Urban Database includes only standing buildings which are Listed). The Gloucester Civic Trust Survey Group remains active in the field of identifying and surveying historic buildings. Individual surveys have been commissioned by the city council of various buildings in its care, including Llanthony Priory, the chapel of St Mary Magdalen's Hospital, and the structures of the King's Board and Scriven's Conduit (pers. comm. Phil Moss). Number 26 Westgate Street, the spectacular 16th-century house in Maverdine Lane, has been surveyed for English Heritage (Price 1994). In 1991 the Gloucester Excavation Unit carried out a rapid building survey of the south-western quadrant of the town as part of archaeological surveys related to the proposed Blackfriars development; this exercise produced much new information. At 47–9 Westgate Street the early 18th-century building stands above a large 13th-century undercroft, and an unprepossessing building at 33 Westgate Street (Fig. 2) incorporates a two-bay timber-framed building with a small stone undercroft (Atkin 1992b, 41; Moss 1993, 53, 56). The discoveries demonstrate how much potential there is for further survey of Gloucester's building stock.

Publication

By 1979 Henry Hurst had published three interim reports and an overview (Hurst 1972; 1974; 1975; 1976). Since then volumes have appeared on Kingsholm (Hurst 1985); the defences (Hurst 1986); the North and East gates (Heighway 1983); and St Oswald's Priory (Heighway and Bryant

Fig. 2:   Number 33 Westgate Street (drawing and recording by Phil Moss).

1999), as well as articles and shorter publications: Malcolm Atkin (1992a) has provided an overview of previous work with bibliography. A number of significant sites of the 1990s have still not been published, including excavations at Gambier Parry Lodge and at Lower Quay Street, but efforts continue to address the problem. With hindsight the most serious gap in the publication record is Henry Hurst's Berkeley Street excavations which remain the only city excavation to examine tenements sites from the Roman through to the medieval period (Hurst 1974, 23–7; Atkin 1992a, 25).

TELLING THE STORY: CHANGES IN PERCEPTION OF GLOUCESTER'S TOPOGRAPHY

The topographical development of the town is a particular interest of mine, and this section will present changes in perspective which have emerged in the last 25 years.

The first topographical maps for Roman Gloucester appeared in Henry Hurst's interim report (Hurst 1974, 20–22). These did not cover the area outside the Roman walls, which of course include a good part of the activities of Roman Gloucester and indeed of all periods. Nevertheless, maps of this kind raise questions which can help to inform future research designs. For instance, the Roman 4th-century map was very nearly blank, and has never been published. The emptiness may result from the inherent uncertainties of pottery dating, or a bias of deposit survival, but it is possible that it is indicative of the economic contrast between the 4th and 2nd centuries in Roman Gloucester. Eventually these earliest topographical maps will be scanned into the Urban Database.

On a different scale, in 1984 I published the first series of plans (Figs. 3A–B) to show the development of Gloucester's topography (Heighway 1984, 360). This was very much a collection of hypotheses, or even speculations. Twenty years on, I have attempted to update this (Figs. 4A–B).

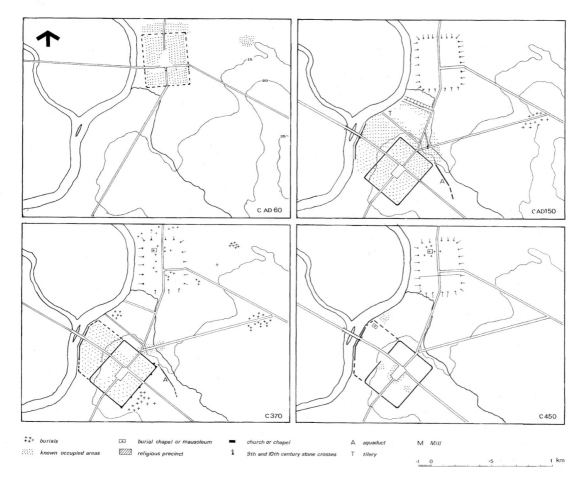

Fig. 3A: *Topographical development of Gloucester c. AD 60 to c. AD 450 as interpreted in 1984 (Heighway 1984, 360). The course of the river Severn is after Rowbotham (1978).*

The drawing has many deficiencies: it is on too small a scale to include the post-medieval period, nor can it take into account the now very numerous sites around the town in the district.

The natural topography of the area of the town of Gloucester forms the background to all these studies. The present town is set on a natural promontory overlooking the Severn, and it is surprising that evidence of pre-Roman settlement on this promontory has not been more frequent. The pre-Roman settlement, as discussed below, is on lower ground further to the north.

An important and influential element of the natural topography was the river Severn and the streams that fed into it. The loop of the river which ran closest to the town of Gloucester has long since silted up and now forms no part of the town's layout, but in the Roman and medieval period this was the position of the quayside and the initiation point of much trade and commerce. In 1978 Fred Rowbotham, who had extensive knowledge of the river Severn and its behaviour,

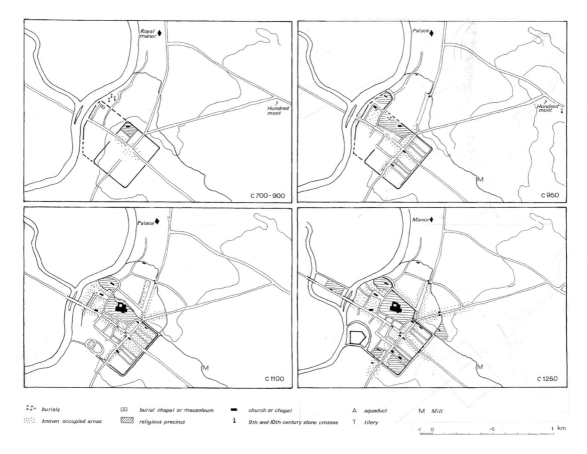

Fig. 3B: Topographical development of Gloucester c.700 to c.1250 as interpreted in 1984 (Heighway 1984, 360). The Saxon hundred moot meeting place is an hypothesis (Heighway 1980).

proposed that the original junction of two loops of the river was just above Gloucester; this would mean that in Roman and Anglo-Saxon times there was one fewer river channel to cross (Rowbotham 1978). Rowbotham's river course was adopted in my topographical drawings of 1984 (Figs. 3A–B) and I have retained it in the more recent drawings (Figs. 4A–B); however, it remains a hypothesis which has not been proved (indeed, it is difficult to know what sort of proof could be adduced). Rowbotham proposed that the break-through of the third channel occurred only in the 12th century, necessitating the building of the Westgate bridge. The adoption of Rowbotham's scheme though accepted by an important recent study (Baker and Holt 2004) has not been universal: see for instance Hurst (e.g. 1999a, 120 fig. 5) or my own recent topographical discussions (e.g. Heighway and Bryant 1999, 3).

Another important topographic element was the Twyver stream which flowed from the east around the city walls and west into the Severn. The contours suggest that the natural course of the Twyver would have been to bypass the town slightly to the north (Heighway and Bryant 1999, 3).[2] It is also likely that the Roman engineers, like their medieval successors, made use of the

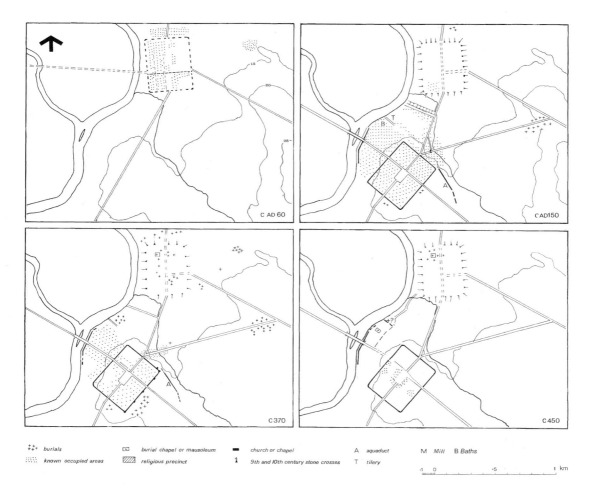

burials
known occupied areas
burial chapel or mausoleum
religious precinct
church or chapel
9th and 10th century stone crosses
A   aquaduct
T   tilery
M   Mill   B Baths

km

Fig. 4A: Topographical development of Gloucester c. *AD 60 to* c. *AD 450 as interpreted in 2004.*

spring waters on the nearby Robinswood Hill to bring fresh drinking water to the town by means of an aqueduct.

The most important contribution to topography has been not an archaeological work but a synthesis of disciplines, the long-awaited *Urban Growth and the Medieval Church*, by Nigel Baker and Richard Holt (2004). This makes full use of post-medieval maps and documentary evidence as well as archaeology and introduces many insights into the topographical and historical past.

Roman Topography

The Roman fortress and *colonia* of *Glevum* are set on the natural promontory overlooking the river Severn, yet it has always been a puzzle that the original fort (or fortress) was located at Kingsholm on the lower ground further north. In 1981, a routine watching brief on the area north of Kingsholm at Gambier Parry Lodge (sometimes known as Coppice Corner: Hurst 1985, 118) uncovered a 1st-century settlement succeeded by a 1st- to 4th-century cemetery. (There is insuf-

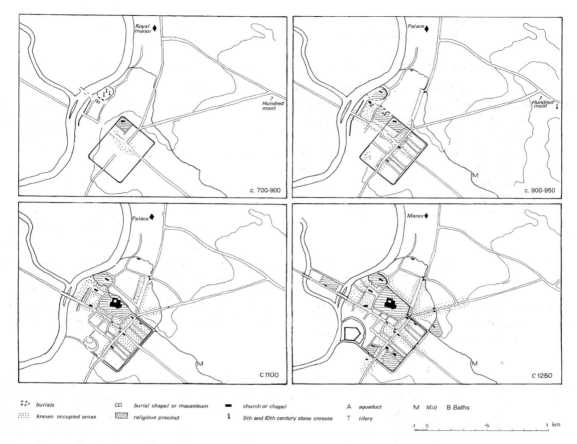

Fig. 4B: Topographical development of Gloucester c.700 to c.1250 as interpreted in 2004.

ficient room for this site on Fig. 4A: the information has had to be compressed into the top of the drawing.) Although the pottery evidence could be consistent with the settlement being contemporary with the first fort at Kingsholm (Timby 1999, 38), the presence of Dobunnic coins does seem to suggest that this settlement was the primary site that dictated the siting of the first Roman fort and hence caused the main line of Ermin Street to head in this direction (Hurst 1999a, 119).

Henry Hurst's excavation at Kingsholm (Hurst 1985), and the many watching briefs in the same area (Garrod and Heighway 1984), had already in 1984 established a chronology for the Kingsholm fort/fortress, showing that it remained in use for a time contemporary with the fortress further south at Gloucester. Hurst judged the available evidence too slight to derive fort limits; however Malcolm Atkin was more daring (or foolhardy) and proposed a two-phase fort (Atkin 1986).

The position of cemeteries (Heighway 1980; Hurst 1986a) is significant. For the Roman town, it indicates the urban limits at different periods. A cemetery south of the town has recently been excavated (Bateman and Williams 2002), and in the last 25 years there have been more discoveries of burials in the Kingsholm area (e.g. Hassall and Tomlin 1984). There have also been further discoveries of both cremations and inhumations along London Road including recently two tombstones (Tomlin and Hassall 2005, 474–7).

The Transition from Roman Town to Mid Saxon Settlement: 5th–9th Centuries

The question of 'continuity' of towns has been endlessly debated in the last 25 years. At Gloucester there is no evidence that the Roman town continued to function as an urban place beyond the early 5th century. Recent work has not changed this picture. Pockets of occupation continue to be evidenced in the 5th century (e.g. on the castle site: Darvill 1988) but the walled area in the 6th–7th century seems to have been largely deserted except for some agricultural use: the Roman west gate for instance may have become a farmstead (site 24/87: Atkin 1992a, 23).

Nevertheless, it was inevitable that the massive Roman remains continued to have a topographic and cultural influence. The minster founded at Gloucester in 679 may have been deliberately placed in a corner of the ruined Roman circuit (though there are alternative sites for the old minster: see Hare 1992). A middle Saxon precinct to the west near the river contained a burial mausoleum, later the church of St Mary de Lode, on the site of a Roman public baths (Heighway 2003; Bryant and Heighway 2003).[3] At the town centre, a late Roman reorganisation involved adaptation of monumental Roman buildings (Heighway in preparation).

There were other locations too which were significant in the Saxon period, like the Kingsholm cemetery, where a high-status early 5th-century burial remained revered until the 10th century, by which time it was close to the site of the Saxon palace. Gloucester was not so much a town as a disparate collection of significant foci.

The Burh

A crucial event for Gloucester's topographic development was the *burh* founded at Gloucester by Æthelflaed of Mercia *c*. AD 900. The most convincing surviving evidence for the refurbishment and laying out of the *burh* is still the overall street pattern of the eastern half of the Roman fortress area (Hurst 1972; Baker and Holt 2004, 20, 65–7, 347, 351). Yet in spite of all the observations of previous decades, no archaeological confirmation for the date of this street pattern has ever been found.

Along with the refurbishing of the Roman town, the *burh* foundation also involved the establishment of a new royal church, the New Minster. This foundation was an integral element of the propaganda which accompanied the new military regime. At the time of its foundation the church was dedicated to St Peter, but before long a raid into Danish territory in East Anglia gained the important relics of St Oswald of Northumbria, which were brought to Gloucester in AD 909 (Hare 1999, 34–5).

Excavations at the New Minster, St Oswald's Priory, took place in 1975–8, with a final season in 1983. The standing ruin which is all that remains of Æthelflaed's church was already famous when the excavations were finally published (Heighway and Bryant 1999) – part of the elevation drawing by Richard Bryant has been reproduced many times and has also been used as the logo of the Society of Church Archaeology. The excavations have put Gloucester on the map of Anglo-Saxon studies: the minster 'could hardly be more significant for our understanding of the first half of the 10th century' (Stocker, 2003, 302); the site is also important for its collection of Anglo-Saxon architecture and sculpture.

St Oswald's must have been a vital element of the early 10th-century topography of the town but the excavations did not deal with the site perimeter and defences. Later medieval sources

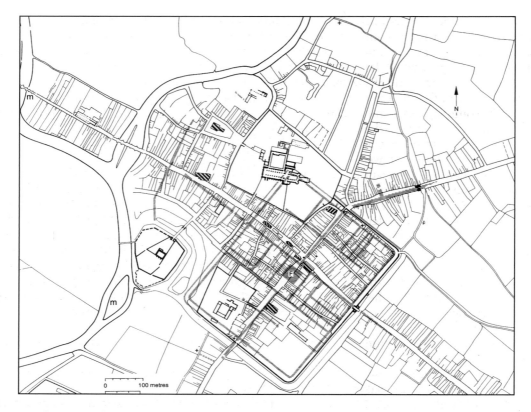

Fig. 5:   Gloucester: the medieval town and the Roman street pattern (after Baker and Holt 2004, 30, fig. 3.2). Reproduced by permission: Nigel Baker and Ashgate publishing.

indicate that St Oswald's stood in its own well-defined precinct (Heighway and Bryant 1999, 8), but it has never been clear how this precinct related to the defence of the *burh*.

The problem is that only the east half of the Roman walled area has the distinctive regular pattern which defines it as the *burh* of AD 900; the same pattern is not evident in the western half whose layout seems to ignore the Roman wall altogether. In 1984 I proposed (Garrod and Heighway 1984; Heighway 1984, 366–8) that the Anglo-Saxon *burh* did not use the western wall of the Roman town, but extended down to the river, where it made use of the riverside wall and a hypothetical Roman extended circuit. The St Oswald's precinct would have been attached to this circuit. Henry Hurst did not accept this; his map of the *burh* retains the Roman walls (Hurst 1986a, 137). I now agree with him, though not for the reasons he gives. I want to detail one key aspect; the line of Westgate Street.

Westgate Street

Medieval/modern Westgate and Eastgate Streets describe a smooth and continuous line from the east gate to the crossing of the river Severn (Fig. 5). It enters from the east through the Roman east gate, but then diverges gently to the north from the Roman line, so that Westgate Street crosses the

Roman wall some 40 metres north of the Roman west gate. On its north side, Westgate Street follows a row of massive Roman columns which Henry Hurst has recently discussed and interpreted (cautiously) as a temple colonnade (Hurst 1999b, 157). These columns have apparently behaved as a magnet which has distorted the whole main street to the north.

Also on the north side of Westgate Street, the medieval south boundary of the abbey precinct crosses the line of the western Roman wall, describing a straight line from its south-eastern corner right to its south-western limit. Neither of these two plan elements, Westgate Street or the abbey wall, show any deviations where they cross the Roman wall; they form one plan-unit, to follow Baker and Holt terminology, and they must have been created after a considerable section of the western wall had been removed.

Henry Hurst claimed that the removal of the western wall took place c.1100 after the building of the Norman abbey (Hurst 1986a, 131). I have in the past argued for a much earlier date (Heighway 1984, 361). My main reason for placing this realignment in the 5th century was excavation near the Cross (Heighway et al. 1979; Heighway and Garrod 1980) which showed that in the late 4th century the buildings north of the Roman street were demolished and levelled and timber buildings were erected on the platforms so created. Not long afterwards, in the early 5th century, the street was eliminated altogether by infilling and by the laying of a metalling over it (Fig. 6). It is conceivable that this metalling, which was very well-made, was part of an urban planning which included the line of columns as a monumental element. Such major topographical changes seemed to me highly likely to initiate the process which re-routed the line of the east/west streets.

There are, however, a number of reasons to place the distortion of Westgate Street much later.

1. A charter of AD 925–6 described St Oswald's defences as 'outside the old wall of the city' (Hare 1999, 36 and 43 n. 21; Baker and Holt 2004, 100).
2. Baker and Holt (2004, 65–7) point out that the mensuration of the eastern *burh* street pattern indicates that the Roman line of Eastgate Street was still in existence when the streets were laid out *c*. AD 900.
3. A watching brief of a sewer trench along Westgate Street (see Fig. 7) seemed to show that demolition of the western wall was very late (Atkin 1992b, 45–7). It is evident that the wall has been re-robbed as late as the 13th century. However for this to happen there must have been masonry in the wall at that date, perhaps not far below the surface of the street, so that wearing down of the street uncovered the blocks which were both a hazard and a source of stone. In turn however this implies that the wall was probably standing well into the post-Roman period.
4. Baker and Holt (2004, 46–7) have discussed the plan unit (1.2) along the north side of Westgate Street and concluded that it was created in the 10th to the early 11th century. The Westgate Street line was thus established by then.

The evidence pulls two ways and I have concluded we must stop thinking in terms of street limits in the medieval or modern sense. After all, we know, also from excavations at 1 Westgate Street, that even in the 10th/11th century the southern street frontage was not defined (a 10th-century building B3 quite close to the street frontage was at a completely different angle to that frontage, retaining the alignment of 9th-century buildings in that area: Heighway et al. 1979, 169). The only hypothesis that fits all the evidence is the suggestion of Patrick Garrod (in Atkin 1992b, 45–6) that the north side of the Roman main street moved north in the early 5th century, but the south limit remained for some centuries: in other words, there was a wide space between the West and East

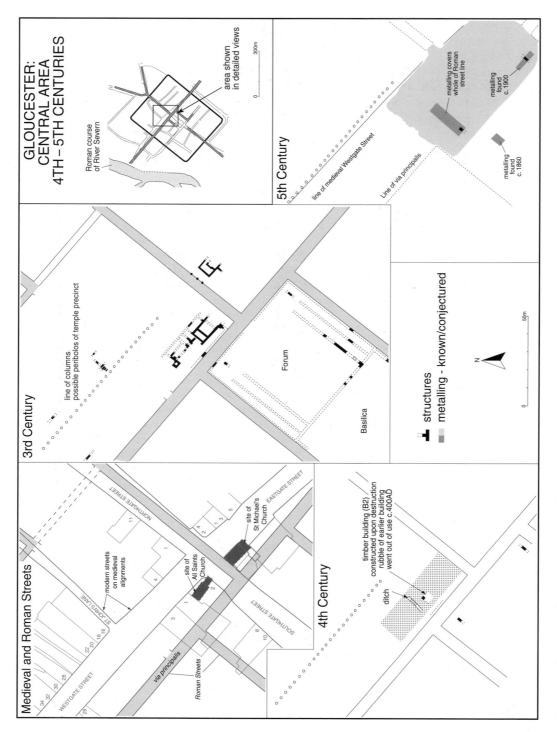

Fig. 6: Gloucester: the re-organisation of the centre of the Roman town in the early 5th century.

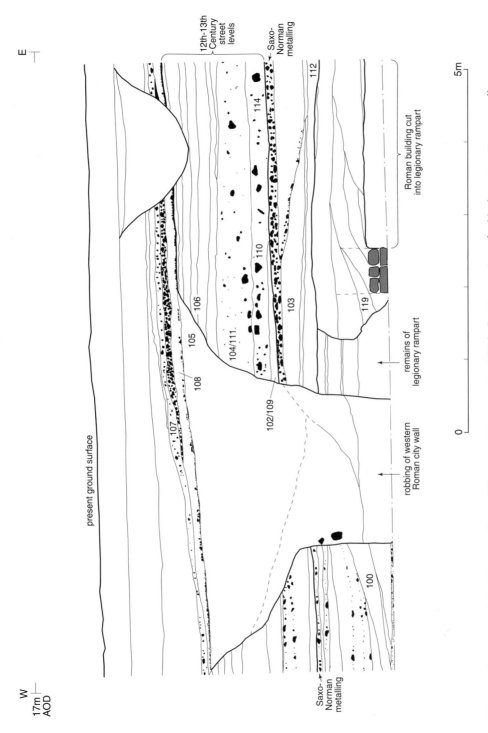

Fig. 7: *Sewer trench in Westgate Street (Gloucester Museum site 9/81) showing section of robbed western Roman wall.*

gates, with no very firm definition except the Roman columns. The *burh* may well have used the Roman walls in the early 10th century when it was created, but not long afterwards the western wall was removed, and the plan unit (Baker and Holt's unit 1.2) north of Westgate Street created. This may have happened in the mid 10th century (Heighway 2003, 8) and had certainly happened by the early 11th (Baker and Holt 2004, 47, 356).

Baker and Holt's suggestion (ibid. 69) that the eastern *burh* layout was centred on the Roman Eastgate Street is very interesting. At first sight it seems to conflict with the archaeology. Observation of the sewer trench up Eastgate Street (site 4/90: Atkin 1991, 26–9) showed that the 60 m-long Roman buildings on the north side of Eastgate Street were robbed to foundation level before the 11th century. The excavator suggests that the rubble deposits covering the demolished building represented road surfaces: in other words the street was already drifting north (Atkin 1991, 29). It is possible that the same process could have occurred here as in Westgate Street; the buildings north of the Roman street were demolished as early as the early 5th century creating a wide space. But in that case, it is hard to see how the new streets of *c*. AD 900 could have been laid out on the Roman street, which would have been out of sight by that time. Was there perhaps a feature which perpetuated the line of the Roman street?

If the 'wide road' hypothesis is correct, the two early churches of St Michael and All Saints are sited in the open space (Fig. 6). St Michael's in particular may have been of early origin: Baker and Holt (2004, 109) suggest it was contemporary with the *burh* foundation. It is very possible that the church of St Michael even *c*. AD 900 perpetuated a relict feature – a stone cross, or a portion surviving from a Roman monumental building. This would be in keeping with what is known of the late 4th-century/early 5th-century replanning, which not only used the 'Westgate columns' as part of the layout, but also involved the deliberate construction of a timber building around a column plinth (Heighway and Garrod 1980, 78).[4] The reason for maintaining the plinth is unclear, but it is evident that the reorganisation was very much a designed process which adapted the previous Roman monuments in specific ways. The site of St Michael's Church was occupied by stone buildings – it is opposite the centre of the forum facade –and these buildings could have been adapted during the urban replanning of the late 4th/early 5th century (Heighway in preparation). These in turn would have influenced the siting of the church.[5] Thus St Michael's or a predecessor feature could have dominated the 9th-century scene just as its 15th-century tower dominates the streetscape today.

Hare Lane

The regular planning of the streets north of the walled town has been suggested as a late Saxon layout: in particular the wide street of Hare Lane has the appearance of an extramural market. Michael Hare has made the suggestion that the lack of evidence for a market may result from the fact that the wide street was created for quite a different purpose, as a processional way whereby kings proceeded in state from the palace at Kingsholm to the minster at Gloucester (Hare 1997).

Medieval

Archaeological evaluations and radar scans provided a revised layout for the first castle, putting it inside, rather than across, the Roman defences (Hurst 1984; Darvill 1988; Atkin 1991, 10). Gloucester Castle must be potentially one of the most significant archaeological monuments, but its status as one of Her Majesty's prisons means that archaeological intervention has been rare. Some watching briefs have been possible, and there is a great deal to be derived from documentary evidence as Henry Hurst (1984) has shown. As a result of evaluations for the 'Blackfriars Development' the topography of this south-western quadrant of the town is now much better understood.

The excavations at St Oswald's Priory established the medieval layout of the Augustinian priory. The layout of the long-vanished church and claustral buildings at Llanthony Priory (Llanthony Secunda) has been recently established by documentary evidence and archaeological evaluation (Watts and Hughes 2004).

The 13th-century map of Gloucester looks much the same at a small scale, but there is much more detail now available, for instance the plot of the churches and general furniture in the middle of medieval Westgate Street (Baker and Holt 2004, 51). The medieval sites are augmented by documents. As well as the work of Baker and Holt, there is also John Rhodes's edition (2002) of the registers of Llanthony Priory. These contain much material for study of the late medieval town. More volumes are in hand and new information is still emerging.

Post-Medieval

Neglect of the archaeology of the post-medieval town has been corrected to some extent by Malcom Atkin (Atkin 1988c; Atkin and Loughlin 1992; Atkin 1992a). The incorporation of the 19th-century maps in the Urban Database will provide a prime source of topographical information. My topographical map, as I have said before, does not include the post-medieval period, but this is largely because there is too much information to summarise: the post-medieval town requires a series of maps of its own. It has many champions – Phil Moss's perspective view of the town *c.*1750 (Fig. 8) is a valuable resource in itself.

CONCLUSION

Although a large excavation would be a wonderful boost to Gloucester's archaeology, large projects have become rare – and have often failed to materialise after years of preparation, like the Blackfriars development. However, I believe there is much to be done with the information we already have. The Urban Database, in its complete form with all drawings from all projects scanned in, has considerable research potential. Although it is funded to provide information for planners, it should be used for 'education' as well. We are stakeholders, and its function should also be to tell us about our past.

Analysis of more sites in the waterfront area, including boreholes, could enlarge our under-standing. Malcolm Atkin showed that quite limited excavation could, with additional non-invasive methods such as radar scanning, produce information about the ancient waterfronts. Late Roman and indeed all burials could benefit from more detailed analysis: this could throw light on the matter of the urban area of the Roman town (Hurst 1986, 116–17), and perhaps the vexed question of where everyone was buried in the 5th–9th centuries. A future programme of analysis of samples from watching briefs, however small, was suggested as long ago as 1985 (Straker and Heighway 1985). Dense waterlogged black layers described as 'organic material' are often seen in the waterfront area. Are they stable sweepings? debris of occupation? animal or human? The question 'what do our finds mean?' is worth asking.

It seems it is not within the remit of the HEROs to carry out synthetic and comparative research; once again it is the local archaeological societies whom we call on to the rescue, as in the good old days of the late 1960s. Professional archaeology, tied as it is to planning functions, is straitjacketed. Its limited funds cannot always provide the interpretative material to present the city's history to the public.

I return to Malcolm Atkin's question, quoted at the outset: – have we done justice to Gloucester's history in the last ten years? Regarding the presentation of archaeology, the answer is – sometimes. The task is not easy. Archaeology may be popular on television, but synthesis and explanation are, when it comes to reality, very difficult, especially when the legislation demands that archaeologists dig very small holes and make very large pronouncements.

However, there is plenty to celebrate. The story of medieval Westgate Street is portrayed in eloquent signing (Phil Moss again) in Westgate Street and St John's Lane. The medieval market buildings and indeed the western Roman city wall are marked out on the street. Llanthony Secunda, once the greatest of the countries medieval priories, is emerging with some success from its former scrap-yard status. The statue of Nerva in Southgate Street is a modern reminder of the Roman past. The Museum has a programme of training digs and museum open days and the scheme to reduce access to the Folk Museum to ten weeks a year has been cancelled.

Yet in 2005 some of Gloucester's finest medieval buildings are again neglected (66 Westgate Street), and it seems a shame to reduce access to the Folk Museum, one of Gloucester's finest medieval buildings and its most interesting museum. The oldest building of all, St Oswald's Priory stands surrounded by a make-shift fence (to guard against falling stone) and is frequently vandalised. Its accompanying explanatory panel (by Phil Moss) has been placed some distance from the monument on the unfashionable side furthest from the main tourist approach: many people do not notice it at all. The site's spectacular collection of late Anglo-Saxon sculpture mostly languishes in the Museum basement.[6] The East Gate chamber is seldom open, the explanatory plaque has disappeared, and the Roman wall under Bell Walk cannot be viewed because of drainage and Health and Safety problems. The great scheme to place Blackfriars at the centre of a heritage centre and shopping complex sadly foundered – indeed Blackfriars, 'the most complete Dominican Friary in Europe', is only open to the public at limited times by prior appointment. Gloucester is still a historic town which keeps its past well hidden.

Archaeologists have to produce technical reports: money for public display and education is seldom available from developer funding. I do not know how to solve this. In any case it is always a challenge to make archaeology relevant and interesting to the non specialist. But we should attempt meaning and synthesis however difficult and risky that may be. I am reminded of Patrick Garrod, who viewing a heap of 9th-century wattle fencing, remarked, 'you spend three hours with a trowel and all you've got is an unlit bonfire'.

ACKNOWLEDGEMENTS

I am grateful to all those who at various times have discussed and commented on this paper. They include Nigel Baker, Phil Greatorex, Neil Holbrook, Phil Moss, John Rhodes and Richard Sermon.

NOTES

1. A survey of the 'Parliament Room' by Rochelle Rowell forms part of her Ph.D. thesis 'The Archaeology of late Monastic Hospitality' (York University, 2000) and is available in the cathedral library.
2. Fulbrook-Leggatt (1964) thought that the whole of the last 3 km (1.5 miles) of the Twyver was an artificial diversion, probably of Roman date: the evidence for canalisation is unequivocal but may represent alteration rather than diversion of the entire stream.

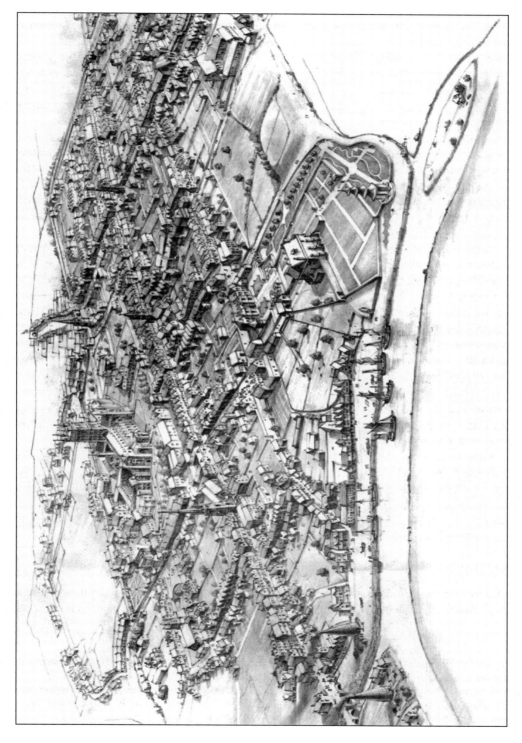

Fig. 8: Gloucester c.1750 (perspective drawing and research by Phil Moss).

3. John Blair has recently offered the interesting suggestion that, since the dating evidence is so uncertain, the 'mausoleum' may have been a product of the 7th century and may have accompanied the founding of the minster of St Peter in 679: Blair 2005, 31 note 90.
4. We suggested it was being used as a table, but was it really this mundane?
5. Baker and Holt's research (2004, 52) seems to indicate that the medieval St Michael's church had its west side at the east side of the 15th-century tower, and was therefore not on the Roman frontage. However John Rhodes (pers. comm.) in his research on the Llanthony registers has found evidence that the tower was actually built inside the footprint of the medieval church, whose west door would have been after all on the Roman frontage of 'Roman Northgate street'.
6. Since this review was composed the Gloucester city council has restored St Oswald's ruin and landscaped the surrounding ground.

BIBLIOGRAPHY

Atkin, M., 1986. 'Excavations in Gloucester 1985; – an interim report', *Glevensis* **20**, 3–12.

Atkin, M., 1988a. 'Marketing Gloucester: The Kingsholm Dig', *Brit. Archaeol.* **8**, 24–8.

Atkin, M., 1988b. 'Post-Medieval Archaeology in Gloucester: A Review', *Post-Med. Archaeol.* **21**, 1–24.

Atkin, M., 1991. 'Archaeological Fieldwork in Gloucester 1990: an interim report', *Glevensis* **25**, 4–32.

Atkin M., 1992a. 'Gloucester Archaeology 1900–1990: An Historical Review', *Trans. BGAS* **110**, 13–36.

Atkin, M., 1992b. 'Archaeological Fieldwork in Gloucester 1991', *Glevensis* **26**, 35–51.

Atkin, M., and Loughlin, W., 1992. *Gloucester and the Civil War: A City Under Seige* (Stroud).

Bagshaw, S., Heighway, C., and Price, A., 2004. 'The South Porch of Gloucester Cathedral: A Study of Nineteenth-Century Stone Repair Types', *J. Brit. Archaeol. Association* **157**, 91–114.

Baker, N., and Holt, R., 2004. *Urban Growth and the Medieval Church: Gloucester and Worcester* (Ashgate Press, Aldershot).

Bateman, C., and Williams, J., 2002. 'The South Gate Cemetery of Roman Gloucester', *Glevensis* **35**, 25–28.

Blair, J., 2005. *The Church in Anglo-Saxon Society* (Oxford).

Bryant, R., and Heighway C., 2003. 'Excavations at St Mary de Lode Gloucester', *Trans. BGAS* **121**, 97–178.

Darvill, T., 1988. 'Excavations on the site of the early Norman castle at Gloucester 1983–84' *Med. Archaeol.* **32**, 1–49.

Fulbrook-Leggatt, L.E.W.O., 1964. 'The River Twyver and the Fullbrook', *Trans. BGAS* **83**, 78–84.

Garrod, A.P., and Heighway, C.M., 1984. *Garrod's Gloucester* (Bristol).

Hare, M., 1992. *The two Anglo-Saxon minsters of Gloucester* (Deerhurst Lecture 1992).

Hare, M., 1997. 'Kings, Crowns and Festivals: the Origins of Gloucester as a Royal Ceremonial Centre', *Trans. BGAS* **115**, 41–78.

Hare, M., 1999. 'The documentary evidence', in Heighway and Bryant 1999.

Hassall, M.W.C., and Tomlin, R.S.O., 1984. 'Roman Britain in 1983. II Inscription, A: Monumental. 1. Gloucester', *Britannia* **15**, 333–52.

Heighway, C.M., 1974. *Archaeology in Gloucester: a policy for city and district* (Gloucester City Council).

Heighway, C.M., 1980. 'Roman cemeteries in Gloucester District', *Trans. BGAS* **98**, 57–72.

Heighway, C.M., 1983. *The East and North Gates of Gloucester* (Bristol).

Heighway C.M., 1984. 'Anglo-Saxon Gloucester', in J. Haslem (ed.), *Anglo Saxon Towns In Southern England* (Chichester).

Heighway, C.M., 2001. *Gloucester Cathedral and precinct: An Archaeological Assessment* (2nd edn.).

Heighway, C.M., 2003. 'Christian Continuity and the early medieval topography of Gloucester', *Glevensis* **36**, 3–12.

Heighway, C.M., and Rhodes, J.F., in preparation. 'St Michael's Church Gloucester: a reconsideration of the excavation of 1956'.

Heighway, C.M., and Bryant, R., 1999. *The Golden Minster: the Anglo-Saxon minster and medieval priory of St. Oswald at Gloucester* (CBA Research Rep. **117**, York)

Heighway, C.M., and Garrod, A.P., 1980. 'Excavations at 1 and 30 Westgate Street', *Britannia* **11**, 73–114.

Heighway, C.M., Garrod, A.P., and Vince, A., 1979. 'Excavations at 1 Westgate Street, Gloucester', *Med. Archaeol.* **23**, 159–213.

Hurst, H., 1972. 'Excavations at Gloucester 1968–1971', *Antiq. J.* **52**, 24–69.

Hurst, H., 1974. 'Excavations at Gloucester 1971–1973', *Antiq. J.* **54**, 8–52.

Hurst, H., 1975. 'Excavations at Gloucester: Third Interim Report: Kingsholm 1966–75', *Antiq. J.* **55**, 267–94.

Hurst, H., 1976. 'Gloucester: A colonia in the West', in K. Branigan and P.J. Fowler, *The Roman West Country: Classical culture and Celtic Society* (Newton Abbot).

Hurst H., 1984. 'The Archaeology of Gloucester Castle: An Introduction', *Trans. BGAS* **102**, 73–128.

Hurst, H., 1985. *Kingsholm* (Gloucester Archaeol. Rep. **1**, Cambridge).

Hurst, H., 1986. *Gloucester: the Roman and later defences* (Gloucester).

Hurst, H. (ed.), 1999. *The Coloniae of Roman Britain: new studies and a review* (Journal of Roman Archaeol. Supplementary Series **36**, Portsmouth, Rhode Island).

Hurst, H., 1999a. 'Topography and identity in Glevum colonia', in Hurst (ed.) 1999, 113–35.

Hurst, H. 1999b. 'Civic Space at Glevum', in Hurst (ed.), 1999, 152–60.

Morris, R.K., 2002. 'Gloucester Cathedral Precinct Buildings Survey' (report for the dean and chapter to accompany their conservation plan).

Moss, P., 1993. *Historic Gloucester: an illustrated guide to the city, its buildings the cathedral and the docks* (Moreton-in-Marsh).

Price, S., 1994. '26 Westgate Street, Gloucester: a report for English Heritage on its History and Architecture' (typescript report).

Rhodes, J. (ed.), 2002. *A Calendar of the Registers of the Priory of Llanthony 1457–66, 1501–25* (Gloucestershire Record Series **15**, BGAS).

Rowbotham, F.W., 1978. 'The River Severn at Gloucester with particular reference to its Roman and medieval channels', *Glevensis* **12**, 4–9.

Sermon, R., 1996. 'Gloucester Archaeology Unit Annual Report 1995', *Glevensis* **29**, 12–23.

Sermon, R., 1999. 'Gloucester Archaeology Unit Annual Report 1998 and 1999', *Glevensis* 33, 17–29.

Stocker, D., 2003. 'Review' of Heighway and Bryant 1999, *Trans. BGAS* **121**, 301–3.

Straker, V., and Heighway, C., 1985. 'Organic matter from medieval deposits outside St Nicholas Church, Gloucester', *Trans. BGAS* **103**, 223–6.

Thomas, A., Holbrook, N., and Bateman, C., 2003. *Later Prehistoric and Romano-British Burial and Settlement at Hucclecote, Gloucestershire* (Cotswold Archaeol., Bristol and Gloucestershire Archaeol. Rep. **2**).

Timby, J., 1999. 'Pottery supply to Gloucester colonia', in Hurst (ed.) 1999, 37–44.

Tomlin, R.S.O., and Hassall, M.W.C., 2005. 'Roman Britain in 2004. III. Inscriptions', *Britannia* **36**, 473–97.

Watts, M., and Hughes, P., 2004. 'Gloucester Quays: Llanthony Priory Redefined?', *Glevensis* **37**, 19–28.

The View from the Gloucestershire Archaeology Service

Jan Wills

INTRODUCTION

Twenty-five years ago archaeology in Gloucestershire was organised very differently from today, and the county council had yet to appoint an archaeologist to its staff. From the early 1980s, minutes of meetings of the Committee for Archaeology in Gloucestershire show concern about development proposals affecting significant archaeological sites in the county and the lack of resources to cope with them. Long before 1980 many local authorities in historic towns had reacted to concerns about the comprehensive urban redevelopment of the early post-War period and the consequent destruction of archaeological sites, by creating archaeological units to carry out excavation in advance of development. Many county councils such as Oxfordshire had also taken the lead in the early development of Sites and Monuments Records (SMRs). The emphasis at this time was on rescue excavation, i.e. dealing with the consequences of development that had already been agreed, and such resources that were available came from public funds, mainly from the Department of the Environment and also for a time through employment schemes run by the Manpower Services Commission. In Gloucestershire major excavation projects were organised by a regional archaeological unit, the Committee for Rescue Archaeology in Avon, Gloucestershire and Somerset (subsequently known as Western Archaeological Trust), by the Gloucester Excavation Unit or by unpaid amateur archaeologists. On the national scene the implications of the then new Ancient Monuments and Archaeological Areas Act 1979 were not yet clear.

This paper, written following the conference, is a brief review of some of the changes affecting the archaeology of Gloucestershire over the last 25 years, focusing in particular on the work of the Gloucestershire County Council Archaeology Service.

RECORDING THE LANDSCAPE OF THE PAST: FROM SMRS TO HERS

The beginnings of the Archaeology Service in Gloucestershire can be identified in 1982 when the county council, with funding from the Department of the Environment, appointed the first Sites and Monuments Record Officer for the county. Work began on a computerised record of archaeological sites, starting with the Ordnance Survey records and an important local index created by the Gloucester and District Archaeological Research Group. This computerised record, together with its paper maps depicting the location of recorded sites and archive files, was the last but one SMR to be created in England, full coverage of the country finally being achieved in the mid 1980s.

Although it initially focussed on archaeological field monuments, the content of the SMR has developed over time to include all types of evidence of the human past. It consequently contains information on archaeological sites, historic buildings, urban archaeological deposits, the historic landscape and historic settlements, covering all periods from the earliest prehistory to a notional cut-off date of the Second World War. This broadening of content is reflected in the current national re-branding of SMRs as Historic Environment Records (HERs).

One of the advantages of the late creation of the Gloucestershire SMR was that it began life as a computerised rather than a paper record. During its 23 years computing has moved on, allowing more sophisticated data structures and retrieval mechanisms to be employed, and, with the advent of Geographical Information Systems (GIS), improved mapping of information. At the time of writing the Gloucestershire SMR uses an Oracle database and ArchGIS, and holds information on over 43,000 items of historic environment data.

In 1982 the SMR was designed as a technical record to be used by professional archaeological staff primarily as a means of identifying threats and problems affecting archaeological sites. It is still the case that the main users of the SMR are the staff of the Archaeology Service for whom it is the key source of archaeological information underpinning their advisory role. It is also widely used by developers and their consultants, who obtain information in order to satisfy the requirements of the planning system, and by land owners and managers, school children, students, researchers and the general public.

The slender resources available to the SMR in 1982 were further diminished by the need for the SMR Officer to spend time dealing with threats and problems affecting the archaeology of the county. In recognition of this the post of County Archaeologist was created in 1985 and an additional member of staff appointed. Since then, the County Archaeology Service has grown to an average staffing level of 20, two thirds of whom are funded from external sources. The range of work carried out includes the curation of the SMR; an advisory service providing archaeological advice on development and land management; archaeological survey and other strategic projects; development–led archaeological fieldwork; outreach and education; and the recording of finds under the Portable Antiquities Scheme.

INFLUENCING THE FUTURE: ARCHAEOLOGICAL ADVICE IN THE PLANNING SYSTEM

One of the most important aspects of the Archaeology Service's advisory role is the protection of archaeological sites through the use of the planning system. During the extensive urban redevelopment and growth of the 1960s and 1970s there was little scope through archaeological or planning legislation to protect sites from damaging development. Where possible rescue archaeology, involving excavation or watching briefs, was undertaken in advance of or during development but inadequate funding meant that many sites were developed without prior recording. Where funding for excavation was available this was often insufficient to ensure that the results of the work were written up for publication, leading to large backlogs of unpublished material.

Change came with the introduction of the Ancient Monuments and Archaeological Areas Act in 1979. For the first time nationally important sites, which had been scheduled as ancient monuments, could be protected from damaging development and preserved *in situ*. One of the first public inquiries under the provisions of this Act was held in Gloucestershire in 1987 following development proposals affecting the Neolithic henge at Condicote in the north of the county.

For the vast majority of archaeological sites in the county, however, improved protection had to wait until changes took place in the planning system. Incremental improvements during the 1980s culminated with the publication of the long awaited Planning Policy Guidance Note (PPG) 16, *Archaeology and Planning*, in 1990. This is one of a series of advisory documents through which central government sets out its policy on key planning issues, and it succinctly articulates the place of archaeology as a material consideration in the planning system. It characterises archaeology as a finite and non-renewable resource fundamentally at risk from damage or destruction caused by development and sets out the mechanisms through which these development pressures can be controlled by the planning system. Key aspects of PPG 16 include a presumption in favour of the preservation of nationally important archaeological remains, whether scheduled or not; the need for archaeological policies in development plans; procedures for the assessment of the impact of individual development proposals on archaeology through desk-based and field evaluation; and a model planning condition to secure archaeological recording in advance of development which puts the onus on the developer to commission this work. PPG 16 also established the importance of local authority archaeological services by identifying SMRs and County Archaeologists as the main sources of archaeological information and advice in the planning process.

Since 1990 the planning system has become an effective mechanism for protecting archaeological sites from development in Gloucestershire, and the systematic assessment of the impact of development on archaeology within the terms of PPG 16 is now a routine part of the planning process. We have an input into local strategic plans, both in advising on policies to provide the framework for decisions on individual development proposals and in looking at the proposed allocations of land for development at the draft plan stage. In development control we advise the county and district planning authorities on the archaeological implications of development, assessing 8–10,000 applications each year. In 2004 we provided archaeological advice on 1,186 planning cases, a small number of which were refused planning permission on archaeological grounds, and provided over 100 briefs for archaeological work. The cost of these processes are shared by the local authority which provides the advisory service, and the developer who has to commission archaeological assessments, evaluations, or other recording once a permission has been given and also to ensure that such work is taken on through post-excavation to publication.

The important emphasis on preservation *in situ* in PPG16 means that there is a realistic opportunity to preserve important sites through the refusal of planning permission on archaeo-logical grounds. However, since 1990 there has also been an unprecedented amount of archaeological excavation both in Gloucestershire and elsewhere, and the vast majority of archaeological recording is now a consequence of the advice given to planning authorities by local authority archaeologists and is carried out to briefs which they provide. An example of this is the recent A417/419 road improvement scheme which generated the most extensive archaeological recording project to date in Gloucestershire, examining a transect across the Cotswolds and the Upper Thames Valley (Mudd *et al.* 1999).

These changes in the planning system have had many other consequences for the practice of archaeology, too many to be discussed in detail here. Amongst them reference must however be made to the much more extensive sampling of the archaeological landscape through evaluation in advance of development, leading to the discovery of entirely new settlements and other human activity, often in areas previously devoid of such evidence. The way professional archaeology is organised has also changed as the transfer of responsibility for the funding of archaeological work to the developer has led to the emergence of a multiplicity of archaeological companies and consultancies tendering competitively for this work.

Parallel advice on historic buildings and conservation areas, PPG 15 entitled *Planning and the Historic Environment*, was introduced in 1994. Although this provides much important advice on the management of the built historic environment some aspects of this document, especially the opportunities to secure the assessment and recording of historic building in advance of development, have not been implemented as widely as they might have been.

THE RURAL LANDSCAPE AT RISK

Through much of the last 25 years there has been a concentration on improving the way in which archaeology can be protected from development through the planning system, with considerable success as outlined above. However, many of the processes which damage archaeology in the rural landscape cannot be controlled by the planning system, and the ancient monuments legislation does not adequately protect even scheduled monuments from damage by cultivation. By 1980 this problem had been the subject of a study which examined the condition of rural archaeological sites, and in particular the effects of arable cultivation, in the Cotswolds (Saville 1980). The major problem of ploughing, even on scheduled monuments, led to the excavation at the Neolithic chambered tomb of Hazleton (Saville 1990) as, at the time, there was no mechanism – other than excavation – for dealing with this problem. More effective ways to protect rural archaeological sites have only recently been secured. As government subsidy moves from agricultural production to environmental protection, the sustainable management of archaeological sites has become one of the objectives of agri-environment schemes. Through Environmentally Sensitive Area (ESA) schemes and Countryside Stewardship (CS) farmers have been able to receive payments for, for example, taking important archaeological sites out of arable cultivation or managing vegetation and erosion. In Gloucestershire we have been advising on ESAs and CS for over 10 years, and the appointment of a Countryside Archaeological Adviser in 2000 enabled us to make significant advances in taking vulnerable archaeological sites out of arable cultivation. Environmental Stewardship, which replaced all previous schemes in early 2005, provides for statutory consultation with local authority archaeological advisers, and archaeological site management options are a significant component of the opportunities now available to farmers.

Not all problems can be dealt with through agri-environment schemes and the County Archaeology Service therefore also runs a Monument Management Scheme with grant aid mainly from English Heritage through which practical conservation work is carried out annually on a range of sites. Currently the largest conservation project of this type is the work at the Iron-Age hillfort of Painswick Beacon where severe erosion, threatening the integrity of the ramparts, has been repaired through work supported by the Heritage Lottery Fund (HLF), English Heritage, English Nature, the Gloucestershire Environmental Trust, the local Painswick Conservation Group and Painswick Parish Council.

NEW DISCOVERIES: RESEARCH AND SURVEY

In addition to its advisory work the County Archaeology Service initiates a wide range of survey and research projects, as well as providing archaeological services to developers. The programme of survey and research is mainly directed towards enhancing knowledge of those areas of the county which are comparatively poorly understood, or improving their management. The results of such projects enhance the SMR and provide a better basis for decision making. Recent examples include work on the small towns of Gloucestershire, historic landscape characterisation and an assessment of the archaeology in areas potentially affected by aggregate extraction. The current focus of survey work is the Forest of Dean, an area where there are far fewer recorded sites than in the rest of the county and a landscape (the wooded central Forest) in which it is difficult to apply conventional survey techniques. The objectives of the Forest of Dean Archaeological Survey are both to research the complex archaeological landscape and to improve its management. The desk-based research and pilot fieldwork stages have now been completed. The latter included the exploration of techniques of rapid walk over survey, environmental sampling, geophysical survey and LiDAR (Light Detection and Ranging) in a wooded environment. The results of this work have enabled a suite of approaches to be devised for more extensive survey in the central area of the Forest over the coming years. These will include further testing of LiDAR, a promising new survey technique for mapping the micro topography of the ground from the air.

INVOLVING THE COMMUNITY: OUTREACH AND EDUCATION

The incorporation of archaeology into the planning and other statutory systems has led to an increased professionalisation of much archaeological work, causing concern that opportunities for the participation of the public in archaeological projects have decreased. While it is true that there are difficulties in involving people in development-led archaeology new opportunities have presented themselves. The Forest of Dean Archaeological Survey for example was designed to involve the local community and to appeal not only to existing local groups and societies but also to those people who have no prior knowledge of archaeology. The Forest of Dean outreach programme has comprised community workshops involving discussion, practical sessions and field visits; community fieldwork projects; newsletters aimed at a non-specialist audience; events such as National Archaeology Day and Heritage Open Days; and regular contributions to local media including community radio. The desire to involve those who have no previous knowledge of archaeology led to the recently completed *Carving History at The Wilderness* project, based at The Wilderness Centre at Mitcheldean and supported by the Heritage Lottery Fund (HLF) Young Roots programme. This year-long project has used archaeology as the inspiration for work with disadvantaged young people, and has just received an HLF award for the best youth project in the South-West region.

THE FUTURE

In his introduction to *Archaeology in Gloucestershire* in 1984 Alan Saville identified urgent problems in the preservation of archaeological sites and historic buildings, and in the local organisation of archaeology, as well as a paucity of archaeological research in the Forest of Dean. I hope that this short review has demonstrated that much has changed since 1984. Both the legislative framework and the organisational framework for the management of archaeology in Gloucestershire have changed for the better, and there is at last a programme of archaeological research in the Forest of Dean as well as an active local archaeological group.

At the time of writing however much that has become familiar over the last 25 years is about to change again. The government's Heritage Protection Review proposes a new unified system of protection for the historic environment, bringing together archaeology and the built heritage into one system and replacing the parallel systems of listing and scheduling. New responsibilities will devolve to local authorities and the government has stated its intention – at long last – to make SMRs a statutory service within local government.

BIBLIOGRAPHY

Mudd, A., Williams, R.J., and Lupton, A., 1999. *Excavations alongside Roman Ermin Street, Gloucestershire and Wiltshire: The Archaeology of the A419/A417 Swindon to Gloucester Road Scheme* (Oxford Archaeol. Unit: 2 volumes).

Saville, A., 1980. *Archaeological sites in the Avon and Gloucestershire Cotswolds* (CRAAGS Surv. **5**, Bristol).

Saville, A., 1990. *Hazleton North. The excavation of a Neolithic long cairn of the Cotswold-Severn group* (HBMCE Archaeological Rep. **13**, London, English Heritage).

The South Gloucestershire Historic Environment Record

David R. Evans

The South Gloucestershire Sites and Monuments Record (SMR) provides a dynamic digest of archaeological and historical sites, structures and find spots which are recorded in the area. It should be regarded as one component of an Historic Environment Record (HER), which includes other, appropriate, data relating to Conservation Areas, Historic Landscape, Listed (and unlisted) structures and related environmental features such as semi-natural woodland. The function of the HER is to provide educational, general and planning advice and information to the people of South Gloucestershire.

The South Gloucestershire Council Historic Environment Record originated in the records maintained by Avon County Council. Its development was quite complicated, but a rough summary is as follows. The initial record was based on a series of record cards and maps which in themselves were based to some degree on the Ordnance Survey Archaeological Service records, supplemented by limited parish survey records. Compilation of the computerised SMR using a Database Manager called SuperFile was begun in 1983 and Manpower Services staff completed much of the initial input of data by 1985/6. A major survey of Marshfield parish was carried out during this period and should have established a standard by which the record could be measured but the opportunity was missed. This said, however, the SMR data for Marshfield was the most comprehensive in the database. Between 1988 and 1993 further records were added mainly, but not entirely, based on projects such as the Severn Barrage Survey, preliminary work for the Second Severn Crossing and early developments at Bradley Stoke. A full time SMR officer partly funded by what is now English Heritage was appointed in 1993.

A considerable backlog, especially of archaeological assessment reports (archaeological grey literature), had accumulated by that time. A major task was therefore to eliminate as much of this backlog as was possible. Local and national journals had also to be examined. Local government reorganisation quickly became an issue when it became apparent that a joint provision for the four successor unitary councils would not be feasible. It was quickly realised that although the database manager was fit for purpose, due to the haphazard construction of the database much data cleaning would be required. It was also accepted that a relational database, which better fitted the event/monument structure becoming the standard for SMRs, should be introduced. The database was transferred to MS FoxPro and considerable data cleaning was undertaken. Upon local government reorganisation in 1996 the paper background material of the SMR was divided between the four successor unitary authorities. Each gained a full database for the former county of Avon with the intention that this would facilitate data exchange.

In 1996/7 data were migrated from SuperFile (via MS FoxPro) to Microsoft Access. At this time a crude link to a Geographical Information System (GIS) was developed. Such a link allowed basic data to be displayed on a computer map base. Two projects initiated under Avon County Council, the Extensive Urban Survey and the Historic Landscape Character Assessment, continued under the successor authorities. Looking back it was the progress of these two projects, which saw the first stage of the transformation of the SMR into a Historic Environment Record (HER). Both began as a paper map-based exercise but it soon became clear that only a computer map-based system would be able to handle and manipulate the data so that they could be presented in a usable format.

At this stage it was realised that although most of the major inconsistencies in the data had been eliminated, a major rethink about how the SMR was structured and how it was developed was required. Therefore, in 1998 a data audit of the existing record was undertaken which resulted in the formulation of a five-year plan for a major overhaul of the database. Although some of these aspirations were overtaken by events and others are still a hope for the future, the main themes of the audit – improving the quality of the data and a full parish-by-parish review of the information – were successfully completed in 2004. All of the main features which appear on First Edition Ordnance Survey maps (c.1880) are now recorded. One aspiration was to have the HER available on the Web. Although a South Gloucestershire based website has not, yet, been established a version of the data can be viewed via the Archaeology Data Service (http://ads.ahds.ac.uk).

Although not directly connected with the development of the HER the appointment of an archaeology promotions officer in 2000 funded by the Heritage Lottery Fund made it possible for a greater involvement for the community in the recording and enhancement of the local heritage. Amongst projects generated by this initiative the construction of a list of buildings of local distinctiveness and a survey of pumps, wells and springs can be highlighted as directly benefiting the HER. A twice-yearly archaeological newsletter was also published, and this continues after the end of the project. A limited amount of fieldwork was also possible within the remit of the project. Three major villas have been sampled and a Saxon burial recorded. Despite reduced staff, limited projects are still being undertaken. Work to improve the presentation of the important coal-mining site at Ram Hill, Westerleigh, is being carried out with considerable local involvement.

What does the HER comprise? All historic and archaeological data contain some element of geographical information and a major change has been the move from a data-centred system to a map-based system. HER data can now be viewed via a series of map layers covering SMR sites (archaeological core data); Scheduled Ancient Monuments; Listed Buildings; Locally Listed Buildings; Registered Parks, Gardens and Battlefields; and settlement cores and excavation sites. But this is not all. A series of digital Ordnance Survey maps, dating approximately to 1880, 1905, 1915 and 1936, together with later Ordnance Survey maps and aerial photographs, forms part of the resource. A separate HER study room which contains considerable amounts of background material, which is not readily available on either the maps or the database, has been established.

Where are we now and where are we going? Although development as outlined above appears to be akin to linear growth, it is in fact much closer to an exponential explosion of data. Although numbers do not tell the whole story, the database has three times the numbers of entries that it had on the establishment of South Gloucestershire in 1996. In many ways the HER appears complete but there is much to do with new data sources to be tapped and new opportunities for exploiting the educational potential of the resource to be explored.

Archaeology in Gloucestershire: Looking Backwards but Mostly Forwards

Alan Saville

It was a very considerable privilege to be invited by Neil Holbrook to participate in the 2004 celebration of Gloucestershire archaeology, 25 years after the conference on the same theme which I organized as part of the Prehistoric Society's summer excursion to the Cotswolds in 1979. Acting as Chairman for the morning session and delivering a summing-up at the end of the day was extremely enjoyable and gratifying, as was the opportunity to hear at first hand the up-to-date accounts of what archaeological work had been taking place in the county over the last two and a half decades. The day brought back pleasant memories of the previous occasion, as indeed did meeting up again with some veterans of that 1979 conference who were still involved in, or at least still interested in, archaeology in Gloucestershire. The conference in 1979 also took place in The Park in Cheltenham, in what was then the College of St Paul and St Mary but which by 2004 had become part of the University of Gloucestershire – an auspicious sign of change.

Just as the 1979 meeting generated a publication – *Archaeology in Gloucestershire* (Saville 1984a) – so has the 2004 conference for which I am penning this minor and confessedly self-indulgent contribution. As I said on the day at the conference, to review the whole wealth of new information presented by the speakers would be unrealistic, and it is now unnecessary since their contributions will be found in the present volume. Instead I will focus on a few themes which struck me at the meeting, or have occurred to me since, that are worthy of further exploration and comment in the context of this volume and its predecessor. In doing so as a non-Gloucestershire resident since 1989 I realize I risk the criticism of being out of touch with local detail, but equally as an interested external observer I have the luxury of expressing my opinions without the constraints of being directly involved.

Whilst in his talk Tim Darvill was able to report a few isolated discoveries from the Palaeolithic and Mesolithic periods, it seemed to me that these earliest phases of prehistory are still very much the 'Cinderella' periods for archaeology in the county and it is perhaps the single category in which we are little further forward than in 1984. Admittedly there have recently been some encouraging national and local prospects for progress in terms of the Lower Palaeolithic. In the far north of the county, the work of the new National Ice Age Network (www.iceage.org.uk), which has grown from the Shotton Project/Midlands Palaeolithic Network based at the University of Birmingham (Buteux and Lang 2002), could lead to new discoveries from the Avon and Severn gravels to expand on previous exciting discoveries from the Twyning area (Whitehead 1988). And in the far south of the county we heard in Bob Jones's talk of new work taking place on the Shirehampton gravels of the Bristol Avon, which have been so productive of early Palaeolithic finds in the past (Lacaille 1954; Roe 1974), but have received little modern attention. The new initiative there may result in the Shirehampton finds being placed in their proper Quaternary context (Bates 2003; www.bristol-city.gov.uk).

It is surprising, however, that hardly any discoveries dating from the Upper Palaeolithic period have been made in Gloucestershire since 1979. The work of Nick Barton and his team at King Arthur's Cave and other adjacent locations in the Wye Valley, mainly just over on the Herefordshire side of the county boundary but including Symonds Yat East rock-shelter in Gloucestershire (Barton 1994; 2005), have made it abundantly clear there was human presence in western Gloucestershire at this period. Just to the south-west in Gwent some surface finds of Upper Palaeolithic artefacts are appearing (Aldhouse-Green 2004, 24), as they are elsewhere in the English Midlands (Cooper and Jacobi 2001; Jacobi *et al.* 2001), and the apparent scanty evidence for this period in Gloucestershire is becoming harder to sustain as a credible reflection of the prehistoric reality.

Similarly I would have expected at least one of the myriad evaluation trenches now being dug throughout the county to have revealed a Mesolithic site of some consequence, but apparently not. One recent summary overview puts the number of known Mesolithic sites in the county as 'over 40' (Mudd *et al.* 1999, 6), very similar to the number I previously listed (Saville 1984b, 75–6). Expert re-examination of museum and private collections and recently excavated assemblages would no doubt produce many further findspots where a few diagnostically Mesolithic artefacts have been found, but more extensive evidence of Mesolithic presence of the type found in truncated form beneath the Hazleton long cairn (Saville 1990, 153–75) or in the estuarine clays of the Severn margins in Wales (Bell *et al.* 2000) must surely be awaiting discovery in Gloucestershire. In terms of research frameworks an emphasis on these earlier periods would be easy to justify.

This brings me to the topic of the distribution within the county of archaeological knowledge for any period. Traditionally the Cotswolds have tended to dominate accounts of much of the county's archaeology, especially in the earlier periods, with the addition of the obvious 'archaeological honeypot' in the Vale provided by Gloucester from the Roman period onwards. As many speakers at the 2004 conference emphasized, this is far from the case today, both because archaeological activity has followed modern development – which is mostly off the Cotswolds proper – and because of fluctuating research interests and opportunities. Thus the new evidence used by speakers was drawn primarily from the Vale and the Upper Thames. In the former there has been a minor revolution in our appreciation and understanding of Severnside activity through time (e.g. Rippon 2001). Whilst most of the spectacular discoveries have been made just outside the county on the Welsh side of the estuary (Bell *et al.* 2000), the remarkable work of John Allen in particular has shown there is a great deal worthy of interest in Gloucestershire on both banks of the Severn (e.g. Allen 2001). In the Upper Thames it is more a question of having expanded our knowledge through a wider dataset since 1979, both through post-excavation projects coming to final publication (e.g. Allen *et al.* 1993) and from new discoveries from continuing survey and excavation (e.g. *British Archaeology* 71 (2003), 6). It is interesting to reflect that at the 1979 conference archaeologists were still coming to terms with the implications of discoveries from the M5 motorway construction through the Vale (Fowler 1977), and in 2004 it was the same with the results from work along the A419/A417 road, particularly in the Upper Thames area (Mudd *et al.* 1999).

However, the concern I expressed in 1984 over the 'paucity of archaeological research which has taken place in Gloucestershire west of the River Severn' (Saville 1984a, 10) is still relevant. It would be very wrong to suggest nothing has changed; Bryan Walters's book (1992) and the energetic efforts of members of the Dean Archaeological Group (DAG) since its inception in the late 1980s have made a huge difference, and the Gloucestershire Archaeology Service's current Forest of Dean Archaeological Survey promises well. Nevertheless, it still cannot be said that west of the Severn in general is fully on the map as far as Gloucestershire archaeology is concerned. One cannot help feeling that it will eventually be this area which will produce some of the most outstanding sites and finds from the whole county, but perhaps this will take a further 25 years to achieve.

In 1979 and 1984 the county of Avon was in existence, and not realizing how historically short-lived it was to be, little attention was given to south Gloucestershire and particularly Bristol in either the conference or the book apart from brief references to medieval pottery and the medieval town. The 2004 conference attempted to remedy this by including a talk on archaeology in Bristol, but there remains a feeling that the potential contribution of Bristol's past to an understanding of the regional picture has still not been fulfilled and that Bristol has not set an example for the region in terms of the way it has managed its own archaeology. With no intention whatever of belittling the work of Bob Jones and many other archaeologists who have wrestled through trying circumstances to recover much archaeological information from the city, I cannot avoid making some critical comment, though on the credit side the support of Bristol City Council for the Severn Estuary Levels Research Committee must be acknowledged. But Bristol is, after all, a major European city with understandable and laudable civic and regional aspirations in many fields, and any dispassionate overview of its achievements in terms of heritage provision – archaeological, historical, and museological – would be forced to conclude that all is not well and has not been so for too long a time. The absence of the heritage, archaeology, and museums in the recently issued *City life: a cultural strategy for Bristol* (www.bristol-city.gov.uk) reinforces this conclusion. When will the city councillors, officials, and politicians wake up to what is going on in heritage terms in comparable cities elsewhere in Europe and when will they show a proper appreciation of the contemporary social and cultural value of Bristol's past for both citizens and visitors alike? My advice to the City Fathers (and Mothers), if I can as an outsider presume to give any, is to commission a comprehensive review, start setting aside a truly meaningful heritage budget, establish the necessary partnerships with English Heritage and others, and begin taking the past more seriously. Creating a Bristol archive centre akin to the London Archaeological Archive and Research Centre (LAARC) would be a good first initiative (www.museumoflondon.org.uk/laarc).

Lack of synthesis in archaeology has become an increasingly critical issue over the last decade or so with the realization that ever more client reports, interims, websites, videos, CDs, and leaflets on archaeological fieldwork are being produced in isolation with no means to integrate findings into coherent overviews. In part of course this is precisely what the present volume is – as was the 1984 volume – designed to address, but there is an obvious limit to the ability of authors in this kind of endeavour to go beyond fully published sources in their research. To delve into the world of 'grey literature', let alone into the storerooms of units and museums (and in so doing to stray beyond one's own specific areas of expertise), is virtually impossible on the basis of academic curiosity alone given the time constraints and work pressures we are all under. What is required is adequate resourcing to allow the accumulated information to be sifted and to come appropriately into the public domain. This might take various forms, such as increased staffing of the county Sites and Monuments Record with the specific aim of period syntheses, the encouragement and financing of postgraduate research (at the University of Gloucestershire?) on relevant topics in conjunction with units and museums, the provision of sabbaticals and post-retirement grants for field archaeologists, and greater access to archives in all forms.

On the question of archives, I was reminded recently, when looking at Peter Leach's (1998) otherwise admirable publication of Ernest Greenfield's work at Great Witcombe Roman villa, of the need to make clear exactly where excavation archives can be accessed. In this case we are told simply that the 'finds ... are in the care of English Heritage' (Leach 1998, ix) and there are many excavation reports still being published which are even less helpful about the whereabouts of the finds. An exemplary recent exception would be Jennings *et al.* (2004, 14), which makes it clear the Thornhill Farm archive is in the Corinium Museum.

Tim Darvill, in the first part of his talk at the 2004 conference, alluded to some of the wider changes taking place in British archaeology which have impacted on what and how archaeology is now undertaken in Gloucestershire. These changes include the introduction of planning guidance (PPG 16) in the early 1990s which has fundamentally altered rescue archaeology by providing a framework for the material consideration of archaeology at all stages of the planning process and for the funding from developers which allows commercial archaeology to flourish. Allied to this, and crucial to the implementation of PPG 16, are the growth of development control archaeology within the County Council and the importance of the local Sites and Monuments Record in this process. This is all a very changed world from 1979, when the existing, constitutionally non-commercial 'regional' archaeological units were almost wholly dependent upon unreliable annual grant-aid from central government and excavation opportunities arose as often as not from 'grape-vine tip-offs'.

Nevertheless, what has accompanied this change is the shift from the kind of large-scale, long-term, research-focused rescue excavation which has done so much to illuminate Gloucestershire's past, such as the work at Uley (Woodward and Leach 1993) and at St Oswald's Priory in Gloucester (Heighway and Bryant 1999) to cite just two examples. (In a non-rescue context one must immediately pay tribute to the enviable tenacity of Eddie Price, not just for continuing his work at Frocester Court, but in recently producing his impressive two-volume report (Price 2000)). Large-scale projects of this kind, however, are of course notoriously difficult and expensive to bring to fruition in terms of final publication, something emphasized most negatively in the county by the Crickley Hill Project, for which the volume on the hillfort defences (Dixon 1994), an exceptionally valuable and innovative report though it was, is the only one to have appeared. By contrast the two-volume publication of work on the A419/A417 (Mudd et al. 1999) appeared extremely rapidly after the completion of fieldwork and all concerned deserve congratulation. Clearly what is required for the future is some way of marrying the technical post-excavation project management skills of modern commercial archaeology to the academic skills formerly deployed on the research-driven rescue excavations.

Another general change in archaeology since 1979, and one which is only just making itself felt in the county, is the introduction of the Portable Antiquities Scheme following on from the Treasure Act 1996, which replaced the previous common law of treasure trove in England. The five annual reports on Treasure which have appeared since the implementation of the Treasure Act in 1997 allow documentation of the Treasure finds from Gloucestershire (Table 1).

In 12 of the 18 cases these Treasure finds were the fruit of metal-detecting, and it is the growth of this hobby, and the realization that the finds being made by it represented a field of archaeological data which was previously largely unknown and/or ignored (even in terms of coin finds), that fuelled the development of the Portable Antiquities Scheme. Gloucestershire has been one of the last counties to acquire coverage under the scheme, and there has only been a Finds Liaison Officer in post since the beginning of 2004. This means that the most recently published report of the Scheme (DCMS 2004b) only includes data from three months of recording, during which 26 finds were reported. Over the coming years it will be interesting to see if the level of finds discovery and reporting starts to match levels in those counties where the scheme is already well established, after making allowances for such factors as the lesser proportion of arable land available for searching in Gloucestershire. Certainly there is no sign as yet of a decline in the popularity of metal-detecting as a pastime and the fact that detectorists in Gloucestershire now have a well-publicized channel for reporting their discoveries under the Scheme must be a major advance. It is not just finds from metal-detecting of course; as Table 1 shows in the case of Treasure,

Table 1: Gloucestershire Treasure finds since 1997.

Findspot	Object	Period	Method of discovery	Allocation	Reference
Bourton-on-the-Water	gold 'bead'	Early–Middle Bronze Age	excavation	Corinium Museum	DCMS 2002, 12
Batsford	gold penannular ring	Late Bronze Age	metal-detecting	Corinium Museum	DCMS 2002, 12
Bourton-on-the-Water	132 coins	Roman	metal-detecting	Corinium Museum	DCMS 2001, 126–7
North Cerney	silver finger-ring	Roman	gardening	returned to finder	DCMS 2000, 12; 2001, 20
Over	14 coins	Roman	metal-detecting	returned to finder	DCMS 2001, 126
Rodborough	25 silver coins	Roman	hedge-clearing	Stroud Museum	DCMS 2004a, 131
Taynton	50 coins	Roman	metal-detecting	returned to finder	DCMS 2001, 123
Taynton	silver finger-ring and 98 coins	Roman	metal-detecting	returned to finder	DCMS 2002, 22
Cirencester	silver decorated belt buckle	5th C	metal-detecting	Corinium Museum	DCMS 2001, 22–3
Sandhurst	silver ingot	Viking	metal-detecting	Gloucester Museum	DCMS 2003, 48
Standish	gold finger-ring	Medieval	metal-detecting	Gloucester Museum	DCMS 2004a, 85
Winchcombe	silver-gilt brooch	Medieval	metal-detecting	returned to finder	DCMS 2003, 53
Wanswell	3 silver coins	16th C	metal-detecting	returned to finder	DCMS 2000, 44
Berkeley	silver-gilt dress-pin	16th C	metal-detecting	Stroud Museum	DCMS 2001, 88–9
Tidenham	118 coins	17th C	metal-detecting	Chepstow Museum	DCMS 2001, 140–1
Tortworth	2 silver coins	17th C	not recorded	returned to finder	DCMS 2000, 44
Winchcombe	coin hoard	17th C	construction work	Cheltenham Museum	DCMS 2000, 45–6
Breadstone	gold posy ring	18th C	not recorded	returned to finder	DCMS 2000, 20

chance finds have been made during gardening, hedge-removal, and construction work, and important archaeological discoveries can be made during any type of ground disturbance. I anticipate that having a designated Liaison Officer to whom these can be reported will profoundly change our understanding of Gloucestershire's past from the perspective of material culture before the next 25 years are over.

From Table 1 it can be seen that museums throughout the county are acquiring Treasure items, but museums are currently in a somewhat contradictory position. Whilst the Portable Antiquities Scheme is responding to, and is itself stimulating, an increased (and increasingly informed) interest in archaeological finds amongst the general public, this is not matched by any increase in any specifically archaeological resourcing for local museums in England, and Gloucestershire has certainly fared no better than most counties in this respect. I wish to avoid specific comment about individual museums in the county, but looked at in general in terms of their archaeological provision the position is arguably well short of satisfactory, even taking into account the impressive new Romano-British displays at the Corinium Museum. One is bound to ask the question as to whether museum archaeology in Gloucestershire would be better served by having fewer museums doing archaeology, or even, heresy though it may seem, a single county museum for archaeology? I fully appreciate this question raises various political issues in terms of local authority organization and funding, and touches on entrenched antipathies, but rationalization of some kind in this area will in the end be unavoidable because of the need to focus resources. Perhaps the answer would be a single archive or heritage study centre for storing all of Gloucestershire's archaeological assemblages and chance finds, and where all archaeological staff would be based, from which representative samples of suitable objects could be drawn for permanent display in the actual museums?

Museums have not been much involved in archaeological publication (the *Archaeology in Gloucestershire* volume of 1984 being unusual in this respect), which has primarily been the preserve within Gloucestershire of the county society – the Bristol and Gloucestershire Archaeological Society – and of local groups, such as the Gloucester and District Archaeological Research Group (GADARG) and DAG, and local archaeological units and companies, and externally of national organizations such as English Heritage and the Council for British Archaeology. It is interesting that the county society has, since 1988, put much of its publishing energy into the very successful Gloucestershire Record Series, of which 18 volumes have now appeared, bucking a trend for publishing such historical studies and very much a personal testimony to the vision and enthusiasm of David Smith, the long-serving Honorary Secretary of the Society. On the archaeological side, however, apart from the introduction of the supplementary reports (with the blue covers) now being issued alongside the *Transactions* on the initiative of Cotswold Archaeology, and the welcome appearance of back numbers of the *Transactions* on open access on the internet, little seems to have changed since 1979. In fact even the single concessionary innovation which Steve Blake and I as editors managed to squeeze agreement for from the remarkably conservative publications committee – the use of an illustration on the front cover from volume 105 onwards – has recently been rescinded, with a blank cover since volume 120 (and I fully expect before long to see the return of the list of contents to the front cover as was the norm up to volume 104[1]). Seasoned *Transactions* watchers may even have noticed that volumes 111 to 115 saw an aberrant and thankfully temporary return to the use of Roman numerals on the cover, not previously seen since volume 55 for 1933. While I have a sneaking respect for the reactionary purity applied to the *Transactions* by the dominant historical wing of the Society, I cannot help but think that the hard line taken on the appearance of the *Transactions* is a reflection of the tension within the Society between the historical and archaeological factions which led, for example, to the 'breakaway' formation of GADARG and necessitated the establishment of the Committee for Archaeology in Gloucestershire. Twenty-five years is a short time in the life of what is one of England's oldest-established county societies, but I would hope that before the next 25 years are over we will have seen some changes in the appearance, method of production, and archaeological content of the *Transactions*. The Society's *Transactions* sit rather uncomfortably these days as the 'dowdy relative' alongside their peer publications, for example the county society journals from adjacent Oxfordshire, Somerset, and Wiltshire.

The 1984 *Archaeology in Gloucestershire* volume was dedicated to Elsie Clifford and Helen O'Neil, two 'amateur' stalwarts who each made a distinctive contribution to the archaeology of Gloucestershire in the 20th century and who in their heydays dominated the scene in an almost 19th-century fashion, which today's practitioners of archaeology would probably find it impossible to imagine. Of the roster of contributors to the 1984 book, only John Drinkwater (happily also present at the 2004 conference) was an amateur archaeologist. This reflects another national change visible in the county, which is the rise of the professional and the concomitant decline of amateur input in field archaeology. Nevertheless, Neil Holbrook in his introduction to the 2004 conference rightly paid tribute to Bernard Rawes, who died in 1995 and who did in a way continue the tradition, though he had to contend (as he often complained) with a much more professional (and hence for him more bureaucratic) system than did Clifford or O'Neil. Bernard's excavation reports are instantly identifiable because of his idiosyncratic style of site illustration (e.g. Rawes 1986; 1991) and I regret the near disappearance of this type of personalized draughtsmanship. The use of 'Autocad' and other technical developments in the archaeological drawing office have led to a kind of homogenization in illustration which Bernard would have found dispiriting. On the other hand archaeological reconstruction drawing seems to be thriving. Several speakers at the 2004 conference commented on the way in which Phil Moss's reconstructions (Phil is another amateur), particularly those using the evidence from the Frocester dig (Price 2000), were an excellent means of bringing the past alive, especially for the general public.

Although it is understandable that individual amateur archaeologists should no longer have such a key role in archaeological fieldwork (Eddie Price being a redoubtable exception), amateur and general public involvement in archaeology in various other ways is probably at an all-time high, and I do not just mean as passive viewers of TV programmes. The Forest of Dean Archaeological Survey is one project involving local groups and individuals, the Portable Antiquities Scheme exists to service the interest in the past acquired by finders of archaeological objects, and local residents attend excavation open-days and other outreach events put on wherever possible by professional field archaeologists and curators. Indeed it was clear from the packed lecture theatre and enthusiastic audience for the 2004 conference that there is a very considerable public interest in the county's past, which bodes well for the next 25 years of archaeology in Gloucestershire. I shall look forward to reading this conference volume when it is published and I hope it enjoys a wide circulation amongst all those sectors of the community in which people value an increased understanding of and respect for the past.

NOTES

1. The present editor of the *Transactions* (JJ) is happy to reassure the author that he has no plans to use the front cover as a contents page.

BIBLIOGRAPHY

Aldhouse-Green, S.H.R., 2004, 'The Palaeolithic', in M. Aldhouse-Green and R. Howell (eds.), *The Gwent County History, volume 1: Gwent in prehistory and early history* (Cardiff, University of Wales Press), 1–28.

Allen, J.R.L., 2001. 'The landscape archaeology of the Lydney Level, Gloucestershire: natural and human transformations over the last two millennia', *Trans. BGAS* **119**, 27–57.

Allen, T.G., Darvill, T.C., Green, L.S., and Jones, M.U., 1993. *Excavations at Roughground Farm, Lechlade, Gloucestershire: a prehistoric and Roman landscape* (Oxford Archaeol. Unit Thames Valley Landscapes: the Cotswold Water Park **1**).

Barton, N., 1994. 'Second interim report on the survey and excavations in the Wye Valley, 1994', *Proc. University Bristol Spelaeological Soc.* **20.1**, 63–73.

Barton, N., 2005. *Ice Age Britain* (London, Batsford/English Heritage).

Bates, M.R., 2003. *A brief review of deposits containing Palaeolithic artefacts in the Shirehampton area of Bristol and their regional context* (Llwnfedwen, Terra Nova Ltd).

Bell, M., Caseldine, A., and Neumann, H., 2000. *Prehistoric intertidal archaeology in the Welsh Severn Estuary* (CBA Research Rep. **120**, York).

Buteux, S.T.E., and Lang, A.T.O., 2002. 'The Shotton Project: the Midlands Palaeolithic Network', *West Midlands Archaeol.* **45**, 15–19.

Cooper, L., and Jacobi, R., 2001. 'Two Late Glacial finds from north-west Leicestershire' *Trans. Leicestershire Archaeol. Hist. Soc.* **75**, 118–21.

DCMS 2000. *Report on the operation of the Treasure Act 24 September 1997–23 September 1998* (London, Department of Culture, Media and Sport).

DCMS 2001. *Treasure Annual report 1998–1999* (London, Department of Culture, Media and Sport).

DCMS 2002. *Treasure Annual report 2000* (London, Department of Culture, Media and Sport).

DCMS 2003. *Treasure Annual report 2001* (London, Department of Culture, Media and Sport).

DCMS 2004a. *Treasure Annual report 2002* (London, Department of Culture, Media and Sport).

DCMS 2004b. *Portable Antiquities Scheme annual report 2003/04* (London, Department of Culture, Media and Sport).

Dixon, P., 1994. *Crickley Hill Volume 1: the hillfort defences* (Crickley Hill Trust and the Department of Archaeol., University of Nottingham).

Fowler, P.J., 1977. 'Archaeology and the M5 motorway, Gloucestershire, 1969–1975: a summary and assessment', *Trans. BGAS* **95**, 40–6.

Heighway, C., and Bryant, R., 1999. *The Golden Minster: the Anglo-Saxon minster and later medieval priory of St Oswald at Gloucester* (CBA Research Rep. **117**, York).

Jacobi, R., Garton, D., and Brown, J., 2001. 'Field-walking and the Late Upper Palaeolithic in Nottinghamshire', *Trans. Thoroton Soc.* **105**, 17–22.

Jennings, D., Muir, J., Palmer, S., and Smith, A., 2004. *Thornhill Farm, Fairford, Gloucestershire: an Iron Age and Roman pastoral site in the Upper Thames Valley* (Oxford Archaeol. Thames Valley Landscapes Monograph **23**).

Lacaille, A.D., 1954. 'Palaeoliths from the lower reaches of the Bristol Avon', *Antiq. J.* **34**, 1–27.

Leach, P., 1998. *Great Witcombe Roman villa, Gloucestershire: a report on excavations by Ernest Greenfield 1960–1973* (BAR Brit. Series **266**, Oxford).

Mudd, A., Williams, R.J., and Lupton, A., 1999. *Excavations alongside Roman Ermin Street, Gloucestershire and Wiltshire: The Archaeology of the A419/A417 Swindon to Gloucester Road Scheme* (Oxford Archaeol. Unit: 2 volumes).

Price, E.G., 2000. *Frocester. A Romano-British settlement, its antecedents and successors* (Stonehouse, Gloucester and District Archaeol. Research Group: 2 volumes).

Rawes, B., 1986. 'The Romano-British settlement at Haymes, Cleeve Hill, near Cheltenham', *Trans. BGAS* **104**, 61–93.

Rawes, B., 1991. 'A prehistoric and Romano-British settlement at Vineyards Farm, Charlton Kings, Gloucestershire', *Trans. BGAS* **109**, 25–89.

Rippon, S. (ed.), 2001. *Estuarine Archaeology: the Severn and beyond* (Exeter, Severn Estuary Levels Research Committee: = *Archaeol. in the Severn Estuary* **11**).

Roe, D.A., 1974. 'Palaeolithic artefacts from the River Avon terraces near Bristol', *Proc. University Bristol Spelaeological Soc.* **13.3**, 319–26.

Saville, A. (ed.), 1984a. *Archaeology in Gloucestershire: from the earliest hunters to the industrial age. Essays dedicated to Helen O'Neil and the late Elsie Clifford* (Cheltenham Art Gallery and Museums and the BGAS).

Saville, A., 1984b. 'Palaeolithic and Mesolithic evidence from Gloucestershire', in A. Saville (ed.) 1984, 59–79.

Saville, A., 1990. *Hazleton North, Gloucestershire, 1979–82: the excavation of a Neolithic long cairn of the Cotswold-Severn group* (HBMCE Archaeological Rep. **13**, London, English Heritage).

Walters, B., 1992. *The archaeology and history of ancient Dean and the Wye Valley* (Cheltenham, Thornhill Press).

Whitehead, P.F., 1988. 'Lower Palaeolithic artefacts from the lower valley of the Warwickshire Avon', in R.J. MacRae and N. Moloney (eds.), *Non-flint stone tools and the Palaeolithic occupation of Britain* (BAR Brit. Series **189**, Oxford), 103–21.

Woodward, A., and Leach, P., 1993. *The Uley shrines. Excavation of a ritual complex on West Hill, Uley, Gloucestershire: 1977–9* (English Heritage Archaeol. Rep. **17**, London).

Index

Compiled by Susan Vaughan

Illustrations are denoted by page numbers in *italics*. The letter n following a page number indicates that the reference will be found in a note.

The following abbreviations have been used in this index: B. & N.E.S. – Bath and North East Somerset; Berks. – Berkshire; Bucks. – Buckinghamshire; Cambs. – Cambridgeshire; Glam. – Glamorgan; Herefs. – Herefordshire; Mon. – Monmouthshire; N. Som – North Somerset; Oxon. – Oxfordshire; S. Glos. – South Gloucestershire; Som. – Somerset; Warks. – Warwickshire; Wilts. – Wiltshire; Worcs. – Worcestershire.